HOMELESSNESS

RECENT TITLES IN DOCUMENTARY AND
REFERENCE GUIDES

Terrorism: A Documentary and Reference Guide
Vincent Burns and Kate Dempsey Peterson

Abortion: A Documentary and Reference Guide
Melody Rose

Civil Liberties and the State: A Documentary and Reference Guide
Christopher Peter Latimer

Culture Wars in America: A Documentary and Reference Guide
Glenn H. Utter

Evolution and Creationism: A Documentary and Reference Guide
Christian C. Young and Mark A. Largent

Gun Control: A Documentary and Reference Guide
Robert J. Spitzer

Islamism: A Documentary and Reference Guide
John Calvert

The Patriot Act: A Documentary and Reference Guide
Herbert N. Foerstel

The Politics of Sexuality: A Documentary and Reference Guide
Raymond A. Smith

U.S. Election Campaigns: A Documentary and Reference Guide
Thomas J. Baldino and Kyle L. Kreider

HOMELESSNESS

A Documentary and Reference Guide

Neil Larry Shumsky

Documentary and Reference Guides

 GREENWOOD

AN IMPRINT OF ABC-CLIO, LLC
Santa Barbara, California • Denver, Colorado • Oxford, England

Library of Congress Cataloging-in-Publication Data

Shumsky, Neil L., 1944–
   Homelessness : a documentary and reference guide / Neil Larry Shumsky.
     p. cm. — (Documentary and reference guides)
   Includes bibliographical references and index.
   ISBN 978–0–313–37700–6 (cloth : alk. paper)—ISBN 978–0–313–37701–3 (ebook)
1. Homelessness—United States—History—Sources. 2. Homelessness—United States—History.
I. Title.
HV4504.S58   2012
362.5'920973—dc23   2011043428

ISBN: 978–0–313–37700–6
EISBN: 978–0–313–37701–3

16 15 14 13 12   1 2 3 4 5

This book is also available on the World Wide Web as an eBook.
Visit www.abc-clio.com for details.

Greenwood
An Imprint of ABC-CLIO, LLC

ABC-CLIO, LLC
130 Cremona Drive, P.O. Box 1911
Santa Barbara, California 93116-1911

This book is printed on acid-free paper (∞)

Manufactured in the United States of America

CONTENTS

Reader's Guide to Documents and Sidebars   vii

Introduction   xi

     Prologue: Vagabonds in England   xxv

Part I   Words and Numbers   1

   1. Words   3

   2. Numbers   11

Part II   Hoboes, Tramps, and Bums, 1790–1930   17

   3. Ben Reitman Defines *Hobo*, *Tramp*, and *Bum*   19

   4. Jack London Explains "the Rods"   25

   5. Train Jumping   31

   6. A Migrant Farm Worker   39

   7. The Extent of the Problem, 1890–1925   45

   8. Country Lodgings   51

   9. The Stem, or Main Stem   59

10. The Hobo Jungle   65

11. "Tramp-Speak" and the Hobo Subculture   71

12. Hobo Songs   81

13. Hobo Politics   89

14. The Hobo College   97

15. Hobohemia Disappears   105

Part III   Migrants and Transients, 1930–1960   111

16. On the Farm   115

17. In the City   123

18. Bonus Army — 131
19. FERA and FTP — 143
20. Bum Brigade — 153
21. Squatters — 163
22. Weedpatch Camp — 169
23. Hooverville — 177
24. Picking Grapes in Lodi — 189
25. Arts and Culture — 197
26. Liquidating the Federal Transient Program — 215

Part IV Street People, Bag Ladies, and Homeless People — 221

Defining Homelessness and Counting Homeless People — 225
27. Charles Dickens Coins the Word — 225
28. Congress Defines *Homeless* — 231
29. Mitch Snyder Claims "Millions" — 237
30. HUD Disagrees Sharply — 245
31. Making Sense of the Conflict — 249
32. The Number of Homeless — 253

Who Are the Homeless? — 263
33. An Overview of the Homeless Population Today — 263
34. Special Populations of Homeless People — 269
35. Homeless Children and Their Families — 287
36. Homeless Veterans — 297
37. Homeless People in Rural Areas — 307
38. Homeless People of Color — 317
39. Homeless Latinos and a Different Perspective — 327

Contending with Homelessness — 335
40. Staying Alive—Homeless People Cope — 335
41. Housing for the Homeless — 345
42. Criminalizing the Homeless — 353
43. Washington Takes the Lead — 363

Bibliography — 375
Index — 379

READER'S GUIDE TO DOCUMENTS AND SIDEBARS

The Control and Regulation of Homeless People
Bonus Army, 133
Bum Brigade, 155
Congress Defines "Homeless," 231
Criminalizing the Homeless, 353
FERA and FTP, 143
The Hobo Jungle, 65
Hobohemia Disappears, 105
Hooverville, 177
Low-Cost Housing Issue Confronts Santa Paula, 349
Picking Grapes in Lodi, 189
Vagabonds in England, xxv

Definitions of Homelessness and Homeless People
Ben Reitman Defines Hobo, Tramp, and Bum, 19
Charles Dickens Coins the Word, 225
Congress Defines Homeless, 231
Defining Homelessness Down, 225
Different Ways of Conceiving Homelessness, 233, 235
Is Homelessness the Most Appropriate Word?, 290
Vagabonds in England, xxv
Words, 3

**Homeless People, Social and Demographic
Characteristics of**
Homeless Adolescents, 289

Homeless Children and Their Families, 287
Homeless Infants, 291
Homeless Latinos and a Different Perspective, 329
Homeless People of Color, 317
Homeless Veterans, 297
An Overview of the Homeless Population Today, 263
The Special Circumstances of Homeless Latinos, 329
Special Populations of Homeless People, 269

Housing
Conditions in Illinois and Chicago, 265
Country Lodgings, 51
Decreases in Publicly Assisted Housing . . ., 347
The Extent of the Problem, 1890–1925, 45
Fieldworkers in California, 170
The Hobo Jungle, 65
Hobohemia, 59
Hobohemia Disappears, 105
Hooverville, 177
Housing for the Homeless, 345
HUD Disagrees Sharply, 245
Low-Cost Housing Issue Confronts Santa Paula, 349
In the City, 123
Inexorable Disease, 165, 166, 167
A Migrant Farm Worker, 39
On the Farm, 115

An Overview of the Homeless Population Today, 263

Squalor and Filth, 166

Squatters, 163

Subsidized Housing for the Homeless, 347

Survival Strategies, 294

Tom Collins Explains His Attitudes toward
   Camp, 172

Literature and Writing about Homeless People

Charles Dickens Coins the Word, 225

Jack London Explains "the Rods," 25

On the Farm, 115

Squatters, 163

Weedpatch Camp, 169

Migrants and Migration (*see* Mobility)

Mobility

Country Lodgings, 51

The Extent of the Problem, 1890–1925, 45

FERA and FTP, 143

The Hobo Jungle, 65

Hobo Songs, 81

Hobohemia Disappears, 105

Jack London Explains "the Rods," 25

A Migrant Farm Worker, 39

Train Jumping, 31

Weedpatch Camp, 169

The Number of Homeless People

Ask the Census Bureau, 255

Backlash over Report Showing Big Drop in L.A.'s
   Homeless Population, 258

Defining Homelessness Down, 225

The Extent of the Problem, 1890–1925, 45

Hobohemia Disappears, 105

How Many People Experience Homelessness?, 255

HUD Disagrees Sharply, 245

Is It Even the Right Question?, 255

L.A. Homeless Population Drops despite Recession,
   259–60

Liquidating the Federal Transient Program, 215

Making Sense of the Conflict, 250

Mitch Snyder Claims Millions, 237

The Number of Homeless, 253

Numbers, 11

Questioning the Accuracy of the Counts, 256, 257

An Overview of the Homeless Population Today, 263

Political Activities of Homeless People

Bonus Army, 133

Hobo Politics, 89

Hobo Songs, 81

Hooverville, 177

Picking Grapes in Lodi, 189

Poverty

Conditions in Illinois and Chicago, 265

The Extent of the Problem, 1890–1925, 45

Fieldworkers in California, 170

Homeless People in Rural Areas, 307

Low-Cost Housing Issue Confronts Santa Paula, 349

In the City, 123

Liquidating the Federal Transient Program, 215

A Migrant Farm Worker, 39

On the Farm, 115

Squatters, 163

Weedpatch Camp, 169

**Recollections, Reminiscences, and Memoirs about
   Homeless People**

Country Lodgings, 51

Homeless Latinos and a Different
   Perspective, 329

On the Farm, 115

Squatters, 163

Weedpatch Camp, 169

**Recollections, Reminiscences, and Memoirs
   by Homeless People**

Bonus Army, 133

The Hobo Jungle, 65

Hooverville, 177
Jack London Explains "the Rods," 25
Train Jumping, 31
"Tramp-speak" and the Hobo Subculture, 71

Rural Homelessness
All Homelessness Is Not the Same, 311
Country Lodgings, 51
And the Differences Can Be Surprising, 309–10, 311
Fieldworkers in California, 170
The Hidden Homeless, 312
The Hobo Jungle, 65
Homeless People in Rural Areas, 307
Liquidating the Federal Transient Program, 215
A Migrant Farm Worker, 39
On the Farm, 115
Picking Grapes in Lodi, 189
Squatters, 163
Weedpatch Camp, 169

Social and Cultural Relations and Institutions of Homeless People
Arts and Culture, 197
The Hobo College, 97
The Hobo Jungle, 65
Hobo Politics, 89
Hobo Songs, 81
Hobohemia, 59
Hooverville, 177
"Tramp-speak" and the Hobo Subculture, 71
Weedpatch Camp, 169

Trains (see Transportation)

Tramps (see Definitions of Homelessness and Homeless People; Mobility)

Transients (see Definitions of Homelessness and Homeless People; Mobility)

Transportation
Jack London Explains "the Rods," 25

A Migrant Farm Worker, 39
Train Jumping, 31

United States Government
Bonus Army, 133
Congress Defines Homeless, 231
Congress Hears about Homeless Veterans, 299
Decreases in Publicly Assisted Housing . . ., 347
FERA and FTP, 143
Homeless Veterans, 297
HUD Disagrees Sharply, 245
The Kansas Transient Service, 145
Liquidating the Federal Transient Program, 215
Tom Collins Explains His Attitudes toward Camp, 172
Washington Takes the Lead, 364
Weedpatch Camp, 169

Urban Homelessness
Hobohemia, 59
Hobohemia Disappears, 105
Hooverville, 177
In the City, 123

Wages (see Poverty)

Work and Labor
Ben Reitman Defines Hobo, Tramp and Bum, 19
Conditions in Illinois and Chicago, 265
Country Lodgings, 51
The Extent of the Problem, 1890–1925, 45
The Hobo Jungle, 65
Hobo Politics, 89
Hobo Songs, 81
Hobohemia Disappears, 105
A Migrant Farm Worker, 39
On the Farm, 115
Picking Grapes in Lodi, 189
Squatters, 163
Vagabonds in England, xxv
Weedpatch Camp, 169

INTRODUCTION

If you don't give it much thought, *homelessness* seems like a simple enough word. Ask people to define the word and they're likely to tell you that it means being without a home. That "definition," or something closely resembling it, might be thought of as "the street definition."

But, if you spend some time thinking about the word *homelessness*, and if you analyze it and take it apart, the subject quickly becomes more complex and less transparent. Uncertainties can arise in your mind and leave you wondering what the word actually means. In fact, the intricacy of defining homelessness requires that the word be deconstructed—taken carefully apart—before some order can be imposed on the topic.

One useful technique to examine the word daringly (but cautiously) is to borrow a system frequently used by teachers of writing. They often tell their students that there are six kinds of questions, each of them represented by a single interrogatory word: what, who, when, where, why, and how. And, to tell any story completely, writers must answer a simple set of questions: (1) What happened? (2) Who did it; that is, who performed the action being considered and whom did it affect? (3) When did it happen? (4) Where did it happen? (5) Why did it occur? (6) How did it all occur, that is, what was the process that created the happening?

Using this simple framework to guide our thinking about *homelessness* in an organized fashion reveals the many dimensions of the topic and begins to provide some understanding of it, while also revealing what is still unknown and what is still uncertain—not to mention why a simple word can become so complex.

1. What is homelessness? How does one go about defining a word that does not represent a concrete, tangible object, something that one cannot touch, something that is an intangible situation, circumstance, or feeling? *Love* is probably the most commonly used example of such a circumstance. We all know that love is out there, and we all experience it at some time in our lives. But we also know that different people explain love differently, and each of us experiences it in different ways.

The same is true of homelessness. In the case of *homelessness*, one way of getting a grip on the word might be to yank it apart and try to understand the meanings of its three component parts: "home," "-less," and "-ness." Let's begin by working backwards, which will take us from easiest to hardest. The part "-ness" doesn't present any real problems. It's pretty much just a suffix that, when attached to an adjective, can transform that adjective into a noun; or, if "-ness" is attached to a noun, it can change the noun into an adjective. So, *happy* can be changed into *happiness*, or the "state of being happy." Or, to take a slightly more complex example, the word *love*, which is already a noun, can be turned into an adjective by attaching the suffix "-ly" to make the adjective *lovely*. But that adjective can be turned back into a noun—*loveliness*—which has a different meaning from the noun we began with—*love*.

Homelessness works the same way, and its complexity becomes a little more understandable. The word starts with a noun, *home*, which is turned into an adjective by adding the suffix "-less" to make the word *homeless* (not having a home), which can then be transformed into a different noun by adding "-ness" to make the word *homelessness*, which could be defined simply as "the state of being without a home."

The second component of the word *homelessness*—the four-letter syllable "-less"—again seems to have a simple meaning, easily determined. It is another suffix, this one meaning "without," or not having something. But, before you even start to think about it, a most sobering question suddenly throws itself at you. What is the meaning of the word *without*? The obvious answer is that "-less" means "not having something." It means something like "the total absence of" something. For example, you see a person walking down the street holding a tin cup, and you think to yourself, "that man is penniless." But, what exactly do you mean by that? Do you mean "that man is very poor"? Or, do you literally mean, "he doesn't have a cent"? And, what if you later learn that, although the man has no actual "cash"—nickels, dimes, quarters, dollar bills, or ten-dollar bills—he owns a large amount of stock in a major corporation. While the man **is**, quite literally, *penniless*, you can hardly think of him as being poor, a man who is without any resources.

The same sort of complication applies to *homeless* and *homelessness*. The words can be used in more than one way; they have several related—but different—meanings. When we call people "homeless" or refer to their "homelessness," are we saying that they literally have no home, no place where they can eat, sleep, keep any possessions, and bathe? They have no abode? Or do we only mean that their place for eating, sleeping, and bathing is unsatisfactory and inadequate? As an example, here is a relevant situation. For many years it was rumored—and later confirmed—that people lived in abandoned tunnels two, three, four, or even five levels beneath Grand Central Station in the heart of New York City. They had found their way deep below the surface of the city, hauled boxes, old lumber, and all kinds of "building materials" down there, and constructed dwellings for themselves. Not as large as most suburban houses, certainly, but they still provided enclosed space. These "tunnel-dwellers" bathed by tapping into underground utility lines, and they got hot water by tapping into steam lines. They got electricity by tying into the power grid. Certainly, few of us would be at all likely to think that that habitation was satisfactory or acceptable (unless we are romanticizing the conditions); we might even consider such living conditions to be subhuman. But is someone who lives in that place, in that fashion, homeless? The "tunnel-dwellers" referred to those underground burrows as their "homes." Even if a middle-class observer who lives in an affluent suburb thinks that a "tunnel-dweller" is homeless, would the person living below ground think that he or she was homeless? Is the suffix "-less" an inflexible term meaning "absolutely, totally without" or does it refer to a shortage or inadequacy of something? If you call a person penniless, are you saying that he has absolutely nothing, or that he is poor, or very, or even extremely poor?

And then we come to the first of the three syllables of *homelessness*—home. What is a "home"? Rephrasing that question in the simplest possible terms, is a "home" the same thing as a house? Perhaps it would be better to ask if a "home" is precisely the same thing as a "residence" or an "abode" of any kind, including not only house but also an apartment, flat, condo, and so on. Does *homelessness* mean only that a person does not have one of those places? Is someone who lives in a million-dollar condo a homeless person? Or, putting it slightly differently is "homelessness" the same condition as "houselessness"? Can you have one of those without having the other? Is it possible to have a home and not have a house? Or, can you have a house but not have a home?

Many sociologists, psychologists, social workers, historians, designers, architects, and practitioners of family therapy strongly maintain that a "home" is much more than a house—it is a place meant to be used for human habitation (not a tunnel under a railroad station, no matter how grand the overhead super-structure), a place where a person has a feeling of belonging, is welcomed, achieves a sense of identity, and to which a person has a sense of emotional attachment.

So, if we put together all of the various permutations and combinations of the different meanings of the syllables "home" and "-less," there are many possible meanings for the words *homeless* and *homelessness*. The question "What is homelessness?" turns out to be much more twisted and nonlinear than it seemed when we first asked the question.

2. Who is homeless? Once again, there are different ways of interpreting this question. At the simplest level, a person who poses the question could be asking for a roster of people. The person inquiring expects to be told the names of everyone who is without a home (whatever that might be and however it might be defined).

But, generally speaking, the question "Who is homeless?" means something broader than "What are the names of the homeless people?" It usually means something much closer to "What sorts of people become homeless?" or "What are the social and demographic characteristics of homeless people?"

But even those questions can be broken down, and different analysts might be seeking different information. One of them might be interested in the sex distribution of homeless people; are they male or are they female? How many of them are men and how many are women? What percentage of them is male and what percentage is female? Are those percentages the same as the percentages of men and women in the society at large, considering everyone and not just the homeless? If one sex has a larger percentage among the homeless population than it does among the population-at-large, how do you account for the discrepancy?

Sex is only one of a whole array of characteristics than can be investigated. Others frequently examined are age, race and/or ethnic group, place of birth, occupation, marital status, income, health, length of homelessness, and current location of a homeless person (urban or rural).

Once again, these characteristics, too, can be subdivided. When considering age, most analysts are less interested in knowing the precise ages of individuals as they are in examining certain periods of age—infancy, childhood, adolescence, adulthood, middle-age, or elderliness. Using these age groupings requires making decisions about the proper boundaries to set among them all—When does infancy end and childhood begin? When does adolescence cease and adulthood occur?

Similar kinds of issues appear when looking at any social or demographic characteristic of a population. In categorizing "nativity" or "place of birth," is one going to look at "born in the United States" and "born outside the United States" or is one going to consider "born in the United States" and "born in Europe," "born in Africa," "born in Asia," and "born in Latin America"? Is one interested in absolute numbers, in percentages, or in comparative statistics between one time period and another to see what changes have taken place?

3. When did people become homeless? "When" is no less complex than "what" or "who." Asking "when" something happened can mean a number of different things. The most obvious of them is the date on the calendar—January 23, March 28, October 31. Perhaps, we won't be so picky and will settle for 1932, 1945, or 1997.

But "when" does not necessarily mean "on what day" or "in what year." It could refer to the age of the participants' lives; at what moment in their lives did they become homeless? Were they children, adolescents, or senior citizens? And, clearly, if that approach is used, "when" can overlap with "who" very neatly.

In addition, "when" can refer to an external event. This could be something like an economic crisis such as the Great Depression. Did many people become homeless at the time of the Depression that lasted throughout the 1930s? Do economic depressions generally produce an increase in the number of homeless people? You can ask questions about "when" without having any specific period of time in mind. You can ask questions such as "When do wars occur?" or "When do people become homeless?" In those cases, you are defining time by the context in which an event occurs, not in terms of calendar markings.

Although a declining economy is almost certainly the external event most commonly said to make people homeless, there is another whole category of events that is widely recognized as causing homelessness: natural disasters. The fire and earthquake that almost leveled San Francisco in 1906 left hundreds, if not thousands, of people living in tents at Golden Gate Park for many months. Hurricane Katrina devastated New Orleans in 2005 and made the dwellings of tens of thousands of its residents uninhabitable, and they became homeless. The great drought and the windstorms that occurred on the southern Great Plains during the 1930s forced thousands of farmers off their land, left them without homes, and caused many of them to go to California where it sometimes took years for them and their families to reestablish themselves and become once again "homed."

War is another significant event that leaves people homeless, and war can easily be associated with "when" as a time that homelessness occurs. Although the terms *war refugees* and *displaced persons* are more frequently thought of in terms of the post–World War II era, they also apply to several other important times in U.S.

history. During and after the Revolutionary War large numbers of American colonists who remained loyal to Great Britain fled north to Canada. During the War of 1812, when the British bombarded Baltimore, Maryland, and burned Washington, DC, thousands of people had to find new homes. And, the devastation in the South after the Civil War left thousands of white Southerners with their homes destroyed and also enabled thousands of black Southerners to leave their homes to find places more appealing and with fewer harsh memories.

4. Where did people become homeless? Once again, the answer to this question is a matter of choice for the investigator and depends on his or her own interests. The investigator can choose the location of the homelessness that he or she wants to study. In the broadest terms, he or she can examine homelessness as a national phenomenon and interpret homelessness in the United States and try to generalize about the phenomenon across the country. This is the path taken by Kenneth Kusmer in his book, *Down and Out, On the Road: The Homeless in American History*, and by Todd DePastino in *Citizen Hobo: How a Century of Homelessness Shaped America*. However, a researcher could also choose to take a narrower look at a section or region of the country as Frank Higbie did in *Indispensable Outcastes: Hobo Workers and Community in the American Midwest, 1880–1930*. One could look at the geography of homelessness in an even narrower location—a single state—such as Joan Crouse did in her study of *The Homeless Transient in the Great Depression; New York State, 1919–1941*. And many researchers have studied homelessness in a single town or city.

If you look more closely at the titles mentioned in the last paragraph, you will also notice that each covers a different time period. Kusmer's book considers homelessness in all parts of the United States from the colonial period to the present; DePastino examines homelessness throughout the United States during a single century; Higbie analyzes a section of the United States, the Midwest, for half of a century; and Crouse looks at a single state, New York, for just over two decades. Obviously, these various authors, if they believed the dates meaningful, could have examined homelessness in their geographic location during any of the other time periods. For example, Crouse could have examined homelessness throughout the United States during the Great Depression, or Higbie could have studied homelessness in the Midwest in the 1950s. So, an author is not necessarily constrained by predefined geographic locations and time periods. Authors can "mix or match" place and time as they think appropriate and meaningful. The word *homelessness* does not have an obvious and easily-understood meaning.

5. Why does homelessness exist? Of all of the questions about homelessness, this is probably the most challenging and controversial. Some social scientists and humanists believe that determining the causes of human behavior and human events is not possible. They argue that human behavior does not work like chemicals in a laboratory, that students of human life are not scientists, and that people are not chemicals; one cannot produce precisely the same conditions in human society an infinite number of times in the same way that a chemist working in a lab can run the same experiment over and over and expect to get the same results. If a chemist mixes oxygen and hydrogen at a certain atmospheric temperature and a certain barometric pressure, he or she will always get the same result: Water will suddenly appear. There are unchangeable physical laws at work in this situation.

But, the same degree of control is not possible when studying human beings and human behavior. Most humanists point out that one cannot produce precisely the same conditions over and over again in human society. The place is never exactly the same, even from day to day. Even if the same people are present, they are not the same because they will have changed over time. And, perhaps most important of all, the time of a second experiment or occurrence can never be exactly the same. Its context has changed, and therefore the experiment will have also changed. The environment or context of an event has changed, which immediately creates a major difference between the first and second events and makes them incomparable.

This way of thinking about human behavior and causation is perhaps the most important difference between humanists who study history, literature, language, and culture, and who believe that each event is unique, and those social scientists who frequently attempt to find larger explanations for events that differ in some respects but seem similar in others. For example, a social scientist might say that there were surely differences between homelessness in the eighteenth century and the present, but both phenomena are described as "homelessness," and to them, the important question is the common characteristics of both. What are they? How do you find them? Where do you look for them?

6. How does homelessness occur? When we examine the "how" of homelessness thoughtfully, after a while, some fascinating realizations spring to mind. First of all, there is a very important issue that frequently gets overlooked: What are the differences between description and causation? For example, if an analyst discovers a statistical correlation between homelessness and alcohol abuse, does that mean the existence of a causal relationship between them? Does alcohol abuse cause homelessness, i.e., if one abuses alcohol, is one more likely to become homeless? What inferences can you draw from a statement such as "30 percent of all homeless people abuse alcohol, but only 20 percent of the entire population abuse alcohol"? Can we deduce that abusing alcohol causes homelessness? Makes it more likely that one will become homeless? How much more likely? If we infer anything about a relationship between alcohol abuse and homelessness, can we also assume that reducing alcohol abuse will reduce the amount of homelessness? Can we predict anything about the likelihood that an alcohol-abusing, homeless individual who ceases to abuse alcohol and becomes a tea-totaler will also cease to be homeless?

Another fundamental question emerges from thinking about the "how" of homelessness. The problem arises from thinking about the individual who is examining homelessness as much as it does from thinking about the homeless people themselves. Some analysts have argued that the basic causes of homelessness, and the conditions that lead to homelessness, are being poor, being a person of color, being of a certain age, having a mental disability, having a physical disability, being deserted by one's spouse, or losing one's job, among many other events that have been put forth. Other analysts have maintained that homelessness results from the general nature and structure of the economy; current economic conditions; the way in which wealth and income are distributed in the society; the various prejudices in a society: racism, feminism, bias against people with any kind of mental or physical disability; classism, or the attitude that people of any particular wealth, whether poverty or affluence, are inferior. Many other similar conditions have also been presented as causes of homelessness, and the processes that have brought about these social conditions are also presented as answers to the question of how homelessness comes about.

But, there is an even more fundamental issue inherent in this discussion. The first group of factors presented as causes of homelessness—poverty, race, unemployment, being handicapped, and so on—are all attributes of an individual. Homelessness is here attributed to some condition that characterizes and distinguishes one individual from another. He is poor, she was deserted by her husband, he is an alcoholic, she abuses drugs—and they are consequently homeless. Therefore, the obvious solution to alleviating homelessness is to change that person's life. He needs to get money, she needs to get her husband back (or another one), he needs to stop drinking, and she needs to stop abusing drugs. All of these are characteristics and the changed behaviors of individuals, and the solution to homelessness is to end the condition adhering to the individual that has caused the homelessness.

The second set of factors mentioned—the extreme degree of poverty in the country, the high level of unemployment, the lack of affordable housing, the growing income disparity between rich and poor, and other similar conditions—are all descriptions of the entire society rather than descriptions of specific individuals. The way to reduce homelessness, therefore, is not by targeting specific individuals and trying to change their circumstances, it is by changing the larger society—by creating more jobs, by raising minimum wages, by building more low-cost houses and apartments, and by making harmful substances (drugs, alcohol) less accessible. This is much more difficult and a much more daunting task. It is hard enough to try to change the life of a single person without even thinking about altering a whole institutional structure.

After thinking about all of these issues, the complexity of homelessness becomes much more obvious. However, such reflection also makes understanding homelessness much more challenging than it did previously, even if the existence of its complexity seems more understandable. Its persistence seems more comprehensible.

And it has persisted. The origins of homelessness are frequently traced back to medieval England where homeless people were labeled *vagabonds*, *vagrants*, and *rogues*. And, as these terms indicate, such people were considered to be criminal rather than law-abiding, wandering rather than settled, and irresponsible rather than dependable. The extent of the loathing toward this part of society is manifest in the extreme punishments meted out to them for what seem to be relatively small transgressions.

Homelessness appeared in the English North American colonies at the moment the first colonists arrived in North America. It can be argued that the first settlers who arrived in Jamestown in 1607 or Plymouth in 1620 or Boston in 1630 were all homeless. There were no dwellings awaiting them. There weren't any apartments that they could rent; there weren't even any hotels where they could stay. More than that, housing was not their construction priority. Their first priority, according to the instructions given the first settlers in Virginia, was to enclose a place for their settlement with a wooden palisade or high fence that would provide protection from enemies, both European and native. Then, they were told, they were to build a storehouse in which to keep their supplies and produce and then to build a church where they could worship God properly. Only after they had built these structures were they free to build houses for themselves. Until then, they could continue to live aboard their ship until it returned to England. Or, as some of them did, they could dig deep dugouts, cover them with branches, and sleep in them. In some cases, these habitations took the form of caves dug into the riverbanks. Under the worst of circumstances, they simply slept unprotected on the open ground.

After time had passed, and the settlers had been able to build rude houses, and later more substantial ones, and when living conditions had noticeably improved, new kinds of homelessness appeared. Old people who lost the ability to support themselves, wives whose husbands died or disappeared, young women who became pregnant without being wives, and anyone who became ill and lost the means of providing for their families could easily lose their housing. In such cases, it was considered appropriate for the local community to provide for them, to arrange housing for them, and for the community to pay someone who was willing to house a person who had no permanent home.

But it also became the law (if not always followed) for towns, especially in New England, to "warn people out," that is, to order strangers who had not received permission to live in the town to return to their place of residence or be fined and jailed. Every person was considered to "belong" to some town or location, and they were expected to remain there. People who wandered from one place to another were considered to be a social threat and a source of social disorder. The same hostility expressed to homeless people for several centuries in England appeared at an early date in the English colonies.

The same practices persisted through the 1600s, but conditions changed during the 1700s. For one thing, as towns and cities grew, people became more anonymous and didn't know their neighbors as well. It became much more difficult for a town to find someone who was willing to house a homeless person for a small return, especially if the homeless person was unknown and was considered an outsider. Furthermore, people were loathe to pay the taxes necessary to subsidize the housing of total strangers who were not known and who were not members of the group. As a result, during the eighteenth century, new institutions such as workhouses and almshouses were established in several cities as places where homeless people could be housed and where they could work to compensate the town that had provided housing for them.

This kind of homelessness, and these ways of treating homeless people, continued into the 1830s and 1840s, but a new moral ideology began to develop. In this new ideology, "home" acquired a sanctified atmosphere in which "Mother" achieved an almost transcendent nature. Family took on a new, almost holy, significance, and as the new urban professional and business middle-class developed, everyone in society was, more than ever, expected to be part of a recognized family that was enshrined as a home within a home. People, especially men, who were not attached to a family were considered to be disorderly agents who had the potential to damage or even destroy society.

These ideas developed, and their significance increased as the nineteenth century passed, but they became particularly important after the Civil War. After 1865, Americans became conscious of the fact that many people were not living according to the precepts of the domestic, home- and family-centered ideology that was becoming dominant. Some of the first groups to be recognized as living outside of this new social paradigm were veterans of the Civil War who never adapted well to the new world of post–Civil War America and ex-slaves who wandered around the country as a way of expressing their new ability to control their own movements and the fact that they were no longer bound to a single location and needing permission to go anywhere else.

At the same time, Americans became conscious of a large group of men whom they called *hoboes*, *tramps*, and *bums*, words which they used interchangeably. After 1870, American magazines and newspapers regularly published articles about the "tramp menace" that was afflicting the United States.

Americans seem to have been fascinated by these people. They wanted to know as much about them as they could—why they wandered rather than being settled, how they supported themselves without a permanent residence, why they lived the kinds of lives that they did. Americans continually asked how many hoboes and tramps there were, and asked about their personal characteristics: age, sex, race, nationality, and so on. Yet, despite this intensive interest, most Americans never achieved a real understanding of the phenomenon. Rather, Americans generally regarded hoboes as an almost subversive element in American society, a group whose nonconforming behavior threatened the social order and the world that was being created in the United States.

In fact, the hoboes and tramps were products of the new social and economic systems that were developing in the country. Major industries, often located in areas outside of major cities, had a strong need for intermittent labor forces. Large ranches needed field workers at planting time and harvest time, not the rest of the year. Outdoor economic activities generally functioned only during certain seasons. Ice-cutting could only be done during the winter, and lumbering could only be done when it was not winter. Mining, usually located in mountainous regions, couldn't be performed when the mines and their bulky output were inaccessible and unable to be moved. Because of the seasonality of these activities, workers moved from one place to another during the year, picking up work where it was available and usually retreating to a convenient large city when the enterprises where they found jobs were functioning at much less than full capacity.

For a number of reasons, this kind of homelessness was clearly declining by the 1920s. For one thing, the economy had so changed that this kind of labor was much less in demand. Newly invented electric refrigerators caused the total disappearance of ice-cutting as a regular activity. The essential completion of the railroad network caused the need for track-layers to disappear completely. The mechanization of farms and the use of new farm machinery, both to plant and to harvest crops, destroyed the need for large armies of laborers to perform these time-intensive jobs. By the 1920s, one of the most important reasons for the appearance of tramps and hoboes—the need for large groups of intermittent laborers—had all but come to an end.

In addition, changed technologies destroyed the way in which hoboes and tramps got from place to place, from one job to another. One of the most significant defining characteristics of these men and women was their particular method of travel. Like other Americans, they rode the rails—but they did so in a unique way. They didn't buy tickets; they just hopped on the train. They might locate themselves on the roof of a car. They might secrete themselves on the small platforms between cars. They might hide themselves in a freight car or gondola. Some of them might even lie on the rods that hung down from a railroad car between the car and the track. But by the 1920s, railroads were using new technologies. Perhaps the most important was the use of diesel rather than steam power. This meant that trains traveled much more rapidly and stopped less often. They were also more powerful and could climb hills much more easily. They never needed to stop at water tanks. As a result of all these changes, there were far fewer times and places that a tramp or hobo could jump aboard a slow-moving train while it was actually moving. The traditional mode of transportation no longer existed.

Finally, the widespread adoption of the motor car during the 1920s meant that there were simply fewer trains moving around the country, and thus there were far fewer trains that hoboes and tramps could use for their own travel. Thus, by the 1930s, the hobo or tramp as he was traditionally known had just about disappeared. They were still around, but they no longer formed a sizeable, recognizable part of the social system. But, while they did exist, they created a separate world—one with its own method of getting around, one with its own culture, and one with its own political and economic systems. They, too, all but disappeared by 1930.

But, while hoboes, tramps, and what has been called Hobohemia disappeared during the 1920s and a little before, homelessness did not disappear. During the 1930s, homelessness took on a new form, and the words to characterize homelessness also changed. Now, homeless people were called *transients* or *migrants*. These people, although homeless, differed in many ways from homeless tramps and hoboes.

The most significant difference between homeless tramps in the 1920s and homeless transients in the 1930s was the different economic context. In the earlier period, although the jobs that employed hoboes were usually temporary positions for a single individual, the job almost always existed from one year to the next. Crops always had to be planted and harvested. Mines always had to be dug, and bulky materials always had to be removed. Timber always had to be harvested and transported. All of these jobs continued even if different people held them.

The nature of the economy, though, changed after 1929. With the onset of the Great Depression, every sector of the economy collapsed, and jobs disappeared by the millions. By 1933, nearly one-fourth of all Americans were unemployed, and many commentators remarked that there were millions of Americans who were under-employed, that is, they only worked part-time or worked for wages that would previously have been considered inadequate.

The search for work pulled Americans from one place to another in hopes of finding some means of support for them and their families. Two groups of workers supplied a large part of the transient population. One group was farmers. Although the Great Depression is usually thought of as beginning in 1929, some sectors of the economy began to feel the Depression much earlier. Farming in particular began to experience a depression in the early 1920s. Demand for agricultural produce declined, and as large farms and ranches (what would later be called agribusiness) began to use modern farm machinery to cut costs, it became almost impossible for traditional farmers to compete. Later, in the mid-1930s, farmers and ranchers in the southern Great Plains began to experience horrendous climatic conditions. Years of drought that left no water for either plants or animals were followed by years of intense heat that dried the land even more and turned the soil into a fine dust. These years were accompanied by unprecedented winds that could blow the fine dust hundreds of miles. Winds carried this dust from Kansas and Oklahoma as far east as Baltimore and New York. In the Great Plains themselves, dust storms could be powerful enough to drown automobiles and even houses in heavy layers of fine powder.

The other sector of the economy to be almost destroyed during the Great Depression was manufacturing. During the 1920s, the United States had begun to develop a consumer-oriented society. In it, U.S. factories produced enormous quantities of manufactured goods that were meant to stimulate and to satisfy the American propensity to purchase manufactured items of all sorts—from cars to refrigerators to radios and washing machines. But with the economy almost dead, and with the growing levels of unemployment, factories stopped producing goods, workers were laid off, and consumers bought little. The result was extraordinary unemployment.

These two groups of people—farmers and factory workers—began leaving their homes trying to find some means of earning an income. After the financial crisis of 1929, many farmers and workers simply abandoned their houses and had them foreclosed. The stresses of daily life in such a troubled economy broke families apart, sending men off in search of work and sending adolescents away from home—either to avoid being a burden on their families or because their parents had told them that could no longer support all of their children.

Once again, Americans were aware of this new homelessness, but they almost never used the word. *Transient* or *migrant* was somehow considered more polite and less pejorative, but they meant the same thing—people who did not have homes as they were traditionally conceived and who, instead or being housed, wandered around the country in search of work.

What truly separated these Depression homeless from the tramp/hobo homeless was the widespread availability of automobile travel. During the 1920s, Henry Ford had made it his goal to put a car in every person's garage, and he was extremely successful, producing automobiles at a much lower cost than ever before and producing automobiles much more basic than ever before. The result was the widespread availability and use of cars for long-distance travel. Large numbers of Americans, from both farms and cities, packed all of their belonging into a car—frequently little more than an old jalopy—and sometimes on top of the car, and headed off to find someplace better. They left behind anything that wouldn't fit into the car, and they set out.

But the car meant that they could travel differently than the hobo. These 1930s-type wanderers frequently wandered with their whole families. It had been thought that women and children were too weak and lacked the physical ability to board and survive on a moving train so hoboes had rarely traveled with a family. Cars were different, and in the 1930s traveling men were accompanied by their families as they searched for work. Some of the places they stayed along the way resembled the hobo jungles of the earlier period, and these homeless people, too, created their own culture and their own political institutions.

One of the great similarities between the homeless people of the 1920s and those of the 1930s is that both groups lost their homeless worlds because of external forces. The hobo world was destroyed by the new technologies of farming, factories, and railroads. World War II ended the homelessness of the 1930s. As much as he tried, President Franklin D. Roosevelt never understood the extent of government spending that was necessary to end the Depression and create enough jobs to employ every worker in the United States. He certainly tried what has been called "pump-priming" on an unprecedented scale, but he had no idea about how much money was really needed. Only the outbreak and subsequent involvement of the United States in World War II created enough demand for war materials that manufacturing was reawakened, millions of jobs were created, and millions of men, and women, too, were provided government jobs—as soldiers and war workers.

At the end of World War II, there was far less homelessness than there had been in the 1920s and 1930s. With a few relatively minor blips, unemployment remained much lower than it had been. The government seemed committed to ensuring that every American could obtain and keep a job, and it provided generous programs designed to keep veterans off the streets and at their workplaces. It also created programs that reduced the size of the labor force in an acceptable way. It created programs that allowed GIs to obtain college educations rather than look for jobs. The general prosperity of the 1950s and 1960s implied to most Americans that the economic problems of the 1930s had been solved and that unemployment and homelessness no longer need concern the country.

Although some Americans remained aware that poverty still existed in the United States, particularly among some ethnic groups and in certain regions such as the Southeast, the Appalachian Mountains, and on Native American reservations, American confidence was so great that in 1964 President Lyndon Johnson could declare a War on Poverty and call for the elimination of poverty from the United States. We know that didn't happen. And we know that poverty has remained an ongoing significant social and economic problem. But the awareness of homelessness ceased to be a significant aspect of U.S. life for several decades. It was not until the 1970s, and particularly the 1980s, that homeless people forced themselves onto the U.S. consciousness by appearing on the streets of cities where they set up temporary residences—sleeping on steam grates for warmth and panhandling coins from strangers.

Americans had mixed reactions to the appearance of hundreds, if not thousands, of homeless people on the streets of major U.S. cities, including the capital, Washington, DC. Some Americans preferred to ignore the issue altogether and close their eyes to it. Others believed that homeless people could work if they wanted and that homelessness had been created by the personal failings of homeless people. Still others didn't care about the homeless people themselves and just wanted to get them off the streets because they considered homeless people to be an unpleasant, visually jarring circumstance that they would prefer not to encounter.

Some Americans, however, viewed homelessness differently. Their experiences during the 1950s and 1960s persuaded them that the U.S. political, social, and economic systems were deeply flawed and that homelessness represented another outcome of those failings. This understanding of the problem provoked a debate that still continues. Its central issue concerns how to solve the problem of homelessness.

The debate rages on several levels. On one, there is a controversy about whether there really is a problem. Are the people living on sidewalks really homeless? Or, do they choose to live like that? Could they work if they wanted? On a second level, those who believe that homelessness is real also debate whether the federal government has a responsibility to alleviate homelessness or if that is each individual's responsibility. What does a society owe to its weakest members? At still a third level, those who think that the government does have a responsibility are divided between those who think that many homeless people bear personal responsibility for their condition while others think that homelessness results from weaknesses in the social, political, and economic systems requiring fundamental change. Those who believe that individuals bear personal responsibility believe that government should only assist those whose condition derives from social, political, or economic causes over which they had no control.

At each of these levels, there is conflict about the nature of the circumstances, the culpability of individuals for their own circumstances, and the question of government responsibility for the welfare of American citizens. These debates, in one form or another, characterize a great deal of the political discourse that dominates the headlines every day—and that seem no closer to resolution than they have ever been.

Prologue

VAGABONDS IN ENGLAND

1 Edw. VI., c.3

- **Document:** These are excerpts from C. J. Ribton-Turner, *A History of Vagrants and Vagrancy and Beggars and Begging* (pp. 89–95), concerning the Parliamentary act formally known as 1 Edward VI., c. 3. The spelling, grammar, and punctuation of the document have been modernized slightly. Also, those sections of the document printed in SMALL CAPITAL LETTERS are not part of the original law. They are summaries by Ribton-Turner, editor of the book from which the document was reproduced.
- **Date:** The law was enacted in 1547.
- **Where:** The law was enacted by the English Parliament in London, England.
- **Significance:** This law, often considered the most Draconian ever enacted against vagrancy in England, reveals increasing hostility toward persons who wandered the countryside rather than living in fixed places and working at permanent jobs. The law is often thought to represent the English origins of attitudes toward poverty, laziness, and homelessness in the United States.

DOCUMENT

Forasmuch as idleness and vagabondry is the mother and root of all thefts, robberies, and all evil acts and other mischiefs, and the multitude of people given thereto have always been here . . . very great and more in number . . . than in some other regions, to the great impoverishment of the realm and danger of the king's . . . subjects, . . . which idleness and vagabondry all the king's . . . noble progenitors . . . and this high court of parliament have often and with great travail . . . [attempted] with goodly acts and statutes to repress, yet until this . . . time it has not had that success which has been wished. . . . Partly by foolish pity and mercy of them who should have seen the . . . goodly laws executed [and] partly by the perverse nature and long-accustomed idleness of the persons given to loitering, the . . . goodly statutes hitherto have had small effect. . . . Idle and vagabond persons being unprofitable members or rather enemies of the commonwealth have been suffered to remain and increase and, . . . if they should be punished by death, whipping, imprisonment or . . . other corporal pain it were not without their deserts for the example of others and to the benefit of the commonwealth. Yet, if they could be brought to be made profitable and do service were much to be wished and desired.

IT [THE LAW] THEN PROCEEDS TO . . . ORDAIN THAT EVERY PERSON NOT IMPOTENT, LOITERING OR WANDERING AND NOT SEEKING WORK, OR LEAVING IT WHEN ENGAGED, SHALL BE TAKEN UP AS A VAGABOND, AND EVERY MASTER WHO HAS OFFERED SUCH IDLE PERSON SERVICE AND LABOR SHALL BE ENTITLED TO BRING HIM BEFORE TWO JUSTICES OF THE PEACE, WHO shall immediately cause the said loiterer to be marked with a hot iron in the breast the mark of V. and . . . judge the said person living . . . idly to such presentor to be his slave, to have and to hold the said slave to him, his executors or assignees for the space of two years.

The slave is to be fed on bread and water or small drink and such refuse meats as the master thinks fit. He [the slave] is to be caused to work by beating, chaining, or otherwise, in whatever work he may be put to, however vile it may be. If such slave runs away, his master may pursue him, and punish him with chains and beating; and if he [the master] brings him [the slave] before two justices of the peace, they are empowered to cause him to be marked on the forehead or ball of the cheek with a hot iron with . . . an S. The master can recover £10 and costs from anyone knowingly detaining his slave. A slave running away a second time is to suffer . . . death as a felon. . . . Infant beggars above five and under fourteen may be forcibly taken as apprentices or servants and kept, males till twenty-four, females till twenty. If they run away, they become slaves. Masters are empowered to let, sell, or give the services of such children, who steal such children. Fathers, mothers, nurses, or bearers about of such children, who steal such children from their service are to become slaves for life to the master of the child.

All vagabonds who are not taken into any service are to be marked on the breast with a V with a hot iron, and then sent to their birthplace with a pass in the following form, "we have taken this bearer vagrantly and to the evil example of others without master, service, or labor whereby to get his living going loitering idly about; and because the same says he was born . . . in the county of S., we have sent him to you . . . till he or she be brought to the place to which he or she has named themselves to be born in, ... There to be nourished and kept in the same city, town, or village in chains either at the common works in mending highways or other common work, or from man to man in order till they . . . be equally charged, to be slave to the . . . city or to the inhabitants of the town or village that he or she were born in." . . . The said city, town, or village shall see the said slave, being able to labor set on work and not live idly . . . upon pain that for every such default that the said slave lives idly by the default of the city, borough, or town, or village by the space of three working days, together the city to forfeit five pounds, a borough or town incorporated forty shillings, and other town or village twenty shilling.

TWO YEARS AFTER [THIS LAW WAS ENACTED], SIR JOHN CHEKE [A TUTOR TO KING EDWARD VI AND THE FIRST REGIUS PROFESSOR OF GREEK AT CAMBRIDGE UNIVERSITY] ... ATTESTED TO ITS FAILURE. Loiterers linger in streets, lurk in ale houses, range in highways; valiant beggars play in towns, and yet complain of need ... [even though] they will never be allured to labor again, contenting themselves better with idle beggary, than with honest and profitable labor. And what more noisome beasts be in a commonwealth? Drones in hives suck out the honey, a small matter, but yet to be looking on by good husbands, caterpillars destroy the fruit, a hurtful thing and well shifted for, by a diligent overseer. Diverse vermin destroy corn, kill pollen, engines and snares be made for them.

But what is a loiterer? A sucker of honey, a spoiler of corn, a destroyer of fruit. Nay, a waster of money, a spoiler of vitals, a sucker of blood, a breaker of orders, a seeker of breaks, a queller of life, a basilisk of the commonwealth, which by company and sight does poison the whole country, and staineth honest minds with the infection of his venom, and so draws the commonwealth to death and destruction.

When we see a great number of flies in a year, we naturally judge like to be a great plague; and having so great a swarming of loitering vagabonds, ready to beg and brawl at every man's door, which declare a greater infection, can we not look for a more grievous and perilous danger than the plague is?

SOURCE: C. J. Ribton-Turner. *A History of Vagrants and Vagrancy and Beggar and Begging.* London: Chapman and Hall, Limited, 1887, 89–95.

ANALYSIS

During the late 1400s and throughout the 1500s, many members of the English political, economic, and social elites, especially those who were literate and left observations of the times, became increasingly concerned about problems that they thought were caused by those whom they variously characterized as rogues, vagabonds, vagrants, beggars, loiterers, and so on. So intense became their alarm that R. H. Tawney, a great English historian who studied and wrote about that period, loudly asserted in 1912 that "the sixteenth century lived in terror of the tramp."

This law, passed by Parliament in 1547, the first year of the reign of King Edward VI, was the most Draconian ever enacted—actually allowing vagabonds to be physically tortured and even enslaved. So harsh was this law that it was repealed only two years after being passed, even though the repealing legislation reasserted its central beliefs about vagabondage.

More recent historians have asked whether the actual number of itinerant or drifting people actually justified the torrent of anxiety that seems to have flooded England at the time. But, while that question is historically important, for the purposes of this particular book, it is almost irrelevant. Apparently, the law represents the common perceptions of influential Englishmen. Their interpretation of developments in England generated a huge amount of parliamentary legislation, which, according to U.S. historians, provided the backdrop against which the British colonies in North America interpreted and responded to vagabonds and how they thought such persons should be treated.

To understand the relationship between vagabondage or vagrancy in England in the fifteenth and sixteenth centuries and homelessness in the United States, one has to recognize that the words *vagabond, vagrant, rogue,* their derivatives, and other similar words are not "perfect" synonyms for *homeless* or *homelessness*. But, homelessness does seem implicitly to have been an aspect of vagrancy and vagabondage. And, it is equally important to remember that, according to the *Oxford English Dictionary,* the word *homeless* was not even coined until the mid-1840s, making it impossible for people in the 1400s and 1500s to discuss it in the same way that we do.

If one goes a step further and asks, "Well, why didn't they invent the word *homeless?*" the answer is complex, but not all that difficult to discern. The English didn't construct that word because the concept was foreign to them. They couldn't imagine that a person was actually without a home. Everyone was attached to some place, even if it was a small area. Everyone had a home, or was at least supposed to. To them, the only sorts of people without homes were those vagabonds and vagrants who were also idle and the "mother and root of all thefts, robberies, and all evil acts and other mischiefs."

The perception that vagabonds, vagrants, migrants, and rogues (who happened to be homeless) were also poor, lazy, criminal, and threatened the social order provides the basis for much of the way homeless people have been dealt with in the United States and explains why they have been viewed as negatively as they have been. Although laws as brutal and severe as the one enacted in England in 1547 have never existed in the United States, attitudes scarcely less negative have been frequently expressed. In 1877, the *Chicago Tribune* suggested how the problem of wandering, homeless people could be solved:

> The simplest plan . . . is to put a little strychnine or arsenic into the meat and other supplies furnished the tramp. This . . . is a warning to other tramps to keep out of the neighborhood, keeps the coroner in good humor, and saves one's chickens and other portable property from constant destruction.

FURTHER READING

Aydelotte, Frank. *Elizabethan Rogues and Vagabonds.* New York: Barnes and Noble, Inc., 1967.

Beier, A. L. *Masterless Men: The Vagrancy Problem in England, 1560–1640.* London: Methuen, 1986.

Dionne, Craig, and Steve Mentz, eds. *Rogues and Early Modern English Culture.* Ann Arbor, MI: University of Michigan Press, 2004.

Howe, Nicholas, ed. *Home and Homelessness in the Medieval and Renaissance World.* Notre Dame, IN: University of Notre Dame Press, 2004.

Ribton-Turner, C. J. *A History of Vagrants and Vagrancy and Beggars and Begging.* London: Chapman and Hall, Limited, 1887.

Woodbridge, Linda. *Vagrancy, Homelessness, and English Renaissance Literature.* Urbana and Chicago, IL: University of Illinois Press, 2001.

Part I

WORDS AND NUMBERS

On the surface, homelessness seems like a relatively simple concept. However, a careful examination reveals that there are many definitions of the word and that many different words have been used to categorize and define homeless people. Having these many definitions and ways of thinking about homelessness makes it extremely difficult to determine the number of homeless people and perhaps even more difficult to develop social and political policies regarding homelessness and homeless people.

1

WORDS

The *Oxford English Dictionary (OED)*

- *Document:* This document contains definitions of "homelessness" and words related to it, and definitions of other words often used as synonyms for a homeless person.
- *Date:* The date given before each quotation is the earliest known date for that usage of the word (except in cases where the early English spelling makes the quotation difficult to read and understand).
- *Where:* Published in Oxford, England, by the Oxford University Press, the *OED* is generally accepted as the authoritative source on the development of English words that have been used throughout the world during the last thousand years.
- *Significance:* The overlapping definitions of these words indicate that the words *homeless* and *homelessness* frequently have a much broader meaning than simply not having a house or permanent residence.

DOCUMENT

homeless, *a.* 1. Having no home or permanent abode. Usually of persons . . . 1782 . . . "Friendless, homeless, unbeloved, unregarded." 1793 . . . "Or was the merchant charged to bring The homeless birds a nest?"
2. Affording no home, dwelling-place. 1797 . . . "Going forth into a new and homeless world."1812 . . . "Thus left by herself on the homeless sea."
homelessness, homeless condition.

* * * *

bum, *n.* 1. A lazy and dissolute person; an habitual loafer or tramp. . . . 1864 . . . "The policemen say that even their old, regular and reliable 'bums' appear to have reformed." 1891 . . . "I don't believe in feeding professional bums."

1926 . . . "A thoroughgoing bum from the road. The term 'bum' is not used here in any cheap or disparaging sense. In those days it meant any kind of a traveling thief."

hobo, orig. *Western U.S.* "An idle shiftless wandering workman, ranking scarcely above the tramp." 1889 . . . "The tramp has changed his name, or rather had it changed for him, and now he is a 'Hobo.'" . . . 1896 . . . "The tramp can scarcely be distinguished from the dyed-in-the wool hoboe."

tramp, *n.* 2. one who travels from place to place on foot, in search of employment, or as a vagrant; also, one who follows an itinerant business, as a hawker. . . . 1808 . . . "A certain class of wandering labourers known by the name of tramps." 1828 . . . "a pedlar; called also a tramper, an itinerant tinker, or one who travels with any kind of wares." 1860 . . . "A wretched woman, who used to traverse the country as a beggar or tramp."

transient, *a.* (*n.*) 2. *colloq.* (orig. *U.S.*). A person who passes through a place, or stays in it only for a short time; *spec.* a "transient guest" at a hotel or boarding-house. Also, a traveler, a tramp, a migrant worker. 1880 . . . "My grandmother held these transients in low esteem." . . . 1893 . . . "On an open, sunny site, and frequented by 'transients' and business men of moderate means." 1894 . . . "Summer residents, transients, and

all, had turned out early." . . . 1941 . . . "Whenever Doober's had rooms to spare a card was put into the ground floor window, and there would be transients for three or four days." 1946 . . . "Piero and the courier were to share a straw mattress in a corridor along with a number of transients only too glad to have a roof over their heads." . . . 1978 . . . "Transients pile in each winter to work the oil patch as soon as the muskeg freezes."

unemployed, *ppl. a.* and *n.* 2. a. Not engaged in any work or occupation; idle; *spec.* temporarily out of work. 1677 . . . "Admit there be in England and Wales a hundred thousand poor people unimployed." . . . 1740 . . . "I remember him three times for some years unemploy'd in any theatre." 1824 . . . "Being unemployed they amused themselves and others with conjectures." . . . 1860 . . . "The vexed question of the destinies of the unemployed workmen." . . . c. Pertaining to, connected with, unemployed persons. 1844 . . . "During this interval he draws the unemployed salary of three hundred rupees per mensem." 1895 . . . "Twenty-four per cent. of its 10,000 members received unemployed benefits."

vagabond, B. *n.* 1. a. One who has no fixed abode or home, and who wanders about from place to place; *spec.* one who does this without regular occupation or obvious

DID YOU KNOW?

In the city, under ordinary circumstances, the homeless man gathers with his kind. Even so, he is very much alone and his contacts with his fellows are relatively formal and distant.

... The flophouse and the cheap hotel compel promiscuity, but do not encourage intimacy or neighborliness. On the outskirts of cities, however, the homeless men have established social centers that they call "jungles," places where the hoboes congregate to pass their leisure time outside the urban centers. The jungle is to the tramp what the campground is to the vagabond who travels by auto. It has for the hobo, perhaps, greater significance, since it becomes a necessary part of his daily life. The evening camp fire for the tourist, on the contrary, is a novelty merely, an experience but not a necessity.

Source: Nels Anderson, *The Hobo: The Sociology of the Homeless Man.* Chicago: University of Chicago Press, 1961, 16. Used by permission of University of Chicago Press.

means of support; an itinerant beggar, idle loafer, or tramp; a vagrant. ... 1575 ... "All wagabondis and idill personis that hes nocht quhairupoun [whereupon] to sustene thame selfis." 1577 ... "The third [sort] consisteth of thriftlesse poore, as the vagabond that will abide no wheres, but runneth vp and downe from place to place (as it were seeking woorke and finding none)." 1605 ... "For shame, betake you to some honest Trade And liue not thus so like a Vagabond." ... 1796 ... "His relations, dishonoured in the public estimation, abandon their home, and become vagabonds." ... 1833 ... "Issuing forth as a vagabond to spread the infection of idleness and vice."

vagrant, *n.* and *a. n.* 1. One of a class of persons who having no settled home or regular work wander from place to place, and maintain themselves by begging or in some other disreputable or dishonest way; an itinerant beggar, idle loafer, or tramp. Vagrants have been the subject of many legal enactments, and by the Act 5 Geo. IV, c. 83 (the Vagrancy Act of 1824, now amended), they were divided into "idle and disorderly persons, rogues and vagabonds, incorrigible rogues and other vagrants". ... 1583 ... "They runne roging like vagarents vp and downe the countries like maisterlesse men." ... 1452 ... "All manere vagraunts, vacabunds and beggers begging oute of the hundred wheras they duelle." 1547 ... " Yf it shall appear .. suche man .. to have been a vagraunte and vacabound or ydle parsone." ... 1856 ... "For the able-bodied vagrant, it is well known that the old English laws had no mercy." 1884 ... "If you dare to trespass on my grounds .. you will be treated as a vagrant or a beggar." 2. One who wanders or roams about; a person who leads a wandering life; a rover. *c*1590 ... "Vagrant, go roam and range about the world, and perish as a vagabond on earth!" ... 1719 ... "In about five Days Time the three Vagrants, tir'd with Wandring, ... came back"

SOURCE: The Oxford English Dictionary. 2nd ed., 1989. *OED* Online. (Oxford: Oxford University Press, 1989), *passim.* Available online at http://dictionary.oed.com. Used by permission.

ANALYSIS

At first glance, the words *homeless* and *homelessness* seem easy to understand. Each word contains two or three syllables, each consisting of four letters that are easily pronounced and whose definitions are not difficult to comprehend. A "home" is the place where one dwells. The first suffix, "-less," means "without," and the second suffix, "-ness," signifies the "the state of." Therefore, looked at in this way, "homeless" means "without a home," and "homelessness" means the "state of being without a home."

But that ease of definition deceives. One recent analyst of homelessness puts it this way:

> To the casual observer, it would appear that defining homelessness would be an easy task. However, this is not the case.

Why not? What makes this apparently straightforward word so complex? One way of answering this question emerges if we dissect *homelessness* into the three component parts—home, -less, and -ness—and look more deeply into their meanings. Start with the word *home*, and consider it only as a noun. The *Oxford English Dictionary* offers eight definitions of *home* as a noun. Each of them has between one and eight sub-

definitions. Probably the one most relevant to understanding homelessness defines a home as "a dwelling-place, house, abode; the fixed residence of a family or household; the seat of domestic life and interests; one's own house; the dwelling in which one habitually lives, or which one regards as one's proper abode." With this definition the word *home* comes close to having the same meaning as "house."

About twenty years ago, a noted architect and architectural historian, Joseph Rykwert, examined the question of the relationship between house and home. He expressed the difference like this:

> "House" means shelter, and implies edges, walls, doors, and roofs—and the whole repertory of the fabric.
>
> "Home" does not require any building, even if a house always does. You can make a home anywhere: a little tinder, even some waste paper, a few matches, or a cigarette lighter is all you need. In our technically advanced civilization, it can be secured with less trouble (but a great deal of equipment) by a VCR tape, which will make flames leap up on your television screen at the push of a button.
>
> But a house must be brick and timber, mortar and trowels, carpentry and masonry, foundations and topping off; and it requires taking thought.

Much more complicated are two other definitions of *home*: "the place of one's dwelling or nurturing, with the conditions, circumstances, and feelings which naturally and properly attach to it" and "a place, region, or state to which one properly belongs, in which one's affections center, or where one finds refuge, rest, or satisfaction." Both of these definitions stress that a home is not only the place where a person dwells. It is something more, it is a particular kind of place, a place for which a person has feelings of affection and with which a person identifies. This way of

DID YOU KNOW?

The real "road" is variously named and variously described. . . . The road proper, or "the turf," as the people who toil along its stretches sometimes prefer to call it, is low life in general. It winds its way through dark alleys and courts to dives and slums, and wherever criminals, hoboes, outcast women, stray and truant children congregate; but it never leads to the smiling windows and doorways of a happy home, except for plunder and crime. There is not a town in the land that it does not touch, and there are but few hamlets that have not sent out at least one adventurer to explore its twists and turnings.

Source: Josiah Flynt [pseud. Josiah Flint Willard], *Tramping with Tramps: Letters and Sketches of Vagabond Life.* New York: The Century Company, 1899, 28.

defining *homelessness* strongly evokes the well-known line in the poem "Death of the Hired Man" (1915) by the American poet Robert Frost. Home, he sang out, is "the place where, when you have to go there, they have to let you in."

Christopher Jencks (1994), a prominent professor of social policy at the Kennedy School at Harvard University, wrote at length about the relationship between *home* and *house*, and he discovered that the relationship between the two words has changed over time.

Many Americans still use the term "home" as a synonym for the place where their family lives. People without family ties are then "homeless" no matter where they live. Building on this conception, American sociologists used to describe men who lived in skid-row hotels as homeless. The label was not based on the fact that these hotels were over-crowded or badly ventilated. Sociologists called these men homeless because they lived alone and seldom saw their kin.

After 1960, as more and more Americans began living alone by choice, the idea that you had a home only if you lived with your family began to lose its grip on the American imagination. By the late 1960s, many Americans thought they had a home if they had a fixed address where they could leave their possessions, return whenever they wished, and sleep in peace. The homeless were in turn defined as people who had no fixed address.

Since 1980, most Americans have adopted an even less demanding view of what it means to have a home. When we talk about the homeless today, we seldom include migrant workers. Today, any private space intended for sleeping can qualify as a home, as long as those who sleep in it have a legal right to be there and can exclude strangers. The homeless have become those who have no private space of their own, no matter how temporary.

Jencks's discussion of the diminished criteria necessary to allow a place to be called a home relates to the second of the three elements of homelessness, -less. What exactly does that syllable mean? Probably the most obvious way to define it is "without"; if you attach the suffix -less to any noun, it means "not having something." Thus, *homeless* means being without a home, *penniless* means being without money, and *topless* means not having a top. But, if we look in the *OED* for a definition of "-less," we discover that this suffix can signify anything from an absolute condition of zero, a total absence, or a complete lack to the less severe condition of scarcity or inadequacy.

And, just as any of the various definitions of *home* or *-less* can be used to define *homelessness*, the same statement applies to the third element of homelessness, *-ness*. How does one define *existence* or *being*? In particular, must a condition be permanent or long-lasting or constant before *-ness* becomes applicable? Or, can a condition described as *-ness* be fleeting, transitory, or short-lived? Can a condition characterized as *-ness* be intermittent, recurring, or on-and-off? How long must a condition exist before it can be recognized with a word that acknowledges its presence?

All of these questions and ambiguities are implied by the many definitions and quotations about *homelessness* provided in the *OED*. The definitions given at the beginning of this chapter somehow refer to wandering, traveling, or migrating. Some of them refer to not having a permanent residence, and all of the definitions interlock with each other. A *bum* is a traveling thief, and a *hobo* is a "wandering" worker and also a tramp. A *tramp* travels from place to place and is a vagrant. A *transient* is also a tramp, and a *vagabond* is said to be an itinerant, tramp, or vagrant. And that last person, a *vagrant*, is characterized as being wandering and itinerant and is also called a tramp. The words all intertwine with each other.

In other words, all of these words do more than resemble each other; they are actual synonyms. That fact is crucial when trying to understand *homelessness*. If all of these words are synonymous, then the characteristics of one word—or person of a particular kind—can be attributed to all of the words or people like that. As a result, the characteristics attributed to all of these words, sometimes explicitly and sometimes indirectly, can also be attributed to *homelessness*.

Two of the characteristics attributed to all of the words are especially important. One is mobility. Many of the definitions refer to transiency, wandering, or traveling. And so, mobility emerges as a key component of *homelessness*. The second characteristic of this group of words has to do with work, employment, or income. All of these words say something about a person's willingness to work or their laziness, their ability or inability to find work, and their income or lack of income. Closely associated with these ideas about labor and toil are other words that refer to a lack of labor, or an attempt to avoid labor—words such as *thievery*, *laziness*, and *idleness*.

The analysis of all of these words makes it clear that *homeless* and *homelessness* are much more complex ideas than the simple definition of "lacking a home." The definitions of *homeless* and *homelessness* include, and sometimes even emphasize, other characteristics than lacking a permanent place of residence.

FURTHER READING

Hitchings, Henry. *The Secret Life of Words: How English Became English*. New York: Farrar, Straus and Giroux, 2008.

Hoad, T. F., ed. *The Concise Dictionary of English Etymology*. Oxford, UK: Oxford University Press, 1986.

Hopper, Kim. "Definitional Quandaries and Other Hazards in Counting the Homeless: An Invited Commentary." *American Journal of Orthopsychiatry*, 65, 3 (July 1995), 340–46.

Hopper, Kim. "Homelessness Old and New: The Matter of Definition." *Housing Policy Debate*, 2, 3 (1991), 757–813.

Liberman, Anatoly. *An Analytic Dictionary of English Etymology: An Introduction*. Minneapolis: University of Minnesota Press, 2008.

Onions, Charles Talbot, ed. *The Oxford English Dictionary of English Etymology*. New York: Oxford University Press, 1966.

Rykwert, Joseph. "House and Home," *Social Research*," 58, 1 (1991), 51–62.

2

NUMBERS

How Many?

- *Document:* This document is a leaflet prepared by the National Coalition for the Homeless (NCH), one of the most prominent organizations in the country advocating for the homeless. As part of this work, it considers the number of homeless people in the United States. This document explains some of the controversies that have surrounded that issue and the disputes that have taken place about it for more than 25 years.
- *Date:* This document was published on the NCH's website in 2009.
- *Where:* The headquarters of the NCH is located in Washington, DC.
- *Significance:* This report from the National Coalition for the Homeless outlines some of the problems that appear when attempts are made to determine how many homeless people there are in the United States.

DOCUMENT

Methodology

Researchers use different methods to measure homelessness. One method attempts to count all the people who are literally homeless on a given day or during a given week (point in time counts). A second method of counting homeless people examines the number of people who are homeless over a given period of time (period prevalence counts).

Choosing between point-in-time counts and period-prevalence counts has significant implications for understanding the magnitude and dynamics of homelessness. The high turnover in the homeless population documented by recent studies . . . suggests that many more people experience homelessness than previously thought, and that most of these people do not remain homeless. Because point-in-time studies give just a "snapshot" picture of homelessness, they only count those who are homeless at a particular time. Over time, however, some people will find housing and escape homelessness while new people will lose housing. . . . Systemic social and economic factors (prolonged unemployment or sudden loss of a job, lack of affordable housing, domestic violence, etc.) are frequently responsible for these episodes of homelessness. Point-in-time studies do not accurately identify these intermittently homeless people, and therefore tend to overestimate the proportion of people who are chronically homeless. . . . For these reasons, point-in-time counts are often criticized as misrepresenting the magnitude and nature of homelessness.

There is another methodological issue that should be considered. Regardless of the time period over which the study was conducted, many people will not be counted because they are not in places researchers can easily find. This group of people, often referred to as "the unsheltered" or "hidden" homeless, frequently stay in automobiles, camp grounds, or other places that researchers cannot effectively search. For instance, a national study . . . found that the most common places people who had been homeless stayed were vehicles (59.2%), and make-shift housing such as tents, caves, or boxcars (24.6%). . . . This suggests that homeless counts may miss significant numbers of people who are literally homeless. . . .

National Estimates of Homelessness

There are several national estimates of homelessness. Many are dated, or based on dated information. For all of the reasons discussed above, none of these estimates is the definitive representation of "how many people are homeless."

In a recent approximation *USA Today* estimated 1.6 million unduplicated persons used transitional housing or emergency shelters. Of these people, approximately 1/3 are members of households with children, a nine percent increase since 2007. Another approximation is from a study done by the National Law Center on Homelessness and Poverty which states that approximately 3.5 million people, 1.35 million of them children, are likely to experience homelessness in a given year (National Law Center on Homelessness and Poverty, 2007).

These numbers, based on findings from the National Law Center on Homelessness and Poverty, Urban Institute and specifically the National Survey of Homeless Assistance Providers, draw their estimates from a study of service providers across the country at two different times of the year in 1996. They found that, on a given night in October, 444,000 people (in 346,000 households) experienced homelessness—which translates to 6.3% of the population of people living in poverty. On a given night in February, 842,000 (in 637,000 households) experienced homelessness—which translates to almost 10% of the population of people living in poverty. Converting these estimates into an annual projection, the numbers that emerge are 2.3 million people (based on the October estimate) and 3.5 million people (based on the February estimate). This translates to approximately 1% of the U.S. population experiencing homelessness each year, 38% (October) to 39% (February) of them being children (Urban Institute 2000).

It is also important to note that this study was based on a national survey of service providers. Since not all people experiencing homelessness utilize service providers, the actual numbers of people experiencing homelessness are likely higher than those found in the study. Thus, we are estimating on the high end of the study's numbers: 3.5 million people, 39% of which are children (Urban Institute 2000).

In early 2007, the National Alliance to End Homelessness reported a point-in-time estimate of 744,313 people experiencing homelessness in January 2005.

Is Homelessness Increasing?

One limited measure in the growth of homelessness is the increase in the number of shelter beds over time. A 1991 study examined homelessness "rates" (the number of shelter beds in a city divided by the city's population) in 182 U.S. cities with populations over 100,000. The study found that homelessness rates tripled between 1981 and 1989 for the 182 cities as a group. . . .

A 1997 review of research conducted over the last decade (1987–1997) in 11 communities and 4 states found that shelter capacity more than doubled in nine communities and three states during that time period. . . . In two communities and two states, shelter capacity tripled over the decade.

These numbers are useful for measuring the growth in shelter beds . . . over time. They indicate a dramatic increase in homelessness in the United States over the past two decades.

By its very nature, homelessness is impossible to measure with 100% accuracy. . . . Recent studies suggest that the United States generates homelessness at a much higher rate than previously thought. Our task in ending homelessness is thus more important now than ever.

SOURCE: National Coalition for the Homeless. "How Many People Experience Homelessness." July 2009. Available online at http://www.nationalhomeless.org/factsheets/How_Many.html. Used by permission.

ANALYSIS

Trying to determine the number of homeless people in the United States at a particular time presents even more problems than defining the word. This complexity exists for two reasons: the definition of the words *homeless* and *homelessness* and the involvedness of counting.

The previous chapter of this book addressed the issue of definition. Obviously, you can't discuss intangible concepts such as "homelessness" unless you have a clear idea of what the word means. Everyone can think differently about a subject such as homelessness; if someone believes that being homeless means living in a house with fewer than two kitchens, that person is not likely to have anyone else agree. If that were a realistic definition of homelessness, almost everyone in the United States would be homeless, and the literature concerning homelessness would be different from its current nature.

Perhaps this point will be clearer if you think about *love*. Like homelessness, love is an intangible concept. It cannot be touched. It has no physical form that defines it and lets people see it. Therefore, different people have different ideas about the meaning of love, and two people talking about the subject can have very different ways of defining the term. Unless they both know what the other means by the term, they cannot have a conversation that they both understand.

Or, take another common word, *democracy*. The leaders of different countries in the world frequently have different ideas about the characteristics of a democratic country or about what makes a country democratic. As a result, one political leader might claim that his or her country is democratic and another say that it is a dictatorship. Therefore, it is extremely difficult to discuss ideas such as love, or democracy, or homelessness. And, the difficulty is compounded in the case of a word such as *homelessness* because there are so many different ways of defining it or characterizing it.

This makes it impossible to determine precisely how many people in a country are homeless now or have been homeless in the past. It is even difficult to estimate the number of homeless people with any real precision. After all, these numbers cannot be determined if you can't specify who should be considered when you are counting. A clear definition of homelessness must be determined before the number of homeless people can be tallied.

The other major difficulty in determining the number of homeless people comes from questions about how the counting is done—not from who is being counted but from who is counting and how they interpret the results of the count. In fact, there are many dimensions of this issue. Who is actually counting people, and do they have any biases that might affect their ability to count accurately? How carefully and systematically do they locate people who should be considered homeless; do they adequately examine every location where homeless people might be located? Does the number of homeless people vary from one day, month, or season to another? When should the count of homeless people be taken; should it be taken on a single day or over several days? Should it be taken during daylight or at night (which would be a better time to be able to find homeless people)? Is it possible to locate all homeless people, or is it possible to take a sample of the homeless population?

The answers to all of these questions affect the number of homeless people said to be part of any given population. That, in turn, can affect how a government or the remainder of the population will react to the homeless population. And that raises still other questions about the relationships among the homeless population, its government, and the rest of the population. Does either the government or the rest of the population have any desire for the number of homeless people to be either larger or smaller? Are there political reasons for wanting to show that there is little homelessness in a country (e.g., to prove that the country is prospering)? Or, is the primary reason for counting to improve the lives of as many people as possible? Do people in the country want to keep taxes as low as possible and therefore want to diminish the number of homeless people so as to avoid an increase in taxes to assist homeless people? Or, are the remainder of the population primarily concerned with issues of the quality of life and social justice and therefore want to identify as many homeless people as possible to help them?

In the United States, there is also an important constitutional point. The Constitution requires that the federal government take a census of all free citizens every 10 years to determine how many seats in the House of Representatives will be apportioned to each state and how taxes will be collected from each state. Does this clause implicitly require that the annual census be accurate down to the last number? Certainly, the Constitution requires a degree of accuracy; there seems to be no point in taking an inaccurate census and then using that number for important purposes. But, since every homeless person cannot be located because they do not have permanent addresses, how accurate must the census be to satisfy the constitutional requirement? Is simply taking a sample of the population and abstracting from that sample an acceptable way of counting the population of the country?

For decades, all of these questions have bedeviled Congress, the Census Bureau, and just about everyone who has cared about or studied homelessness. These questions recur every 10 years when the census is being prepared and taken, and they will almost certainly continue to be raised every decade in the future.

FURTHER READING

Hopper, Kim. "Definitional Quandaries and Other Hazards in Counting the Homeless: An Invited Commentary," *American Journal of Orthopsychiatry*, 65, 3 (July 1995), 340–47.

Part II

HOBOES, TRAMPS, AND BUMS, 1790–1930

In the British colonies in North America and in the early republic of the United States, the villages, towns, and small cities recognized that some people had no homes. However, they perceived those people somewhat differently. They thought of them as being disabled or injured in some way; they might experience some mental or physical disability, or they might have been abandoned by a spouse, or left orphaned by the death of parents, or suffered from some disaster such as a fire that had destroyed all of their possessions. The people in these small communities knew their neighbors, felt a sense of responsibility for them, and tried, as a community, to provide for them, or at least assist them. However, they had relatively little sympathy for people who had wandered into their communities uninvited. Such people belonged somewhere else and should return there or be returned there, and communities would "warn them out."

As the eighteenth century wore on, the size of communities grew, and citizens ceased to know all of their neighbors as well as they had in the past. People began to feel a less-pressing need to assist others with problems, but, without wanting to neglect them completely, they established places where they could be housed and fed but where they were expected to work in return for their upkeep and maintenance. These workhouses and almshouses, as they were known, became more common as towns and cities grew larger and the 1800s passed.

After the Civil War, the number of people whom we might call homeless began to increase rapidly, and Americans began to hear that the country was being plagued by a "tramp menace." And, as they heard about this danger from ministers, politicians, and the press, they began to wonder how many tramps there really were in the country, why there were so many, and what to do about them.

Most Americans in the late nineteenth century never received or developed a satisfactory view of what was going on. Although they recognized that some people were the unwitting and unwilling victims of circumstance—sickness, injury, abandonment, death—they perceived most wandering people as lazy bums, laggards who simply refused to work to care for themselves and their families.

Most Americans didn't understand the nature of the national economy and that various industries needed large numbers of temporary employees, rather than stable numbers of year-round employees. Certain industries or sectors of the economy, especially agriculture, only needed workers at times when large amounts of work had to be done in a short period of time, such as planting or harvesting. As a result, they didn't understand that there were thousands of people in the country who didn't work and live in the same place all year round. Rather, they wandered from place to place following the seasons of industry and going where jobs took them.

Because most Americans didn't understand the migratory patterns and annual life cycles of these migratory laborers, they also didn't recognize other important characteristics of their lives. They didn't understand that those wanderers were not vagrants locating themselves by stealing rides on trains and that their lives required them to be able to move readily from one job to another with little cost. They didn't understand that these "bums" had their own geographies in "hobo jungles" and "the main stem," that they had their own political organizations, their own vocabularies, and their own songs—in other words, their own distinct subculture within the United States.

3

BEN REITMAN DEFINES *HOBO*, *TRAMP, AND BUM*

Quotations about Ben Reitman

- **Documents:** The documents present definitions of some words frequently used by Chicagoans to describe homeless people at the end of the nineteenth and the early twentieth century: *hobo, tramp,* and *bum.* The person who provided the definitions was Dr. Ben Reitman, a Chicago physician who treated primarily homeless people and prostitutes and who was sometimes referred to as the "King of the hoboes." Some of the selections are direct quotes taken from Reitman's published or spoken words, and others are indirect quotes.
- **Date:** Reitman gave all of these definitions between 1907 and 1923.
- **Where:** The statements were all made in Chicago either by Reitman or by people who knew him and heard him.
- **Significance:** These statements reveal how members of the hobo community defined themselves and how they distinguished among hoboes, tramps, and bums.

DOCUMENTS

1. Ben Reitman defines *hobo, tramp,* and *bum*:

A hobo works and wanders, a tramp dreams and wanders, and a bum drinks and wanders.

SOURCE: Quoted in Eddy Joe Cotton, *Hobo: A Young Man's Thoughts on Trains and Tramping in America.* New York: Harmony Books, 2002. Cotton does not indicate his source for the quotation.

* * *

2. Another definition said to be given by Reitman:

A tramp is a man who doesn't work, who apparently doesn't want to work, who lives without working, and who is constantly traveling. A hobo is a non-skilled, non-employed laborer without money, looking for work. A bum is a man who hangs around a low class saloon and begs or earns a few pennies a day in order to obtain drink. He is usually an inebriate.

SOURCE: Roger A. Bruns, *The Damnedest Radical: The Life and World of Ben Reitman, Chicago's Celebrated Social Reformer, Hobo King, and Whorehouse Physician.* Urbana, IL, and Chicago: University of Illinois Press, 2001. This quotation and this terminology ascribed to Reitman have been cited many times. See, e.g., Tim Cresswell, *The Tramp in America.* London: Reaktion Books, 2001.

* * *

3. This is a third attempt by Reitman to define *hobo, tramp,* and *bum.* On this occasion, he was quoted by a journalist who heard him speaking at a meeting:

The doc has systematized his information about vagrants. He wants, first of all, to have the public differentiate an itinerant vagrant from just a common vagrant. "A vagrant, you know, is a man who has no visible means of support," he ran on last night. "But all such do not wander, do not tramp about. Some stay in one place. Those who are penniless and content to remain in one place I will not consider.

"Itinerant vagrants are sub-divided into well-defined classes: 1. Tramp, [a man] who dreams and wanders, a victim of wanderlust, who globe-trots without money. 2. Hobo, [a man] who works and wanders but who doesn't work long in one place. 3. Bum, [a man] who drinks and wanders. And each of these last classes are again sub-divided. Among the tramps, for instance, there is the tramp criminal, who is dodging around to escape the police. The criminal tramp is a man who is wandering about for the pure love of going, but who isn't above turning off a trick now and then as a little side affair.

"Then there is the neuropathic tramp. That's what I am. A neuropathic tramp is simply a man who is crazy about batting around. It is a sort of disease, a simple form of insanity. Instead of having fits of epilepsy or imagining that he is a Napoleon, the itinerant vagrant has fugues. The most common form of the fugue is ambulatory automatism.

DID YOU KNOW?

Poem about Ben Reitman

He understands all—he knows all.
All that they try to express, he
    already knows.
Their lives he has lived, their deaths
    he has died.
Their loves he has known, their sins
    he has committed.
And their he sits among them.

Holding them all, idealist and prostitute,
    student and moron, conservative and
    radical, the believer and the scoffer.
What is it that all these souls find in
    this one man?

Against each other they would fight to
    the death.
Yet in him they find a common
    meeting ground.

Source: The Papers of Benjamin Lewis Reitman, M.D. Box 1, Folder 8, February 7, 1934. Special Collections Department, University of Illinois at Chicago. Used by permission.

DID YOU KNOW?

Reitman's letterhead read:

DR. BEN L. REITMAN
Physician and Sociologist

Work Limited to the Diagnosis,
Prevention, and Treatment of
Venereal and Social Problems

His two-room suite was across State Street from Marshall Field & Company. The reception room was drab and untidy. It had an old couch, several straight chairs, and a desk usually occupied by his secretary/assistant. There was a constant stream of persons coming and going as in the office of any successful medical practitioner, but there the similarity ended, for Reitman's visitors were not only prostitutes and pimps but also radicals, politicians, and academicians. Reitman lectured regularly at the University of Chicago, at the Dil Pickle Club, and unofficially chaired the almost daylong discussions in his reception room. In the midst of an intense argument on unemployment and welfare a flashily dressed pimp would saunter in, nod to the company, and proceed to the inner office; Reitman would finish his sentence and follow. Generally in a moment or two they would be out and the discussion would resume, the pimp sometimes staying to listen or participate.

... Dr. Reitman was a large man of imposing presence, with untidy black hair, and a full beard in later years. He usually wore a black foulard tie and carried a cane and a black slouch hat when he went out. Niver often went to lunch with Reitman at Berghoff's on Adams Street in the basement. Reitman's favorite meal there was pig's knuckles and sauerkraut. He would noisily suck out the marrow and smack his lips in enjoyment. His political and social philosophy is not so easily described. ... Reitman wrote to Niver, "I'm an Anarchist and think all governments wrong and harmful and built upon violence. Only freedom in all of its loveliness, cooperation to share and share alike will bring peace on earth. Let me repeat again with Walt Whitman, 'I swear I ask for nothing for myself that I do not want for all man.'"

Source: Franklin Rosemont, ed., *The Rise and Fall of the Dil Pickle: Jazz-Age Chicago's Wildest & Most Outrageously Creative Bohemian Nightspot.* Chicago, IL: Charles H. Kerr Publishing Company, 2004, 163–64.

"When I say that a man tramps I mean that he travels by foot or by train. In the latter case beating his way. America is the only country in the world where vagrants make a habit of beating their way on the trains.

"A hobo is always looking for work as he goes; a real tramp never does. The hobo is the sort of fellow who works in the wheat fields of the Dakotas in the Fall, in the orange groves of California in the Winter, on the railroads of Wyoming in the Spring, and on the fruit farms of Michigan in the Summer. He is often a printer and sometimes mends umbrellas. He is usually a good worker, but he won't stay long in one place.

"The old rosy ways of the bum have passed. Time was when he hung around saloons, and when the beer kegs were put out he drained them of their contents. In those days there was always a little left in every keg. He was the man with a tomato can on a string. But now every saloon of any account has an air-pump that draws out of the keg the very last drop of liquid before it is taken from its bunk."

SOURCE: "Bread Lines Badly Managed—President of Chicago Tramps Here to Champion Needs of Vagrants." *New York Times*, December 2, 1907.

ANALYSIS

If you define *homelessness* as "not having a permanent physical abode," then homelessness has existed in the present-day United States from the moment that English settlers reached Virginia in 1607. If you define homelessness in a narrow way and say that it is the "condition of being without a permanent place to live," then everyone who entered North America as a colonist in the earliest years of the European occupation was homeless. After all, when they set foot on land for the first time, there were no houses for them to buy or rent, no apartments to rent, and no hotels where they could stay until they made more permanent arrangements. Even after settlers had thrown together nasty places where they could sleep, eat, and store their few possessions temporarily, these shelters could hardly be considered homes. The first English settlers in Virginia dug holes in the ground that had a depth about half the height of a dwelling's normal walls. They then threw a rudimentary frame over this burrow and covered it with tree branches, mud, and leaves. These dugouts, as they literally were, remained the colonists' dwellings until their leaders thought the colony well-established and secure enough for some men to break away from providing food and defending the settlement and turn to putting up more traditional dwellings.

Even after the first Englishmen had provided more satisfactory housing, they were still homeless if a broader definition of homelessness is used. The first English settlers in 1607 were all men. No women are known to have arrived in Jamestown until 1619. Therefore, the first houses can hardly be described as places that provided the kind of emotional fulfillment so often said to be a major component of making a house into a home.

However, although homeless people lived in Virginia and the other colonies throughout the colonial period, they were never referred to as *homeless*. That word didn't enter the English vocabulary until about 1800 when an English writer is credited with using it for the first time. Even then, the word didn't become commonly used for many decades, probably until well into the twentieth century.

As a result, there is no evidence that people wrote about, talked about, described, or analyzed the condition that would today be called "homelessness" or the people who would be called "homeless." Instead, other terminology was used to refer to them, words that were mentioned and discussed earlier in this book. This alternate vocabulary continued in use throughout the nineteenth and most of the twentieth centuries. Consequently, to analyze and understand homelessness, one has to explore social conditions and vocabulary deeply to discover those people who were homeless.

The first large, identifiable group of people in the United States whom contemporary historians consider to have been homeless attracted widespread attention after the Civil War. At the time, instead of being called homeless, they were generally labeled tramps, hoboes, or bums. And, their most important characteristics were generally thought to be frequent mobility and difficulty obtaining regular employment.

It is important to recognize that most people, both then and now, have used the three words—*tramp, hobo, bum*—interchangeably and perceived no differences among them. But regardless of their usage generally, hobo leaders made clear distinctions and defined the words and the people they represented differently from each other. In doing so, their distinctions and their definitions emphasized mobility and work—whether a person worked and moved, worked and didn't move, did not work but did move, and neither worked nor moved.

Perhaps no one tried more diligently than Ben Reitman to define the words *hobo, tramp,* and *bum*. Reitman has been described as "the damnedest radical" in Chicago, and he participated in as many unconventional (for the times) activities as anyone in the city, perhaps even in the country. Reitman (1879–1942) was born in St. Paul, Minnesota, but grew up in the more squalid sections of Chicago where he developed an unorthodox set of interests and a highly nonconformist lifestyle. Reitman left home when he was 10 and spent several years wandering throughout the United States. After he returned to Chicago permanently, he attended high school, graduated from the College of Physicians and Surgeons, and earned the right to practice medicine in

Illinois in 1904. As a physician, he developed a highly unusual practice. Many prostitutes in the city consulted Reitman because of his unusual practices and beliefs. He had much more open-minded sexual attitudes than most doctors in the city—certainly more tolerant than most people in general. He thought that prostitution should be legalized, and he badly wanted to protect prostitutes from venereal disease. He established the first clinic for the treatment and prevention of venereal disease at the Cook County Jail, and he was willing to perform illegal abortions for women who wanted them.

In politics, Reitman was an outspoken anarchist. Through his anarchist political activities, he met Emma Goldman, the most well-known and feared woman radical in the United States, perhaps of anyone in the country. The pair fell passionately in love and began a torrid love affair that lasted, intermittently, for several decades. Among their most important political goals was securing and guaranteeing the right of free speech, a cause that brought them into regular conflict with the political establishment.

Throughout his life, Reitman maintained close associations with the hobo community. He was one of the founding members of the Hobo College in Chicago and has sometimes been called its founder. This was a place financed by William Eads, "the millionaire hobo," where wandering men gathered to read books, swap stories, and hear lectures by noted speakers, teachers, and intellectuals on topics ranging from venereal disease to vagrancy laws and from personal hygiene to politics. Reitman also published the life story of a hobo who, unlike most of them, was a woman. This book, whose title page read *Sister of the Road: The Autobiography of Boxcar Bertha, as told to Dr. Ben Reitman*, was actually a novel. There was no single Bertha Thompson, and Reitman based the narrative on the lives of three women hoboes he had known. However, it was so realistic and convincing that, even today, people writing about tramps and hoboes believe that Boxcar Bertha was a real person and that Reitman did nothing more than record her reminiscences. So aware of hoboes and Hobohemia was Reitman that he became known as "King of the hoboes."

In reading Reitman's definitions, notice how his vocabulary changed over time and that he used different words to describe homeless people at different times. In the earliest of the documents, he not only puts hoboes, tramps, and bums in a hierarchical order, but he also lists them as subgroups of vagrants. The changing relationships among these terms strongly suggest that Reitman's thinking about the subject had also changed.

FURTHER READING

Bruns, Roger A. *The Damndest Radical: The Life and World of Ben Reitman, Chicago's Celebrated Social Reformer, Hobo King, and Whorehouse Physician.* Urbana, IL: University of Illinois Press, 2001. (Originally published 1987)

Reitman, Ben L. *The Second Oldest Profession: A Study of the Prostitute's "Business Manager."* New York: Vanguard Press, 1931.

Reitman, Ben L. *Sister of the Road: The Autobiography of Box-Car Bertha, as Told to Dr. Ben L. Reitman.* New York: Harper & Row, 1937.

4

JACK LONDON EXPLAINS "THE RODS"

"Rods and Gunnels"

- *Document:* This document is a selection from a magazine article by U.S. author Jack London describing one way a hobo could ride the train without buying a ticket.
- *Date:* The article was published in August 1902.
- *Where:* It was published in the United States.
- *Significance:* The article graphically depicts how a hobo might sneak aboard a train and find somewhere to hide. It also indicates how important train-riding was to hoboes by showing the great risks they took to travel for free.

DOCUMENT

. . . In professional Trampland "riding the rods" has a specific meaning. . . . [When] the ordinary tramp . . . hears "riding the rods" . . . he confuses them with gunnels. . . .

Now, what are the gunnels? . . . [T]hey are "the truss rods which, after the fashion of bridge trusses, support the middle stretch of the car between trucks." They are heavy iron rods which run lengthwise with the car, and which differ in number and shape according to the make of the car. While they occur on passenger coaches, no one ever dreams on riding them except on freight cars. And by those who know and set the pace in Trampland, they are known as "gunnels." And be it remarked parenthetically that criteria are required in Trampland as well as any other land. Somebody must set the pace, give the law, sanction usage.

Anybody with arms and legs can ride the gunnels. It requires no special trick or nerve. . . .

But to "ride the rods" requires nerve, and skill, and daring. And, by the way, there is but one rod, and it is on passenger coaches. . . .

A four-wheel truck is oblong in shape, and is divided into halves by a cross-partition. . . . Between this cross-partition and the axis is a small lateral rod, three to four feet in length, running parallel with both the partition and the axle. This is the *rod*. There is more often than not another rod, running longitudinally, the air-brake rod. These rods cross each other; but woe to the tyro who takes his seat on the brake rod! It is not *the* rod, and the chance is large that the tyro's remains will worry and puzzle the county coroner.

Let me explain how such a rod is ridden. . . . [F]or clearness let me describe it in the first person.

The train is pulling out and going as fast as a man can run. . . . I stand alongside the track. The train is approaching. With a quick eye I select the coach and truck—the for'ard truck, so that sheltered by the cross-partition, I shall avoid "punching the wind." I begin to run gently in the direction the train is going. As "my" truck comes closer I hit up my pace, and just before it reaches me I make one swift spurt, so that when it is abreast of me the respective velocities of the train and myself are nearly equalized. At this moment (and it must be the moment of moments neither the moment before nor the moment after), at this moment I suddenly stoop, reach under the car, and seize the first gunnel; and at this same instant,

When hoboes decided to ride trains without first buying tickets, they needed to find places where they could remain hidden, unseen by officials or employees of the railroad company. Sometimes they rode on the platforms or connections between train cars; sometimes they found vacant space within the cargo of boxcars; and sometimes they squeezed into the narrow space between the wheels of a train car and the bottom of the car's interior. Sometimes, as in this picture, they rode on the top of a railroad car where they could not be seen by anyone inside the train while it was moving. (Library of Congress)

I lift my feet from the ground swing my body under the car and bring my feet to rest on the break-beam. The posture is undignified and perilous. My feet are really resting, my whole weight is supported by my arms, the car above me is rolling and jolting, and my back is toward the rails singing beneath.

But, hand over hand, I haul myself in till I am standing in a doubled position on the break beam. It will be noted that I am still *outside* the truck. Between the top of the truck and the bottom of the car is a narrow space, barely sufficient to admit a man's body. Through this I squeeze, in such manner that my feet will remain *outside* the truck on the brake beam, my stomach is pressed against the *top* of the truck, and my head and shoulders unsupported are *inside* the truck. I say "unsupported," and I mean it for beneath my chest is the rapidly revolving axle. This I dare not touch, but must thrust my head and trunk, snake fashion, over and past it till I can lay my hands on either the brake-rod or the cross-rod. This done, my head and shoulders are now lower than my hips (which are on top of the truck), and I must draw my hips, legs, and feet over and down across that moving axle without touching. Squirming and twisting, this is accomplished, and I sit down on the cross-rod, back resting against the side of the truck, one shoulder against the cross-partition, the other within a couple of inches of the other wheel. More than once I have had a

DID YOU KNOW?

Nels Anderson Goes Cross-Country

. . . [A] passenger express pulled in, a dozen strides away from me. No one was there in either direction watching. So came another impulsive decision. I crawled unsure under out of sight, inside a truck on a brakebeam. Less than two hours later came Canon City. The train stopped at the point of entering the yards, possibly to get signals. I got off, thankful for that short ride. From here, one could get a freight train west.

Two minutes later, I was opposite the station. The passenger express was still there. . . . [N]o police or other watchers were in sight. Again I crawled under the same car to sit on the same brakebeam. That turned out to be an all night ride, the temperature dropping slowly until the Continental Divide was reached . . . something to be grateful for, the cool helped keep me awake. Down the west slope the temperature rose, but now daylight was there and keeping awake was no problem. By mid-forenoon my Denver and Rio Grande train had come to the hot desert of eastern Utah. Now began my worry about keeping awake. The wind blowing under was warm and hot by turns, often sand or dust coming with it. One did well not to get ditched in this stretch of desert. It was well past noon. Already I had been about twenty-four hours on that seat, with one arm gripping the frame of the truck. Muscles here and there were aching. The fear of weariness became more a worry than fear of going to sleep.

Source: Nels Anderson, *The American Hobo: An Autobiography.* Leiden, Netherlands: E. J. Brill, 1975. 100. Used by permission of Koninklijke Brill NV.

wheel rasp against my shoe or whizz greasily against my shoulder. Six or eight inches beneath me are the ties, bounding along at thirty, forty, or fifty miles an hour, and all in the world is a slender swaying rod as thick as a man's first finger. Dirt and gravel are flying, the car is bounding overhead, the earth flashing away beneath, and rumble and roar, and . . . this is "riding the rods."

. . . The point of this article is: *that when the lesser local tramps are themselves ignorant of much of the real "road," the stray and passing sociologist, dealing only with the lesser local tramps, must stand in corresponding ignorance.* Such investigators do not deal with the genuine "profesh" [tramp or hobo word meaning "professional tramp"]. The tramps they probe and dissect are mere creatures without perspective, incapable of "sizing up" or understanding the Underworld in which they live. These are the *canaille* and *bourgeoisie*, these "gay cats," "bindle stiffs," "stake men," "shovel bums," "musher," "fakirs," and "stew bums." As well might the Man from Mars get a lucid and philosophic exposition of twentieth-century sub-lunary society from a denizen of Mulberry Street as the stray and passing sociologist get a clear and searching exposition of the "road" from these men.

SOURCE: Jack London. "Rods and Gunnels." *The Bookman*, XV (August 1902), 241–44.

ANALYSIS

Every author who wrote about hoboes and tramps between roughly 1870 and 1930 remarked on their mobility—that they were constantly on the go and never stayed in one place for very long. Wandering and its implication of homelessness probably received more attention than any other characteristic of hobo or tramp life. More than that, every commentator agreed that to hoboes and tramps the most important way of getting from place to place was riding on trains. They understood that walking was an important way of getting around, but getting around under one's own steam was primarily used for traveling short distances. Going any distance meant "riding the rails."

The centrality of movement to the lives of hoboes and tramps is an obvious part of the reason that it received more attention than any other aspect of hobo and tramp life. It is safe to say that almost no account of hobo or tramp life written during this period does not discuss mobility. In many cases, mobility is the central topic of these accounts. This is so whether an author was himself a hobo or simply an observer.

However, there is another reason for the great interest in train-riding by hoboes themselves as well by outside writers and their readers. Hoboes and tramps did not get on trains and ride them like other passengers. They did not go up to a ticket counter, buy a ticket, board the train, and then take the seat assigned to them. They couldn't do that because they lacked the money needed. If they wanted to ride the train, they had to find ways of riding for free.

And that is what they did. In great numbers—they tried to sneak aboard trains and hide themselves where they could remain undetected until they were ready to depart. They would ride on the roof of a car, on the platform between two cars, or inside a freight car. The most gripping and attention-grabbing manner of riding for free was to secrete oneself in the substructure of a railroad car where a man would hang precariously only a few inches above the track bed. This way of copping a ride was so fascinating because every aspect of it seemed almost impossible to understand. How did a man get under there? How did he stay there? How did he avoid the dangers of being there?

One of the most popular writers in the United States in the years just after 1900 was Jack London, the author of such naturalistic novels as *The Sea-Wolf*, *White Fang*, and *The Call of the Wild*. But, before he became one of the most popular authors of the time, London had been a hobo and also a newspaper columnist. During that time in his life, he wrote a series of magazine articles about hobo life. And one of those articles explained the technique of "riding the gunnels" and how a hobo could secrete himself underneath a moving train car. While London has almost certainly romanticized the subject, it was nevertheless a common practice of some hoboes and tramps. The article illustrates the importance of train-riding to hoboes and tramps by disclosing how willing some of them were to undertake this difficult feat and accept its life-threatening nature in return for free travel.

FURTHER READING

A-No. 1, b. 1872. *From Coast to Coast with Jack London; by A-No. 1, b. 1872, the Famous Tramp, Written by Himself from Personal Experience*. Erie, PA: The A-no 1 Publishing Company, 1917.

Foner, Philip Sheldon. *Jack London, American Rebel*. New York: Citadel Press, 1964.

Gypsy Moon. *Done and Been: Steel Rail Chronicles of American Hoboes*. Bloomington, IN: Indiana University Press, 1996.

Lennon, John. "Can a Hobo Share a Box-Car? Jack London, the Industrial Army, and the Politics of (In)visibility." *American Studies*, 48, 4 (Winter 2007), 5–30.

Limbaugh, Ronald H. "Before Kilroy: Confessions of a Professional Tramp." *Pacific Historian*, 27, 3 (1983), 50–52.

Walcutt, Charles Child. *Jack London*. Minneapolis, MN: University of Minnesota Press, 1966.

5

TRAIN JUMPING

Letters from a Tramp

- *Document:* This document is a more detailed description of how hoboes and tramps rode trains.
- *Date:* The article was published December 1901.
- *Where:* The article describes events that occurred in the United States. Its author lived in Connecticut.
- *Significance:* The article provides a more complete description of catching train rides than Jack London. The author, a minister and a professor at Trinity College in Hartford, Connecticut, based it on letters that he received from a hobo ("Roving Bill," mentioned in the article) with whom he corresponded regularly.

DOCUMENT

I shall be permitted . . . a brief digression on the subject of "train jumping," which is the most characteristic feature of American tramping.

. . . [I]t may be stated as a general proposition that the Ho-Bo only walks when walking will better his purpose.

For shorter distances and ordinary occasions the freight train is employed. A place is selected where the up-hill grade compels a slackening of speed, and then with a quick run and spring the train is boarded—nearly always successfully, but occasionally there is an accident; the railroad returns suggest that there may be an aggregate mounting into the thousands annually. A man . . . told me that while on the way down from Hartford he saw a tramp run over by one train as he was making ready to jump another. And it was a gruesome reflection that one of them made: "When we fall off there is a fight between the towns as to which shall furnish the box!" To stay on a train thus boarded, whether it is made up of box cars or open ones—"gondólies" they call these latter—requires, of course, some sort of consent on the part of the hands [workers on the train]. They [the hoboes] may be able to evade apprehension for a while, by running about over the cars, but observation they can hardly hope to escape. It follows that the brakeman must be actively or passively consenting parties—considering especially that the general rules of all the companies are against the practice.

A young student friend of mine, finding that he had lost the last passenger train of a Saturday night, brought into requisition skill acquired as a boy in "stumping" other boys of the town in jumping on and off passing trains, and "jumped" a freight. Great was his amusement when the brakeman, instead of rebuking or threatening him, began from his throne of the brake-wheel, to give him pointers as to the best way of hanging on. . . .

Not infrequently, the brakeman demands compensation of other sort for winking at the violation of orders. I have more than once heard it said by tramps that, with tobacco, or a pint bottle, they can go anywhere. This is not mathematically accurate, I dare say, but there is no doubt something in it. One man has told me that in default of these creature comforts inquiry is sometimes made after personal property, as knife or razor, and on one occasion his necktie was demanded.

There are, of course, all kinds of brakemen: and they vary greatly with the [rail]road [company]. But the life of freight brakemen is a rough and dangerous one, neither inviting nor fostering gentleness of character. Many of them have passed to and fro from life on the road to life along the road. And this naturally gives them sympathy with wanderers.

The safer and more common methods of riding have been alluded to. When comparative concealment is desired, the "blind-baggage"—i.e., the end of the baggage car toward the tender—is a favorite, because not much visited by the "Con[ductor]," who is always dreaded above

Boarding a train without attracting attention was challenging. If hoboes tried to sneak aboard while a train wasn't moving, a guard or watchman could easily see them, apprehend them, and have them legally prosecuted. Hoboes responded by finding ways to board a train surreptitiously. One was to wait in a vacant place alongside the railroad tracks just beyond the station. When a train approached but hadn't yet built up speed, hoboes would run alongside it to gain momentum and then, when a suitable place on the train was next to them, they would grab a handhold and literally launch themselves into the train's interior. (North Bank Fred)

any of the crew. The "bumpers" come next—the man stands on one, with his back braced against the end of the car—I have counted a dozen this way on as many trains, successive evenings; less frequently the man straddles the two, steadying himself with his hands.

The box car is often entered by springing the door off its iron way at the side opposite the seal. A party going one way will do this for a party going the opposite direction and then, when all are in, spring the door back again. Since everything externally is in the best of order long trips may be made in this manner without disturbance or interruption.

DID YOU KNOW?

Blackie and Joe Take a Ride

... Running silently, Blackie led him across tracks, stumbling over points, avoiding lights.... They were now near enough to the station for Joe to see the wide platforms and hurrying crowds.

"Now, listen!" said Blackie, "She begins to pick up speed pretty soon after starting. We must catch her before she's goin' too fast. When she starts, we runs towards her.... When we get by the engine, we grab the steps on the front car.... You follow me and do what I do. There's a handrail ... you can grab ... to help swing yourself up...."

... Slowly [the train] began to slide towards them.

"Come on," cried Blackie, and he began to run towards the approaching monster....

When he got to within a few feet of the train, Blackie stopped. As the engine reached him, he began to run with it, Joe following all the time. Blackie let the engine and tender catch him up, and then, catching hold of a steel handle, he jumped on to a step. From there onto another step, and then to the projecting ledge of the front baggage-car. Leaning well forward, he held out his hand.

With a wild jump, Joe had caught the handle and leapt on to the narrow step. He caught Blackie's hand, and in an instant was on the ledge of the baggage-car.

... The train leaped forward, gathering ever greater speed. Wind rushed by them and sparks flew back....

... On the ledge ... there was sufficient space for five or six men to stand closely together.... [They], therefore, were comfortable—according to hobo standards....

It was cold, and Blackie prepared to face the weather. He turned up his coat-collar under his overalls, and fastened it with a safety-pin.... He took off his soft felt hat, folded it, and put it in the bosom of his shirt. Then, he took a cap from his pocket and pulled it well over his eyes. He knotted a large black handkerchief at the back of his neck and pulled it up over his face, so that it hung down just under his eyes.... This was to keep the dirt, smuts, and sparks from his face and mouth. Then he put on his gauntlet gloves, so that his hands should not become frozen, holding on to the steel handles through the long hours. Carefully, Joe followed his example....

... "Every time she stops," Blackie told Joe, "we must jump off, as the train slows down. Then we run forward, round the station, and catch her again when she starts. We can't stay on because they usually search her for hobos, when she stops."

Through the cold night they raced on. The rain had stopped, and some frozen stars appeared. On through the

Now and then the prisoner is exposed to danger of starvation. A case of this kind has been related to me—where only the accidental visit of a train hand saved a man from death. The brakeman inspected the intruder's papers, and, finding that they showed him to be in good standing in his union, took him out, fed him up and then replaced him—to finish his journey in peace....

A railway accident, whether by water or fire, is a very serious affair to passengers of this sort. You have doubtless read more than once, as I have, of tramps drowned like rats, or burned or crushed to death, while stealing rides in this fashion.

Riding the trucks is done in various ways. A locomotive engineer ... has shown me the precise spot from which he had taken out two men at one time. It was on the rear truck of the tender. They were resting face downward on the truck beam, with just eleven inches of vertical space for their bodies, by actual measurement. He also showed me the little cage under the "cow-catcher" of his rather old-style engine, whence he had once extracted two tramps. And it so happened that the week following this relation, as his engine drew up close to another train, a man crept out from the same spot and started calmly off for the neighboring station, simply remarking, "Seems to me you run up pretty tight!"

"Yes, and what if we'd happened to hit?" was the rejoinder.

To which the tramp replied, "Oh, I'm used to that. I'm not afraid."

And when you come to think of it, a place inside the cow-catcher is not much less safe than one anywhere else on the train. Still, it must be a little billowy and a trifle airy withal.

The same engineer showed me another place from which he had seen tramps issue forth—the old fashioned tool-box, still occasionally found under some of the cars. It is about three feet wide and two and a half high, and has a convenient flat-door at the end. It is always very greasy and dirty, and must be excessively dark. Otherwise, it ought to be commodious enough.

The rods, referred to in the formula "riding the rods," are the truss rods which, after the fashion of bridge trusses, support the middle stretch of the car between trucks. They are generally in pairs, from one to four feet apart, and the body may be supported upon the pair crosswise, resting commonly upon a plank, and I have heard of one case of slinging a hammock from the rods. The plank, called by some a "ticket," is liable to work off and let the body down—a fatal lapse. To prevent this, the plank is roughly grooved to allow the rods to fit in and catch. . . . [T]his sort of riding is too hazardous to be much used. And the same is true, tho in less measure, of truck-riding.

But I am neglecting "Roving Bill." In the letter which I began to quote a little while ago, he . . . pronounces the Southern people in the South very charitable. . . .

I stayed at a place . . . one day near Lake City, Fla., on the G.S.F.R.R. [Gulf Stream and Florida Rail Road], a farm house. He was no old Rebel soldier; he gave me my dinner and treated me kindly. He said there was an Irish Ho-Bo stopped there one morning and knocked. He went to the door. The son of Erin says: "I don't want anything to eat but I just want to borrow your looking glass. I want to see how an Irishman looks starving to death." He told him to come in and he got his feed.

. . . Let us go back now to the letter, which is a long one, starting at Boston and ending at Manchester, N.H. . . .

I arrived at Nashua last night. Met a fellow H.B. yesterday. He did not know where he was going. Had no particular point of view. We took an empty box car. The air was chilly. I slept very comfortable; my feet got a little cold towards morning. My partner got very cold. I could hear him shivering and shaking every time I was awake during the night. He left me this morning. He said he was going to bum some Priest for a quarter as he wanted to get a shave and get something to eat. . . . I met an old Irishman last Sunday on the Rail Road between Lowell and Boston. He stopped and asked me for a match. I accommodated him. He said he had worked in Lowell ever since last Christmas and now he was walking out of the town. He said the drink was the cause. Today being Decoration Day I did not do much faking [repairing umbrellas]. I had a part of a loaf of Bread. I done on that for Breakfast and dinner and then I made fifteen cents fixing an umbrella. I got some crackers and cheese for supper.

. . . [He] evidently moves; for his next begins. "I am now in sight of the city of Manchester, N.H." Later he accounts for mistakes, bad spelling and writing on the plea of the numerous "inconveniences" under which he has been writing. "The muskeetoes is very troublesome today," he half apologetically remarks. Furthermore: "As I sit on the ground, my back against a pine tree, my knee for a desk, it is not as comfortable as it is in an easy chair in library or office."

SOURCE: John J. McCook. "Letters from the Diary of a Tramp; Train Jumping—a Digression; Nature; the South." *The Independent*, LIII, 2766 (December 5, 1901), 2880–88.

---

sleeping land rushed the long express. Inside the passengers sat, warm and soft, on the upholstered seats, or lay sleeping in their berths. And on the prow of the giant land-ship stood . . . muffled figures, shivering but dauntless, carried on—through bitter cold and smoke and turmoil, danger of arrest or of beating—toward the harvest jobs that would earn them sustenance for a short while.

Source: Charles Ashleigh, *Rambling Kid*. Charles H. Kerr, 1984. Used by permission of Charles H. Kerr Publishing Co.

ANALYSIS

John J. McCook was a Protestant minister and professor at Trinity College in Hartford, Connecticut. At some point in his life, he became interested in the large number of hoboes he saw around him, and he began collecting information about them. He had questionnaires printed that he sent to police chiefs across the United States asking them about the hoboes in their cities. McCook initially sent out nearly 1,000 of these surveys, and he received several hundred in return.

While he was gathering information, McCook began to correspond with a hobo named William Aspinwall. Although the two men never actually met, they corresponded for several years and exchanged several hundred letters. On the basis of these letters, McCook published a series of articles in the journal *The Independent* in which he tried to depict and explain hobo life to his readers.

In this particular article, he makes several important points. First, he reveals the places on a train where hoboes commonly hid themselves. Although he does not mention hoboes riding on the roofs of cars or underneath them, he does refer to freight cars and couplings as places where hoboes frequently concealed themselves. Second, he identifies some of the less-recognized dangers faced by hoboes. As well as being run over, they could fall from trains and receive severe injuries; and, if the doors of a car became unexpectedly locked, a hobo inside could either starve to death or freeze to death in winter. If he was trapped in a refrigerator car, he could freeze irrespective of the season.

Finally, and perhaps most importantly, McCook indicates that hoboes were not as isolated and disaffiliated as some analysts have argued. There were relationships among hoboes, even among those who did not know each other well but simply met as they traveled. These relationships could be long-lasting if the two men decided to travel together, or they could be intermittent and perhaps renewed if two men happened upon each other on another occasion. It is significant that many hobo or tramp biographies and reminiscences mention situations when two acquaintances just happened to arrive at the same place, at the same time, by chance.

McCook also points out that hoboes could have friendly relationships with the men who worked on the trains. He directly argues that the presence of hoboes could not remain unknown to brakemen or conductors and that the railroad men were at least complicit in the hoboes' presence. Just as interesting, McCook suggests that these relationships had an economic or material nature; the hoboes expected to give, and the trainmen expected to receive, some kind of economic payment, even if it was small.

Such payments were not usually monetary, and they were not usually of great value, but they were important. They made hoboes feel as if they were not riding the trains without giving any compensation, and they allowed the trainmen to feel that they were less guilty of violating company rules by letting people ride for free. Finally, these "donations" probably had some additional meaning if the form of payment was a material item whose image was less than totally positive—tobacco, liquor, or occasionally even sexual favors.

FURTHER READING

Cotton, Eddy Joe. *Hobo: A Young Man's Thoughts on Trains and Tramping in America.* New York: Harmony Books, 2002.

Gypsy Moon. [Schmidt, Jacqueline]. *Done and Been: Steel Rail Chronicles of American Hoboes.* Bloomington, IN: Indiana University Press, 1996.

Kasindorf, M. "A New Breed of Hobos." *Newsweek*, 100 (August 16, 1982), 30–31.

Livingston, L. R. "Riding the rods with A-no.1." *American Heritage*, 7 (August 1976), 94–95.

Spence, Clark C. "Knights of the Fast Freight." *American Heritage*, 27, 5 (August 1976), 50–97.

Spence, Clark C. "Knights of the Tie and Rail—Tramps and Hoboes in the West." *Western Historical Quarterly*, 2, 1 (Spring 1971), 4–19.

Williams, Clifford. *One More Train to Ride: The Underground World of Modern American Hoboes.* Bloomington, IN: Indiana University Press, 2003.

6

A MIGRANT FARM WORKER

A Hobo's Recollections

- *Document:* An interviewer who was investigating hobo life reports on one of his informants. In this section of the report, the interviewer reveals what Thomas Lee told him about the working conditions, traveling, and riding trains that a hobo might experience.
- *Date:* The report was written in 1914.
- *Where:* Thomas Lee's travels took him through Minnesota, North Dakota, and Montana.
- *Significance:* The interview reveals how frequently a hobo moved around and how heavily he relied on trains for transportation. It also indicates that Lee's primary motivation for wandering was to find work.

DOCUMENT

THOMAS LEE. 58 years; a pretty strong man still; can do hard work preferably outside. Irish. Came to the United States with his parents when he was five years old. Single. He could not get the woman he wanted. Homeless, no relatives, no friends. Does not know any trade. When he was nineteen years old he started to learn moulding. After a year of learning he discovered that he did not like it. He wanted to drive horses which he liked very much. This is the reason he became a laborer.

He wanted to earn and save money to buy a farm and to start to raise horses, but he always failed. In the periods of unemployment, which often occurs in the position of a laborer, he used up his saved money. After years of struggle, hopes, and disappointments, he gave up the idea of becoming a farmer. After that he did not care to save money; when he had it he "blew it in."

A year ago he was in Minneapolis; when he arrived he "rested" a week, drinking mostly beer, going to the shows and to the girls. "A man can't get along without that—it's God's arrangement." When his money was almost gone he got a job through a private employment office; he had to pay his last dollar in advance for fees, and was shipped free into North Dakota into a railroad camp replacing ties; ten hours a day; pay $2 a day; $4 [a week] for sleeping place and board. He slept in a boxcar, one man in a bunk, bunks two stories high; ten men in a car, the air was foul; men themselves cleaned the cars, no spittoons; bedding was an old mattress; he cleaned his but others slept dirty. The board was poor—mostly cold storage products; work was pretty heavy; worked Sundays, fifteen hours for $3 on a Sunday. After three weeks he quit it; he did not like the heavy dirty work and the poor board. The prices of the goods in the Commissary Store were 30% higher than in the private stores, but the goods were alright as everywhere. Both the store and board were furnished by the Boarding Co.

He went to Mavil, N.D. and hired himself as a helper to a thrasher, who employed twenty-five men; he worked from sunrise to sun-down—thirteen hours a day; pay $2.50 a day and board at the farmers', the grubs were good; the men slept in a hay barn, although dusty but clean and without vermin. The work was hard and quite exhausting; the thrasher was a good man. In sixteen days the job was finished. He jumped a freight train to Minneapolis. In two days he had such a "good time" that from $45 he had only a few dollars left. He then got a job through a private employment office paying $1 in advance. He was shipped free to Duluth to a railroad camp to do surfacing on the Great Northern, 25 miles from Duluth; ten hours a day, $2 a day, and for camp and board $4. He slept in a boxcar, one man in a bunk; the bunks were two-story high; fifteen men in a car. The air in the cars were foul; every morning the men had headaches and bad tastes in their mouths. There was no man in charge of cleaning the cars; no spittoons; the board was good although cold storage grubs; worked ten hours a day. He freighted back to Duluth, and "rested" there a week. Every cent was gone. He then got a job through a Boarding Co. who charged him $1 for fees which was afterwards taken off from his wages. The shipment to Hibbing, Minn. was free. The work was in a railway construction camp—surfacing; ten hours a day; $2 per day; $4 for board; the bedding and board were pretty clean and good. He worked three weeks and quit because he earned enough money and wanted to start his journey toward Chicago, where he felt better than anywhere else in the world. He jumped a freight to Duluth; spent one day there—"just having a little time." He then went to Superior and spent another day there. From there he jumped a freight to St. Paul where after he spent a day took a freight to La Crosse, Wis. where he found work in a railway camp, 25 miles from La Crosse; 10 hours a day; $1.75; for board $3.75; slept in an overcrowded boxcar; one man in a bunk; the bunks were two-story high; the bedding was dirty and lousy; he cleaned and cleaned but could not get rid of the vermin. The board was very poor—meats spoiled; he could stand this job only eight days. Went back to La Crosse and spent a day there, then jumped a freight train to Milwaukee—in October. Here he "rested" a week—had just a "little time," did not look for work. The next job he found himself in a railway "extra gang," fourteen miles from Milwaukee, raising rails and shoveling earth which was pretty hard work; ten hours a day; $1.75 a day; $4 for board; the sleeping place, board and foreman were good; he worked one month. The wages were then lowered from $1.75 to $1.65; he and four other men: 2 Polish and 2 Irish, quit on account of the reduction. After coming back on a work train to Milwaukee last Dec. 1st, he lived in "Ideal" lodging house, paying 10¢ per night, and 15¢ to 20¢ per meal in restaurants. He will stay here for a few days more, and then jump a freight to Chicago. If he gets hold of anything there he will stay there for the winter and in spring will return to Milwaukee and then to Superior for the purpose of working in the north where the climate is cooler.

He has never asked for public charity. He has done very little begging. In the former times he has stolen money from his friends when they were drunk, but he has left this habit because he was caught and jailed which made more trouble than the money was worth.

He expects a poor winter in getting jobs. He has heard that many factories have reduced their production considerably so that the factory workers are looking for jobs of any kind and pressing upon the common laborer. He has heard that the depression was nothing more than a wall street trick played against the pending currency bill. If this is true, he does not know; but he is inclined to believe in this explanation of the coming crisis.

He does not know much about labor organizations—thinks they are necessary and good for those only who belong to them. He has never had a chance to join one.

SOURCE: Quoted in Roger A. Bruns, *Knights of the Road: A Hobo History*. Methuen, New York: Fairfield Graphics, 1980, 140–43.

ANALYSIS

In 1914, the federal government became alarmed about the labor unrest that was developing in U.S. cities. One way it thought to relieve the conflict that seemed so threatening was by establishing a Commission on Industrial Relations to investigate labor conditions. It was supposed to recommend ways to restore social tranquility.

One important aspect of the Commission's work was to examine the daily life of the hobo and tramp army that seemed so frightening and then try to find ways to solve the problems. Of all the Commission's investigators, none was more assiduous and hard-working than Peter Speek. Born in Russia, Speek had fled there after the Revolution of 1905. An outspoken newspaper editor, Speek knew that a life-sentence to Siberia loomed over him if he stayed in Russia. He came to the United States, earned a degree in sociology at the University of Wisconsin, and began to work for the Industrial Commission.

His ability to speak several languages allowed him to get close to hoboes and interview many of them. By the time he was finished with this work, he had conducted more than 100 interviews. His subjects seem to have told their stories with great sincerity and equal honesty.

Two of the subjects that Speek tried to explore most intensively were why men had become hoboes and the nature of a hobo's everyday life. He especially wanted to get past the stereotypical notion that hoboes were simply lazy men who refused to work and who suffered from a serious case of wanderlust.

In one of Speek's most incisive interviews, Thomas Lee told him that he had not been successful with women; nor had he been successful raising horses. So, he took to the road. Lee also reveals, in just a few pages, that he was constantly on the move, going from one place to another, always by jumping a ride on a train. Moreover, his wandering was not random. He followed a regular route, returning to the same places in a loose order. He also seems to say that while he moved throughout the northern Great Plains States, Chicago was the farthest limit of his travels. Chicago was the city where he could spend the winter when there was little outdoor work to be done in the prairies. Lee also told Speek about the nature of his work, the low wages that he received, and the generally unpleasant living conditions.

But perhaps Lee's statement is most important for its clear revelation that he was not wandering aimlessly because he had "itchy feet" and liked to travel. Rather, he was continuously seeking work that would pay him a decent wage, be somewhat pleasant, and allow him to live in moderately decent conditions. He was not simply a "bum" or "vagrant" as many Americans would have considered him. He also revealed that he had many of the same desires and wants of middle-class Americans: a family, a clean place to live, decent working conditions, and wages that would allow him to support himself.

FURTHER READING

Hall, Greg. *Harvest Wobblies: The Industrial Workers of the World and Agricultural Laborers in the American West, 1905–1930*. Corvallis, OR: Oregon State University Press, 2001.

7

THE EXTENT OF THE PROBLEM, 1890–1925

How Many Were There?

- **Document:** The document is part of an analysis of the magnitude of homelessness and the characteristics of the homeless population between 1890 and 1925. The lead author was a practicing psychiatrist, the founder and president of the National Council on Family Homelessness, and a professor at the Harvard University Medical School.
- **Date:** The article was originally published in 1992.
- **Where:** The article was originally published in the *Journal of Public Policy*, which is published by Cambridge University Press in England.
- **Significance:** The article gives insight into the number of homeless people in the United States between 1890 and 1925. It also confirms the difficulty of determining the size of the hobo population definitively and also the changing terminology used to refer to homeless people.

DOCUMENT

Counting the homeless is a formidable if not impossible task, and because of serious methodological problems, the numbers, then and now, are not well suited to comparisons. However, given this caveat, we can make various general statements. The number of homeless persons has always ebbed and flowed with fluctuations in the national economy. Although the overall economy expanded during the period from 1890 to 1925, for example, the nation still experienced severe bouts of economic depression and unemployment which were associated with proportionately larger numbers of homeless persons. During the crash of 1873, 38,000 men lost their homes. As the economy recovered during the 1880s, the number of homeless persons declined, but by 1890 the homeless population increased to 45,000, then doubled to approximately 90,000 within three years. During this period nearly

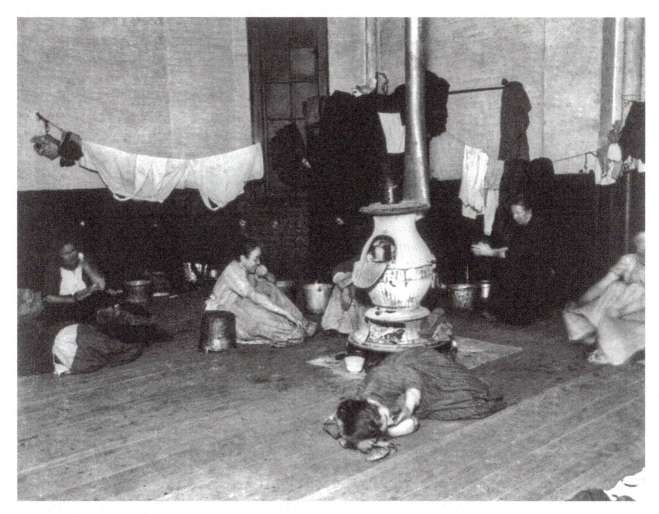

No one knows exactly how many homeless people lived in American cities during the late-nineteenth and early-twentieth centuries. After all, there was no way of locating them all to count them. However, the number was so staggering that police stations commonly served as nighttime shelters for homeless people during the winter. Most stations that provided warmth and allowed homeless people to sleep on the floor admitted only men and excluded women. Occasionally, though, they did admit women as shown in this picture taken by Jacob Riis, the first well-known American photojournalist. (Library of Congress)

16,000 businesses collapsed, unemployment hovered around 3 million, and the economy functioned at 25 to 30 percent below capacity.

Conservative estimates of the numbers of tramps who rode the rails between 1890 and 1925 range from 100,000 to 500,000. These numbers, while difficult to verify, are based on records kept by big-city shelters, the railroads, and charitable facilities such as poorhouses and jails. During its first eleven years (1902–1912) the New York City Municipal Lodging House sheltered about 542,000 men, 62,000 women, and 18,000 children. The Wayfarer's Lodge in Philadelphia housed 28,000 men annually from 1900 to 1907. During the same period, Chicago institutions sheltered approximately 40,000 to 60,000 homeless each year. The growth of lodging houses throughout the country also reflected the alarming increase in the numbers of vagrants. In 1890, poorhouses were available in only six large cities; twenty years later most cities had a sizable number.

... Homelessness is merely one phase in a cycle of extreme poverty. A decrease in income or increase in expenses places persons living below the poverty level at high risk of becoming homeless. Not surprisingly, surges in the poverty rate are mirrored by increasing numbers of homeless people.

In 1904, Robert Hunter asserted that no fewer than 10 million Americans, 12 percent of the population, were living in poverty. These people were unable "to obtain those necessaries which will permit them to maintain a state of physical efficiency"; they were "underclothed, underfed, and miserably housed."

Hunter, using the few available cost-of-living studies, fixed the poverty line at $460 per year for a family of five in the industrial states of the Northeast and Midwest, and at $300 per year in the rural South. On the basis of scattered statistics, Hunter asserted that the 350,000 railroad trackmen and carmen earned less than $375 per year in the North, and less than $150 in the South. Cotton mill workers averaged $360 in the North and $235 in the South. Sixty percent of the coal miners earned less than $450 in the Mid-Atlantic States, nearly 30 percent of the work force earned less than $300.

At times, even such low-paying jobs as these were scarce. For example, Frederick [Jackson] Turner, a contemporary expert on the frontier, argued that the depression of the 1890s "did violence to the comfortable assumption that ample employment awaited the worthy and the willing." And "when the poor face the necessity of becoming paupers," he continued, "when they must apply for charity if they are to live at all, many desert their families and enter the ranks of vagrancy." As [Alexander] Keyssar noted [in his historical study of unemployment], "By the end of the Progressive Era, unemployment had become a major item on the nation's list of social problems."

... [F]ollowing a period of abnormal unemployment during the winter of 1914–1915, the Advisory Social Service Committee of the New York's Municipal Lodging House found that 90 percent of the men they studied had been without work for over one week and nearly two-thirds for over a month. Fewer than 15 percent, however, had been unemployed for over six months and nearly two-thirds claimed to have been stably employed for an average of 12.2 months during the preceding five years. ...

Housing

During 1890–1929, housing production in cities throughout the United States generally lagged behind housing needs. Housing starts between 1890 and 1914, 1919 and 1930, and in 1930 fell far short of the 1899 figure of 342,000 starts, while the number of persons per household remained fairly high. (1890, 5.0; 1900, 4.8; 1910, 4.5; 1920, 4.3; 1930, 4.1) ... The housing boom that began in 1905 and lasted until World War I began to meet housing demand, but the war caused a severe setback in housing construction, which was restored by the mid-1920s. However, the Great Depression and World War II again created housing shortages.

Two important trends shed some light on the origins of the housing shortage during the period. The first was the population boom. Between 1890 and 1930, the U.S. population almost doubled as 60 million people were added to the nation's total. Immigration accounted for 37 percent of the increase. Because these "new wave" immigrants settled in port cities where they landed or gravitated to factory and mining towns, housing shortages were particularly acute—and housing conditions particularly crowded and squalid—in these areas. Still, as the National Housing Association conferences made clear at the turn of the century, housing shortages and rank housing conditions during this period were not confined to urban areas.

A second trend was urban migration. In 1890, 35 percent of the population lived in urban areas. By 1900 the number increased to 39 percent, by 1910 to 46 percent, by 1920 to 52 percent, and by 1930 the number climbed to 56 percent of the population. . . .

In *Recent Trends in American Housing* (1931), Edith Wood summarized the housing situation during the period from 1905 to 1929 as follows.

> The housing shortage at the end of the War came as a surprise to most people in the United States. . . . In 1917 and 1918 almost no building was done except by the Federal government. Private building was expected to resume briskly as soon as the War was over. It started to do so, but halted. The cost of a home— labor and materials—had doubled.
>
> The volume of home-building in 1919, instead of reducing the shortage, was only 59 percent of normal. That of 1920 reached only 37 percent of normal. . . . The maximum shortage was at the end of 1921, when it reached at least one and a quarter million. Then the tide turned. Nineteen twenty-two held its own. Each year thereafter showed substantial gains. By 1926 the end of the shortage was in sight. By 1928 it had been reached. In a nationwide numerical sense, there was no longer a housing shortage. We were back to where we were before the War, with qualitative rather than quantitative needs. So far as net progress was concerned, we had lost ten years.

Wood reported that during the period of housing shortages housing standards plummeted and rents soared. Housing structures fell into disrepair, single-family units were turned into apartments, existing apartments were divided into even smaller rental units, unsound vacant housing was occupied, and doubling up of families was common. Jacob Riis eloquently exposed the wretched housing conditions in New York City's tenements in his classic study of *How the Other Half Lives*. Overcrowding was rampant in all housing arrangements.

> The density of New York's Lower East Side—1000 people per acre—exceeded that of any European or even Asian city; its closest rival was one district in Bombay. During the post–Civil War Era, cities on the Eastern seaboard were congested with tides of foreign immigrants heaped on top of a native population streaming in from the countryside; by 1900, New York's population had tripled and Boston's more than doubled. The housing have-nots packed themselves tightly into cellars and tenements of appalling squalor; deprived of adequate light, air, heat, and running water. Two or three families typically shared a dwelling unit (often a single room) and scores of families shared an outside toilet.

SOURCE: Ellen Bassuk and Deborah Franklin, "Homelessness Past and Present: The Case of the United States, 1890–1925." *New England Journal of Policy Planning*, 8, 1 (1992). Used by permission.

ANALYSIS

The authors of this study had several goals. They explained their central goal at the very beginning of the essay (before the selection given here)—to determine whether "various experts" were correct when they have claimed that "the characteristics of homeless people, as well as the causes of homelessness, have changed" (from 1890–1925 to the present). They present their answer immediately after posing the problem: "A careful historical review has proved otherwise."

As they developed this thesis, they almost inevitably had to consider the questions of how to define homelessness and how many people were actually homeless in the United States between 1890 and 1925. To do this, they examined the historical literature about hoboes, tramps, and vagrants and reached the conclusion that, "Today we refer to the entire population [of hoboes, tramps, and vagrants] as 'homeless,' a term that implies a broad continuum of economic and residential instability as well as disconnection from community and family ties." In other words, these authors, too, see a continuous pathway of words between *vagrant, tramp, hobo, bum,* and *homeless person.*

And, in answering the question of how many homeless people there were in the country between 1890 and 1925, they acknowledge that "Counting the homeless is a formidable if not impossible task." Because of this near-impossibility, they avoid presenting a single number of the homeless population. They don't even give a narrow range of numbers (e.g., from 100,000 to 150,000). Instead, they have adopted two other strategies. One is to present a wide range of numbers to give a sense of the likely dimensions of the phenomenon with the implication that either number is substantial (as when they state that estimates of the number of tramps who rode the railroads between 1890 and 1925 range from 100,000 to 500,000). Their other strategy for presenting information about the numbers of homeless people is to present a number for a much more limited segment of the homeless population with the result that a careful reader will ask something like, "Well, if one homeless shelter in Philadelphia alone housed 28,000 men annually, how many men did all the shelters in the city service? And, how many homeless people must there have been in the whole country?" The authors have made the point that the number of homeless people was substantial in a much more effective and persuasive way than if they had reported that one particular observer estimated that there were more than half a million homeless people in the United States in 1893 (the year of one of the most serious depressions in U.S. history).

FURTHER READING

Solenberger, Alice Willard. *One Thousand Homeless Men: A Study of Original Records (1911).* New York: Charities Publication Committee, 1911.

8

COUNTRY LODGINGS

Mary Dodge Woodward's Diary

- *Document:* This document is a selection from the reminiscences of Mary Dodge Woodward who lived on a wheat farm in the Dakota Territory during the 1880s.
- *Date:* Ms. Woodward kept a diary from 1884 to 1889 that was published in 1937.
- *Where:* The events described here took place in the Dakota Territory.
- *Significance:* In telling about her life on a wheat farm in the Dakota Territory in the 1880s, Mary Dodge Woodward revealed the importance of tramp or migrant labor to farmers in the last decades of the nineteenth century. She also provided much information about the lives and work of "homeless" agricultural laborers.

DOCUMENT

July 20

... The men are haying, all thirteen of them, and we send their dinners to the fields. I have to rack my brains every day to contrive meals for them.

Tonight I went out of doors, and there by the corner of the house, stood three tramps. They wanted to sleep in the barn, so Walter took them some blankets. ... The country is full of men tramping about and begging at farm houses where they stop to hire out. I have fed several the past week and so have my neighbors. Fortunately we are too far from the [railroad] tracks to be bothered with regular tramps, but they go by the [grain] elevators in droves.

July 31

... We hired two men today, one called The Kid, the other Boyd, a deserter from Warner's brigade.

August 27

... Our boys finished harvesting all the wheat and oats. McKay, who is to thresh, with his crew of twenty men, his tents, and his cookhouse are already on the grounds. The outfit looks very picturesque among the shocks of wheat. ... The country teems with threshing machines. I could see eight this morning, each with a crew of from two to thirty men which makes lively times.

September 2

... [S]omeone must have prayed too hard for rain. McKays have to board two threshing crews all through it. They have six tents, two cook-cars, and four cooks. Walter set some of his men to plowing, and others to moving oats from one building to another.

September 19

... The boys who sleep [in the granary] got frightened, left their beds, and came down to sleep in the barn. They say the grain cracked all night.

April 11

I am glad that we can have the same men that were here last year. They planted eighty acres yesterday which is a big day's work, as seeding is the hardest part of farming in Dakota. The men walk between eighteen and twenty miles a day besides lifting sacks, filling seeders, and managing horses.

April 19

... The boys at the granary have callers as they often do on Sunday. It seems to be a novelty to the neighbor boys to come here, almost as good as going to town. The men live in a large room in the granary, and none of us women go there except on Mondays to change and air and make the beds.

August 11

Harvest has started, now there will be no rest for man, woman, or beast until frost which comes, thank heaven, early here. I was nearly beside myself getting dinner for thirteen men besides carpenters and tinners. ... I baked seventeen loaves of bread today, making seventy-four since last Sunday, not to mention twenty-one pies, and puddings, cakes, and doughnuts.

The men cut one hundred acres today. All four of our harvesters are being used as well as three which were hired to cut by the acre.

September 18

... Bill Miller ... had come into Fargo from a farm where he had worked through harvest and threshing, earning sixty dollars. He started drinking, went to sleep at the Minnesota House, and in the morning found that he had not one cent. Somebody had gone through his clothes in the night. Half of the money that is earned in Dakota goes in that manner, and the poor boys work so very hard to earn it.

August 22

We have eighteen men now. Every bed is full, even to the lounge.

Every person and every horse is at work with might and main to secure the wheat crop from storms. . . . There have been eight men along looking for work. Patrick Haines left. He could not stand farm work longer. He was a barber in Philadelphia who had gotten out of money in Fargo [now in North Dakota]. Frank Brady came just after the Fourth, ragged and dirty with not one cent in his pocket. Now he had fifty dollars which burns him; so he must strike out for Mapleton where, I fear, he will deposit it in a saloon.

December 11

The boys have commenced sawing and hauling ice on the Sheyenne. Ice is a hard-earned luxury when one has to procure it in such extreme cold. They cut great shining blocks. . . . they can hardly haul more than one load a day. There is nothing much for men to do here in winter, and unless they have homes of their own, they leave here when fall comes.

July 11

The new man was left alone in the cellar, digging, when I happened to look out and saw him a mile off, going to Mapleton. He did not even ask for his wages for one day.

August 1

We now have twenty men, all the dining room will hold. We have put a second table at the end of the extension table, leaving just room enough at the ends to get by. We can seat nineteen men and every seat is occupied. . . . The sheets and pillowcases for the twelve beds make big washings. I pound the men's in a barrel so that they need no rubbing. The carpenters usually overlap the harvesters, and I think they will this year.

August 13

Our family has increased until there are thirty-two. We have put a cook stove in the blacksmith shop. The men have taken all the machinery from the machine house and put in tables with bunks overhead, making fine new living quarters. We have a man cook and he has taken sixteen men at his table out there.

August 16

. . . The place presents a lively appearance now, while there are fifteen teams at work and thirty men besides the family. . . . We make up twenty beds and still some of the men sleep in the barn. The men are stacking wheat.

September 2

. . . A load of threshers went to Fargo today who, altogether, drew checks for seventy dollars which they will deposit, mostly in saloons. The towns are full of men who have sweated and toiled, and many will have their money and go out as they came in, with nothing, and winter coming on. One of the boys came back and drew the rest of his money, about eighty dollars, and hurried to town to finish his spree.

September 20

... The harvesters did a pretty clean job of picking up when they left, stealing five new blankets, some tools, and other things, the rascals.

July 30

A new man came today and started plowing. ... The boys said they saw him in Fargo in a drunken condition, so I presume he is dead broke and obliged to come into the country to work. He looks as though work would come hard. The country is full of such men in summer and fall who work like slaves and then leave every cent in the saloons. I feel sorry for them.

August 1

... I fed one great tramp. The country is full of them. Many are not regular tramps, but men hunting work who have come too soon—before the harvest is ready. The Waltz boys came from Kingston to work through harvest.

September 27

Two of our boys who have often disagreed flew at each other in the barn and had a regular fist fight. ... Jim Markham went to the field and plowed awhile, but concluded that if he stayed Dutch Henry would not give up the feud so he left. Walter hired the first man who came along as we cannot afford to have a plow stand idle.

SOURCE: Mary Dodge Woodward, *The Checkered Years: Excerpts from the Diary of Mary Dodge Woodward Written while Living on a Bonanza Farm in Dakota Territory during the Years 1884–1889.* Ed. Mary Boynton Cowdrey. Caldwell, Idaho: The Caxton Printers, Ltd., 1937. Used by permission of Caxton Press.

ANALYSIS

The reminiscences of Mary Dodge Woodward explain a lot about how agriculture, especially wheat farming, had developed in the northern Great Plains by the middle of the 1880s. Beginning in the 1870s, the character of farms changed dramatically. The small individual farmer and the family farm so praised and esteemed since the days of Thomas Jefferson were quickly disappearing. They were being replaced by large-scale operations known as "bonanza farms" employing large labor forces and making the most of modern technology, tools, and machines. This was the beginning of what is now called agribusiness.

These new "plantations" had been made possible by the invention of new farm machinery, the availability of cheap land, the growth of larger markets for food in Eastern cities, and the ongoing development of the railroad system, which allowed enormous crops of wheat to be transported easily and cheaply throughout the country. All of that is reflected in Woodward's reminiscences, and it is not just coincidence that the first of the bonanza farms could be found in Minnesota and the Dakota Territory in the mid-1870s, precisely the place where Woodward was living at the time she was writing this.

However, her memoirs also reveal a great deal about another aspect of the new farms—their labor forces and the laborers' lives. Early in the diary, Woodward's family "farm" had 12 hired men living and working there. By the end of the story, there were 30. Woodward doesn't explain directly how these laborers and the foremen made contact with each other, but she refers several times to men wandering around the countryside and knocking on doors in search of work. She also mentions on one occasion hiring a man who just showed up at the house. This suggests that at least some of the hired hands were wandering hoboes. However, in another entry, Woodward expresses pleasure in the fact that the men working in the fields were the same ones who had been there the previous year. This comment suggests that some kind of interaction took place that allowed the men to return to the farm without having face-to-face contact with the person in charge of hiring.

Woodward also says a lot about the lives of these homeless men. For one thing, she mentions the different kinds of work that they did and when they could do it. In the spring, homeless laborers planted crops. In the fall, they harvested them, and in the winter, when there was no farm work to be done, they cut ice from the frozen rivers.

While they were doing agricultural labor in Woodward's fields, many of their needs were provided for them. There were sleeping accommodations—sometimes in a large room that served as a bunkhouse or dormitory, but on occasion in a granary. On at least one occasion, noises being made by crackling wheat scared some of the men and they asked permission to resort to the barn. Woodward doesn't indicate if the men had to pay for the right to sleep on the farm, or how much they might have been charged, but the tone of her diary suggests that sleeping accommodations were a part of a man's wages.

In addition to a place to sleep, the men received food and other services. Woodward talks about having to "rack her brains" to figure out menus for meals, but she also mentions a cook who prepared meals and could feed as many as 16 men at his own table. Additionally, she mentions that she herself baked food for the men. On one occasion, she noted that she had baked 17 loaves of bread that day and that she had baked more than 70 so far during that week. And, during an undefined period of time, she had recently baked 21 pies, cakes, and other sweets.

As well as providing some of the men's food, Woodward also reveals that she kept their bed-linens clean and washed. In one entry, she refers to washing sheets, and in another she talks about airing their bedding and changing it.

Woodward seems to have had at least a somewhat ambiguous or ambivalent attitude toward individual members of the labor force. On the one hand, she is cognizant of how hard they work. She seems to understand why they visit a nearby town on Saturday evenings and spend their money, or have it stolen, or do other things that she doesn't mention explicitly. On the other hand, she seems to have had a much less positive attitude toward the man who quit his job on the first day of his being employed. At one point, she refers to being "bothered" by tramps. And, throughout the diary, she implies negative feelings about the men's going to town on Saturday nights and throwing away their hard-earned money in saloons. Perhaps her most manifest statement of disapprobation appears in the entry in which she noted that some departing harvesters had stolen "five new blankets." And, she sums up the entry with the phrase "the rascals."

Although Woodward's diary reflects the perspective of the land-owning, labor-employing class, most of the hired hands would probably have thought her farm a good place to work. It was convenient to the railroad. The boss (or at least one of his family members) seemed not to be overtly hostile. The food seems to have been at least edible and included more than the minimal (pies and cakes, for example). According to Woodward, she even tended to their bedding. In all likelihood, Woodward has provided a picture of a farm that provided high-quality living arrangements for its hobo and tramp laborers.

FURTHER READING

Woirol, Gregory R. *In the Floating Army: F. C. Mills on Itinerant Life in California, 1914.* Urbana and Chicago, IL: University of Illinois Press, 1992.

9

THE STEM, OR MAIN STEM

Hobohemia

- *Document:* This document describes that section of U.S. cities where hoboes lived when they were in the city.
- *Date:* The selection is taken from a book published in 2003, but it concerns events and circumstances that occurred in the 10 or 15 years before the United States entered World War I.
- *Where:* The book was published in Chicago, but it refers to all large U.S. cities.
- *Significance:* The selection describes the facilities and institutions available to hoboes when they returned to a city and took up residence in "the main stem." It begins to suggest that there was in fact a distinctive culture that hoboes and tramps—homeless people—created for themselves.

DOCUMENT

Metropolises with expansive hinterlands boasted particularly robust main stems that virtually defined their city centers. Minneapolis's Gateway district . . . was a key hobo resort of the Midwest, accommodating 105 lodging houses and 6,000 men. On the West Coast, San Francisco's South of Market was the largest hobo mecca, lodging upward of 40,000 men per night by World War I. Dwarfing even these was Chicago's hobohemian district. . . . In 1908, one researcher estimated that between 40,000 and 60,000 men took shelter in the neighborhood's 200 to 300 lodging houses and hotels. . . .

Why did such crowds flock to the main stem? The greatest single lure was . . . the labor market. . . . Districts [like these] . . . functioned less as a source of work for hoboes than as an infrastructure for housing, marketing, and transporting their labor to the hinterlands. . . . The tracks that carried grain, cattle, coal, iron, and other raw materials . . . also conveyed hundreds of thousands of workers who supplied seasonal labor to an area stretching west to Omaha, east to Pittsburgh, south to Nashville, and north to Minneapolis. . . .

By the turn of the century [1900], job seeking in the hobohemian "slave markets" invariably involved a visit to an employment agency. . . . [T]hose specializing in the marketing of hobo labor were the most numerous, shipped the farthest, and had the greatest turnover of customers. . . . [M]any opened only during the frenzied hiring seasons of spring and summer. . . . The sidewalks outside of Minneapolis's eighteen employment agencies got so crowded during the early summer that men stood "so close together you couldn't put a newspaper between their elbows."

While employment agencies embodied the main stem's core economic function, lodging houses defined the district as a homeless man's resort and lent the main stem much of its unique "character." Incoming migrants frequently made it their first order of business to survey their sleeping options, which, depending upon their cash reserves, ranged from a hotel to a park bench. . . .

> ## DID YOU KNOW?
>
> ### A Contemporary Historian Defines the Main Stem
>
> The gathering place for transients in the city was a well-defined sub-area known in the tramp's argot as "the main stem." The main stem formed around cheap lodging houses. . . . The evolution of the main stem was often rapid. Homeless men completely changed the face of the Minneapolis Gateway area between 1880 and 1900. In San Francisco the South of Market, which still had well-to-do residents in the 1860s had become a haven for miners, sailors, farm laborers and other transients by 1880, with half the city's lodging houses. A full three-quarters of the buildings in New York's Bowery area at the turn of the [twentieth] century catered to homeless men.
>
> . . . Transient men found on the main stem all the places they needed, not only cheap hotels and lodging houses but also second-hand clothing stores, employment agencies, saloons, inexpensive safes and restaurants, and brothels.
>
> *Source:* John C. Schneider, "Tramping Workers, 1890–1920: A Subcultural View," in Eric H. Monkkonen, *Walking to Work: Tramps in America, 1790–1935.* Lincoln, NE, and London: University of Nebraska Press, 1984, 224–25.

. . . Commercial lodging houses for the general market of tramping workers . . . made their first appearance in depreciated sections of working-class neighborhoods . . . after the Civil War. The depressions of the Gilded Age inspired many urban property owners to convert commercial spaces of all sorts, from workshops and warehouses to theaters and factories, into makeshift lodging houses. . . . Numerous . . . late-nineteenth-century slum investigators lavished attention on the most notorious "flops" and "stale-beer dives" of homeless-man districts, where tramps paid a penny or two a night for the privilege of sleeping on a cellar floor.

Despite such sensational . . . reports, most lodging choices along the main stem were not so grim. Virtually all hoboes, it is true, spent some nights without shelter . . . during seasons when demand for lodgings outstripped supply. Some homeless men, from time to time, also slept in saloons, whose owners often accommodated paying customers. But most hoboes on the main stem found room in commercial lodging houses that varied in price and comfort.

For ten to fifteen cents, a lodger could pass the night in a hammock, rough bunk, or cot in an open dormitory ward. For double the price, he could get a dilapidated bed in a partitioned cubicle or "cage." Cubicles were merely stalls, measuring as little as five by seven feet, constructed of wood or corrugated iron partitions. Although a three- to five-story lodging house might hold several hundred cubicles that were all open to the ceiling, these cells nonetheless provided a modicum of private space. At the same time, they remained at least half as expensive as a cheap hotel room.

For lodging house owners, partitions could double or triple rent potential. Consequently, cubicles rapidly became a hobohemian standard by the turn of the century [1900].

In addition to supplying the bare necessities of work and shelter, the main stem also offered brighter attractions that engendered its reputation as "the Rialto" of the hobo.... [Some hoboes] romped in "hobohemia's playground," enjoying the saloons, brothels, gambling resorts, vaudeville, houses, fortune-tellers, cigar stores, barbershops, secondhand stores, and other commercial establishments catering to the tastes of homeless men. Despite their poverty, hoboes frequently arrived on the main stem with wages in hand, looking to spend them in convivial surroundings.

...On the main stem, during periods of layoff, [hoboes] met and intermingled, spent their money, and participated in organizational life to a degree unimaginable in the mines, forests, construction sites, and harvest fields where hoboes labored. Encounters in the city gave the hobo world a sense of continuity and coherence despite the almost constant migrations such a life entailed. Renewing old friendships and meeting up with acquaintances from previous jobs were common activities on the main stem.... Through these reunions and other contact, hoboes garnered information on job prospects, housing, and transportation. They also shared ideas and participated in activities not really expressed or pursued while on the job.

SOURCE: Todd De Pastino, *Citizen Hobo: How a Century of Homelessness Shaped America.* Chicago and London: University of Chicago Press, 2003. Copyright (c) 2003 by the University of Chicago Press. Used by permission of University of Chicago Press.

ANALYSIS

When hoboes descended from trains in more rural, less populated areas on the outskirts of a city, they often settled in "hobo jungles," at least for a short time. And, when they arrived in cities, they also headed for a specific location—a district of the city known as the "Stem" or "Main Stem." This area of large cities was a place where a hobo could satisfy all of his needs easily and cheaply.

The location of the "Stem" was known to every hobo who visited a city, usually before he got there, but found easily enough once he had arrived. It was most often located near the railroad yard, thus providing easy access to transportation, and it was the place to which all hoboes headed. All a man needed to do to find the "Stem" was to follow the line of other men departing from the railroad station.

Although these districts were always important to hoboes, they took on added significance when rural activities—farming, mining, lumbering—shut down because of the weather. Men needed a place to hole up for the winter and counted on surviving with whatever money that they had saved during the working seasons. Then, when winter drew to a close, the "Stem" provided access to employment offices where men could find work for the upcoming season and not have to wander about searching for it.

But the "Stem" provided much more than convenience and access to jobs. It also provided cheap housing, food, entertainment, clothing, tobacco, and alcohol. Whatever a hobo sought, he could find it in the "Stem." As John Schneider put it so eloquently, for hoboes "the Stem" was their neighborhood.

FURTHER READING

Anderson, Nels. *The American Hobo: An Autobiography.* Leiden, Neth: Brill, 1975.

Anderson, Nels. *The Hobo: The Sociology of the Homeless Man.* Chicago, IL: University of Chicago Press, 1923.

Anderson, Nels. *On Hoboes and Homelessness.* Ed. Raffaele Rauty. Chicago, IL: University of Chicago Press, 1998.

Bogue, Donald. *Skid Row in American Cities.* Chicago, IL: University of Chicago Press, 1983.

Edge, W. *The Main Stem.* New York: Vanguard, 1927.

Schneider, John C. "Skid Row as an Urban Neighborhood." *Urbanism Past and Present*, 9, 1 (1984), 10–20.

VanderKooi, Ronald. "The *Main Stem*: Skid Row Revisited." *Society*, 10, 6 (September 1973), 64–71.

10

THE HOBO JUNGLE

The Hobo Jungle

- *Document:* This document is taken from the first scholarly study of hoboes to be published. It is generally considered to have been the initial truly professional sociology text on the subject.
- *Date:* The book was written in 1923.
- *Where:* The book was published in Chicago, but the author was writing about hoboes and tramps throughout the United States.
- *Significance:* The book takes a sympathetic attitude toward homeless men. The author had himself been a hobo before he went to college and then graduate school. He based the book on his own experiences, and he was also one of the first academic sociologists to use participant observation as an important means of gathering information. Because of his own experiences, Nels Anderson could recognize and understand the behaviors and beliefs of homeless hoboes more clearly than most other observers at the time. The document also describes another neighborhood where hoboes and tramps gathered and interacted.

DOCUMENT

On the outskirts of cities . . . the homeless men have established social centers that they call "jungles," places where the hoboes congregate to pass their leisure time outside the urban centers. The jungle . . . becomes a necessary part of his daily life.

Accessibility to a railroad is only one of the requirements of a good jungle. It should be located in a dry and shady place that permits sleeping on the ground. There should be plenty of water for cooking and bathing and wood enough to keep the [cooking] pot boiling. If there is a general store nearby where bread, meat, and vegetables may be had, so much the better. For those who have no money but enough courage to "bum lumps," it is well that the jungles be not too far from a town, though far enough to escape the attention of the natives and officials. . . .

Jungle camps may be divided into two classes—the temporary and the permanent, or continuous. Temporary jungles are merely stopover or relay stations inhabited intermittently. . . . Men stranded temporarily in a town usually seek a secluded spot at the edge of a village, not too far from the railroad. . . . Men on the road look for other places where men preceding them have camped. There they are likely to find pots and kettles in which to cook food or wash dishes. . . .

The continuous or permanent jungles are seldom deserted, at least in summer. There is usually someone there to keep the fire burning and usually there are men and boys occupied at various tasks—cooking, washing or boiling clothes, shaving, sewing, bathing, and reading.

Women are [not] often found . . . in the jungles. Here is an institution where the hobo is his own housewife. He not only cooks his own food, but has even invented dishes that are peculiar to jungle life. . . .

The hobo who lives in the jungles has proved that he has become domesticated without the aid of women. He has established the habit of keeping his clothes and his person clean. . . . The hobo learns here the housewife's art of keeping pots clean and the camp in order. The man who cannot, or will not, learn the few elementary principles of housekeeping is likely to fare ill in the jungle.

. . . There may be newspapers from different cities brought in by men traveling different directions. Travelers meeting this way have much of common interest to talk about and conversation is enlivened with questions of concern. . . . The jungle is always astir with life and movement, and the hobo enters into this life as he does no other. Here he turns his back on the world and faces his fellows and is at ease.

The average man of the road has had a variety of experience. . . . In the jungles there is always an audience for anyone who wants to talk, whether of his thoughts, his experiences, or his observations. There is plenty of opportunity to tell stories. The art of telling a story is diligently cultivated . . . in the assemblies about the fire. This vagabond existence tends to enrich the personality, and long practice has developed in some of these men an art of personal narrative that has declined elsewhere. . . .

DID YOU KNOW?

Jungle Sociability

As I capered along the track, trying to get warm, I spied a jungle, or hobo camp, fifty yards to one side of the railroad. A pile of old railroad ties half concealed by bushes was snapping and crackling with jovial flame and smoke. I approached the jungle along the banks of a small stream.

There was only one 'bo at the fire, an auburn-haired giant in a dirty red undershirt and dangling suspenders. He was shaving in such fashion as I had never seen any one shave before. In lieu of a razor, he used strips of broken glass, and propped up before him in the crotch of a willow-tree was a tiny pocket-mirror. . . . After four or five strokes with a sliver of glass, he threw it away and selected another from a heap of shattered window-panes at the base of the tree. He kept breaking the glass again and again to insure a shaving edge.

"Hello, brother," he blared, spraying me with a tiny mist of soap-suds.

"Howdy."

. . . "How's ridin'?"

"Good."

. . . The man grunted and went on with his scraping. I warmed myself at the fire; then in accordance with jungle etiquette, which demands that the newcomer forage firewood, I returned to the railroad, and, finding an old tie, I lugged it over and threw it on the blaze

Source: Glen H. Mullin, *Adventures of a Scholar Tramp.* New York and London: The Century Company, 1925, 294–95.

DID YOU KNOW?

Jungle Rules

... Hobos had what was called the code of the road and also had what was known as the rule of the jungle. Many hobo camps wouldn't allow a drunk to light there, and dope fiends and trouble-makers of any kind usually got beaten up and ejected bodily as soon as they were found out. They used to say, "Junkies have no place in the jungle." This jungle rule was good, for it contributed to better, more respectable living.

Hobo discipline was inflexible. There were no appeals and no plea bargaining in the jungle. The true tramp didn't ride trains. They walked the highways and byways. They were less prone to work for what they got than was a true hobo. They usually had some kind of a gimmick such as peddling pencils, thread, buttons, soap, shoe strings, and so on from house to house....

There were quite a few escaped convicts and fugitives from county jails and state penal farms, chain gangs, road gang work camps, and so on. There were also a lot of jack-rollers (muggers), dips (pickpockets), second-story men (burglars), and a goodly percentage of genuine professional yeggs (hoodlums) known as Pete men (safe blowers) and heisters (stickup men) and all manner of petty thieves, referred to as hand-burglars.

These people used to infiltrate the hobo jungles and mingle ... there was never any true comradeship between the true hoboes and the hoodlum element of jungle society. The two groups had nothing in common and managed to survive together by an unwritten law, to wit: "You leave me alone and I won't bother you."

Source: Charles Elmer Fox, *Tales of an American Hobo.* Iowa City: University of Iowa Press, 1989, pp. 2–3.

... In every permanent camp, there is likely to be a permanent group that makes the camp its headquarters.... As a rule, however, the jungle is extremely hospitable and democratic.

The freedom of the jungles is, however, limited by a code of etiquette. Jungle laws are unwritten, but strictly adhered to. The breaking of these rules, if intentional, leads to expulsion, forced labor, or physical punishment.

Jungle crimes include (1) making fire by night in jungles subject to raids; (2) "hi-jacking" or robbing men at night when sleeping in the jungles; "buzzing" or making the jungle a permanent hangout for jungle "buzzards" who subsist on the leavings of meals; (4) [*sic*] wasting food or destroying it after eating is a serious crime; (5) leaving pots and other utensils dirty after using; (6) cooking without first hustling fuel; (7) destroying jungle equipment. In addition ... men are supposed to use cooking cans for cooking only; "boiling up" cans for washing clothing, coffee cans to cook coffee etc. After using, guests are expected to clean utensils, dry them, and leave them turned bottom side up so that they will not fill with rainwater and rust. They are expected to keep the camp clean. To enforce such common-sense rules self-appointed committees come into existence.

... The part played by the jungles as an agency of discipline for the men of the road cannot be overestimated. Here hobo tradition and law are formulated and transmitted. It is the nursery of tramp lore. Here the fledgling learns to behave like an old-timer. In the jungles the slang of the road and the cant of the tramp class is coined and circulated. It may originate elsewhere but here it gets recognition. The stories and songs current among the men of the road, the sentiments, the attitudes, and the philosophy of the migratory laborer are all given due airing. In short, every idea and ideal that finds lodgment in the tramp's fancy may be expressed here in the wayside forum where anyone who thinks may speak, whether he be a jester or a sage.

Suspicion and hostility are the universal attitudes of the town or small city to the hobo and the tramp. Accordingly, the so-called floater custom of passing vagrants on to other communities is widespread. The net effect of this policy is to intensify the antisocial attitude of the homeless man and to release and accentuate criminal tendencies. The small town is helpless to cope with the situation. As things are, its action perhaps cannot be different. Agriculture, as it becomes organized upon a capitalistic basis is increasingly dependent upon seasonal labor. . . . The report of the Commission on Industrial Relations states:

> The attempts to regulate movements of migratory workers by local organizations have, without exception, proved failures. This must necessarily be true no matter how well planned or well managed such local organizations may be. The problem cannot be handled except on a national scale and by methods and machinery which are proportioned to the enormous size and complexity of the problem.

SOURCE: Nels Anderson, *The Hobo: The Sociology of the Homeless Man*. Chicago, IL: University of Chicago Press, 1923. Used by permission of University of Chicago Press.

ANALYSIS

Hoboes had another possible destination besides the Main Stem when they exited a train—a hobo jungle. These venues could have either a country setting or a city setting, but either way they had their own character and did not replicate homeless areas in either the city or the country.

The best way to characterize these "jungles" is to say that were permanent settled locations that generally did not have more than a few permanent residents. That is to say, the population was always coming and going, and few people stayed there for long periods. The jungle was a scene of constant population movement.

If one of these "jungles" had a rural location, it was frequently located in a secluded spot near the railroad tracks. Men going there could find it easily, but it might well escape the attention of a casual passerby. Hoboes knew the location of a "jungle" by word-of-mouth communication or by discerning signs and symbols that other hoboes had left behind to guide newcomers.

If a "jungle" had an urban location, it was also located near the train tracks, but it developed in a place that outsiders would probably overlook—in a somewhat desolate area that attracted few unwelcome intruders. Locations such as the piers beneath a bridge or the abandoned path of a river that had changed its course are other places where a "jungle" might develop.

But whether a "jungle" had an urban or a rural setting, generally it possessed the same sort of physical character. Nothing here could be called a building. At most, there were shelters, or lean-tos that had been cobbled together with whatever material could be found easily. These huts lasted only as long as someone was using them. In these jungles, there was usually a fire that provided warmth and also a source of heat

---

DID YOU KNOW?

Jungle Friendliness

That evening I came to a hobo jungle where three or four men were cooking. I stopped and sat down. I wasn't scared, but I was ready to run. One fellow about forty years old was cooking some liver in old flattened-out can. He had a little sack. He took out bread and some cheese; the coffee was already made. The other fellows came together, and they had a stew and were eating it. Christ, was I hungry, but they never said a word. The fellow with the liver took his time and when it was all ready, he set it down on a clean place he had made, and he too started to eat. I was watching every bite but not saying a word. All at once he said, "Where you from, kid?" I said, "New York," and he said, "Eat yet?" I said no, and he just made a motion with his hand for me to come over and sit down, which I did. He let me clean up the biggest part of the grub.

Source: Henry E. McGuckin, *Memoirs of a Wobbly*. Chicago, IL: Charles H. Kerr Publishing Company, 1987, 9–10.

The Model Jungle

One jungle must be mentioned, that outside Coffeyville, Kansas, remembered partly because it was larger than most and nearest the model one reads about. There was water, as I recall, a small stream. I stayed there much of one day except once to go rustling food. There were large cans and I had soap, so I used the time to wash and dry my clothes. Others were doing the same. Doing things together opened the way to talk. One of those men, with whom I shared the sandwiches I had gathered, was definitely the type of tramp who dreams and wanders. . . . His way of begging was to go to stores; ask the butcher for a bone to boil, ask the baker for some old bread, try to get a potato, a carrot, and an onion from the grocer. With salt which he carried, that made a good stew, and that he was making for his day, over a half-gallon, which he shared with me and a couple of men known to him and with whom he did most of his talking. All were workers when they could find jobs but if not they were able to make out.

Source: Nels Anderson, *The American Hobo: An Autobiography.* Leiden, Netherlands: E. J. Brill, 1975, 95–96. Used by permission of Koninklijke Brill NV.

for cooking. The most common item on the menu was "mulligan stew." A large pot of water was kept constantly hot, and it was expected that each new arrival would contribute something to the mixture—whether it was some meat, some vegetables, or even some kind of bread. If a man didn't have anything, he was expected to go out and find something or to perform domestic chores: "sweeping the ground, finding and chopping firewood, or washing pots and utensils. Most often, there was a pot of coffee kept permanently hot, and anyone could have a cup as desired."

Pots, dishes, and utensils came from many different origins. A typical pot for the stew was a large can, the sort that had once contained tomatoes. The typical bowl was a smaller can. Eating and cooking utensils—knives, forks, spoons, ladles, and so on—might have been taken from a shelter or home where a man was once fed or the man might have brought them with him when he began tramping. In some cases, if a man found suitable materials, he might even fabricate his utensils. But, however cooking implements were acquired, one of the basic rules of these "jungles" was that no one was allowed to remove any eating or cooking equipment. It belonged to the camp, and while a person was allowed to use these tools, he had to clean them when he was done and leave them behind when he left.

In fact, a widely understood set of rules prevailed in all "hobo jungles." They were similar from one "jungle" to another, and experienced travelers knew both the permissible and the forbidden behaviors. If they didn't, or if someone was new to this life and uninformed, someone would make it his business to educate them.

The "jungles" appealed to wandering laborers for a number of reasons. First, and this is easily understood, a man could find them and get to them easily. They were convenient and accessible. But second, at the same time, they were at least somewhat distanced from the larger society. Most hoboes and tramps preferred to have some solitude before they entered a new town or city. Their appearance was not attractive. They might not have bathed recently; they might not have shaved recently; they might not have combed their hair recently; their clothes might be ragged and filthy from riding a long distance on the roof of a train car—or even beneath one. This kind of travel was not conducive to cleanliness. These "jungles" provided a place where a tramp could attempt to make himself look at least semi-respectable before he entered a town to find food, look for work, enter a store, or go into a saloon.

FURTHER READING

Forbes, J. "Tramp, or, Caste in the jungle." *The Outlook*, 98 (August 19, 1911), 869–75.

11

"TRAMP-SPEAK" AND THE HOBO SUBCULTURE

The Q, the P.A., and the Dope

- *Document:* The document contains a list of words, and their definitions, that were commonly used by hoboes. Like many subcultures, hoboes had their own distinctive jargon that allowed them to communicate with each other without being understood by anyone else standing nearby.
- *Date:* The document is part of a book published in 1899.
- *Where:* The book was published in Massachusetts, but it reflects a part of the hobo's world that existed across the country.
- *Significance:* The word list shows that hoboes had their own vocabulary that was known to everyone who spent time hoboing, an important sign that they constituted a separate subculture in the United States.

DOCUMENT

The Tramp's Jargon

Almost the first thing that one remarks on getting acquainted with tramps is their peculiar language. In every country where they live, they have dialects of their own choosing and making, and the stranger who goes among them must learn to speak there before he can associate with them on terms of intimacy. Indeed, the "tenderfoot" in tramp life, the beginner, is recognized by his ignorance of the "lingo." The way he carries himself, shakes hands, and begs are also signs by which the "professional" [hobo] determines the newcomer's standing in the brotherhood; but they are not unmistakable as his use of the tramp dialect, and it is seldom necessary talk with him for more than a few minutes to discover how long he has been on the road.

Glossary

BALDY: an old man

BALL: a dollar

BATTER: to beg

BEEFER: one who "squeals" on, or gives away, a tramp or criminal

BLANKET-STIFF: a Western tramp; he generally carries a blanket with him on his travels

BLIND-BAGGAGE: the front end of a baggage-car having no door

BLOKE: a fellow; synonymous with "plug," "mug," and "stiff"

BLOWED-IN-THE-GLASS STIFF: a trustworthy "pal"; a professional

'BO: a hoboBRAKEY: a brakeman

BUGHOUSE: crazy

BULL: a policeman

BUNDLE: plunder from a robbery

CHEW: to eat or feed

CHEW THE RAG: to talk

CHI (pronounced "shi"): Chicago

CINCIE: Cincinnati

CON: a conductor

COOLER: a dark cell

COP: a policeman. To be "copped" is to be arrested. A "fly-cop" is a detective

CRIB: a saloon or gambling-place; more or less synonymous with "joint" and "hang-out"

CROAK: to die, or to kill

CROCUS: a doctor

CROOK: a professional criminal. "Crooked work" means thieving

DEAD: reformed. A "dead" criminal is either discouraged or reformed

DICER: a hat

DIP: a pickpocket

DITCH, OR BE DITCHED: to get into trouble or to fail at what one has undertaken. To be "ditched" when riding on trains means to be put off, or to get locked into a car

DOPE, THE: the Baltimore and Ohio Railroad

DOSS: *noun*, sleep; *verb*, to sleep

DUMP: a lodging-house or restaurant; synonymous with hang-out

ELBOW: a detective

FAWNY MAN: a peddler of bogus jewelry

FINGER, FLATTY: a policeman, synonymous with "bull"

FLAGGED: when a man is paid by criminals or tramps to be "flagged," it means that he is permitted to go unmolested

FLICKER: *noun*, a faint; *verb*. To faint or pretend to faint

GAG: any begging trick

GALWAY: a begging priest

GAY-CAT: an amateur tramp who works when his begging courage fails him

GHOST-STORY: any statement or report that is not true. When told to young boys it means a "faked" story of tramp life

GRAFT: a line of business; synonymous with "spiel"

GRAFTER: pickpocket

GUN: a fellow; more or less synonymous with "bloke," "stiff," "mug," and "plug"

GUY: a fellow

HAND-OUT: a bundle of food handed out to a beggar at the back door

HANG-OUT: the hobo's home

HIT THE ROAD: to go tramping

HOBO: a tramp. Derivation obscure. Farmer's "Americanisms" gives: "HO-BOY or HAUT-BOY: a New York night-scavenger"

HOISTER, OR HYSTER: a shoplifter

HOOSIER: a "farmer." Everybody who does not know the world as the hobo knows it is to him a "farmer," "hoosier," or "outsider"

HORN, THE: a triangular extension of the Chicago, Burlington and Quincy Railroad . . .

HORSTILE: angry, unfriendly, hostile

JIGGER: a sore, artificially made, to excite sympathy

JIGGERED: "done," beaten. When used as an exclamation, as in "I'll be jiggered," it means "I'll be damned," or words to that effect

JOCKER: a tramp who travels with a boy and "jockers" him—trains him as a beggar and protects him from persecution by others

JOINT: practically, any place where tramps congregate, drink, and feel at home

KIP-HOUSE: a lodging-house

KIP TOWN: a good lodging-house

LEATHER: a pocket-book. "To reef a leather" means that the pickpocket pulls out the lining of a pocket containing the "leather"; this is frequently the best way of capturing a pocket-book

LIGHTHOUSE: one who knows every detective by sight, and can "tip him off" to his comrades

MAIN GUY: the leader

MARK: a person or house "good" for a food, clothes, or money

MEAL-TICKET: a person "good" for a meal

MONKEY: the tramp's nickname, as "New Orleans Blackie," "Mississippi Red," etc.

MOOCH: to beg; also to "light out," "clear out"

MOOCHER: a beggar . . .

MUG: *noun*, a fellow; *verb*, to photograph

MUSH-FAKIR: an umbrella-mender. The umbrellas which he collects are frequently not returned

OFFICE: to "give the office" is to give a signal to a confederate. It is usually done by raising the hat

ON THE HOG: on the tramp; also, "busted," "dead broke"

P.A.: Pennsylvania

PAPER: stocks and bonds

PEN: a penitentiary

PENNSYLVANIA SALVE: apple-butter

PENNYWEIGHTERS: jewelry thieves

PETER: a safe thief. "Knock-out drops" are also "peter"

PHILLIE: Philadelphia

PLUG: a fellow: synonymous with "bloke" and "stiff"

POKE-OUT: a lunch; synonymous with "hand-out"

POUND THE EAR: to sleep

PRUSHUN: a tramp boy. An "ex-prushun" is one who has served his apprenticeship as a "kid" and is "looking for revenge," i.e., for a lad that he can "snare" and "jocker" as he himself was "snared" and "jockered"

PUNK AND PLASTER: bread and butter

PUSH: a gang

Q: the Chicago, Burlington and Quincy Railroad

QUEER, The: money

REPEATER, or REVOLVER: an old-timer; a professional criminal and a "blowed-in-the-glass" tramp

RINGER: a bell

RUBE: a "hoosier" or "farmer"

SAPS: a clubbing with weapons, made from saplings; synonymous with "timber" (see below)

SCOFF: *noun*, food, "nourishment"; *verb*, to "feed," to "gorge"

SCREW: a prison turnkey

SET-DOWN: a square meal

SETTLED: in prison

SHACK: a [railroad] brakeman

SHATIN' ON ME UPPERS: . . . to be dead broke

SHOVE: a gang

SHOVER: a man who passes counterfeit money

SIDE-DOOR PULLMAN: a box-car

SINKER: a dollar; synonymous with "ball"

SLOPE: to run away

SLOPPING-UP: a big drunk

SNARE: to entice a boy into tramp life

SNEAKS: flat or house thieves. A bank sneak is a bank thief.

SNIPE: cigar butts . . .

SONG AND DANCE: a begging story or trick

SPARK: a diamond

SPIEL: something to peddle. Hoboes often carry needles, pins, court-plaster and the like. On meeting one another, they ask, "What's your spiel?" ("What are you hawking?")

SPIKED: upset, chagrined, disappointed, disgusted

SQUEALER: one who gives away the gang

STAKE-MAN: a fellow who holds a position only long enough to get a "stake"—enough money to keep him in "booze" and tobacco while he is on the road. The tramps call him a "gay-cat."

STALL: the pickpocket's companion

STIFF: a fellow; synonymous with "bloke" and "plug"

SUCKER: a victim of both tramps and criminals

THROW THE FEET: to beg, "hustle," or do anything that involves much action

TIMBER: a clubbing at the hands of the toughs of a town unfriendly to tramps (see "saps")

TOMATO-CAN VAG: the outcast of Hoboland; a tramp of the lowest order, who drains the dregs of a beer-barrel into an empty tomato-can and drinks them; he generally lives on the refuse that he finds in scavenger barrels

TOOT THE RINGER: ring the bell

TURF: the road, or low life in general

TURF IT: to be on the road

YAP: *noun*, a farmer or "hoosier"; *verb*, to say or to tell

YORK: New York City

SOURCE: Josiah Flynt [Josiah Flint Willard]. *Tramping with Tramps: Studies and Sketches of Vagabond Life*. New York: The Century Co., 1899. 381–98.

ANALYSIS

Recognizing that hobo jungles and stems were distinct places inhabited by hoboes, tramps, and people who provided goods and services to them—housing, food, entertainment, and so on—suggests another way of thinking about hoboes

Kind lady lives here | Jail | Dog | Officer lives here

Religious talk gets meal | Don't go this way | Go this way | Hold your tongue

Food for work | Keep away | Catch train here | Good place for a handout

Most hoboes and tramps traveled alone. It was simply too difficult for a family to accommodate to the difficulties of jumping trains. However, the fact that hoboes wandered by themselves did not mean that they were totally isolated from everyone else and had no social contact with other people. One way in which they overcame isolation was by developing a unique way of communicating with each other. They informally created a widely understood pictorial language that transmitted information to each other. When a hobo inscribed one of these signs on a wall or a post or a tree, hoboes who came later learned about nearby conditions. Was the neighborhood safe or dangerous? Were residents close at hand likely to be hostile or friendly? Would the local population give hand-outs to a panhandler or slam the door in a hobo's face? Was law enforcement rigid or lenient? This means of communication tied homeless people into a kind of community that would not have existed otherwise. (ABC-CLIO)

and their world. In his book about *The Hobo*, Nels Anderson pointed out that hoboes living in the jungle had their own set of gender roles, a political system of rules and leadership, and a communications system that involved both written and verbal language. The ability to exchange information openly shaped social relationships and affected power relationships. Seeing hoboes and the hobo jungle in this way strongly suggests that "Hobohemia" was actually a distinct subculture within the United States.

Although the concept of subculture existed before 1979, in that year Dick Hebdige, a media theorist and sociologist, asserted that subcultures, in addition to being part of a larger culture, challenged the larger culture by criticizing it and posing alternatives to it. Oftentimes, the values, attitudes, behaviors, and institutions of a subculture are posed in terms directly counter to those of the larger culture. Moreover, Hebdige contended that subcultures are comprised of individuals who feel alienated from the larger society and allow them to develop a sense of identity apart from it. According to him, members of a subculture indicate their sense of belonging to it by creating or adopting a distinctive style, including fashions, mannerisms, and speech. Also, and importantly, a subculture and its members have strong attachments to particular places.

About 30 years later, in 2007, Ken Gelder, a professor of English and a prominent student of literary and film studies, expanded Hebdige's conceptualization of subcultures and clarified it. According to his analysis, a subculture's distinctiveness may be based on linguistics, aesthetics, religion, politics, sex, geography, or a combination of these factors. Gelder was particularly forceful in his discussion of "subcultural geographies" and the nature of the relationship to a particular place between a subculture and its members.

The widespread existence of stems and "hobo jungles" strongly indicates that Hobohemia was a distinct subculture in the United States. But, the existence of these separate geographies is not the only indication that hoboes created a distinct subculture. Looking at Hobohemia and comparing it to Gelder's list of possible subcultural characteristics (listed in the previous paragraph), it becomes clear that Hobohemia displayed many of these prerequisites of "subculturalness," certainly enough of them to qualify as a distinct subculture. And, between Gelder's list and Anderson's description of the hobo jungle, a strong overlap exists.

Hobohemia possessed a distinct jargon or argot, produced its own artistic works, and created its own political institutions. Unfortunately, many of these have not been generally recognized. In some cases this is because the larger society looks down on and disparages objects or items produced by a subculture and associated with the subculture. At the same time, some aspects of the subculture can be taken over—expropriated—by the larger society and woven into the larger culture. When that occurs, the origins of an object are frequently lost and its relationship to the subculture is overwhelmed as it becomes part of the larger society.

One of the most important aspects of any culture or subculture is its own distinctive manner of communicating. This can occur in many different ways—speaking, writing words and letters, drawing pictures, dancing, or acting dramatically in films or plays. Language is critical in this process, and nothing defines groups of people more clearly than possessing a distinct but commonly understood language. Certainly, not knowing a group's language makes it hard for an outsider to enter the group. While some subcultures do have totally distinct languages, many of them have only a specialized vocabulary, argot, or jargon. For example, if a person wanted to enter the subculture of baseball, he or she would have to understand the words *catcher, pitcher, base, ball, strike, out,* and all of those other words that make it possible to talk about the game.

The existence of a distinct argot, or jargon, appears in the writings of almost every hobo author—in novels, stories, autobiographies, reminiscences, and every other form of written communication. It also exists in the writings of almost every outside observer who wrote about hoboes and the hobo world.

One almost blatant example occurs in a magazine article written by Jack London, the hugely popular American novelist in the years around 1900. London has laced this article with words and terms that were recognized by a hobo but must have been unintelligible to anyone with no familiarity of the hobo world. At the end of the article, London tosses off a string of these unfamiliar words in rapid succession. He must either have been assuming that readers understood these words or he was rubbing their ignorance in their faces, making them feel stupid, uninformed, and uneducated. In either case, he did not define these words to make his article understandable to any literate person. The list of words that he tossed off included *profesh*, *gay cat*, *bindle stiff*, *stake man*, *shovel bum*, *musher*, *fakir*, and *stew bum*.

Everything hoboes wrote about their world in those decades reveals the existence of a special vocabulary that they used to describe that world. Moreover, they had a separate and even more distinctive way of communicating with each other. Both hoboes and outside observers frequently remarked that tramps left markings on walls or sidewalks as messages for tramps coming later. These well-known marks told the "reader" what he could expect at the nearest house or store or neighborhood—whether the people were friendly, whether they would provide food or a place to sleep, whether they were likely to offer some cash, or whether they were more likely to summon the police.

Many observers have tried to catalogue both of these vocabularies—the verbal and the pictorial—and make them understandable to the broader public. Although there are only a few relatively small "dictionaries" of the pictorial language, a number of hoboes or observers of hoboes generated vocabulary lists. Several of them identified between 100 and 200 words, but some lists were much longer. The list in this document contains about 125 words and was assembled by Josiah Flint Willard, who wrote using the pen-name Josiah Flynt. Flynt came from a comfortable family, but he was interested in hobo life so he disguised himself as a hobo and lived among hoboes as a way of understanding them. When he returned to his comfortable life, he wrote an account of his experiences. To this, he appended a list of hobo words. Although Flynt's list is accurate and does not define any of the words incorrectly, it is not all-inclusive. Another author who collected and defined hobo words came up with more than 1,700, including all of those mentioned by Flynt and London.

The hoboes understood the importance of language and words and seemed to have sensed that their special vocabulary was a part of their unique culture. Because they recognized that new hoboes did not understand the language, they also considered it proper and appropriate for an older, more experienced tramp to teach this lingo to a newcomer, especially a younger man trying to enter hobo society. Doing this was considered important for another reason. Tramps and hoboes used knowledge of the jargon as an indication of someone's identity. When a stranger appeared, or approached them, they wanted to know if that person could be trusted or if he was potentially threatening. They considered his ability to speak their language as a good way of determining his attitude and his purpose.

FURTHER READING

Hader, J. J. "Honk honk hobo". *The Survey*, 60 (August 1, 1928), 453–55.
"HOBO Signs." *American Heritage*, 27 (August 1976), 93.
Horn. P. "Signs to the Open Road—the Hobo's Helper." *Psychology Today*, 9 (May 1976), 32.
Ponsler, Marge. "Tell a Story about Hobo Signs." *Design Magazine*, 74 (Winter 1972), 4–7.
Richards, Stan, and Associates. *Hobo Signs*. New York: Barlenmir House, 1974.
Samolar, Charlie. "The Argot of the Vagabond." *American Speech*, 2, 9 (June 1927), 385–93.

12

HOBO SONGS

- *Documents:* This chapter provides the lyrics of three songs that were widely known and frequently sung by hoboes.
- *Date:* The precise dates when the songs were written and first sung is generally not known. However, they are usually thought to have been written between 1890 and 1930.
- *Where:* The songs were sung across the United States wherever hoboes were to be found.
- *Significance:* The songs are an important indication that hoboes created a distinct subculture in the United States. They also reveal what hoboes were thinking about and disclose some of their attitudes toward U.S. society, culture, and institutions. The songs provide both a way of understanding hoboes, but, more importantly, a way of hoboes to communicate with each other at first glance.

DOCUMENTS

HELLELUJAH*

O, why don't you work
As other men do?
How in hell can I work
When there's no work to do?

Chorus
Hellelujah, I'm a bum!
Hellelujah, bum again!

---

*Every printed version of this song which does not recognize its hobo origins prints the word as Hallelujah.

Hellelujah give us a handout—
To revive us again

O, why don't you save
All the money you earn?
If I did not eat,
I'd have money to burn
(Repeat chorus)

O, I like my boss
He's a good friend of mine.
That's why I am starving
Out in the bread line!
(Repeat chorus)

I can't buy a job
For I ain't got the dough;
So I ride in a box-car,
For I'm a hobo.
(Repeat chorus)

Whenever I get
All the money I earn,
The boss will be broke
And to work he must turn!
(Repeat chorus)

MY WANDERING BOY

Where is my wandering boy tonight?
The boy of his mother's pride?
He's counting the ties with his bed on his back,
Or else he's bummin' a ride.

Chorus
Oh, where is my boy tonight?
Oh, where is my boy tonight?
He is on the head end of an overland train,
That's where your boy is tonight.

His heart may be pure as the morning dew,
But his clothes are a sight to see.
He's pulled for a vag [vagrant], his excuses won't do.
"Thirty days," says the judge you see.

Chorus
Oh, where is my boy tonight?
Oh, where is my boy tonight?
The chilly winds blow, to the lockup he goes,
That's where your boy is tonight.

"I was looking for work, oh judge," he said.
Says the judge, "I have heard that before."
So to join the chain-gang off he's led,
To hammer the rocks some more.

Chorus
Oh, where is my boy tonight?
Oh, where is my boy tonight?
To strike many blows for his country he goes,
That's where your boy is tonight.

Don't search for your wandering boy tonight,
Let him play the old game if he will.
A worker, a bum, he'll never go right,
As long as he's a wage slave still.

Chorus
Oh, where is my boy tonight?
His money is out of sight.
Wherever he blows, up against it he goes,
"23" for your boy tonight.

THE PREACHER AND THE SLAVE

Long-haired preachers come out every night,
Try to tell you what's wrong and what's right;
But when asked how 'bout something to eat,
They will answer with voices so sweet:

Chorus
You will eat, bye and bye,
In the glorious land above the sky;
Work and pray, live on hay;
You'll get pie in the sky when you die. That's a lie.

The starvation army they play,
They sing, and they clap, and they pray.
'Till they get all your coins on the drum,
Then they'll tell you when you're on the bum.

Repeat *Chorus*

Holy Rollers and jumpers come out,
They holler, they jump, and they shout.
Give your money to Jesus they say,
He will cure all diseases today.

Repeat *Chorus*

If you fight hard for children and wife,
Try to get something good in this life—
You're a sinner and bad man, they tell,
When you die, you will sure go to hell.

Repeat *Chorus*

Workingmen of all countries unite;
Side by side, we for freedom will fight.
When the world and its wealth we have gained,
To the grafters we will sing this refrain:

Repeat *Chorus*

You will eat, bye and bye,
When you've learned how to cook and to fly
Chop some wood, twill do you good.
And you'll eat in the sweet bye and bye.

ANALYSIS

Hoboes sang. Actually, they sang a lot. And, not only did they sing, but hoboes wrote most of the songs that they sang. At least they wrote the lyrics even if they didn't always write the musical score. Perhaps most important of all for making the case that hoboes formed a subculture, they were able to transmit their music tradition to their successors.

The most well-known, beloved, and memorable hobo songs were parodies of songs commonly known by the U.S. people. Songwriters parodied the original lyrics of a popular song and sang them to the tune used in the original version. The best of these songs were extremely clever, twisting the original lyrics to be applicable to the world of tramps and hoboes. For example, in one famous hobo song, "the Salvation Army" becomes "the Starvation Army." In another, the line "you'll be high in the sky, bye-and-bye" is transformed into "there'll be pie in the sky when you die, that's a lie."

Like these two examples, many of these songs have a needle-like sharpness and accuracy that belies what the words say. For example, the song reference to the Starvation Army is making the sarcastic point that the Salvation Army talks a good line about helping hoboes and providing them with food but in actuality does little of any significance. And the song about pie in the sky, "that's a lie," is scoffing at Christian churches that believe there is a heavenly afterlife where all of life's troubles and sorrows have disappeared.

Given the large number of hobo songs that have been discovered, and also given the rich heritage of hobo singing, it seems strange that knowledge of this tradition is so sparse. One almost has to wonder why awareness of the songs has slipped under the radar and why they are so little known. Here, once again, just like with hobo vocabulary, some of the creations of tramps and hoboes were rejected, discarded, or found meaningless by the larger society. Other hobo musical creations, however, were appropriated by other institutions or organizations such as the International Workers of the Word (IWW) and the International Brotherhood of Welfare Assistance. And some of the songs were even taken over and sanitized by U.S. society itself.

Several well-known songs generally thought to be IWW songs almost certainly began as hobo songs. For example, "The Preacher and the Slave," which has been called "the IWW's signature song," was almost certainly first sung by tramps as "Hellelujah, Bum Again" before the IWW incorporated it into their songbooks. The words of the song and the constant refrain, "I'm a bum," as well as accounts by several hoboes seem clearly to mark it as a hobo song.

The same can be said about another song often attributed to the IWW. "My Wandering Boy," a song that first appeared in the IWW's songbook in 1905 and was claimed to be a Wobbly song, seems to have predated the chartering of the IWW in 1905 and contains words and language that are consistent with hobo thinking and speaking.

Some of the confusion and misinterpretation of the origins of these songs results from the fact that many of the songwriters who can be identified were hoboes who joined the IWW either while they were still hoboing or soon afterward. This is certainly true of three men who wrote some of the most famous songs associated with the IWW: Harry K. McClintock ("Helleluhah, Bum Again"), Joe Hill ("Casey Jones—the Union Scab," "The Tramp," "Ta-Ra-Ra Boom De-Ay"), and Ralph Chaplin ("Solidarity Forever"). The precise year in which the songwriters composed these songs is unknown; the words and the ideas that they express are just as reflective of the hobo world as the Wobbly world. Possibly they wrote and first performed these songs in the hobo world, took them to the Wobblies when they joined that organization, and the songs become known as IWW songs. In any event, they can easily be attributed to the perceptions of the author as a hobo as well as to an IWW mentality.

There are two other indications that some of these songs began as hobo songs. First, the IWW, one of whose major goals was creating a universal union of all workingmen, worked hard to enroll hoboes as members. It cajoled them, threatened them, and gladly welcomed them. Hoboes who were known to have written songs about the darker moments of their life would certainly have been prime targets for the IWW. Second, there are some songs that contain imagery suggestive of both hoboes and of the IWW. However, in almost all of those cases, the IWW imagery occurs toward the end of the song, suggesting that these stanzas might have been later additions after a man had joined the IWW and was modifying the song to be more applicable and relevant.

There is one last reason why some of the songs are frequently not attributed to hoboes and are not thought of as hobo songs. Over time, some of these songs have passed into the general "American songbook" and therefore transcend being identified with any distinct segment or subculture of U.S. society. They have become part of the American tradition. In 1927 Carl Sandburg included "The Preacher and the Slave" in his *American Songbook*, thus claiming it as an American folksong. Perhaps the most ironic theft of a hobo song by mainstream U.S. folk musicology is "The Big Rock Candy Mountain." Originally sung by hoboes as the tale of an older man who seduced an adolescent boy into joining him on the road, American singers, especially Burl Ives, modified the lyrics drastically. Ives cleaned up the lyrics, removing all references to sex, alcohol, and tobacco to make it socially acceptable. After he recorded the song, it became canonized as an icon of American folk music. Once that had happened, the song would never again be thought of as a hobo classic. If the song is ever included in a collection of American songs, it is always said to have an "unknown author." If one ever looks for the original lyrics, they are extremely difficult to find, and the song's original tale has been lost.

FURTHER READING

Green, Archie, David Roediger, Franklin Rosemont, and Salvatore Salerno, eds. *The Big Red Songbook*. Chicago, IL: Charles H. Kerr Publishing Company, 2007.
Greenway, John. *American Folksongs of Protest*. New York: Octagon Books, 1970.

13

HOBO POLITICS

The I.W.W.

- **Document:** The following document consists of selections from "The I.W.W.," an article that appeared in *The Atlantic Monthly* in November 1917. Its author had been Executive Secretary of the State Immigration and Housing Commission of California. In 1918, the U.S. government assigned him to investigate examine the cases of two union organizers charged with murder in the Wheatland Riot that year in California—one of the most notorious instances in the history of U.S. labor.
- **Date:** The article was published in 1917.
- **Where:** The magazine *The Atlantic Monthly* is published in Boston, Massachusetts.
- **Significance:** This article formulates a clear connection between hoboes and the IWW and explains why the two were as tightly intertwined as the author believed.

DOCUMENT

. . . It is perhaps of value to quote the language of one of the most influential of the I.W.W. leaders.

You ask me why the I.W.W. is not patriotic to the United States. If you were a bum without a blanket; if you had left your wife and kids when you went West for a job, and had never located them since; if your job never kept you long enough in a place to qualify you to vote; if you slept in a lousy, sour bunkhouse, and ate food just as rotten as they could give you and get by with it; if deputy sheriffs shot your cooking cans full of holes and spilled your grub on the ground; if your wages were lowered on you when the bosses thought they had you down; if there was one law for [Henry] Ford, [the automobile manufacturer], [Herman] Suhr [a Wobbly organizer convicted of murder], and [Tom] Mooney [a radical activist convicted of a bombing in 1916], and another for [Harry] Thaw [who murdered the architect Stanford White]; if every person who represented law and order and the nation beat you up, railroaded you to jail, and the good Christian people cheered and told them to go to it, how in hell do you expect a man to be patriotic?

. . . The American I.W.W. is a neglected and lonely hobo worker, usually malnourished, and in need of medical care. He is as far from being a scheming syndicalist [economic and political radical] . . . as the imagination might conceive. His proved sabotage activities in the West total up a few hop kiln buntings. Compared to the widespread sabotage in prison industries, where a startlingly large percentage of materials is intentionally ruined, the I.W.W. performance is not worth mentioning.

. . . The I.W.W. is a union of unskilled workers in large part employed in agriculture and in the production of raw materials. While the I.W.W. appeared in the East at Lawrence [Mass.], Paterson [New Jersey], and certain other places, at the height of strike activity, its normal habitat is in the upper middle West and the far West. . . .

DID YOU KNOW?

A Political Sensibility

There were intellectuals among the hoboes. The Industrial Workers of the World (IWW) was on West Madison Street, its headquarters from about 1905 on. It was at first active from Chicago westward, to organize the hobo workers. It would use these mobile men as messengers to spread the idea of "One Big Union." . . .

Westward, the IWW continued working with the "bummery." Strong locals, for example, were formed in the western lumber industry. Each summer, the organizers were in the harvest fields. Some who were not official representatives at all would go about signing up members and keeping the initiation fees. Many of these hobo organizers were serious believers in the One-Big-Union ideal when the workers of the world would become a mighty force and would put down grafting employers. It was a song-promoting movement, giving out its little red songbook "to fan the flames of discontent." The story of the movement is but marginally important except as it pertains to the occasional intellectual hobo. While he went out to jobs, he spent more time than most hoboes in the cities, not drinking but talking. . . . Mostly they were soapboxers.

Source: Nels Anderson, *The American Hobo: An Autobiography.* Leiden, Netherlands: E. J. Brill, 1975, 177. Used by permission of Koninklijke Brill NV.

It is fortunate for our analysis that the I.W.W. membership in the West is consistently of one type, and one which has had a uniform economic experience. It is made up of migratory workers currently called hobo labor. The terms "hobo miner," "hobo lumber-jack," and "blanket stiff" are familiar and necessary in accurate descriptions of Western labor conditions. Very few of these migratory workers have lived long enough in any one place to establish a legal residence and to vote, and they are also womanless. Only about ten percent have been married, and these, for the most part, either have lost their wives or have deserted them. Many claim to be "working out," and expect eventually to return to their families. But examination usually discloses the fact that they have not sent money home recently, or received letters. They are "floaters" in every social sense. . . .

The membership of the I.W.W. which pays regular dues is an uncertain and volatile thing. While a careful study in California in 1915 showed but forty-five hundred affiliated members of the I.W.W. in that state, it was very evident that the functioning and striking membership was double this, or more. In the State of

Washington, in the lumber strike of this year, the I.W.W. membership was most probably not over three thousand; but the number of those active in the strike and joining in support of the I.W.W. numbered approximately seven thousand. . . .

. . . Its numerous headquarters are the result of the energy of local secretaries. They are not places for executive direction so much as gregarious centres where the lodging-house inhabitant or the hobo with his blanket can find light, a stove, and companionship. In the prohibition states of the West, the I.W.W. hall has been the only social substitute for the saloon for these people. The migratory workers have almost all seen better economic and social days, and carry down into their disorganized labor level traditions, if only faint ones, of some degree of dignity and intellectual life. To these old-time desires the headquarters cater. In times of strike and disorder, the headquarters becomes the centre of the direct propaganda of action; but when this is over, its character changes to that of a rest-house, and as such is unique in the unskilled workers' history.

. . . The combination of low wages, the unskilled nature of the work, and its great irregularity tends to break the habit and desire for stable industry among the workers. Millions drift into migrating from one industrial centre to another in search of work. In these centres nearly all saloon-keepers run an employment-agency business of a more or less informal kind, and to the saloon the job-hunter turns. In return for the job it is his obligation to drink up part of his pay-check, and if he is a married man, his history here becomes marked by a recital of excuses sent to the distant wife instead of money. The worker slides down the scale and out of his industry, and joins the millions of unskilled or ex-skilled who float back and forth from Pennsylvania to Missouri and from the lumber camps to the Gulf States and California. They lie up in the winter in the cheap lodging-houses, in a state of pseudo-hibernation. Thirty dollars plus a few weeks of ice-cutting enables them to weather the winter through. . . .

In one San Francisco lodging-house, out of two hundred and fifty beds, there were eight with outside ventilation. A New York study disclosed that the lodging-house inmates were eleven times more tubercular than the average population. The beds seldom have linen, and the covers are usually dirty quilts which have to be regularly fumigated during the winter on account of vermin. The migratory worker lies up for the winter with a thirty-dollar stake. . . . In a ten-year period the Chicago police stations gave lodging to 1,275,463 homeless men, and the municipal lodging-house to 370,655. Only 20 percent of those were residents of Chicago.

In the spring this labor group drifts out toward the first work. In the main, they "beat their way." Between 1901 and 1905, 23,964 trespassers were killed on American railroads and 25,236 injured. These were largely tramps and hobos. The railroad companies calculated that at a given time there were 500,000 hobos beating their way or waiting at stations to catch on a train, or walking the tracks. This group might be called the fraction of the migratory millions actually in transit. Numerous statistical studies show that the average term of employment of the migratory worker is between ten and fourteen days. With a stake of ten dollars, he will retire to a hobo camp beside some stream—his "jungle" as the road vernacular has it—and, adding his daily quarter or half of a dollar to the "Mulligan fund," he will live on until the stake is gone. If he inclines to live further on the charity of the newcomers, he is styled a "jungle buzzard" and cast forth. He then resumes his haphazard search for a job, the only economic plan in his mind being a faint realization that about August he must begin to accumulate his thirty-dollar winter stake. Each year finds him physically in worse disrepair, psychologically more hopeless, morally more bitter and anti-social. His importance to our nation's future lies in the uncomfortable fact that proportionally he is increasing in number and his recruiting group above is increasing in unrest and economic instability.

SOURCE: Carleton H. Parker. "The I.W.W." *The Atlantic Monthly*, 120, 5 (November 1917).

ANALYSIS

The acquisition of hobo songs by the IWW and claiming them as their own is of more than passing significance. Certainly, it is an important detail in explaining some of the popularity of the Wobbly movement. The songs—and especially their tunes—were known by many Americans who therefore felt more sympathy for the IWW than they might have otherwise. The expropriation of these songs also reveals something about the origins of the IWW and where it got some of its members. It has been long known, and several historians have written, that many hoboes joined the IWW. But, the confiscation of these songs also discloses that Hobohemia had an important political component.

The precise nature of that relationship has never been made clear. The large number of hoboes who joined this radical political movement makes one wonder how instrumental hoboes actually were in creating the IWW or if it was just a matter of the IWW seeking out hoboes and persuading/urging/cajoling them to join their organization. While one would like to answer this question, unfortunately that is not possible. No one at the time made any effort to identify exactly who became hoboes or who joined the IWW, and no one attempted to sort out the nature of the relationship, although Carleton H. Parker certainly seemed to believe that it was a two-way street.

We do know two things, though. First, there was some relationship between hoboism and the IWW; the overlapping of so many songs makes that clear. Second, the political consciousness of hoboes and Hobohemia predated the formation of the IWW by at least a decade. Hoboes, as a group, first seem to have expressed themselves politically in 1894 when they joined Coxey's Army; only later did they join the IWW. This political consciousness has not been widely recognized, probably because hoboes did not form a separate political organization that represented only them. As a result, their involvement in other political movements has been overlooked, and when acting as members of Coxey's Army or as Wobblies, their identity as hoboes was hidden by their allegiance to an alternative movement or organization that did not outwardly reflect hobo culture, values, and behavior. Perhaps Carleton Parker saw the relationship more clearly than any other contemporary observer.

Coxey's Army appeared in 1894. That year, a businessman from Massilon, Ohio—one Jacob Coxey—tried to organize an army of unemployed men to march on Washington, DC. He thought that they could effectively protest against the terrible, and still worsening, economic conditions in the United States, which was entering the worst depression in the country's history up to that time. Coxey told the press that he hoped 100,000 men would join in this great procession.

This great number of followers did not appear. When "General" Coxey and his group departed Masillon, Ohio, on Easter Sunday, March 25, 1894, it is estimated that he was leading only 100 men. By the time they reached Washington, DC, the band of soldiers had grown to perhaps 500. However, across the country, comparable forces were preparing to join them, and similar regiments appeared far and wide, especially in the far West—in California, Colorado, Oregon, Washington, and Montana.

All of these troops identified with Coxey's expeditionary unit, wanted to join it, and hoped to deliver the same message to the country: The federal government, and especially Congress, had the responsibility of finding ways to solve the country's economic problems. The Western contingents were delayed in reaching Washington only because of problems with their transportation, not because of any hesitation to participate.

Who were these men? Whom did they represent? Nobody knows exactly. However, we do know that the newspapers constantly referred to them as bums or tramps or hoboes, any one of which designated homelessness. In *The Damnedest Radical*, a biography of Dr. Ben Reitman, Roger Bruns relates a conversation that took place between Reitman and Coxey. The interesting aspect of the discourse is not that Reitman and Coxey had any disagreement about who had participated in the march, only what terminology should be used to characterize them.

In a conversation with Ben, General Coxey claimed, "The trouble with these movements of the unemployed is that people fail to recognize that there are men honestly seeking employment. They think they are a lot of ruffians and property destroyers. They call all [men who are] out of work hobos."

"A lot you know about hobos," Reitman gently shot back. "When you led your Army of 3,000 to Washington . . . you were at the head of a mob of unemployed hobos. A hobo is a man tramping around looking for work."

"That's not the way I've heard the word used," Coxey responded. . . . A hobo is a good-for-nothing fellow who would rather beg or steal, or even starve than work. I never led hobos to Washington."

Reitman and Coxey were clearly talking about the same men—those who were unemployed and had no permanent home—but they used different words to describe them.

Reitman and Coxey were both using the terms in a different way from most newspaper reporters at the time. One recent historian studying the protesters who marched on Washington has noted that at the end of the nineteenth century journalists regularly used words like *hobo* and *tramp* to "transform working-class radicals."

One of the clearest ways of seeing how hoboes became involved in politics and active members of the IWW is by looking at specific individuals and tracking the progression of their lives. Probably the man who became the most famous Wobbly in the United States was Joe Hill. Born in Sweden, he and five siblings were orphaned when he was a teenager. As a result, he and one of his brothers migrated to the United States in 1902. As one biography puts it, "Little is known of Hill's doings or whereabouts for the next 12 years." Nevertheless, some general details are widely accepted. Again, quoting from one of his biographies, he "was an itinerant worker, who moved around the west, hopping freight trains, going from job to job." That is, he was a hobo.

Using slightly different words, but expressing the same essential idea, another biographer identifies Hill as "a songwriter, itinerant laborer, and union organizer." He seems to have joined the IWW about 1910, become active in the organization, and begun traveling and recruiting members on its behalf. He delivered speeches, authored poems, and wrote songs (perhaps his most noted accomplishment). In 1915, he was indicted for, convicted of, and executed by the state of Utah in a highly controversial trial that many people, both then and now, think to have been a travesty of justice.

Like Joe Hill, Len De Caux made the transition from being a hobo to becoming a Wobbly. After his Wobbly days, he became publicity director of the Congress of Industrial Organizations (CIO), which became one of the most powerful unions in the United States during the 1930s and which merged with the American Federation of Labor (AFL) in 1955 to form the AFL-CIO. Fortunately, De Caux wrote several books including a biography in which he explicitly described his first acquaintance with the IWW and his ultimate participation.

Other than a few anecdotes, however, we know little about the attraction of the IWW to hoboes. The writings of Carleton H. Parker and his wife, Cornelia Stratton Parker, fill in some of the blank spots. Parker was briefly a bond trader and journalist, but he became an economist who taught at the University of California in San Francisco. From that position, he was appointed Executive Director of the State Immigration and Housing Commission of California. During his short career, he published many articles about housing conditions and was always cognizant of the overlap between hoboism and Wobblyism. Parker died in 1918 at the age of 40, and his widow wrote a biography that provides additional insight into his thinking.

FURTHER READING

De Caux, Len. *Labor Radical: From the Wobblies to CIO, a Personal History*. Boston, MA: Beacon Press, 1970.

Hall, Greg. *Harvest Wobblies: The Industrial Workers of the World and Agricultural Laborers in the American West, 1905–1930*. Corvallis, OR: Oregon State University, 2001.

Palmateer, Dmitri. "Charity and the Tramp: Itinerancy, Unemployment, and Municipal Government from Coxey to the Unemployed League." *Oregon Historical Quarterly*, 107, 3 (Summer 2006), 8–53.

Worth, Cedric. "Brotherhood of Man and the Wobblies." *North American Review*, 227 (April 1929), 487–92.

14

THE HOBO COLLEGE

The Hobo College

- *Document:* The document describes the origin, purpose, and nature of the Hobo College. The author himself was both a student there and later a teacher.
- *Date:* The book was published in 1956.
- *Where:* The book concerns events that occurred in Chicago during the first few decades of the twentieth century, but it also describes happenings that took place in other cities.
- *Significance:* The selection describes the goals of the Hobo College, how it attempted to meet those goals, and the nature of students there. It is also further evidence that there was a community among the hoboes that can legitimately be considered to have been a distinct subculture whose members had clear goals and a strong sense of their own aspirations.

DOCUMENT

. . . [James Eads How] decided that he would distribute his wealth in helping the migratory worker—the hobo, whom he addressed ever after as brother.

. . . He [How] lived on the coarsest and simplest fare himself and when solicited gave his "brother" only "coffee and ——" or an apple. He believed it was wrong for him to dine while millions in the world were hungry or starving.

When he was finally educated [as a physician at Harvard University] and experienced, he came to Chicago, which had become the hobo capital of America with its 60,000 or more homeless men, to begin his life work. He organized the International Brotherhood [Welfare] Association which maintained little dingy halls where men could sleep free and get "coffee ——." The local organizations were never self-supporting. They were subsidized by How.

In the midst of the depression of 1913–14, he and an interested group of some dozen men including Irving St. John Tucker opened what was then the first Hobo College at Congress Street near Wabash. He thought that he could bring something worth-while to his "brothers" through education.

Students came and competent faculties taught. The incomparable Mary Garden sang as a feature of the first Commencement program in 1917 and diplomas were given to well over one hundred students.

The text of this diploma read:

BE IT KNOWN TO ALL THE WORLD
THAT A HOBO HAS BEEN A STUDENT
AT THE HOBO COLLEGE and has attended the lectures, discussions, clinics, musicals, readings and visits to art galleries and theatres.

He has also expressed a desire to get an education, better his own condition and help build a world that will be without unemployment, poverty, wars, prostitution, ignorance, and injustice. He pledges himself individually to live a clean, honest, manly life, and to take care of his health and morals, and abstain from all habits that undermine his health and better nature. He agrees to cooperate with all people and organizations that are really trying to abolish poverty and misery, and to work to build a better world in which to live.

Dr. Ben Reitman, erstwhile King of the Hoboes, was Director of this College and what he lacked in understanding of an educational institution he made up for in his first-hand knowledge, enriched daily, of the problems of his Hobohemian students. Moreover, he was so eminently successful in interpreting to teachers the value of working with him as unsalaried volunteer[s] that the faculty list soon included such scholars and teachers as are named here, with the subjects they taught: Herman Adler, Mental Hygiene; Preston Bradley, Public Speaking; E. L. Schaub, Philosophy; E. W. Burgess, Sociology; David Rotman, Psychiatry; John Landeson, Criminology; and somewhere in the list, Frank O. Beck, Social Pathology. Jim Tully, the author was also on the staff.

DID YOU KNOW?

"Hobo College" Opens

James Eads How Proposes to Show Pupils How to Get Jobs

The "Hobo College" came into being yesterday at 202 Bowery under the direction of James Eads How, the "millionaire hobo" of Chicago. The books are now said to be open to any full-fledged hobo desiring courses in such subjects as "sociology," "industrial law," and "public speaking."

The "college," How explained, is the outgrowth of institutions which, he said, have been conducted in Chicago and Cincinnati. "The idea has taken hold in other cities," he said, and if we can educate discharged soldiers and inveterate hoboes so that they can get jobs, our purpose will be accomplished. The classes will continue all Summer, and we will operate an employment agency on a small scale.

The idea, it appears, is to open the day with a search for employment. The applicant arrives between 9 and 9:30 o'clock and is sent out to interview a prospective employer. If he fails to find a job, he returns at 11 o'clock, and is invited to take part in the college courses. These continue until 2:30 o'clock, when a "jungle luncheon" is served.

"We will have three major subjects in the college," How said. "In economics, or sociology, we will try to give the pupils an idea of labor conditions. The course in public speaking will enable the students to talk more intelligently and should increase their chances of getting positions."

The courses will be held Tuesdays, Wednesdays, and Thursdays. The reading room of the "College" will be open at all hours.

Source: The New York Times, June 11, 1919.

DID YOU KNOW?

The College Campus

Firsthand accounts describe a room with a capacity for 150, ramshackle furniture, a lending library of discarded books from the public library, and walls displaying portraits of Mark Twain, Karl Marx, and Charles Darwin made by alumni. Handbills and posters advertised "classes" on topics including successful panhandling, "how to survive without eating," street speaking, the history of vagrancy, philosophy of the road and the curiously dubbed, "Will the Coming Christ be a Hobo." Occasionally actors and musicians at the Hobo College, including noted actor Richard Bennett and company and a remarkable performance by opera star Mary Garden. More importantly, the Hobo College recorded the homeless the chance to express and educate themselves, share their ideas, songs and poetry, and provide a place where they could be treated with respect.

Source: Mark Moscato, "Editor's Choice—Hobo 101: The down and out found strength and hope in Ben Reitman's Hobo College, USA." (Street Roots, USA) Street News Service.

. . . Your opinion, no doubt, is that the main run of hoboes can not qualify intellectually for such high-brow courses. This was the unsupported position of the general public until a study was made of a thousand men of this class. Of this number only 89 were found to be feeble-minded, epileptic, or insane. While the average intelligence of the [ho]boes was lower than that of the same number of small businessmen, yet among the hoboes there was a higher per cent of mentally superior persons. The intelligence of the group was as high or higher than that of the adult males tested in military camps. Students of vagabond life are universally surprised at the intellectual curiosity and ability of the migratory worker.

Psychology students at Northwestern University gave the army Alpha intelligence tests to 80 students of Hobo College and found that they were higher intellectually on the average than were seniors in the University.

. . . The Hobohemian life begins by breaking ties. First with the family and then with the community. It ends with severing all associations with static people and roving over the face of the earth. The hobo becomes thus not only a "homeless" man but a man without a cause, without a country, without, in fact, any type of responsible associations.

The Hobo College was set up to meet just this need for ties, however futile the effort might have seemed in the eyes of the general public. . . . Its first aim was to furnish an opportunity for the [ho]boes to exchange experiences and to maintain, though only for a short season, some sort of corporate existence and experience.

At the end of every course I presented at the College I stressed the idea that a romantic passion for freedom was not enough. The highest achievement of a human life was to establish and maintain purposeful communications with other human lives. The [ho]bo rolls along, missing the security and the glory of an attachment to the earth, to a cause, and also the stability and satisfaction of a recognized, worthwhile position in the scheme of things.

A Hobo's Prayer
Almighty God, heavenly father who has blessed us hobos with good health and avid appetites and made this world a bountiful and plentiful place for all of us bipeds with towering possibilities: Give us common sense enough to wander and roam the world, and make the freights warmer and safer to ride in. Make the "town-clowns" more humane, sandwiches easier to get, and the chickens come closer to the "jungles" that we hobos might have

chicken-stew oftener. Abolish, O Lord, the lousy flophouses and ungodly vagrancy laws and their concomitants, the rock-piles. Send us, O Lord, more sunshine and less winter, so we can enjoy our leisure time more, and grant us the privilege to ride the "cushions" gratis. For these simple and elemental things we will forever praise thee, O Lord! Amen.

SOURCE: Frank O. Beck, *Hobohemia*. Rindge, NH: Richard R. Smith, Publisher, Ind. 1956. Used by permission of Charles H. Kerr Publishing Co.

When someone hears or reads words such as "homeless" or "hobo" or "tramp," a stereotypical reaction is to picture a person who is dirty and unkempt—unwashed with uncombed hair, bad breath and raggedy clothing—in other words, a bum. The picture of the Hobo College refutes that image and presents a very different view. Taken at a lecture delivered at the Hobo College in Chicago, the men depicted here are all quite presentable. Some of them wear clothing that suggests membership in the middle class, and some of them wear working-class attire, but all of them look respectable enough to be classified well above the category of "derelict," even though some of them were probably homeless. Their very presence at a public lecture on a serious topic at a place called a college suggests that these men, regardless of their economic status, had a clear consciousness of the world around them and cared deeply about it. (Chicago History Museum)

ANALYSIS

The richness of hobo culture and society surprises almost everyone who has had little or no personal contact with hoboes and their world. For many people, perhaps most, it is hard to think of hobo jungles or the main stem producing literature, music, or educational institutions. Those activities don't fit into stereotyped views of hoboes. And yet, they did exist.

Many of the most highly regarded writers in the United States at the end of the nineteenth or beginning of the twentieth centuries spent time as homeless hoboes, and their experiences informed their writing. Other writers, who themselves had not participated in Hobohemia, nevertheless used it and its residents as important parts of their novels or stories. A list of these authors would include, among others, Frank Norris, Theodore Dreiser, Jack London, Upton Sinclair, and Stephen Crane, some of the greatest authors ever produced in the United States.

Even more numerous are hobo autobiographies, reminiscences, and memoirs. One student of this literature has identified nearly 40 such works that were published in the United States between 1890 and 1940. Even more, he has found these autobiographies to have enough common characteristics that he has labeled them "a genre of American literature."

Among these shared characteristics, perhaps the most important in thinking about the culture of Hobohemia was these authors' representation of themselves as intellectuals. As John Allen, a professor of English, has pointed out, during the Progressive Era professional writers and intellectuals went into the slums and on the road for inspiration and material. Such "crossing over" between classes blurs the apparent distinction between tramps and intellectuals. A subculture of intellectual tramps and hoboes (centered in Chicago) also contributed to this blurring.

Allen's specific reference to Chicago reflects the fact that the Windy City, because of its position at the center of the railroad system in the United States, also became the center of the hobo world. It was probably here that the use of the terms *stem* and *main stem* originated. But, there is more to it than that. Chicago was also home to one of the most unexpected institutions of Hobohemia, one that indicates that homeless men, or poor men, or men without families, or men without blue- or white-collar jobs, cannot necessarily, or even generally, be categorized as unintelligent, unthinking, or mentally unstable.

The existence of the Hobo College strongly suggests that the residents of the hobo subculture had many of the same values as the larger U.S. society, even while developing and maintaining their own subculture. Among those values were education and the use of analytical thinking skills to understand, evaluate, and critique the nature of social, political, and economic conditions and institutions. As Nels Anderson described the situation in his autobiography, published in 1975, "There were intellectuals among the hoboes." And even though Anderson had some reservations about the hobo college, which he said was only "euphemistically called the Hobo College," he also characterized it as "a point at which hoboes of serious bent would gather," men who "spent more time than most hoboes in the cities, not drinking but talking."

Two most unusual men created the Hobo College. One was James Eads How who provided funding for the college. Known as the "Millionaire Hobo," How came from a wealthy family and was the grandson of a prominent engineer, James Buchanan Eads, who had built the Eads Bridge that crossed the Mississippi River at St. Louis. During his youth, however, James Eads How concluded that it was not right for one individual to control such great wealth, and he decided to use his fortune for the betterment of mankind. He himself adopted the life of a hobo. Along the way, he established and financed a newspaper for hoboes, *The Hobo News*. He also provided the money to found six hobo colleges, the most important being in Chicago. How once described the objects of the colleges as teaching "three major subjects. In economics or sociology, we will try to give the pupils an idea of labor conditions. The course in public speaking will enable the pupils to talk more intelligently and improve their chances of getting positions."

The college in Chicago, certainly the most well-known and vibrant of these institutions, was founded in collaboration with Dr. Ben Reitman. Reitman was a Chicago physician who had lived as a hobo, maintained relations with the hobo world, and was an active political provocateur. He belonged to the Socialist Party, interacted with anarchists in the United States, and was the long-time lover of the most feared and reviled anarchist in the country, Emma Goldman. Reitman was one of the early members of the Dil Pickle Society in Chicago where he came to know and befriend such figures as Carl Sandburg, Sherwood Anderson, Clarence Darrow, Lucy Parsons, Ben Hecht, Vachel Lindsay, Ralph Chaplin, and Harriet Monroe. Reitman met How at a meeting of the International Brotherhood Welfare Association, another organization founded by How, became his protégé, and took on the task of opening the college in Chicago.

FURTHER READING

Bruns, Roger A. *The Damndest Radical: The Life and Times of Ben Reitman, Chicago's Social Reformer, Hobo King and Whorehouse Physician*. Urbana, IL: University of Illinois Press, 1986.

15

HOBOHEMIA DISAPPEARS

The End of Tramping

- *Document:* The document explains how "the stem" or "Hobohemia" disappeared. It considers why and when the section of large U.S. cities in which hobo culture flourished seems to have vanished.
- *Date:* The article was published in 1999 but describes events that occurred during the 1950s and 1960s.
- *Where:* The specific events analyzed in the document took place in Philadelphia, Pennsylvania, but they were repeated in almost every large U.S. city.
- *Significance:* The document discusses the social, political, and economic forces that led to the disappearance of hobo districts in U.S. cities.

DOCUMENT

After the mid-1920s, the declining demand for casual, migratory labor reduced job opportunities and increased economic hardship among the homeless population. Being habitually homeless became an additional liability as the Great Depression subsequently developed and millions of newly unemployed and destitute men also became homeless in the 1930s. This situation eased only at the onset of World War II, when the war effort offered employment to all who were able to work. After the war, prolonged economic prosperity expanded work opportunities elsewhere and this, along with increased veterans' benefits and an expanded social welfare system, continued the trend of reducing the number of young men who would once have taken up life as itinerant laborers. Those who remained were, as a group, older, more disabled, and less attached to the labor force than their predecessors.

The demand for itinerant labor never returned in the decades following World War II, and as a result greater emphasis was placed on the homeless population's social isolation, aversion toward structured responsibility, and opposition to conventional status orientation. The labor niche that they once occupied was no longer there to serve as a prop against images of drunken men, squalid flophouses, and panhandlers. The term "derelict" joined older terms of vagrant, hobo, and bum, and more [people] clearly defined homeless men as failures, threats, and objects of fascination. While the homeless population was always judged to a large extent by their moral failings, their work was also able to support urban districts that catered to their unique needs. In the absence of a viable economic function, the districts in which homeless men congregated contracted and took on a perversely exotic appeal for both tourists and sociologists. . . . In recognition of these social, structural and demographic changes, urban concentrations of homeless men in Philadelphia and elsewhere became, in the early 1950s, known as "Skid Row."

. . . Since 1952, proponents of Skid Row clearance described the area as declining and blighted. But the Skid Row population, by the accounts available, held steady throughout the period of preparations for urban renewal and only declined owing to the implementation of the renewal projects from 1963 to 1976. Research also indicates that perceived pathologies such as alcoholism and disability, though prominent, were limited to a minority of Skid Row residents and that the main means of support for Philadelphia's and other cities' skid row residents were not welfare benefits but retirement pensions and wages from irregular, temporary labor stints. This income, while usually meager, kept most of the homeless population lodged in private accommodations on a given night. Skid Row was perhaps not as large as the turn-of-the-century ["main stem"], but neither did it appear to be dying a natural death.

The size of Skid Row did not change until the local political economy took an active interest in Skid Row whose location was ever closer to an expanding and more image-conscious CBD [Central Business District]. . . . Philadelphia's local economic interests not only helped broker the spatial redevelopment of this area but also took a leadership role in planning the social rehabilitation of its residents. . . .

. . . Characterizing Skid Row's problem in terms of social as well as physical blight led to a policy response that was consistent with the ambivalent mixture of fear and sympathy that has been traditionally shown toward the homeless population and their urban habitat. Philadelphia . . . became the sight of a major research effort . . . which highlighted the pathologies associated with homelessness, especially alcoholism, as responsible for the blighted Skid Row environment. This reinforced, on the one hand, popular reactions of sympathy in response to the homeless man's miserable existence [and] his human weakness. . . . On the other hand, this research also legitimated the homeless population's pariah status

---

DID YOU KNOW?

A Changing Economy

[In 1922] his kind of work was coming to a close. The advent of machinery was threatening the grain-harvest jobs. Ice-making machinery would soon replace making ice on the lakes. Soon there would be no more construction of the railroads. On levee work, the dredges and drag lines would soon replace the team outfits. Even that favorite winter retreat of miners, lumbering, was about to be mechanized.

Source: Anderson, Nels. *Men on the Move.* Chicago, IL: University of Chicago Press, 1940, 12

DID YOU KNOW?

Extinction

Both tramps and hoboes are anachronisms bound for extinction. It does not take a particularly astute observer to see the imminent doom of the hobo, the migratory workers. A presage of it is found in the Middle Western wheat harvest for years the summer stomping ground for hobo hordes. As the harvest has become more mechanized, the employment of hoboes has decreased, and for two years now, like the buffalo herds before them, the hoboes have failed to come through.

At the same time, automobiles have made it possible for any college sophomore to bum the breadth of the continent. No special determination or fortitude is required to qualify as a tramp nowadays, and presently the tramping fraternity, with all of its lore, must break up before the influx of gaycats who have neither any respect for tramp-dom's tradition nor any desire to make tramping a lifetime occupation.

Source: George Milburn. *The Hobo's Hornbook.* Introduction. Quoted in Nels Anderson, *Men on the Move.* Chicago: University of Chicago Press, 1940, 38.

and the fiercely negative community reactions to the prospect of Skid Row relocating to another area of the city. . . .

. . . Like virtually all other cities, Philadelphia, while in the process of destroying Skid Row and scattering its residents, all but ignored Skid Row's historical function as an inexpensive refuge for the economically and socially down and out. Skid Row's position as a buffer zone that separated a population, widely held as deviant, from the rest of the city became harder to maintain as other uses, particularly transportation and tourism, encroached upon this area. Optimistic assessments of economic prosperity ascertained these areas [Skid Row] as obsolete. Since one of the primary goals of Skid Row's planned demise was for this socially undesirable area not to arise elsewhere, no provisions were made to replace the skid row's unique supply of often squalid but cheap housing, known as single-room occupancy (SRO) housing.

SOURCE: Stephen Metraux, "Waiting for the Wrecking Ball; Skid Row in Postindustrial Philadelphia." *Journal of Urban History,* 25, 5 (July 1999). Reprinted by permission of SAGE Publications.

ANALYSIS

By 1920, hoboes had created a distinct subculture in the hearts of cities in the United States. These districts, generally called the "stem" or "main stem," housed a group of homeless people referred to by any number of names—*tramps, bums, hoboes,* and *vagrants,* for example. A careful look, however, discloses that their lives had much more substance than those terms suggest. The denizens of Hobohemia had a singular way of riding trains not used by anyone else; they also spoke in a coded vocabulary that was comprehended only by other members of the subculture. They produced a literature and body of writing, and other authors (including some of the finest in American literature) used them as the protagonists of their own prose. Members of this generally undetected subculture wrote and sang songs that grew directly out of the political, social, and economic institutions of that subculture but were appropriated by the larger culture or other organizations within it. It is even accurate to say that hoboes had political interests, participated in politics, and made an unmistakable political presence.

However, despite the vibrancy of this subculture in the first few decades of the twentieth century, one could probably wander endlessly through the streets of those same cities today and stumble upon only faint traces of that subculture. This circumstance raises several important questions: What has happened to that subculture, and where has it gone? Why has Hobohemia vanished?

The answers to these questions are not deeply hidden. To find them, one simply needs to recognize that the circumstances producing the subculture and Hobohemia have disappeared. And, as they disappeared, so did Hobohemia and its subculture. Although other reasons could also be mentioned, a few stand out from the rest—the changing U.S. economy, the declining significance of trains and the changing technology of railroad operations, the rapid adoption of automobiles as the most important form of transportation in the United States, and the outbreak of World War II.

During the 1920s, new kinds of machinery were developed for nearly every sector of the economy in which hoboes found jobs. As a consequence, the demand for labor on farms, in mining, and in logging declined—providing much less reason for the existence of migratory labor. Railroads became much less significant in the United States than they had been for decades, a trend that would continue throughout the twentieth century. As this happened, there were fewer and fewer trains that hoboes could use to get from place to place.

Moreover, the technology of trains changed. As train engines became more powerful and climbed grades more rapidly, and as new technologies made trains less dependent on regular supplies of water, trains had to slow much less often to climb hills or stop at water tanks; in consequence, the possibilities for men to climb on and off of trains shrank simultaneously. As people in the United States began relying on automobiles as their primary means of transportation and the speed of cars on highways increased, it simply became more difficult to catch a ride on passing trains or animal-driven vehicles in rural areas. Finally, when the United States entered World War II, the employment situation in the country changed dramatically. Hundreds of thousands of men entered military service, removing them from the pool of floating labor; hundreds of thousands of other men went to work in the factories and businesses supplying war materials. By the first few years of the 1940s, the huge pool of wandering U.S. labor had evaporated.

When the war ended, previous conditions did not return. Rural industries did not return to earlier methods of production, and trains became an even less significant element of the U.S. transportation system. By then, the suburban ideal of single-family homes surrounded by vegetation and removed from urban areas was being thoroughly absorbed into U.S. culture and society, partly because of its representation in the movies and on television. As part of this transformation, the federal government encouraged returning veterans to buy suburban homes and gave them incentives to do so, effectively removing a substantial number of them from Hobohemia. Finally, by the middle of the 1950s, Americans had begun to perceive the dense, congested central sections of their cities as decaying, deteriorating, and degenerating, especially compared to the green, bucolic, and healthsome atmosphere (so perceived) of suburban areas. The result was a widespread demand for urban renewal, renovation, and gentrification, which ultimately caused the leveling of older buildings and developments. Districts that had housed the main stem now became defined as centers of urban blight and social disorder that did not measure up to the standards of the suburban ideal in which the proper "home" meant a married man and woman, their own children, a single-family house on its own land, an adult employed husband whose earnings supported the family, and his adult wife who raised their children and served as caretaker for everyone else in the family.

The article concludes by commenting on the dynamics of urban renewal and the forces behind its implementation. It especially emphasizes the point of view and values of those who favored urban renewal and their attitudes about people characterized as homeless. In doing so, it remarks on the lack of consideration given to the perceptions and attitudes of homeless people themselves.

FURTHER READING

Hirschoff, E. C., and J. Hart. *Down and Out: The Life and Death of Minneapolis's Skid Row.* Minneapolis: University of Minnesota Press, 2002.

Lee, Barrett. "The Disappearance of Skid Row: Some Ecological Evidence." *Urban Affairs Quarterly,* 16 (1980), 81–107.

Part III

MIGRANTS AND TRANSIENTS, 1930–1960

By 1920, Hobohemia, the Stem, the Main Stem was clearly past its glory days. The changes in the economy had significantly lessened the demand for an army of itinerant farm workers and labor in many of the seasonal, rural industries where men found jobs—logging, laying railroad tracks, mining, lumbering, and cutting ice, for example. The changing technology of railroads had slowly destroyed trains as a means of transportation that provided cheap—essentially free—transportation across the country. The use of diesel engines, more powerful engines that moved at greater speeds and didn't need to slow down to take on water or climb hills, ended the possibility of climbing on board when a train was moving slowly or even stopped in out-of-the-way places. Redesigned railroad cars did not have the rods, gunnels, and platforms between cars where hoboes could take it easy until they reached their destination. Also, the greater speed of new locomotives substantially increased the danger of riding atop a train car. The chances of being hit by a piece of flying gravel, not to mention the chance of being thrown to the ground by the motion of the train, simply made hitching a ride without a ticket too dangerous for even the most intrepid among them.

The Stems that had provided a base for hoboes' wandering, a place where they could return during winter when there was no rural work, where hoboes had created their own neighborhoods and a distinct subculture, slowly began to die. They certainly did not have the same vitality as Hobohemia with its rich artistic and intellectual character. It would take another 20 or 25 years, but by the middle of the 1950s, the Stem had fallen to being Skid Row, a section of the city that was almost universally considered to be an area of bums—single, male, laborers who didn't work, spent whatever excess money they had on drink, and provided a palpable danger to anyone who encountered them.

At about the same time as Hobohemia was clearly slipping downhill, a new kind of homeless person suddenly showed up in the United States. These were folks whose lives had been wrenched apart by the economic problems resulting from the Great Depression. Farmers began to experience a severe agricultural depression in the 1920s when declining prices of agricultural products made it impossible for thousands of them to compete successfully. Because of their declining incomes, farmers who had borrowed money from banks found that their farms, which they had used as collateral for their loans, were foreclosed on, and they had to find somewhere to go.

Going to a city did not present a desirable alternative. In addition to the farmers' preference for a rural landscape and style of life, cities were experiencing their own catastrophic years. After the stock market crash in

October 1929, banks began to fail, factories ceased production, and millions of Americans lost their jobs. The level of unemployment rose consistently until 1933, and, on the day that President Franklin D. Roosevelt was sworn into office, just about 25 percent of the workforce was unemployed.

As a result, the country once again became the setting for a vast army of wandering men, both rural and urban, looking for some way to support themselves and their families. But these men differed from men who had tramped in the previous era of homelessness. Whereas those men had generally wandered alone, the new homeless men traveled with wives, children, and all their belongings. Instead of traveling by train, the new homeless traveled with their whole families. Thousands of them had acquired trucks and cars, and they now loaded them up with everything that they could carry— from pots and pans to furniture, from clothing to farm tools, from children's toys to whatever books they might have acquired—and on top of this ragtag mixture of possessions they piled wives, children, and sometimes household animals.

Almost all of these people went west—toward California—a never-ending caravan—which they had heard was the next best thing to the Garden of Eden. A sizeable number of them never got that far, headed somewhere else or even returned to the place they had just abandoned. But several hundred thousand of them did make it all the way to the Pacific Ocean—only to find out that the stories about easy life and easy living in the Golden State were so much cant. The large growers in California's fields of fruit and vegetables had allowed stories to be spread about the great need for more agricultural workers with the expected result: A huge over-supply of potential agricultural labor showed up looking for any kind of work, which they could sometimes find at wage rates that would not allow individuals to support themselves alone, much less a wife and children. The camps that the growers provided to the workers could hardly be described, their conditions were so horrible. Many of them were nothing but dry riverbeds, and others had no shade from the blinding, blistering California sun. Many of the camps had no running water and no sanitary facilities. Nevertheless, Midwestern farmers who had lost everything and had nowhere to go continued coming to California hoping to find better conditions. The growers were able to severely mistreat the transient workers because of their close ties to the political establishment in Sacramento who supported them almost reflexively.

By the middle of the 1930s, some Californians had ceased to have any sympathy for the transient farmworkers. It seemed to them that the newcomers were taking jobs that should go to people who lived in California, and they also resented having their tax money used to provide aid and assistance to people who they thought had no right to be there. This hostility reached its height in the late summer and early fall of 1935. That is when the Chief of Police of Los Angeles decided unilaterally to post 136 Los Angeles police officers at the road sites where major highways entered California from Oregon, Nevada, and Arizona. His intent was, in short, to keep people who had few, if any, resources from entering the state.

In the meantime, the federal government had begun to accept some level of responsibility for homeless people. One of the first pieces of New Deal legislation to be passed by Congress and signed by Roosevelt in the spring of 1933 was the Federal Emergency Relief Agency (FERA). One of its subdivisions was the Federal Transient Program (FTP), whose authorization explicitly allowed it to provide aid to states to give assistance to people who did not have legal residence in the state, in other words, the transient farmworkers who had not already lived in California for at least one year.

Unfortunately, the congressional bill that created the FERA and FTP had authorized their existence for only two years. As a result, in 1935, the two agencies were unexpectedly dismembered, leaving hundreds of residents of their camps with nowhere to go.

Despite loud protests from the staff at the FTP, and also from residents who had created less miserable homes at the FTP camps, Roosevelt refused to back down and attempt to extend the life of these agencies although he could almost certainly have accomplished that with little effort. It has been suggested that his motivation was to direct the resources used by the FTP to other agencies. Some historians have argued that the rise of such demagogues as Huey Long, Father Coughlin, and Francis Townsend (who all looked as if they might be contenders for the Democratic Party's presidential nomination in 1936) changed Roosevelt's path to try to win over those men's followers.

In any event, both the FERA and the FTP were dismantled, and much of their work, especially that concerning agriculture, was turned over to the new Farm Security Administration (FSA), which was assigned the project of building some model camps for transient farmworkers. It was at one of the first of these to be constructed that John Steinbeck met its manager, Tom Collins, who became a good friend and who supplied Steinbeck with much of the material that he used to write The Grapes of Wrath.

16

ON THE FARM

"Whose Names Are Unknown"

- *Document:* This document is taken from a novel written by Sanora Babb, a woman who was born and grew up in the Panhandle of Oklahoma. It presents a firsthand view of life in the Dust Bowl and the subsequent migration of farmers from Oklahoma and surrounding states to the agricultural regions of California.

- *Date:* The story takes place in the 1930s and was written at that time, but it wasn't published until 2004. It had been accepted for publication by a major publisher in 1939, but the editor withdrew the offer when John Steinbeck's *The Grapes of Wrath* appeared and became a national bestseller. He, the editor, didn't think that there would be a market for two novels about the same aspect of the Depression.

- *Where:* The story is set in Oklahoma and California. After sitting in a desk drawer for 65 years, it was published to rave reviews by the University of Oklahoma Press. Some reviewers compared it favorably to *The Grapes of Wrath*.

- *Significance:* The novel presents an intimate portrait of the lives of people in Oklahoma during the first part of the 1930s and then in the agricultural valleys of California. In a personal way, its characters reveal their attitudes, feelings, and reasons for moving from Oklahoma to California; the book reveals how and why they became homeless.

DOCUMENT

...She was getting ready to pour boiling water in a pail when she heard Milt running to the house, not fast but running. His shoes sounded out on the bare hard ground.

"Julie! Julie!" he called from the door. . . . "Come out!" She put the teakettle on the stove and hurried up the steps. He was standing with his hands in the hip pockets of his overalls looking at the rapidly changing sky.

"She's coming!" he said. She stood beside him and they watched the high moving wall of dust spread from east to west in a semi-circle that rose into the sky and bent over at its crest like a terrible mountainous wave about to plunge down upon them. The cool spring air held a sudden faint smell of dust.

. . . "Look!" he said again, and they stood together not saying anything, awed by this new attack of nature. It was an evil monster coming on in mysterious, footloose silence. It was magnificent and horrible like a nightmare of destiny towering over their slight world that had every day before this impressed upon them its vast unconquerable might. Grains of dust sounded against their shoes in a low flurry. The open land beyond was blotted out as the brown mass struck the edge of the field.

"She's on the wheat now. It's a gonner. It'll cover it up. Funny though, it's so quiet and not as thick as it looked. Maybe it'll stay in the air and blow past."

"No wind," Julia said in surprise. The truck crept in into the gate. . . .

The old man helped the little girls from the truck.

. . . "Looks like the end of the world," he said, trying to be cheerful.

"Think it'll get us?" Milt asked.

"We'll know as soon as it's over. I don't think it's as bad as it looks." . . .

The air was thick now. Some of the green field showed, fluttering below the low wind. Lonnie ran to Milt and held onto his trouser leg.

"What is it, Papa?" she asked. "A still cyclone?" He looked at her and laughed.

. . . Milt watched the dust until the last of the wheat was covered.

"We'd better go in or we'll choke," he said bitterly. The dust rolled over them in thin clouds, stealthy, quiet, moving as if by an obscure power. There was no sound. They retreated into the dugout. Milt was last. He shielded his eyes and nose and looked over the house and he could see nothing but dust before his eyes. The barn was a mere shadow. He noticed in surprise that the dust was fine and soft. . . . He felt it in his throat like fur and had to cough. . . . As he went down into the room, he saw the dust like a mist.

"Look how it's sitting in around the windows," Julia said. "How will we sleep in this?"

"We'll sleep," the old man said wearily. "When you're tired you sleep."

"Well, we'll have to milk. We'll wait awhile. Maybe it will slacken. I can scald the pails and put cloths over them." They watched the windows for a sign of clearing, but the dust kept on in a monotonous soundless deluge.

Finally, Julia and the old man tied handkerchiefs about their mouths and noses and went out to milk. Milt sat on the bed waiting to look at the wheat. When they came back, he had not moved. They shook the dust from their clothes onto the steps and pulled the kerchiefs off. The upper parts of their faces were dark.

"Whew!" they said together, spitting the powdery film off their tongues.

"Let up any yet?" Milt asked

"No," the old man said. "This is a real siege. Worse than any so far I wager. It won't stop all night."

"How can you tell?"

"Can't for sure. Somethin' steady about the way it's coming. Like the way a steady rain falls different from a shower."

"Wish to hell it was rain! Next year we won't be able to plant if it don't stop. If the top soil's not gone, it'll be covered up. If all of us farmers wasn't so stubborn we wouldn't have planted this year!"

"Well, we have to take the bitter with the sweet," the old man said laconically.

"Where in hell is the sweet?"

The old man nodded his head sidewise in a sharp movement and made the clucking sound with his tongue and teeth. He had said the wrong thing.

"I'll go out and look around," Milt said.

"Wait till we eat," Julia said impatiently. "Dust or no dust, we have to eat." She drew her finger along the oilcloth table cover and it left a trail in the dust. She wiped it off carefully and sat the lard can with a pan of potatoes in her lap. The peelings fell away paper-thin with no waste. When she dipped into the lard can where she kept the flour, she noticed how low it was and scooped the cup cautiously so as not to strike the bottom and call Milt's attention to it. In the silence, they heard the dog scratching and whining at the door.

"Let him in," Milt said. . . . "It's even too much for Rusty."

SOURCE: Sanora Babb. *Whose Names Are Unknown, A Novel.* Norman, OK: University of Oklahoma Press, 2004. Used by permission of University of Oklahoma Press.

ANALYSIS

People frequently think that the Great Depression began in October 1929 with the collapse of stock values on the New York Stock Exchange. The Depression is then thought to have accelerated with the failure of business and manufacturing, rising unemployment, and the almost complete breakdown of the financial system, including both the banking system and securities exchanges. But, while all of those events happened, and while all of them had severe consequences for homelessness in the country, the initial events of the Depression occurred earlier and hundreds of miles away from New York or other large cities in the East. They took place in the western parts of the country across the Mississippi River, and they happened in the agricultural sector of the economy, not manufacturing or finance.

The roots of the agricultural Depression can be traced back to World War I and even earlier. Between about 1870 and 1910, U.S. farmers grew unprecedented amounts of crops. Farms produced so bountifully that indexed food prices dropped by about 30 percent during those decades. But things began to change after 1919.

Perhaps the first catalyst of change originated in Europe. A few years earlier, in 1912 and 1913, astute observers sensed a general war looming on the horizon. Knowing that wars destroyed agriculture by devastating fields and turning farmers into fighters, European governments began to stockpile food, especially grain. By 1913, this increased demand for grain had already begun to raise the prices that U.S.

farmers received for their produce. Not recognizing that, in all probability, this situation was temporary and would cease when the war ended and European agriculture had recovered, U.S. farmers increased their production even more. And, once the United States entered the war in 1917, demand increased once again, and farmers again responded by growing more food.

To finance the costs associated with boosting output—buying more land, hiring larger work forces, and acquiring better machines and tools—farmers borrowed money from banks. After the war ended in November 1918, the men who had survived the war began returning to their farms all across Europe; European agricultural production began returning to its prewar levels. By 1921, it had just about done so.

In retrospect, the result was not surprising. The prices for U.S. agricultural commodities plummeted as the worldwide production of food increased again. Supply far exceeded demand, and food prices collapsed. As the prices of individual commodities—a bushel of wheat, a bale of cotton, a basket of apples—declined, farmers felt impelled to produce even more, thinking that greater production would balance a smaller price per unit and let them maintain their current level of income. The problem arose when too many farmers took similar actions and grew even more. This still larger production, with no increased demand, again forced prices to fall rapidly.

As prices fell, and farmers were unable to maintain their already reduced incomes, they were unable to repay the money that they had borrowed to increase production. At the same time, they faced a new kind of competition. The more widespread use of newly devised agricultural machinery occurred on large farms. This machinery was more cost-effective there and allowed large producers to undercut the prices received by smaller farmers. The single individual working his family farm simply could not compete successfully with the beginning of "agribusiness."

U.S. agriculture was in serious trouble by 1930, but it became even worse in the southern Great Plains, an area that became known as the "Dust Bowl." In 1933 and 1934, the region began to experience horrendous climatic conditions. First, an extended drought dried up the water supply. The area received much less rain than usual, and the rain that did fall was not enough to support traditional modes of agriculture much less the intensive agriculture now being practiced.

Then, intense heat began to accompany the drought. But this was not just any normal heat; it was unprecedented. On July 24, 1934, the temperature in Oklahoma skyrocketed to 117°F. The severity of the heat can hardly be imagined—especially when one realizes that this was the 17th consecutive day of temperatures exceeding 100°F. Fields were already parched, and rivers and streams had vanished. But more was yet to come. As if drought and heat weren't bad enough, a plague of grasshoppers that can only be described as being "of biblical proportions" suddenly dropped from the skies. Clouds of these voracious insects darkened the skies, descended on farms and ranches, and devoured everything in sight. The insects leveled the fields.

Later analysts realized that the damage caused by heat and drought were not entirely caused by nature. The climatic problems also contained social and technological causes. Because the new methods of agricultural were so much more efficient than human labor and did the work of planting and harvesting so much more quickly, landowners began replacing farm laborers with machines. Even small farmers who had survived now felt that they had to have the newest and best reapers, rakers, binders, and tractors to compete successfully. They went into debt, or even greater debt, to buy these extraordinary new tools for themselves. But, there was a hidden trap. To make the new machinery cost-effective, farmers had to devote all of their land to growing just a single crop, wheat, rather than a full complement of vegetables.

This new single-crop agriculture—growing only wheat—intensified the problems caused by drought, heat, wind, and grasshoppers. Growing only a single crop depleted the soil of necessary nutrients, which could not be quickly restored. The only way to do that would have been for farmers to leave their land fallow or plant another crop. To farmers, taking either of these actions would have been a gamble that presented another threat to their already diminished incomes, a risk that they simply couldn't take. So, the land became less productive because of a combination of both the natural conditions and the new way of growing wheat.

At the same time, another situation exacerbated the water shortages. Because the land was not flat in the Dust Bowl area, but had gently sloping hills, it was easier to grow crops in rows going down the hills rather then running across them. This meant that when rainfall did occur, it followed the furrows away from the plants rather than staying in nearby channels and remaining available to them. The result was an even lower water table and less water saved for use in the future.

The grasshopper plague can also be partly attributed to the system of agriculture. Although the famers certainly did nothing directly to cause the plague of grasshoppers, growing only wheat had a significant effect. The grasshoppers devoured the wheat greedily and reproduced abundantly. Giving them vast quantities of this favorite food was disastrous. Had at least some of the acreage been used for growing some other crop—one that did not promote gluttony by the insects—the damage would have been less.

Then, one last catastrophe occurred. Great winds began to blow—but not just any winds. These were windstorms of cyclonic power, windstorms of incredible, unimaginable force that devastated millions of acres of productive farmland. The winds demolished natural and human-made objects, but they also destroyed the land itself. Their force could launch the dried-out soil into huge clouds of dust—now of a powdery consistency—hundreds of miles. So fierce were the winds that the interiors of buildings could be coated with a heavy layer of red dust even if all the doors and windows of a building were shut. People walked around with cloth masks over their noses. So powerful were these windstorms that the sky blackened and, as many people commented, turned day into night. So violent were these storms that they propelled clouds of dust into New York, Boston, and Chicago.

As hard as it is to believe, the situation worsened in1935. Pictures are barely adequate to reveal the dimensions of events. In March and April, 12 consecutive days of ferocious wind battered Kansas. Objects as large as cars were completely buried in dust and disappeared from view. In her diary, one woman wondered if the end of the world had arrived. One day, April 14, 1935, exceeded all others in its horror. That day, the windstorms never ceased. There was no natural light at all, and a person couldn't see things directly in front of him or her.

Many people had had enough. About 500,000 residents of the Dust Bowl decided to abandon the place that the poet Walt Whitman had called "the inexhaustible land of wheat." Nothing remained to exhaust. About 300,000 of the migrants made for California. Although not all of them came from Oklahoma, they became known as "Okies" and sometimes "Arkies" (people from Arkansas). They had heard tales of bumper cotton crops in California, and they knew how to harvest. They imagined that they could get back on their feet in the "Golden State" and create brighter futures for themselves there. They loaded their families as well as everything they owned into beaten-up cars and trucks, and they headed west.

Before long, the number of workers expecting to find jobs as agricultural laborers in California far exceeded the number of workers needed by farmers and ranchers. Seeking any work to provide for themselves, the newcomers became agricultural migrants, roaming the state in search of jobs, acting much like the hoboes of previous times. Whether they found jobs or not, they were homeless, and their lives were wretched. Their living conditions were ghastly. The Berkeley *Gazette* referred to "hungry Dust Bowl refugees living in the fields and woods like animals." Another newspaper lamented the fact that the "migrants lived in almost unimaginable filth."

Perhaps the most famous literary portrait of migrant farm laborers in Oklahoma and California during the Depression was the great novel *The Grapes of Wrath*, by John Steinbeck. This novel did more than any other document to call attention to the misery of conditions on rural farms and sensitize the U.S. public to homelessness. Its ability to increase American awareness of these problems was magnified when the book received a Pulitzer Prize and was turned into an award-winning film starring the movie icon Henry Fonda. (Several decades later, Steinbeck also received the Nobel Prize, and his citation expressly mentioned *The Grapes of Wrath*.)

The novel had its origin in 1937 when the *San Francisco News* asked John Steinbeck to study conditions in the San Joaquin Valley, one of California's richest agricultural regions, and write a report about them. Steinbeck wrote a series of seven articles for the newspaper in which he elucidated the horrible conditions without holding anything back. A year later, the articles were collected, supplemented with an eighth chapter, and published as a small book entitled *The Harvest Gypsies*. Steinbeck subsequently used these articles, his other observations, and information given to him as the basis for the novel.

FURTHER READING

Adams, Jane, and D. Gorton. "This Land Ain't My Land: The Eviction of Sharecroppers by the Farm Security Administration." *Agricultural History*, 83, 3 (Summer 2009), 323–51.

Cook, Benjamin I., Ron L. Miller, and Richard Seager. "Amplification of the North American 'Dust Bowl' Drought through Human-Induced Land Degradation." *Proceedings of the National Academy of Sciences of the United States of America*, 106, 13 (March 31, 2009), 4997–5001.

17

IN THE CITY

Foreclosure

- *Document:* This document is taken from a history of the Federal Home Loan Bank during the 1930s. It explains how bank policies contributed to the housing crisis and how new federal policies developed to alleviate the economic catastrophe.
- *Date:* The book was published in May 1938.
- *Where:* It was published in Washington, DC.
- *Significance:* The history shows that Congress recognized the extent of the housing crisis in the country and explains why changes in financial policies were necessary. In presenting its case, the document indicates the magnitude of the housing crisis and why so many people had their mortgages foreclosed and their houses taken from them.

DOCUMENT

[The report concludes with the following 14 reasons for the establishment of a home loan system run by the federal government:]

(1) Figures show that home ownership in the United States is declining and that we are drifting into a nation of tenants. The principal reason is an insufficient amount of low-cost, long-term, installment mortgage money. The home loan bank bill is designed to place long-term funds in the hands of local institutions. Thus, a debt-free home ownership can be created as borrowers reduce their debt from month to month. . . .

(2) Thousands of people who have borrowed money on their homes are having difficulty meeting their contracted payments. With the investors in the lending institutions withdrawing money, pressure is created which prevents

the lending institutions from carrying the borrower without payments until conditions improve or from reducing his monthly payments. If the home financing institutions had a place to raise money on their mortgages, they could greatly assist borrowers. . . .

(3) Many homes are being lost through [banks'] calling or refusing to renew straight mortgages. Owners who have never failed to pay interest charges are denied renewals [and they] are threatened with foreclosures. . . .

(4) Home ownership has been commended and urged by our men in public life and leaders in all phases of American life. Millions of our thriftiest and most patriotic citizens have purchased their homes and now own them free from debt or with only small remaining mortgage balances. . . . Today these people from the common walks of life cannot borrow on these homes to tide them through the vicissitudes of unemployment, reduced income, sickness and the like. . . .

(5) The investment in the homes of the country is a significant and imposing portion of our national wealth. Much of the decline in the values of residential real estate has been due to the lack of credit during the last two years. Foreclosures and inability to borrow on homes create distress conditions and low prices in homes, which are supposed to be the most stable of property and investments. Home owners must have funds before business can recover. . . .

(6) Hundreds of small banks which have closed could have carried on if they had had a way of raising money on their good mortgages. Building and loan associations have disappointed thousands of their investors in that they have been unable to return their savings within reasonable notice. . . .

(7) With funds available for needed repairs, additions and modernization of homes already erected, thousands of men now unemployed can be put to work. There are also many who have saved for years with the intention of building [houses] when conditions were "right" who would build now, when labor and materials are the cheapest they have been in years, if they could secure assistance in mortgage money without bonuses and without incurring the dangers of short-term financing. . . .

(8) Funds for home owners should be available at low cost and in liberal amounts at all times. The home owner should not be subjected to the vicissitudes of the general money market. The smaller communities, as a rule, are without sufficient mortgage funds for home-financing demands at all times. In the years where there has been ample money in some parts of the country, there have been high rates and scarcity in others. . . .

(9) The establishment of this system will enable thousands of deserving citizens who have been induced to undertake home ownership in the wrong way, namely by a short-term mortgage which is now coming due, to save their equities. . . .

(10) Home ownership, as a national objective, will be permanently injured by the thousands of foreclosures that are now being made on homes, unless through the establishment of a credit system to prevent the recurrence. . . .

(11) The home loan bank system will eliminate the costly and burdensome second mortgage by enabling local lending institutions to make advances up to 70 and 80 percent of sound value....

(12) Unless there is a restoration in confidence in realty values, hundreds of towns and cities having heavy bonded indebtedness and depending on the collection of . . . taxes upon real estate, principally homes, for the repayment of their debts and interest will have their credit permanently destroyed....

(13) The years 1920–21 and 1929–32 demonstrated a permanent need for a reserve system for the home-financing institutions, just as commerce and industry has the Federal Reserve System and agriculture has the Federal Farm Loan System. It will stabilize these thrift and home-financing institutions; will improve and standardize mortgage practices; will decrease costs of mortgage money; and will regulate the supply of mortgage credit....

(14) This measure is an important and integral part of the comprehensive program for economic recovery undertaken by Congress. . . . [N]o consideration has been given to the home owner who, after all, is the backbone of our Nation. Mortgages have been foreclosed; families have lost their homes and savings they have had in them, and many wage earners who own property are in want. A great injustice results if those who own their homes are not given relief in the present emergency.

SOURCE: [Federal Home Loan Bank Board], *The Federal Home Loan Bank Board and Its Agencies*. Washington, DC: [GPO], 1938.

ANALYSIS

Hobohemia, as this book has described it, slowly began to disappear in the 1920s—not totally by any means, but to a noticeable degree. As the country became more prosperous during that decade, not everyone benefited but many did. Many factors caused the increased prosperity, but one noticeable cause was the increased production of more consumer goods in urban factories. Automobiles are the best example, but there was a whole range of new manufactured consumer items. As this new manufacturing developed, the need for more factory workers also increased. Many Americans began to receive weekly wages more regularly than before, when hourly wages were the common form of compensation. Therefore, many of them had less need to wander from place to place and search for employment. As many of them settled in cities with more stable jobs, they located themselves and their families in apartments, flats, double-deckers, or tenements and they ceased to be homeless in the same way as the tramps and hoboes before the 1920s.

These conditions lasted throughout the 1920s. There was less discussion of "the tramp problem" by politicians or the media, and there was less public consciousness of a large population of vagrants who lacked "normal and usual" housing. To most observers, the economy was constantly growing and would continue to do so indefinitely. Most people who thought about hoboes and tramps probably thought they would soon disappear in the United States. That perception of American society and economy came to an abrupt end in the fall of 1929. One result was the appearance of homeless people very different from hoboes, tramps, and bums.

On September 3, 1929, the Dow Jones Industrial Average (DJIA)—the most well-known index of the value of stocks listed on the New York Stock Exchange (NYSE)—reached an all-time high. When the NYSE closed for the day, the DJIA stood at 381.17. At that time, only a few people realized that the DJIA was about to begin a slow but accelerating decline that would become known as the Great Crash or the Stock Market Crash of 1929. To most Americans, the Crash has always marked the beginning of the Great Depression, the most severe economic collapse in U.S. history.

Two weeks after reaching its high, at the close of trading on September 17, the DJIA had lost just about 3.3 percent of its value, closing at 368.52. And, two weeks after that, on October 1, the Dow had lost another 7 percent of its value, falling to 342.57. For the next three weeks, the DJIA moved up and down, falling to 305.85, another decline of nearly 10 percent. Then, on October 24, "Black Thursday," a frenzy of selling swept over the NYSE. Although declines in stock prices were not enormous, only about 2 percent of their aggregate value, the number of shares sold on the New York Stock Exchange that day was more than double the volume of any previous day in history, about 12,900,000 shares.

A relatively calm day, October 25, sometimes called "Black Friday," was followed by two cataclysmic days, "Black Monday" and "Black Tuesday." On Monday, October 28, the DJIA shrank from 301.22 to 260.64, a drop of 13.5 percent, and on Tuesday, October 29, it took another big hit, dropping to 230.07 and giving up still another 11.5 percent of its value. Altogether, the declines amounted to nearly one-third of the total value of all the stocks listed on the New York Stock Exchange.

During the next two years, the stock market continued its collapse, reaching its nadir on December 2, 1933, when the Dow closed at 55.91. In other words, during the time between late October 1929 and December 1932, two months more than three years, the aggregate value of all the shares of stock listed on the New York Stock exchange lost about 85 percent of their total value.

This tremendous, unprecedented, and almost totally unforeseen disintegration of the stock market affected every other sector of the U.S. economy and was a key element in bringing on the Great Depression. Perhaps the most reliable indicator of a country's economic health—in this case, unhealthiness is probably a better word—is changes in the country's Gross Domestic Product (GDP), the total value of all the goods and services the economy produced during the last year. Using this measure, one can truly say that the U.S. economy was on its deathbed after October 1929. Between 1929 and 1931, GDP declined from $103.6 billion to $76.5 billion, a decline of 21.7 percent. But 1931 was not the bottom. During the next two years, GDP sank by another $20 billion, bringing the total decline to more than $47 billion, about 45 percent. After 1933, the economy slowly began to recover, then sank again in 1938, and it did not reach its 1929 level again until 1941.

As GDP collapsed, the number of unemployed people in the country ballooned. From 1,550,000 (3.2% of the labor force) in 1929, the number of people without work began to skyrocket. It nearly tripled in one year, exceeding 4,350,000 (8.7% of the labor force) in 1930, climbing to 8,020,000 (15.9% of the labor force) in 1931, and 12,060,000 (23.6% of the labor force) in 1932. The unemployment rate finally peaked in 1933 when roughly one-fourth of Americans were jobless, 12,830,000 people, 24.9 percent of the labor force. Not until 1943 did the unemployment rate fall back to its 1929 level.

The rising unemployment rate meant tremendous drops in personal income for many Americans. According to the Bureau of Economic Analysis in the Department of Commerce, before the Stock Market Crash in 1929 and the onset of the Great Depression, disposable personal income in the United States was $83.2 billion. After 1929, disposable income, like GDP and the level of employment, tanked. It declined to $74.6 billion in 1930, $64.2 billion in 1931, $49.1 billion in 1932, and $46.0 billion in 1933. Like the stock market, the disposable income of the American people had declined about 45 percent during those years.

The loss of jobs and income was accompanied by an increasing number of homeless people. Obviously, people had less money to spend on shelter as well as on food, clothing, medical care, and other necessities. The quality of housing deteriorated for some people, and for some it disappeared altogether. Even without adequate statistics that "prove" that homelessness increased during the early 1930s, other evidence supports the proposition. Personal accounts including diaries, letters, and reminiscences all suggest that the number of homeless people was increasing. Media coverage of homelessness intensified as magazines, newspapers, and movies all portrayed homelessness occurring at unprecedented levels, and the rapid development of photojournalism allowed the subject to be clearly displayed and given a new kind of immediacy. Government reports and the reports of private charitable and philanthropic agencies show that homelessness was becoming an ever-growing social problem.

Perhaps the most telling evidence of increasing homelessness can be found in a massive study of the Federal Home Loan Bank Board. In it, David Bridewell, assistant to the general counsel of the Home Owners Loan Corporation, the Federal Home Loan Board, and the Federal Savings and Loan Corporation, wrote that at the beginning of 1934 more than 50 percent of all home loan mortgages in urban areas of the United States were in default—that is, the owner had failed to make mortgage payments when they were due. The average length of delinquency was an unheard-of 15 months. This means that, on average, people who had missed paying a monthly mortgage had not done so for 15 months. Technically, banks could have foreclosed, or taken away from their owners, more than half of the houses in the United States.

This housing and mortgage crisis clearly encompassed far more people than just those who were previously considered poor or impoverished. A large part of the middle class—people who had once been prosperous enough to purchase a home—either lost, or were in danger of losing, their houses because they could no longer make the monthly payments.

Just as important as all of those factors, one has to recognize and understand the relationship between housing and the general financial system. The collapse of the housing market was instrumental in provoking and fueling the collapse of the financial system. When people buy houses, they do not normally pay the full price of the house with their own money. Most people don't have nearly enough liquid cash to do that. Instead, they borrow money from a bank and assume a debt known as a mortgage.

Where does the bank acquire the large sums of money that it lends to homebuyers? In essence, banks borrow money from their depositors. The money that a person deposits in a bank is a debt that the bank owes the depositor. And the bank now lends that money to borrowers, especially homebuyers. This works for banks because they charge the homebuyer/borrower a higher rate of interest to use the bank's money than the bank has to pay the person who has deposited money in the bank.

So, there is a stream of debt. The homebuyer borrows money from the bank, and, in essence, the bank borrows money from its depositors. As long as everyone involved pays their debts on time, all is well. Serious trouble transpires when people are unable to pay their debts. The homebuyer is unable to make his or her monthly payment to the bank. Unless it has ample reserves of cash—enough to give its depositors if they want to withdraw their money—the bank will not have enough money to repay the depositors who want cash. If this cycle continues for any length of time, the bank will close, and all of its depositors will lose their money.

This is what happened between 1929 and 1933—not just because of the housing crisis but because of bad banking policies. During the 1920s, banks made bad loans to many people—to homebuyers, to businessmen making risky investments, and to people speculating in the stock market. Banks *should* be careful when they lend money, trying to make sure that borrowers will have the ability to repay their loans. But, that does not always happen. Bankers sometimes, as in the 1920s, take an optimistic view of their clients and of the economic conditions and assume that people will be able to pay back the money they had borrowed.

Throughout the 1920s, banks made risky and unsafe loans—they made loans that were too large for individuals to handle, and they made loans for assets, such as stocks, that could easily lose their value. When those things happened and borrowers could not repay the bank, the bank had no choice but to close its doors. And, as news spread of one bank's closing, people worried about other banks and decided to withdraw their money from them. The result could be, as there was in 1929, a run of people withdrawing their money from every bank and thus forcing almost all the banks to fail.

The banks expected to have adequate funds when the people who had borrowed money to buy houses repaid their mortgages. But when the economy collapsed and people lost their jobs, they lost the income that they needed to make mortgage payments to the bank. The result was that the bank foreclosed on the house and took it away from the person who had bought it. The bank then hoped to sell the house to recover the money it had loaned to the purchaser. But, when so many houses were being repossessed and banks were trying to sell such a large number of houses at the same time, the value of houses declined; it was a matter of supply and demand. The situation turned into a horrible cyclical crisis. People lost their jobs. Then they used up their savings to pay expenses and ran out of savings, or they lost their savings when banks failed, and they couldn't pay their mortgages. The banks sold the houses at low prices—too low to recover the amount of money they needed to repay their depositors. And the cycle went on and on and on.

In 1931, as the housing and financial crises worsened, President Herbert Hoover sent a message to Congress requesting the creation of a Federal Home Loan Bank to regulate the banking industry and protect banks. After holding hearings in January, February, and March 1932, the House of Representatives' Committee on Banking and Currency reported 14 reasons favoring the establishment of a Federal Home Loan Bank. They make the magnitude of the housing crisis unmistakably clear and explain the relationship between the housing and financial crises, thus illustrating why a new and different kind of homelessness appeared in the country.

18

BONUS ARMY

Homeless Vets Meet the Army

- *Document:* This article appeared in *The Nation* magazine in August 1932, just as the Bonus Army was being rousted from its encampments in Washington, DC.
- *Date:* The events took place mostly in the summer of 1932, especially in July.
- *Where:* The events described in the article occurred in a part of Washington, DC, called the Anacostia flats, the site of the largest encampment of the Bonus Marchers.
- *Significance:* This contemporary journalistic account of the Bonus Army shows how some Americans, in this case veterans of World War I, were responding to homelessness in the early 1930s. Not incidentally, it also shows how the federal government and the Hoover administration reacted to them. Although the events described here relate specifically to the early payment of the Veterans' Bonus and to the homelessness experienced by World War I veterans, they foreshadow the later question of whether the federal government has any responsibility for ensuring that all Americans have decent housing. Is decent housing a basic civil right of all Americans? The national government's response to the Bonus Army was its first unequivocal response to that issue.

DOCUMENT

Hoover's campaign for reelection was launched Thursday, July 28, at Pennsylvania Avenue and Third Street [in Washington, DC] with four troops of cavalry, four companies of infantry, a mounted machine-gun squadron, six whippet tanks, 300 city policemen and a squad of Secret Service men and Treasury agents. Among the results immediately achieved were the following:

Two veterans of the World War shot to death; one eleven-weeks-old baby in a grave condition from gas, shock, and exposure; one eight-year-old boy partially blinded by gas; two policemen's skulls fractured; one bystander shot through the shoulder; one veteran's ear severed with a cavalry saber; one veteran stabbed in the hip with a bayonet; more than a dozen veterans, policemen, and soldiers injured by bricks and clubs; upward of 1,000 men, women, and children gassed, including policemen, reporters, ambulance drivers, and residents of Washington; and approximately $10,000 worth of property destroyed by fire, including clothing, food, and temporary shelters of the veterans and a large amount of building material owned by a government contractor.

The political results are less impressive. Indeed, among high officials of the Administration there is fast-growing apprehension that the great exploit was planned and executed with more daring than judgment, and that, as a campaign effort, it may prove to be one of the deadliest boomerangs in political history. That fear already has found expression in two public statements by the gallant Secretary of War, Pat Hurley, seeking to justify the employment of [tear] gas bombs, tanks, sabers, bayonets, and fire against unarmed men, women, and children. One of them, as I shall presently show, is such a tissue of known and demonstrable falsehoods that utter panic must have prompted it.

The circumstances surrounding the use of troops and modern implements of war to evict these people from their miserable hovels and to drive them from the capital force me to the reluctant conclusion that the whole affair was deliberately conceived and carried out for a political purpose—namely, to persuade the American people that their government was threatened with actual overthrow, and that the courage and decisiveness of Herbert Hoover had averted revolution. It is no secret that Mr. Hoover and his advisers hope to make "Hoover versus radicalism" the leading issue of the campaign. The presence of the unemployed veterans and their families in the capital presented an opportunity to show the country

DID YOU KNOW?

Bonus Army

Evalyn Walsh McLean whose husband owned the Washington Post and who herself owned the Hope Diamond remembers her encounter with the Bonus Marchers.

I felt that crowd of men, women, and children never should have been permitted to swarm across the continent. But I could remember when those same men, with others, had been cheered as they marched down Pennsylvania Avenue. While I recalled those wartime parades, I was reading in the newspapers that the bonus army men were going hungry in Washington.

That night I woke up before I had been asleep an hour. I got to thinking about those poor devils marching around the capital. . . . It was one o'clock, and the Capitol was beautifully lighted. I wished then for the power to turn off the lights and use the money thereby saved to feed the hungry.

When . . . I rode among the bivouacked men I was horrified to see plain evidence of hunger in their faces; I heard them trying to cadge cigarettes from one another. Some were lying on the sidewalks, unkempt heads pillowed on their arms. A few clusters were shuffling around. I went up to one of them, a fellow with eyes deeply sunken in his head.

"Have you eaten?" He shook his head.

Just then I saw General Glassford, superintendent of the Washington police. He said, "I'm going to get some coffee for them."

"All right," I said, "I am going to Childs'."

It was two o'clock when I walked into that white restaurant. A man came up to take my order. "Do you serve sandwiches? I want a thousand," I said. "And a thousand packages of cigarettes."

"But, lady—"

"I want them right away. I haven't got a nickel with me, but you can trust me. I am Mrs. McLean."

Well, he called the manager into the conference, and before long they were slicing bread with a machine; and what with Glassford's coffee also (he was spending his own money) we two fed all the hungry ones who were in sight.

. . . [Another] day Waters, the so-called commander, came to my house and said: "I'm desperate. Unless these men are fed, I can't say what won't happen to this town." . . .

That night I telephoned to Vice-President Charlie Curtis. I told him I was speaking for Waters, who was standing by my chair. I said: "These men are in a desperate situation, and unless something is done for them, unless they are fed, there is bound to be a lot of trouble. They have no money, nor any food."

Charlie Curtis told me that he was calling a secret meeting of senators and would send a delegation of them to the House [of Representatives] to urge immediate action on the Howell bill, providing money to send the bonus army members back to their homes."

Source: Evalyn Walsh McLean, *Father Struck It Rich.* Boston: Little, Brown & Co., 1936, 303–5.

that the danger of "insurrection" was real and that the Administration had prepared to meet it. To accomplish this object it was necessary to provoke actual conflict, and that is what the Administration proceeded to do. A simple review of the salient facts would seem to make this apparent.

For several weeks the men and their families had been encamped in Washington, some occupying abandoned and partially wrecked buildings and shacks on downtown plots owned by the government, but a large majority existing in crude shelters erected by themselves on a large government-owned field on the opposite bank of the Anacostia River. Excepting a small unit of Communists, which the main body promptly outlawed, the behavior of the men was characterized by extraordinary discipline and restraint. To one who visited their camps many times and talked to scores of them, any suggestion that they constituted a threat against the government is preposterous. Even the Communist gestures were confined mainly to two futile attempts to parade before the White House, which got them nothing but broken heads, jail sentences, and fines. The attitude of the great majority was one of good-humored and patient fortitude under incredibly primitive conditions of existence. In a thousand ways they exhibited the instinct to make comedy out of their own vicissitudes—an instinct as characteristic now as it was in France. The so-called "bonus army" in actuality was an army of unemployed men who believed they had a special claim on the government and came here asking the government to give them relief unless it was ready to provide work. Bonus or no bonus, they would not have come if they had had jobs. Any assertion to the contrary is ridiculous.

Save for the feeble gestures of the isolated Communist group there was no trouble until that fatal Thursday, due in part to the remarkable tact and common sense of General [Pelham] Glassford, the chief of police, in part to the discipline enforced by the leaders of the camps, and in part to the essentially law-abiding instincts of the men themselves. The worthy [Secretary of War Patrick] Hurley mouths indignant phrases about "panhandling" and "forced tribute from citizens," but in all my visits to the camps I was never asked for anything more valuable than a cigarette—and I am a fairly prosperous-looking citizen. As soon as Congress adjourned there was a steady exodus of the campers, as attested by the daily statements of the Veterans' Bureau, dutifully reported by the Associated Press and Administration newspapers. Responsible officials repeatedly declared it was only a matter of days until all would be gone.

But suddenly someone high in authority decided the government must have immediate possession of the partially razed block bounded by Third and Fourth Streets and Pennsylvania and Missouri Avenues, where about 1,500 were existing in abandoned buildings and makeshift huts. Most of these people were from Texas, California, the Carolinas, Nebraska, West Virginia, and Florida, which are not exactly hotbeds of "radicalism." Instructions went from the Treasury to the District [of Columbia] commissioners to have the police evict the squatters. On two occasions, Glassford convinced the commissioners that the police had no authority to conduct such evictions, and pointed out that the procedure for eviction is definitely prescribed by law. On Wednesday there was a conference at the White House attended by Hurley, Attorney General [William] Mitchell, and General Douglas MacArthur, chief of staff of the army. On Thursday morning Glassford was informed that Treasury agents would begin evacuation of a part of the block, and that if anyone resisted eviction he was to be arrested for disorderly conduct. This meant that the actual eviction would be done by the police, and so it worked out. Someone had devised a technicality for getting around the law. Glassford's protests were unavailing. It was obvious that irresistible pressure had been applied to the commissioners. . . .

The trouble was that someone in authority had determined to force the issue. Two District commissioners reported to President Hoover that the civil authorities were "unable to maintain order," and within a few minutes infantry, cavalry, machine-gunners, and tanks were on their way from Fort Myer and Fort Washington. . . .

When the troops arrived they actually were cheered by the veterans on the south sidewalk of Pennsylvania Avenue. A cavalry officer spurred up to the curb and shouted: "Get the hell out of here." Infantrymen with fixed bayonets and trench helmets deployed along the south curb, forcing the veterans back into the contested block. Cavalry deployed along the north side, riding their horses up on the sidewalk and compelling policemen, reporters, and photographers to climb on automobiles to escape being trampled. A crowd of three or four thousand spectators had congregated in the vacant lot on the north side of the avenue. A command was given, and the cavalry charged the crowd with drawn sabers. Men, women, and children fled shrieking across the broken ground, falling into excavations as they strove to avoid the rearing hoofs and saber points. Meantime, the

Hostility toward homeless people has existed throughout U.S history. Probably, however, no single incident reveals the intensity of that antipathy more clearly than the events that occurred in Washington, DC, in the spring and summer of 1932. After thousands of veterans of World War I gathered in the country's capital to request aid from the federal government, President Herbert Hoover mobilized the national army, ordered them to level the men's encampments, and told the army to drive the homeless men from the city. This is one of only a very few incidents when the United States government (as opposed to state and local governments) turned its armed force against U.S citizens. As such, it reveals a great deal about public attitudes toward homeless people in the United States. (Library of Congress)

infantry on the south side had adjusted gas masks and were hurling tear [gas] bombs into the block into which they had just driven the veterans. Secretary Hurley states that "the building occupied by the women and children was protected, and no one was permitted to molest them."

What he means by "the building" I do not know, because scores of shanties and tents in the block were occupied by women and children. I know that I saw dozens of women grab their children and stagger out of the area with streaming, blinded eyes while the [tear gas] bombs fizzed and popped all around them. I saw a woman stand on the Missouri Avenue side and plead with a non-commissioned officer to let her rescue a suitcase which, she told him, contained all the spare clothing of herself and her child, and I heard him reply: "Get out of here, lady, before you get hurt," as he calmly set fire to her shanty.

"No one was injured after the coming of the troops," declares the veracious Mr. Hurley. I saw one of his own blood-splashed cavalrymen put into an ambulance, apparently unconscious, as several of his comrades pursued a fugitive into a filling station, trampling a woman in their charge. Simultaneously an ear was shorn from the head of a Tennessee veteran by a cavalry saber. As a matter of fact, there was hardly a minute when an ambulance did not dash in and dash off with a victim. I was in that hapless mass of policemen, reporters, and spectators at Third and C Streets a few minutes later when an order was given from a staff officer's car, and a company of infantry came up on the double quick, tossing [tear] gas bombs right and left. Some exploded on the sidewalk. Some fell in front yards jammed with Negro women and children. One appeared to land on the front porch of a residence. Two small girls fell to the sidewalk, choking and screaming. . . .

Secretary Hurley defiantly announced that "statements made to the effect that the billets of the marchers were fired by troops is a falsehood." On the day when he first made this declaration, it appeared in dozens of newspapers which also published a graphic . . . photograph of an infantryman applying a torch to a veteran's shanty. I am only one of numerous reporters who stood by while the soldiers set fire to many such shelters. In the official apologia, the Secretary asserts that "the shacks and tents at Anacostia were set on fire by the bonus marchers before the troops crossed the Anacostia Bridge." I was there when the troops crossed. They celebrated their arrival at the Anacostia terminus of the bridge by tossing [tear] gas bombs into a throng of spectators who booed and refused to "get back" as soon as ordered. About fifteen minutes after their arrival in the camp, the troops set fire to two improvised barracks. These were the first fires. Prior to this General MacArthur had summoned all available reporters and told them that "operations are completely suspended," that "our objective has been accomplished," that "the camp is virtually abandoned," and that it would "not be burned." Soon after making that statement he departed for the White House. When the two barracks ignited by the soldiers had been burning fiercely for at least thirty minutes, the veterans began firing their own shelters as they abandoned them. On the high embankment which bounds the plain opposite the Anacostia River, thousands of veterans had gathered, and with them mingled thousands of Anacostia residents, all intent on the lurid spectacle below. Promptly at midnight (General MacArthur had gone to the White House more than an hour earlier) a long and shadowy line of infantry and cavalry advanced across the fiery plain toward the embankment. Sabers and bayonets gleamed in the red light cast by the flames. Virtually everyone had deserted the camp; it seemed incredible that the offensive would be pushed still further. It seemed so to the veterans and the residents of Anacostia—but an officer had told me earlier in the evening that the strategy was to drive all the campers "into the open country of Maryland." . . .

For many blocks along the embankment similar scenes were being enacted. With "unparalleled humanity and kindliness," the troops tossed scores of [tear] gas bombs into the vast crowds lining the hillside, driving them back to the main thoroughfare of Anacostia. Automobilists, unable either to turn or back up, abandoned their vehicles and ran from the stinging fumes and menacing bayonets. Within five yards of the main business corner, a veteran carrying an American flag failed to move rapidly enough, and I saw a gleaming blade sink into his hip. Moaning, he staggered toward a drug store, still clutching his flag.

Chief Glassford, who was in the best position to know, has said that it was "unnecessary." But, although a brilliant soldier and an even more brilliant policeman, he is not a politician. The politicians had decided it was necessary. It was necessary to dramatize the issue of "Hoover versus radicalism." One hitch has developed. The President has asserted that less than half of the campers were men who had actually served under the flag, and Hurley assures us that the disorders were led by "reds" and "agitators." How unfortunate, then, that those killed were bona fide veterans of the World War, entitled to honorable burial in Arlington [National Cemetery]! But how much more tragic it is that, in a crisis like this, the United States Government should be under the control of such a trip of adventurers as Hoover, Hurley, and Mills!

SOURCE: Paul Y. Anderson, "Tear-Gas, Bayonets, and Votes," *The Nation*, August 17, 1932. Used by permission.

ANALYSIS

The Bonus March had its origins in 1924. That year, Congress authorized a so-called Soldiers' Bonus to be paid every veteran of World War I. Everyone who had served in the American Armed Forces during the Great War was to receive $1.00 for every day that he had been stationed in the United States and $1.25 for every day he had spent overseas. However, there was a catch. The money was not to be distributed immediately after the legislation was enacted. The bill provided that those eligible to receive the Bonus would receive "compensation certificates" that could not be redeemed for 20 years, until 1945.

Now, in 1932, with the Depression worsening and unemployment skyrocketing, Congressman Wright Patman (D-Tex) introduced a bill calling for immediate payment of the bonus. All over the country, unemployed homeless men began discussing the prospects of receiving their bonuses earlier than they had expected. Among them was Walter Waters, an unemployed cannery supervisor in Portland, Oregon.

As Waters talked about the issue with other veterans, he hit upon the idea that a "march on Washington" might pressure Congress into passing Patman's bill. During the spring of 1932, Waters began sensing enthusiasm for his idea, and, in May of that year, he and about 300 others began the long journey from the Pacific Coast to the nation's capital. Eighteen days later, after both walking and hitching rides on trains, they reached Washington.

As news of their expedition spread across the country, more and more men, some with their families, undertook to join them. By the end of May, the number of arriving veterans had already overwhelmed Washington's charitable and religious missions.

Pelham D. Glassford, the Chief of Police, was providing housing for them in unused government buildings and spending his own money to buy food for them. On May 29, Glassford met with Waters, and, during their conversation, asked how many men Waters thought might ultimately arrive in Washington. Not really having any idea how many veterans were on the way, Waters blurted out, "20,000."

This bold prediction turned out to be perceptive. Day by day, hundreds of men poured into the capital. On the evening of June 7, an estimated 8,000 of them marched down Pennsylvania Avenue in front of 100,000 spectators. And still they kept coming. They built, and stayed in, camps spread over at least 20 different locations ranging from torn-down buildings at the foot of Pennsylvania Avenue to the country home that a former governor of New Hampshire made available to them.

Mired in mud flats along the Anacostia River, Camp Marks was the largest of the camps, housing about 10,000 men—many accompanied by their wives and children. Named in honor of a compassionate Washington police officer, the settlement, one of the first to be called a "Hooverville," sheltered its occupants under every kind of usable odds and ends. According to a description in the Washington *Star*,

> Every scrap of material which can possibly be fitted into a shelter of any kind is being dragged out of the big junk pile on the hill above the camp. There are shelters built of egg crates, of paper boxes, of rusty bed springs, . . . of newspapers, of scraps of junked automobiles, of old wall-paper, of pieces of corrugated iron roofing, of tin and bed ticking, of the rusty frames of beds, of tin cans, of rusty fence wire, of straw, or parts of baby carriages, of fence stakes, of auto seats. The man who can salvage an auto top from the dump has a mansion in this strange city.

The reporter saw one man living in a barrel of grass, another in a casket set on trestles, and still another in a piano box that he had labeled "Academy of Music." Wherever they housed themselves, these squatters slogged through deep mud after rains, fought swarms of flies in the light of day, and struggled with multitudes of mosquitoes in the dark of night.

In June, Congress considered Patman's bonus bill. After the House of Representatives passed it, the Senate considered the question. On June 17, the Senate voted 62 to15 against passage. Anxious to leave town for the summer recess, and as a sop to the thousands of men camped out in Washington, Congress on July 7 appropriated $100,000 to *lend* the men and allow them to purchase transportation home.

A few hundred marchers did depart, but others arrived and took their places. Anxiety in the federal government mounted. On July 14, Vice President Charles Curtis, fearing chaos and disorder, tried to take matters into his own hands. He commanded the Marines to clear the Capitol grounds of Bonus Marchers. The Vice President backed down after being reminded that only the President had power to call out the armed forces.

But confrontation between the United States military and the Bonus Marchers was coming soon enough. Two days after Curtis's misguided order, a crowd estimated at about 17,000 gathered in front of the Capitol to await the adjournment of Congress. That morning, the Marchers' leaders also dispatched a delegation of representatives to the White House, hoping to meet with President Hoover and discuss their needs and their requests.

This mission returned about noon carrying word that the President had refused to see them. Hoover also announced that he would not be making his traditional closing-day visit to Congress, a blatant attempt to avoid confronting the marchers. Additionally, he had ordered the city's police to close the White House gates and to clear Pennsylvania Avenue and adjacent streets of all pedestrians and traffic. While the police were following the President's orders, three demonstrators were arrested and dragged off to jail.

Ten days later, Waters's suspicion that the federal government desperately wanted to get rid of the Bonus Army was validated. At the only meeting ever held between the administration and representatives of the Bonus Army, Secretary of War Patrick Hurley told Waters that, "You and your army have no business in Washington." According to Waters, Hurley also told him that, "We are not in sympathy with your being here. We will not co-operate in any way with your being here. We are interested only in getting you out of the district. At the first sign of disorder or bloodshed in the B[onus].E[xpeditionary].F[orce]., you will all get out. And we have plenty of troops to put you out."

Over the next few days, Waters negotiated with government officials about abandoning some of the sites where Bonus Marchers had bivouacked. He thought that he reached an accommodation with the administration. But, four days ahead of the schedule that had been worked out, Waters received a written order to evacuate about 200 men from one of the sites within the next 10 minutes. Waters actually completed the evacuation quickly, but not before a skirmish had broken out between the police and a group of marchers.

Order was quickly restored, but it was too late to arrange a peaceful settlement. President Hoover had been informed of the fracas and decided that the time to act had arrived. He called out the Army, a decision reported in the afternoon newspapers. Around five o'clock that afternoon, four cavalry troops appeared with their sabers raised. Six tanks followed them, and behind the tanks jogged helmeted infantrymen with tear-gas canisters dangling from their belts and bayonets drawn. Leading the forces was General Douglas MacArthur on a white horse. Right beside him marched two other Army officers who would gain greater fame during World War II, Major Dwight D. Eisenhower and Major George Patton.

Homelessness, poverty, and events like the Bonus Army had an extraordinary effect on the American people. As the economy continued its collapse following the stock market crash of 1929, they could not avoid realizing what was happening. They saw more and more people standing in breadlines; they saw increasing numbers of people sleeping in parks and on the streets. They couldn't avoid hearing talk on the radio about the continued decline of stock prices, and they were bombarded with newspaper stories about the hard times. If one read a newspaper or listened to the radio, one knew about the Bonus Army.

What made matters even worse was the fact that no one seemed to have any idea about what to do or how to fix the economy. Unfortunately, the federal government provided little, if any, leadership or direction. It was incapable of doing anything, to a large extent because of President Hoover.

President Herbert Hoover, who had been elected in a landslide in 1928, had a particular set of values and beliefs that prevented him from favoring direct government intervention in the economy or providing assistance to individuals in need. His position on the national economy rested on the concept of voluntarism. He believed that a partnership between public and private institutions was the most effective way to achieve high long-term economic growth. Hoover believed that too much intervention or coercion by the government would destroy individualism and self-reliance, which he considered two of the most important American values. He expressed all of this in a little book that he wrote, *American Individualism*.

Hoover's ideals and values about the proper relationship between individuals and the economy were sorely tested by the onset of the Great Depression. Hoover also had the misfortune of having as his Secretary of the Treasury Andrew Mellon, thought to be the third wealthiest person in the United States, topped by only John D. Rockefeller and Henry Ford. Mellon was a banker from Pittsburgh and one of the founders of the Aluminum Corporation of America (Alcoa). He advised Hoover to leave the economy alone and told the President that the economic calamity was just a normal part of the business cycle. It was simply purging itself of weak links. He counseled Hoover "to liquidate labor, liquidate stocks, liquidate farmers, liquidate real estate . . . it will purge the rottenness out of the system. High costs of living and high living will come down. People will work harder, live a more moral life. Values will be adjusted, and enterprising people will pick up from less competent people." He also advocated spending cuts to balance the federal budget, and he argued against fiscal stimulus measures.

Although no one knows how much weight Hoover gave to Mellon's recommendations or if he based specific policies on them, Hoover clearly viewed the government's role in the economy much as Mellon did. This was disastrous in 1932 when Hoover had to contend with the Bonus March. Frequently called the Bonus Army or the Bonus Expeditionary Force—a reference identifying and equating the marchers with the Allied Expeditionary Force, America's World War troops—these men considered themselves soldiers and the American economy as the enemy. They wanted the federal government to help them fight this adversary.

Unfortunately, Hoover did not understand the reasons for the veterans' request, and neither did MacArthur. He was later quoted as saying that the Bonus Army was "beyond the shadow of a doubt" ready to seize control of the government, and the rationale for his actions was the danger of communist inspired revolution. This explanation persuaded very few people.

What people did realize was the unwillingness of the federal government to take any responsibility for providing decent housing to Americans suffering from poverty and homelessness through no fault of their own. Even veterans of the recent conflagration in Europe, men who found themselves with no income, no home, and no prospects, men who came to Washington, DC, where they lived in miserable, jerry-built hovels while they appealed to the government for help, found the U.S. Army turned against them by a federal government totally opposed to giving veterans a few hundred dollars, much less a decent place to live. This conflict between homeless people and governments at every level—federal, state, and local—would continue throughout the Great Depression and can still be seen today.

FURTHER READING

"Bonus Army Has Evaporated." *Review of Reviews*, 86 (September 1932), 18.

Bonus march [electronic resource] / [Bureau of Investigation]. [Washington, D.C.]: U.S. Bureau of Investigation, 2000.

Brown, Ernest Francis. "Bonus Army Marches to Defeat." *Current History*, 36 (September 1932), 684–688.

Daniels, Roger. *The Bonus March: An Episode of the Great Depression*. Westport, CT: Greenwood Pub. Co., 1971.

Dickson, Paul and Thomas B. Allen. *The Bonus Army: An American Epic*. New York: Walker and Company, 2004.

Dickson, Paul, and Thomas E. Allen, "Marching on History." *Smithsonian*, 33, 11 (February 2003), 84–95.

Kingseed, Wyatt. "A Promise Denied." *American History*, 39, 2 (June 2004) 28–35.

Kusmer, Kenneth L. "The Bonus Army: An American Epic." *Indiana Magazine of History*, 103, 1(March 2007), 115–18.

Liebovich, Louis. *Press Reaction to the Bonus March of 1932: A Re-Evaluation of the Impact of an American Tragedy*. Columbia, SC: Association for Education in Journalism and Mass Communication, 1990.

MacArthur, Douglas. "Soldier's Work between Two Wars." *Life*, 57 (July 3, 1964), 56+.

McGoff, K. "Bonus Army." *American History Illustrated*, 12 (February 1978) p. 28–37.

Weaver, John D. "Bonus Army." *American Heritage*, 14 (June 1963), 18–23+.

19

FERA AND FTP

Agency Recommendations

- *Document:* The document is a selection from a report written by the National Committee on the Care of Transient and Homeless. This organization was one of the strongest and most vocal supporters of the establishment of a federal agency such as the Federal Transient Program (FTP). This report explains their motivations for favoring such a government agency.
- *Date:* The survey was published in 1934.
- *Where:* The survey was published in New York.
- *Significance:* The report says that the Federal Transient Program had been successful. It also indicates the failings of the program, makes suggestions for improvement, and recommends that it be continued. The selection reveals the attitude of the FTP toward homeless people, who it thought they were, and how the problem of homelessness might be solved. It is also one of the first documents that directly expresses a relationship among homelessness, poverty, and unemployment.

DOCUMENT

The prevention of transiency through better social, recreational, and educational processes within community life is a main objective. . . .

The root social causes of transiency may be largely identical with those of homelessness. Homelessness and transiency are probably aspects of common social problems, and might well be thought of as the problem of the unattached. . . . Treatment should center upon prevention . . . and a more united attack upon the social causes within each community. . . .

I. The Problem of Transiency and Its Prevention

... There is little positive knowledge of the causes of transiency, and the F.E.R.A. (Federal Emergency Relief Agency) must have an opportunity ... to get at these causes. ... It should develop programs looking to the prevention of transiency and to the readjustment to normal life patterns of men and families already transient.

We urge intensive co-operation of the F.E.R.A. with all agencies ... which are seeking to stabilize individuals and to assure them adequate educational, industrial, and other opportunities for establishing personal effectiveness and economic security. ...

If the program of care offered to the transient is to be adequate to his needs, it must be attractive enough to counteract the lure of the open road. ... The Committee specifically recommends in this connection:

1. That the problems of youth in their home communities be given special attention, to the end that the restlessness and frustration engendered by present economic conditions and personal psychological and social conditions may be offset by increased educational, vocational, life guidance, recreational, and cultural activities. ...

2. That the best experience obtainable from subsistence homesteading, rural rehabilitation, youth groups ... be drawn upon for the framing of preventive and rehabilitative programs for young unemployed persons.

3. That the state and local relief administrations be constantly reminded of the effect of inadequate relief on the solidarity of the family group, emphasizing the possibility of older children or husbands taking to the road in order to escape intolerable economic conditions at home and that the home relief departments be equipped with sufficient case work facilities to detect incipient family breakdown, whether caused by social, economic, or personal factors.

4. That a better liaison be established between transient bureaus and emergency relief bureaus for the adjustment of such transients as are

---

DID YOU KNOW?

The Kansas Transient Service

In early 1933, the FERA [Federal Emergency Relief Administration] invited states to register their plans for the establishment of a transient service. Each plan had to provide information on the extent and the nature of the problem that migrants posed, indicate how those problems would be tackled, and to give an estimate of the cost of the proposal. The federal government indicated that states should establish a separate facility for the generation of transients, where they would immediately be assigned to a social worker who would provide full casework facilities. Bona fide transients could expect food, shelter, and clothing to be provided according to their needs. They would also receive medical attention. Transport would be available to take them either to their place of legal residence, or to another location that would be decided on after consultation with a social worker. ... Finally, suitable employment provided through local work projects, or resulting from registration with employment bureaus, was an essential part of the plan. Seasonal migratory workers were not considered transients, nor were intrastate migrants or the state's homeless; all were judged a local responsibility. ...

[All] states were obliged to fulfill certain conditions before they could claim their cash grants. For example, each had to start collecting statistical information that could be transmitted to Washington in the form requested. This data eventually made possible the creation of an accurate picture of the transient problem across the nation. ... It also provided the basis for several valuable and innovative empirical studies on the causes and the effects of transiency. ... Within two weeks, the FERA had approved the plan. ...

The next step was to establish the creation of two types of service centers and also camps that would form part of a national network. ... Reference centers became the first port of call for transients. After registration, each migrant received immediate but temporary care which included food and lodging, and had the opportunity to meet a social worker.

The next step was the referral of families, single men, and boys to a treatment center where the process of rehabilitation would begin. At the treatment center, families and individuals received a medical examination, accommodation was provided, and work began on a plan that was intended to bring their wandering to a halt. ...

Separate treatment centers were established for both families and single males, though single females and boys

---

less than fourteen years of age were accommodated in family centers. The family centers were supervised by trained social workers but the transient families were lodged in houses in various parts of the towns in which the centers were located. ... Unattached males, on the other hand, were lodged in single buildings near places where they might find work. Strenuous efforts were made to find appropriate, continuous work for all transients who were considered fit for employment. The significance of regular work in the path toward a normal life was stressed by the FERA and was echoed by all Kansas officials. Indeed, the FERA proposal was that all able-bodied transients should perform thirty hours work each week in exchange for their subsistence and a small cash allowance.

Source: Fearon, Peter. "Relief for Wanderers: The Transit Service in Kansas, 1933–35." *Great Plains Quarterly* (2006), 248–50. Available online at http://digitalcommons.unl.edu/greatplains quarterly/62

returned to settings from which they had formerly fled.

The Committee recognizes that not all transiency is socially undesirable, however, and believes that a differentiation must be made between aimless wandering and the legitimate migration of workers in search of employment and of young people seeking new opportunities. It recommends:

5. That the migration of workers be regulated by developing improved local public employment services where accurate information as to the state of the job market in all sections of the country may be available to persons who find it necessary to leave home in search of work.

6. That a migratory worker served by the transient bureaus be cared for in a manner that will decrease his need for further wandering without impairing his chance of securing employment.

7. Industry should be required, in its "codes of fair practice," to make proper provision for its seasonal labor requirements. Industrial agriculture should similarly be required to regularize its labor needs.

SOURCE: Ellery F. Reed, *Federal Transit Program: An Evaluative Survey, May to July, 1934.* New York: The Committee on Care of Transient and Homeless, 1934.

ANALYSIS

On July 18, 1932, following orders from President Hoover, the United States Army, under the command of General Douglas MacArthur and Major George Patton and Major Dwight Eisenhower, began to advance on the largest encampment of the Bonus Army in Washington, DC. With little trouble, the troops quickly dispersed the protestors and finished their work by setting the camp on fire.

Newspapers trumpeted these events across their front pages. While a few of them praised the military action, most of them condemned the government and military with unrestrained passion. The *New York Times* devoted its first three pages entirely to coverage of the fighting in the nation's capital. The *Washington Daily News* editorialized about these events in ominous and foreboding terms: "The mightiest government in the world chasing unarmed men, women, and children with Army tanks. If the Army must be called out to make war on unarmed citizens, this is no longer America."

One individual who clearly understood the significance of the Army's attack on ex-soldiers was Franklin D. Roosevelt. Then governor of New York and the nominee of the Democratic Party for the presidency that year, FDR told one of his close advisers that the incident assured his election as President. Looking at pictures in the newspapers, Governor Roosevelt called them "scenes from a nightmare." Later, he told another of his advisers that "what Hoover should have done was to meet with the leaders of the Bonus Army when they asked for an interview. When two hundred or so marched up to the White House, Hoover should have sent out coffee and sandwiches and asked a delegation in. Instead he let Pat Hurley [Secretary of War] and Doug MacArthur do their thing." In FDR's opinion, "MacArthur has just prevented Hoover's reelection."

By the time of the presidential election in November 1932, the United States was nearing the bottom of the Great Depression. The unemployment rate had just about peaked, and Herbert Hoover's popularity had just about vanished. It had probably sunk so low that Roosevelt would have been elected under any circumstances. Nevertheless, the Bonus Army debacle probably sealed the fates of both Hoover and Roosevelt.

This fact contains a certain amount of irony. FDR was misunderstood by Hoover and large parts of the American public. After Roosevelt received the Democratic presidential nomination in early July, Hoover was delighted. He believed that Roosevelt would be the easiest Democratic candidate to defeat. The diaries of Theodore Joslin, Hoover's press secretary, indicate that Hoover had deliberately done things to assist Roosevelt's nomination because of that belief. Hoover could hardly have been more misguided. In November Roosevelt won the election by one of the largest majorities of any President in U.S. history.

> ## DID YOU KNOW?
>
> ### FSA Farm Workers' Camps
>
> [The] fifteen standard farm workers camps' [operated by the Farm Security Administration (FSA)] provide minimum facilities for shelter, sanitation, and orderly community living. Each has tent platforms and metal shelters for separate family living, ranging from around 125 in the smaller camps to 300 in the larger projects. The 15 camps now operating have a total capacity of 3,300 families. There is a central community building with an auditorium, stage, kitchen, and facilities for nursery school, adult classes, women's activities and like interests that can be commonly conducted and shared; central utilities with showers, flush toilets, and laundry arrangements; a health center building for use by doctors and nurses of the Public Health Service and the Agricultural Workers Health and Medical Association, and a quarantine or isolation unit for communicable disease.
>
> Each community has a sewage and garbage disposal unit, a central water supply, water-heating plant, surfaced streets, and electric street lighting. A manager's residence, office, and storage building are provided for administrative purposes. Athletic grounds and recreational facilities of a simple type, such as horseshoe courts and baseball lots for adults, swings, bars, and slides have developed from natural desires and needs until they have become a feature in every community.
>
> *Source:* "Testimony of Laurence I. Hewes, Jr.," US Cong., House, Select Committee to Investigate the Interstate Migration of Destitute Citizens, 76th Cong., 3rd Sess., *Interstate Migration.* Washington, DC: Government Printing Office, 1941. Part 6, 2604–97.

Another irony is that, during the presidential campaign, Roosevelt's position on paying the bonus before its due date did not differ from Hoover's at all. Perhaps because he did not want to appear to agree with Hoover, perhaps because he did not want to alienate a large and important bloc of voters, perhaps because he did not think it was appropriate for a candidate to comment on a tense political situation while it was occurring, Roosevelt never publicly expressed his opposition to Patman's Bonus Bill. However, he clearly communicated his attitude to close advisers and a few others in private. As early as April 1931, well before the Bonus Army appeared, FDR said that it would be "unthinkable" to pay the bonus ahead of schedule while the Federal Treasury was running annual deficits. In October 1932, a month before the election, he said that the federal government could not "consider anticipation of a bonus payment until it has a balanced budget." And then on

DID YOU KNOW?

Harry Hopkins Explains Who the Migrants Are

Those who went over the hill in search of work were the transients. They were not bums, though in many communities they inherited the opprobrium that attaches to bums. Nor were they hoboes or professional migratory laborers, although circumstances threw them into the same labor reserve. They were industrial workers, artisans, laborers, who, after years of settled life, were forced by necessity to seek employment in new places. They were dispossessed farmers, travelling westward with their families as their fathers had done before them. They were young men who had never had a chance to work, and who could no longer remain dependent on their burdened parents. They were country people looking for work in the city and city people looking for security in the country. They were negroes following in the usual road of opportunity northward. They were the aged, the tuberculous and the otherwise infirm, moving to the widely toured climes of Florida, California, and the Southwest in the hope that the favorable climate would somehow mitigate the rigors of poverty.

Source: Harry L. Hopkins, *Spending to Save: The Complete Story of Relief.* New York: W. W. & Company, 1936, 126.

March 2, 1933, on the eve of his inauguration, Roosevelt used his radio address to request that veterans give him their support and cooperation, implying that putting off paying the bonus would be in the spirit of their wartime service and sacrifice.

Roosevelt continued to treat the bonus issue with a light touch during the first few months of his presidency. In May 1933, two months into his term as President, a second but smaller bonus army arrived in Washington to urge Congress to authorize early payment of the bonus. When they arrived, Roosevelt and the new administration treated them very differently from Hoover who had refused to meet their representatives. When Roosevelt learned that the new Army was coming to Washington, he arranged to have 9,000 of them housed in an abandoned army fort in Virginia about 10 miles from Washington. He also allocated funds to feed them, provide medical care, and transport them between the fort and the capital.

More than that, he responded in a very personal and unexpected way. He asked one of his advisers to take First Lady Eleanor Roosevelt, to visit the camp and meet with the men. Most emphatically, he also told her to tell the marchers that she was coming on his behalf. At the site of the veterans' new base, with no prior notice of her coming and with no secret service agents surrounding her, Mrs. Roosevelt sloshed through the mud to visit the men. She later wrote in her memoirs,

> Very hesitatingly, I got out [of the car] and walked over to where I saw a line-up of men waiting for food. They looked at me curiously and one of them asked my name and what I wanted. When I said I [was the President's wife and that I] just wanted to see how they were getting on, they asked me to join them.

The men could not believe that she was actually the President's wife [remember that there was no television then and most of the men had probably never seen a picture of her], but she did persuade them of her identity. Then, she had lunch with them and spent an hour or so visiting. She was particularly careful to tell them about her experiences in Washington during the war, when she prepared coffee and sandwiches for soldiers and visited the wounded. The men were so entranced with her that they insisted on singing popular songs to her.

Two weeks later, on May 19, FDR himself met with three leaders of the Second Bonus Army at the White House. While they met, about 3,000 veterans marched down Pennsylvania Avenue. An editorial in *the New York Times* described Roosevelt's actions as a "rational and friendly and human way of dealing with a human problem. Perhaps also the President had learned something from the mistakes of his predecessor."

During the next few years, Congress twice passed versions of the Bonus Bill. On both occasions, Roosevelt vetoed it. The first time, the House of Representatives overrode his veto, but the Senate upheld it. On the second occasion, Roosevelt let it be known that he would veto the bill but would not be upset if Congress overrode his veto. Both houses of Congress then voted to override Roosevelt's veto, and the Treasury Department quickly prepared to redeem the veterans' certificates.

Roosevelt clearly had mixed feelings about the Bonus Bill, but whatever his reservations, he always showed compassion and understanding of the veterans' position. He made sure not to alienate them, and he showed much more political savvy than had Hoover.

At the same time, he understood the connections between unemployment, poverty, and homelessness. In the next few months, he took quick action with regard to housing conditions in the United States, not just as they affected veterans but as they affected all Americans. This was the first time that the federal government ever considered housing and homelessness to be appropriate concerns and a subject for the federal government to consider.

FDR took two important actions with regard to housing and homelessness. On April 5, 1933, just a month after his inauguration, the President issued Executive Order 6101, which created the Civilian Conservation Corps (CCC). This became one of Americans' favorite New Deal programs because of its emphasis on preserving and protecting the natural environment and natural resources—forestry, flood protection, soil erosion, and other similar topics. But the program had another purpose—to provide housing for homeless young men and to keep them off the road. The CCC was authorized to provide housing, food, and small wages to 250,000 men between the ages of 16 and 24. They were to be housed in clean, sanitary, healthful, and respectable camps where they could perform conservation projects, be safe, and not be a problem for either their families or society.

One month after he established the CCC for young men, FDR issued another executive order that modified the first. This amendment allowed 25,000 veterans of the World War, of any age, to join the CCC with preference given to 2,000 men who had participated in the Second Bonus Army. Clearly, despite his equivocations about the Bonus Bill, Roosevelt felt some urgency to address their concerns.

Roosevelt's other major effort to address the national housing problem was a provision of the Federal Emergency Relief Act (FERA). Also passed by Congress in May 1933, it was one of the major pieces of New Deal legislation passed in the famous

---

DID YOU KNOW?

Harry Hopkins Explains Who Was Unemployed

Hopkins was well aware of the innovative nature of the FERA and knew that he would have to convince the American public that it was really not radical. To do this, he used rhetoric that would appeal to most Americans. In his typical fashion, Hopkins insisted that the unemployed were folks just like all of us. In a radio address he asked:

> Who are these fellow citizens? Are they tramps? Are they ne'er-do-wells? Are they unemployables? Are they people who are no good and incompetent? Take a look at them, if you have not, and see who they are. There is hardly a person listening in who does not know of an intimate friend, people whom you have known all your life, fine, hard-working, upstanding men and whom who have gone overboard and been caught up in this relief structure of ours. They are carpenters, bricklayers, artisans, architects, engineers, clerks, stenographers, doctors, dentists, farmers, ministers, the whole crowd is caught in this thing, the finest people in America. That is who they are—or were before they lost their jobs.

Source: Hopkins, June. *Harry Hopkins: Sudden Hero, Brash Reformer.* New York: St. Martin's Press, 1999, 162–63.

DID YOU KNOW?

Ending the Transient Program

Eventually the epidemic diminished and finally went away, leaving us with a much larger problem on our hands. This was the problem of how to phase out the Transient Program when its parent organization, the Federal Emergency Relief Administration, was coming to an end. This was part of the grand design of 1935, wherein Roosevelt said that he wanted to get the federal government out of "this business of relief." He was talking about the sweeping general relief that characterized the FERA program. What he wanted in its place were highly differentiated and specialized programs for people with different needs. The Works Progress Administration program was for the needy unemployed. Federally-aided state assistance helped the needy aged, blind, and widows (with disability added later). The Social Security Act established an insurance program for the retired aged (wives and widows were added in 1939) as well as an unemployment insurance for those losing their jobs in the future. The Resettlement Program in the Agriculture Department provided assistance and loans for displaced farmers and farm workers. There was no place for the Transient Program in this grand design, so to the great dismay of its friends and supporters the program ended.

Every effort was made to get women, children, and the aged back to their place of legal residence. Many transients, however, had lived and worked in a way that deprived them of such legal residence. I especially remember a delegation of over-age lumbermen from Maine pleading for a continuation of the program. In some states special provision was made for hardship cases. The camps and work projects were transferred to the WPA.

Most of us felt sadness, not because it was such a great solution to the complex of problems that produced the phenomena of transiency and homelessness but because so much good will and effort had gone into the program. Not until the seventies did the Supreme Court rule that residence laws were unconstitutional as a condition for assistance. But our present day problem with the homeless makes clear that there is much more to the problem of homelessness than such legalities, however important.

Source: Elizabeth Wickenden, "Reminiscences of the Program for Transients and Homeless in the Thirties," Rick Beard, ed., *On Being Homeless: Historical Perspectives.* New York: Museum of the City of New York, 1987.

Hundred Days. It began by explaining that the law was being enacted because "the present economic depression has created a serious emergency due to widespread unemployment and increasing inadequacy of State and local relief funds." It therefore appropriated $500,000,000 to the Reconstruction Finance Corporation to make grants to individual states "to aid in meeting the costs of relief and work relief, and relieving the hardship and suffering caused by unemployment in the form of money, service, materials, and/or commodities to provide the necessities of life to persons in need . . . *whether resident, transient, or homeless.*"

The part of the last clause just quoted is critical to recognizing the New Deal's housing efforts. Traditionally, on the rare occasions when an individual state assisted people in need, that assistance was limited to legal "residents." In most states, that meant that a person had to have lived in that state for more than one year to be eligible for publicly provided assistance. That limitation meant that tens of thousands of people who were moving around the country in search of work and a place to live had residency in no state and therefore did not qualify for public assistance. By legislating that federal money could be granted to states to assist people in need, even if they were transients or homeless, the federal government was accepting and assuming some responsibility to care for homeless people.

To accomplish the goal of helping states to help people, FERA established a separate division, the Federal Transient Program (FTP). This subdivision was essentially an umbrella agency meant to help every state create its own Transient Program to assist all applicants for aid, regardless of their residency status.

Thus, this act contains several important provisions. First, it strongly implied that "transients" were essentially "homeless" people. Second, this was the first occasion on which the federal government directly assumed any responsibility to care for transients and explicitly used the word *homeless* in referring to them. Third, the FTP functioned in essentially the same way as the CCC. It established camps where people could obtain decent housing, food, and medical care. The main difference between FTP camps and CCC camps was the age requirement for admission to CCC camps (which was reduced in an important way). However, it is also important to acknowledge the President's ambivalent attitude. FERA was given only a two-year lifespan in the legislation. Although it could be renewed, it wasn't, and that would have serious consequences for many of the camps' residents.

At the end of July 1934, The Committee on Care of Transient and Homeless, an organization that had lobbied heavily for the establishment of an agency like the FTP, evaluated the program's first year. It carefully examined every aspect of the program from the composition of the transient population to the conditions of the housing provided, the food, medical care, religion, education, and leisure provided for the residents of the camps. It then offered a list of recommendations—42 of them, not counting all the parts of each recommendation. Reading these recommendations reveals why the program was established and its goals, who was thought to be homeless, and what was necessary to "cure" them of this condition. It also indicates who the program—and thus the government—thought constituted the bulk of the homeless population.

FURTHER READING

Baldwin, Stanley. *The Rise and Decline of the Farm Security Administration.* Chapel Hill, NC: University of North Carolina Press, 1968.

Charles, Searle F. *Minister of Relief: Harry Hopkins and the Depression.* Syracuse, NY: Syracuse University Press, 1963.

Hopkins, Harry L. *Spending to Save: The Complete Story of Relief.* New York: W. W. Norton & Company, Inc., 1936.

Stein, Walter J. "A New Deal Experiment with Guided Democracy: The FSA Migrant Camps in California." *Canadian Historical Association Historical Papers,* 1970, 132–46.

Wickenden, Elizabeth. "Reminiscences of the Program for Transients and Homeless in the Thirties." In *On Being Homeless: Historical Perspectives.* Ed. Rick Beard. New York: Museum of the City of New York, 1987.

Williams, Edward Ainsworth. *Federal Aid for Relief.* New York: Columbia University Press, 1939.

20

BUM BRIGADE

Not Welcome

- *Document:* The selections are excerpts of articles from a newspaper in Los Angeles, California. They describe the attempt of the Los Angeles Chief of Police to block homeless transients from entering California in 1935 and 1936.
- *Date:* The articles appeared in the Los Angeles *Herald-Express* between August 1935 and February 1936.
- *Where:* The articles discuss events that originated in Los Angeles and occurred at the borders of California with Arizona, Nevada, and Oregon.
- *Significance:* The articles disclose the extent of hostility toward transients to California and reveal how far California officials were willing to take their hostility.

DOCUMENT

Los Angeles *Herald-Express*, August 24, 1935

Stay Away from California Warning to Transient Hordes

Indigent transients heading for California today were warned by H. A. Carleton, director of the Federal Transient Service, "to stay away from California."

Carleton declared they would be sent back to their home States on arrival here due to closing of Transient relief shelters and barring of Works Progress Administration work relief in the State to all transients registered after August 1.

"California is carrying approximately 7 percent of the entire national relief load, one of the heaviest of any State in the Union," said Carleton. "A large part of this load was occasioned by thousands of penniless families from other States who have literally overrun California."

Carleton estimated the transient influx at 1,000 a day.

* * *

Los Angeles *Herald-Express*, February 4, 1936

Indigents Barred at Arizona Line

While a tumultuous row was raging in city council over Police Chief James E. Davis "expeditionary force" of policemen to halt the indigents over California's far-flung borders, the lid was successfully clamped on the Arizona-California line today.

The spectacular row in the council broke out when Councilman P. P. Christensen, consistent critic of Davis, introduced a resolution demanding by whose authority the police chief was sending 136 of his "coppers" to the State line "trenches."

At the same time Deputy Chief Homer Cross said the entry ports on the Arizona boundary had been blocked against transients in an effort to hold the "flood of criminals" and divert the stream of penniless transients.

Within 3 more days, Cross estimated, the blockade would be similarly effective on the Oregon and Nevada lines. . . .

The skirmish began right after Councilman Evan Lewis took the floor to argue in favor of Christensen's resolution.

Meantime, from Sacramento to Phoenix, Ariz., the reverberations resounded. At the California capital Deputy Attorney General Jess Hession declared he believed Davis' methods illegal. Governor Frank F. Merriam withheld comment but State Senator Thomas Scollan, who had brought about defeat of an indigent-barring law at the last session, characterized the "expeditionary forces" as "damnable, absurd, and asinine."

. . . Councilman Earl C. Gay also took the floor and hotly opposed Lewis and Christensen. "As usual," Mr. Gay said, "Mr. Lewis is talking about something he knows nothing about." His face flushed and making no effort to hide his indignation, Councilman Lewis leaped to his feet. His first remarks were drowned by the gavel of Council President Robert L. Burns, who tried to leave the floor to Gay. Lewis remained on his feet and continued to shout as Burns loudly pounded for order. Half a dozen other councilmen tried to gain the floor. Gay then resumed his argument insisting that the action of the police chief probably was dictated by the police commission.

DID YOU KNOW?

Bum Brigade

[The] chief of police of the city of Los Angeles established a border patrol at some 16 border stations at which, throughout the months of November and December 1935 and January, February, March, and April, 1936 were on duty in an effort to turn back all incoming migrants. The practice of the border patrol during the time it was in operation was outlined as follows: (1) all incoming trains, passenger and freight, were searched for persons evading payment of train fare; (2) Such persons once detected were charged with suspicion of vagrancy and evasion of payment of fare, both misdemeanors; (3) Such persons were then taken before magistrates where they were given a choice of leaving the state or serving jail terms; (4) All highways and secondary roads were carefully watched and persons having no apparent means of support were, as the phrase was, "discouraged" from entering California. This border patrol was established, incidentally, despite the fact that on February 18, 1936 the attorney-general of California had rendered an opinion to the effect that the patrol was illegal. . . .

When the border patrol was abandoned, an effort was made to get at the situation through legislative action, and in the 1935 session of the legislature, assembly bill No. 2459 was introduced. . . . This bill, if enacted, would have had the effect of preventing so-called paupers, indigents, and transients from entering the state. . . . [O]n January 23, 1939, assembly bill NO. 1356 was introduced, which, if enacted, would have had the same effect.

Source: "Statement of Gov. Culbert L. Olson, of California," in United States House of Representatives. Select Committee to Investigate the Interstate Migration of Destitute Citizens. 76th Cong. 3rd Sess., *Interstate Migration*. Washington, DC: Government Printing Office, 1941. Part 6, 2232–36.

DID YOU KNOW?

Bills Introduced into the California Legislature

Assembly Bill 980
Introduced January 24, 1935

Section 1. Section 717 is hereby added to the Political Code to read as follows:

"717. State police officers shall be stationed at all points where a highway crosses the border of a state and in all unincorporated towns within the state which are situated at or near the border of the State. If any state agency maintains an inspection force at any such point, the officers or officers comprising such force may be sworn in as State police, at the discretion of the chief."

****

Assembly Bill 2459
Introduced May 16, 1935

An Act to prevent the entry into California of paupers, vagabonds, indigent persons, persons likely to become public charges, providing means for enforcing the same and prescribing penalties for the violation thereof, declaring the urgency thereof, and providing it shall take effect immediately.

The people of the State of California do enact as follows:

SECTION 1. Large numbers of paupers, vagabonds, indigent persons and persons likely to become public charges have been, and are, coming into this State, burdening the relief roles, creating further unemployment in the State, and subjecting our workers to competition with pauper labor. This influx of unemployed and unemployables at the present time seriously threatens the safety and welfare of the people of this State, and, if continued, will destroy the State. In order to protect this State and the people thereof from pauper labor; also to save this State and its people from impossible financial burdens in caring for vast numbers of paupers and indigent persons; also to preserve the peace, health, and safety; also to preserve the standard of living of the people of this State and to maintain the general welfare and to protect and defend this State, it is imperatively necessary that hereafter no paupers, vagabonds, indigent persons or persons likely to become public charges, shall be allowed to enter or shall enter this State.

SEC. 2. All paupers, vagabonds, indigent persons are hereby prohibited from entering the State of California.

Asks Legal Opinion

The Christensen resolution was amended and sent to the city attorney's office requesting that official's legal opinion. . . .

Orders Outlined

"Tactical orders" under which the city police were seeking to dam the tide of trouble at the border were outlined by S. L. Harman, assistant secretary of the Los Angeles Chamber of Commerce. He said police and civic authorities were seeking to stop at the State line, persons riding trains without paying fares, give these persons the option of leaving the State or serving jail terms and finally, to discourage from entering California all auto parties without apparent sources of support.

In the sieve of the widespread border patrol, the officers by fingerprinting methods, expected to catch or at least keep out of California a considerable number of wanted criminals, Harman said.

* * *

Los Angeles *Herald-Express*, February 6, 1936

Rule Guard at Border Legal

Flaying critics of Los Angeles' swift war on jobless, penniless winter nomads, Mayor Frank L. Shaw today revealed an opinion by City Attorney Ray L. Chesebro stating that the police reinforcements of the border patrol, was authorized by the city's charter.

Meantime, against hesitant cooperation and even outspoken opposition from Arizona, Nevada and Oregon, Police Chief James E. Davis' flying squadrons of 136 police officers, succeeded in turning back hundreds of indigents and has caused at one border port . . . a 50 percent drop in incoming hordes.

No Dumping Ground

Mayor Shaw declared Los Angeles would not be the dumping ground of charity-seekers fleeing from the more vigorous winters in practically every other State in the Union. He declared that on January 31, when the police commission showed him the gravity of the winter indigent problem with its trail of crime and added relief burdens, he asked City Attorney Chesebro for the legal opinion and received authority for Davis to set up the police "foreign legion."

"It is important to note," Mayor Shaw said, "that Los Angeles is facing a desperate situation if we permit every incoming freight train to bring us a new shipment of unemployed, penniless vagrants, to consume the relief so seriously needed by our needy people and to create a crime menace almost beyond conceivable control.

"Officials of cities and States en route will not permit these transients to leave the trains, preferring for their own safety that the problem should be dumped in Los Angeles.

"Our own recourse is to reinforce the sheriffs of the border counties with men loaned from the Los Angeles Police Department who can turn back the front ranks of these oncoming hordes promptly and in such numbers that the invasion can be halted at its sources as soon as the news reaches the east.

"We are simply trying to apply an ounce of sensible prevention to save a pound of costly cure later on. Critics of the plan have either not taken pains to examine facts or, for mysterious reasons of their own, are content to see Los Angeles filled with a homeless indigent army of thousands recruited from every State in the Union and threatening every security and hope of our own working people.

"It is noteworthy that the critics have no constructive proposals of their own to offer with reference to this very real problem."

> **Assembly Bill 1356**
> Introduced January 23, 1939
>
> *An Act to prevent the entry into the State of California of paupers, vagabonds, and fugitives from justice, providing for enforcement of this Act and prescribing penalties for the violation thereof*
>
> SECTION 1. Large numbers of paupers, vagabonds, and fugitives from justice have, and unless restrained will continue to, come into this State, and have created a problem of relief and law enforcement. This influx of such persons is detrimental to the interests of this State and this statute is enacted in the exercise of the police power of this State as a matter of self-preservation, and to prevent the overburdening of facilities of the State for the relief of destitution and for law enforcement.
>
> The legislature hereby declares that the enactment and enforcement of this act is essential to the welfare of the people of this State.
>
> SEC. 2. All paupers, vagabonds, and fugitives from justice are hereby prohibited from entering the State of California.
>
> *Source:* Printed in US Cong., House, Hearings before the Select Committee to Investigate the Interstate Migration of Destitute Citizens. 76th Cong. 3rd Sess., *Interstate Migration.* Washington, DC: Government Printing Office, 1941.

Slap at Faction

The mayor's tart remarks were interpreted in city hall circles as a slap at the council faction which yesterday maneuvered a unanimous request from the council to City Attorney Chesebro for an opinion on specific points not covered by the opinion Chesebro gave the mayor.

A possible major development today was the suggestion of Governor Frank F. Merriam at Sacramento for a meeting of western State Governors to seek means of halting the westward tide of jobless.

"There are stations in Arizona," Governor Merriam said, "where chambers of commerce furnish gasoline to itinerants to help them along to California."

Speaking on the much-questioned legality of Los Angeles' far-flung expeditionary force, the Governor said, "I guess Los Angeles can do it, its city boundaries go almost that far."

Governor B. B. Moeur, of Arizona declared, according to Phoenix dispatches, that Los Angeles was bluffing.

In 1936, nearly one-third of California's labor force was unemployed. At the same time, thousands of Americans from other states continued flocking to California. They were drawn there by (incorrect) media reports and propaganda distributed by large farmers and agricultural organizations saying that jobs and prosperity still existed in the Golden State. In response to the continued influx of people, the Los Angeles Chief of Police, James Davis, deployed 125 (some sources say 136) police officers to the state's borders with Arizona, Nevada, and Oregon. Their orders were to bar immigrants from entering California. This small army became known as the "bum brigade." Although the troops were withdrawn in about six weeks, hostility toward homeless people continued. In 1938, a group calling itself the California Citizen Association demanded that the federal government return immigrants to their home states, and more than 100,000 people signed their petitions. Many Californians ceased talking about "the poor" or pauperized "Okies" and began labeling them as "freeloaders," "chiselers," and "crooks." California's legislature even passed a law making it illegal to bring an indigent person into the state. Nationally, hostility toward the poor and the homeless diminished only after the onset of World War II ended the Great Depression and brought renewed prosperity to the United States. (Bettmann/Corbis)

Charges "Scare"

"What the Los Angeles police are trying to do is unconstitutional," he said. "They are simply trying to scare travelers away by threats of fingerprinting. I am investigating."

On the Oregon front, Governor Charles H. Martin said at Salem that the situation was alarming and that he was investigating through the State police force whether California's border could be closed to transients.

At Carson City, Nevada's Governor, Richard Kirman, said he was "not excited" by the transients' ban, but was watching a possible high tide of border-halted indigents, hurled back onto Nevada relief agencies. As the "war" went into its second day, wires hummed with communiqués from the local front.

. . . Sergeant D. Douglas, in charge of the "expeditionary force," reported to Davis that his men were halting tramps riding the "blind baggage" or railway trains and hitchhiking into the State in autos. Of 16 men stopped at one port, Douglas reported 8 were found to have police records.

Sworn in as local deputies in the counties in which they are stationed, the officers of the squadron were taking hoboes off freight cars, tenders, and blind baggage compartments and holding them on two charges, vagrancy and evading railroad fares. Railroads are cooperating with the police, Chief Davis said. He explained the only reason the railroads had not succeeded earlier in halting the westward influx of tramps was lack of special officers. Some freights carry 50 or 60 hoboes Davis said, and the men on the train crew are helpless to throw them off.

The chief, meantime, defended his plan on the ground that in sending 136 of his men to the State's outposts he has taken a "humane and legal course and the only one that will work."

. . . "If we wait until these thousands of indigents scatter over the 460 square miles of Incorporated Los Angeles, the police department will have little control over them, but if we stop them at the arteries now being guarded, the situation is considerably simplified. If this is done, we confidently expect a 20 percent decrease in the crime total in the next 12 months. Records show that 65 to 85 percent of migratory indigents come to southern California. Fingerprinting of vagrants and street beggars recently showed that approximately 60 percent of these have criminal records. If we remember that to obtain government work one must have been a resident in the

State at least a year [he is referring to being able to participate in a state relief program], it can readily be seen that the hordes of immigrants are not coming to California for work. They are coming to get on relief rolls, to beg, and to steal."

The chief said he expected hoboland's grapevine would promptly pass the word to jungle camps.

* * *

Los Angeles *Herald-Examiner*, February 19, 1936

Group Demands Los Angeles Police: 136 Recalled from California Border

A formal demand that Police Chief James E. Davis' "foreign legion" be withdrawn from California's borders was filed with the police commission today by the American Civil Liberties Union, which asked that the police squads be returned to the city. Clinton J. Taft, California director of the union, said his organization was prepared to seek a court injunction if necessary to stop the police patrol. At the same time, written protests against the "bum blockade" program were filed with the police board by the Hollenbeck Borough Voluntary Board and the Hollywood Open Forum. While the protests were being received the police commission approved the allocation of an additional $1000 to the border patrol of 136 policemen, effective today; another $1000 for February 20, and a third $1000 effective February 21.

SOURCE: Los Angeles Herald-Examiner, August 1935 to February 1936.

ANALYSIS

The events that occurred in Washington during the summer of 1935 are unprecedented in the history of the United States. Never before and never since has either the President or Vice President used or attempted to use the armed forces of the United States literally to attack citizens of the United States. The only occasions on which federal troops have been used inside the country are on those rare occasions that a group of citizens seems likely to block enforcement of a federal law. Certainly there have been occasions when the National Guard was called out, but that has almost always been to protect a group that was being threatened, as at moments during the civil rights era. But this event was of a different magnitude.

Unfortunately, the same cannot be said about relations between a state government and the American people. It happened on many occasions in the South when state and local governments attempted to control the black populations. It happened during the protests that occurred against the Vietnam War during the 1960s, and it also happened in Chicago during the Democratic Party convention in 1968.

It also happened in 1935 and 1936 during the migration of tens of thousands of Dust Bowlers to California. As about half a million people fled the Dust Bowl and sought better places to live, a large proportion of them decided to go to California.

21

SQUATTERS

Harvest Gypsies

- *Document:* This document is excerpted from a newspaper article describing living and housing conditions in the agricultural valleys of California during the Great Depression. Most especially, it concerns the housing available for migrant agricultural workers during that era. The selection is from one part of a series of seven articles that John Steinbeck wrote in 1936 and that became an important source that he used to write *The Grapes of Wrath*.
- *Date:* The article was published in 1936.
- *Where:* The article concerns conditions that existed in the agricultural regions of California, especially the Salinas and San Joaquin Valleys. It was published by one of San Francisco's major daily newspapers.
- *Significance:* Steinbeck's writings, both his articles and *The Grapes of Wrath*, were the most influential sources that informed the general public about the deplorable housing conditions that existed for homeless migrant agricultural workers during the Depression. They had an immediate affect on the public and brought about cries for reform and the creation of more acceptable housing for the migrants.

DOCUMENT

The squatters' camps are located all over California. Let us see what a typical one is like. It is located on the banks of a river, near an irrigation ditch or on a side road where a spring of water is available. From a distance it looks like a city dump, and well it may, for the city dumps are the sources for the material of which it is built. You can see a litter of dirty rags and scrap iron, of houses built of weeds, or flattened cans or of paper. It is only on close approach that it can be seen that these are homes.

Here is a house built by a family who have tried to maintain neatness. The house is about 10 feet by 10 feet, and it is built completely of corrugated paper. The roof is peaked, the walls are tacked to a wooden frame. The dirt floor is swept clean, and along the irrigation or in the muddy river the wife of the family scrubs clothes without soap and tries to rinse out the mud in muddy water. The spirit of this family is not quite broken, for the children, three of them, still have clothes, and the family possesses three quilts and a soggy, lumpy mattress. But the money so needed for food cannot be used for soap or for clothes.

With the first rain the carefully built house will slop down into a brown, pulpy mush; in a few months the clothes will fray off the children's bodies while the lack of nourishing food will subject the whole family to pneumonia when the first cold hits.

Five years ago this family had fifty acres of land and a thousand dollars in the bank. The wife belonged to a sewing circle and the man was a member of the grange. They raised chickens, pigs, pigeons and vegetables and fruit for their own use; and their land produced the tall corn of the Middle West. Now they have nothing.

If the husband works every harvest without delay and works the maximum time, he may make four hundred dollars this year. But if anything happens, if his old car breaks down, if he is late and misses a harvest or two, he will have to feed his whole family on as little as one hundred and fifty [dollars].

. . . Here, in the faces of the husband and his wife, you begin to see an expression you will notice on every face; not worry, but absolute terror of the starvation that crowds in against the borders of the camp. This man has tried to make a toilet by digging a hole in the ground near his paper house and surrounding it with an old piece of burlap. But he will only do things like that this year.

He is a newcomer and his spirit and decency and his own sense of his own dignity have not been quite wiped out. Next year he will be like his next door neighbor.

This is a family of six; a man, his wife, and four children. They live in a tent the color of the ground. Rot has set in on the canvas so that the flaps and the sides hang in tatters and are held together with bits of rusty baling wire. There is one bed in the family and that is a big tick lying on the ground inside the tent.

They have one quilt and a piece of canvas for bedding. The sleeping arrangement is clever, Mother and father lie down together and the children in between them. Then, heading the other way, the other two children lie, the little ones. If the mother and father sleep with their legs spread wide, there is room for the legs of the children.

There is more filth here. The tent is full of flies clinging to the apple box that is the dinner table, buzzing about the fouled clothes of the children, particularly the baby; who has not been bathed nor cleaned for several days.

DID YOU KNOW?

Squatters

Even for those who did not travel, living conditions were ghastly. The new migrants pitched tents along irrigation ditches or on the side of a road close to a spring of water. Some built houses out of corrugated paper tacked to wooden frames. Most camps had no toilets and no clean water. Public health officials grew alarmed. Outbreaks of smallpox, tuberculosis, malaria, and pneumonia were common in camps.

Source: Constitutional Rights Foundation. Bill of Rights in Action. Summer 2005 (21:3). "Dust Bowl Exodus: How Drought and Depression Took Their Toll." Available online at http://www.crf-usa.org/bill-of-rights-in-action/bria-21-3-a.html.

DID YOU KNOW?

… The investigators found that the housing situation was indescribably wretched. One investigator reported that he had found a two-room cabin in which forty-one people from Southeastern Oklahoma were living; another described a one-room shack in which fifteen men, women, and children, "festering sores of humanity," lived in "unimaginable filth." … Most of the boasted "model camps" maintained by the growers were found to be without baths, showers, or plumbing; in most districts, the workers bathed in and drank from irrigation ditches. Eighteen families were found living near Kingsburg, under a bridge. Workers in large numbers were found living in shacks built of linoleum and cardboard cartons; in tents improvised of gunny sacks on canal banks with coffee cans serving for chimneys on their makeshift stoves; in some cases, a bit of carpet or sacking had been tacked against a tree for shelter. One investigator found an entire tent city consisting of "dirty, torn tents and makeshift shacks in a sea of mud."

Living and sanitary conditions are a serious and irritating factor in the unrest we found in the Imperial Valley. We visited the quarters of the cities where live Mexicans, Negroes, and others. We inspected the temporary camps of the pea-pickers, and know that they are similar to the camps that will serve as places of abode of workers in the fields when melons are gathered. This report must state that we find filth, squalor, an entire absence of sanitation, and a crowding of human beings into totally inadequate tents or crude structures built of boards, weeds, and anything that was found at hand to give a pitiful semblance of a home at its worst. During the warm weather when the temperature rises considerably above 100 degrees, the flies and insects become a pest, the children are fretful, the attitude of some of the parents can be imagined, and innumerable inconveniences add to the general discomfort.

Source: Quoted in US Resettlement Administration, Paul S. Taylor, "The Migrants and California's Future: The Trek to California, and the Trek in California" (ms. University of Texas Library, Austin, Texas).

The family has been on the road longer than the builder of the paper house. There is no toilet here, but there is a clump of willows nearby where human feces lie exposed to the flies—the same flies that are in the tent.

Two weeks ago, there was another child, a four year old boy. For a few weeks they had noticed that he was kind of lackadaisical, that his eyes had been feverish.

They had given him the best place in the bed, between father and mother. But, one night he went into convulsions and died, and the next morning the coroner's wagon took him away. It was one step down.

They know pretty well that it was a diet of fresh fruit, beans, and little else that caused his death. He had no milk for months. With his death there came a change of mind in his family. The father and mother now feel that paralyzed dullness with which the mind protects itself against too much sorrow and too much pain.

And this father will not be able to make a maximum of four hundred dollars a year any more because he is no longer alert; he isn't quick at piece work, and he is not able to fight clear of the dullness that has settled on him. His spirit is losing caste rapidly.

The dullness shows in the faces of this family, and in addition there is a sullenness that makes them taciturn. Sometimes they still start the older children off to school, but the ragged little things will not go; they hide in bushes or wander off by themselves until it is time to go back to the tent, because they are scorned in the school.

The better-dressed children shout and jeer, the teachers are quite impatient with these additions to their duties, and the parents of the "nice" children do not want to have disease carriers in the schools. The father of this family once had a little grocery store and his family lived in back of it so that even the children could wait on the counter. When the drought set in there was no trade for the store any more.

This is the middle class of the squatters' camp. In a few months this family will slip down to the lower class. Dignity is all gone, and spirit has turned to sullen anger before it dies.

The next door neighbor family of [a] man, wife and three children of from three to nine years of age, have built a house by driving willow branches into the ground and wattling weeds, tin, old paper and strips of carpet against them.

A few branches are placed over the top to keep out the noonday sun. It would not turn water at all. There is no bed.

Somewhere the family has found a big piece of old carpet. It is on the ground. To go to bed the members lie on the ground and fold the carpet over them.

The three year old child has a gunny sack tied about his middle for clothing. He has the swollen belly caused by malnutrition.

He sits on the ground in the sun in front of the house, and the little black fruit files buzz in circles and land on his closed eyes and crawl up his nose until he weakly brushes them away.

... The first year he had a little milk, but he has had none since.

He will die in a very short time. . . .

... The husband was a share-cropper once, but he couldn't make it go. Now he has lost even the desire to talk.

He will not look directly at you for that requires will, and will needs strength. He is a bad field worker for the same reason. It takes him a long time to make up his mind, so he is always late in moving and late in arriving in the fields. His top wage, when he can find work now, which isn't often, is a dollar a day.

> ## DID YOU KNOW?
>
> There is a continual epidemic of measles, mumps, whooping cough, scarlet fever, and a few cases of small pox among the children. One little boy had infantile paralysis, another diphtheria. They had been admitted to the hospital, but were sent home long before they were able to continue life in a leaky tent. If one child in a family gets a contagious disease, because of the impossibility of isolation, all of them are usually in bed at one time. In one trailer, I found a family of eight children, all in two beds with the measles. The mother who had just recovered from them was sitting on a box nursing a very young baby, also feverish and broken out with measles. One little girl, about eight, squeezed in bed with the others, was very ill with pneumonia. They had no food at all, and no gas for the car and they were miles from a town.
>
> Source: Babb, Sanora, and Dorothy Babb, *On the Dirty Plate Trail: Remembering the Dust Bowl Refugee Camps.* Wixson, Douglas, ed. Austin: University of Texas Press, 2007, 108–9.

The children do not even go to the willow any more. They squat where they are and kick a little dirt. The father is vaguely aware that there is a culture of hookworm in the mud along the river bank. He knows the children will get in on their bare feet.

But he hasn't the will or the energy to resist. Too many things have happened to him. This is the lower class of the camp.

... This is the squatters' camp. Some are a little better, some much worse. I have described three typical families. In some of the camps there are as many as three hundred families like these. Some are so far from water that it must be bought at five cents a bucket.

SOURCE: John Steinbeck, "The Harvest Gypsies: Article 2." *San Francisco News,* October 6, 1936.

ANALYSIS

The novelist John Steinbeck did more than anyone else to publicize the living conditions, including the housing, of migrants from the Great Plains to California during the 1930s. In 1936, just after his first novels had received praise and he was becoming recognized as an important writer, the *San Francisco News* hired him to go to the Salinas and San Joaquin Valleys and investigate the living conditions of the migrant farm workers there.

Steinbeck made several trips through the whole area to gather information about the conditions being experienced by the transient farmers. While he was there, he met Tom Collins, the superintendent of the Arvin camp established by the Farm Security Administration, the fictional Weedpatch that Steinbeck created in *The Grapes of Wrath*. Collins was a tireless advocate for the homeless migrants, and he acted as Steinbeck's guide and teacher. He informed Steinbeck about where to go to get the information that he needed. Apparently, he also loaned Steinbeck the notes he had been keeping about the situation of agricultural laborers. Collins also introduced Steinbeck to Julia Babb, and she, too, loaned Steinbeck her notes. Steinbeck apparently used the observations of Collins and Babb as well as his own experiences to construct *The Grapes of Wrath*.

Steinbeck also used these sources when he wrote seven articles for the *San Francisco News*, which published them between October 5 and October 12, 1936. He wrote them in a style reminiscent to that adopted by the Muckrakers of the Progressive Era who wanted their journalism to bring about social, political, and economic change in the United States. In very much the same way, Steinbeck intended for his articles not only to inform his readers about conditions but also to arouse their passions and especially their anger about those conditions. He, too, hoped to bring about changes.

In 1938, the Simon J. Lubin society collected all seven of Steinbeck's articles into a single text, added an eighth chapter, and published them as a small book. Although Steinbeck had titled his series of articles "The Harvest Gypsies," the Lubin Society renamed it *Their Blood Is Strong*.

A year later, Steinbeck published his great novel *The Grapes of Wrath*. He based the book on the same information that he had used to write the articles. The difference was that the articles were nonfiction and factual. Steinbeck intended them to be an actual picture of conditions as they existed. In contrast, *The Grapes of Wrath* was an artistic composition. He took the same information and presented it differently to engage his readers' attention more strongly. While the characters and situations in *The Grapes of Wrath* were composite pictures constructed by Steinbeck out of his many and various observations, the characters and situations he reported in the "Harvest Gypsies" articles were a journalistic report of what he had seen.

Although the "Harvest Gypsies" articles attracted little attention outside of California, *The Grapes of Wrath* achieved almost instantaneous notice and success. It quickly became a national bestseller and brought national attention to the plight of the "Okies." It also established Steinbeck as one of America's great novelists. He received the Pulitzer Prize for *The Grapes of Wrath* in 1940, and in 1962 he received the Nobel Prize for literature with special mention given to *The Grapes of Wrath*.

FURTHER READING

McWilliams, Carey. *Factories in the Field: The Story of Migratory Farm Labor in California*. Boston, MA: Little, Brown and Co., 1939.

Wixson, Douglas. *On the Dirty Plate Trail: Remembering the Dust Bowl Refugee Camps*. Texts by Sanora Babb; Photographs by Dorothy Babb. Austin: University of Texas Press, 2007.

22

WEEDPATCH CAMP

A Sympathetic Overview

- *Document:* This document is a selection from *Factories in the Field*, an analysis of agricultural conditions in California that was published only a few months after *The Grapes of Wrath*. However, while Steinbeck's work is a magnificent novel, the volume by Carey McWilliams is a journalistic *tour de force*.

- *Date:* The book was published in 1939 and describes events between roughly 1936 and 1939.

- *Where:* The events described in the book occurred in the agricultural heartland of California.

- *Significance:* The book reinforced and supported the picture that Steinbeck had drawn of modern agriculture and the oppression of migrant fieldworkers. From that time on, there could be little doubt that both Steinbeck and McWilliams were describing and analyzing conditions accurately. In this selection, McWilliams is describing conditions in what many people considered to be the model camp for migrant workers, and it was frequently held up as an example of the kind of camp and housing that could be constructed. Ironically, this presentation of the "best" camp may have done more to shape the public thinking about the housing of migratory workers. "If this," they wondered, "is the best housing that can be provided, what must the worst be like?" Unfortunately, some of McWilliams's comments allowed some members of his middle-class readership to overlook the physical and economic shortcomings of the migratory camps and see only what they considered to be the deficiencies of the migratory workers.

DOCUMENT

... The camps may be described as small collective communities. Applicants to the camp must present a card showing that they have registered for such with the United States Employment Service. If admitted to the camp, they are assigned living quarters for which they pay a rental fee of ten cents a day. The camps are laid out, in sections, as small communities. The living quarters consist of platform tents, with kitchenettes and outdoor privies. Diesel heating units provide hot and cold water. The general buildings consist of a utility unit, an isolation unit, a: delousing unit, assembly room, nursery, first-aid unit and child clinic library, a garage pergola and grease rack ... office and living quarters for the general manager, a warehouse, pumphouse, hose-cart, shed, incinerator, shower baths and sanitary units, laundry units and clotheslines. It would be difficult to overemphasize the importance of the fact that the camps provide migratory workers, for the first time, with an adequate supply of decent drinking water and proper sanitation.

The managers have been carefully instructed to establish a large measure of self-government in the camps. What they have attempted to do is introduce the "town-hall" type of government. The Campers' Committee, for example, attends to all matters of discipline and law and order within the camp, and settles all controversial issues. Under the manager's supervision, each person is expected to contribute two hours' work a week for the upkeep of the camp, and in cases where a family cannot pay the ten-cents-a-day fee, they are supposed to work two hours a day. A Recreation and Entertainment Committee has charge of various social and athletic activities.... A Child Welfare Committee and Good Neighbors Committee have charge of various aspects of camp. Every effort is made to induce the campers to solve their own problems. The Good Neighbors Committee, for example, collects and repairs old clothes for those in need. Without exception, our resident managers report that their methods meet with an excellent response on the part of the workers, who show, when encouraged, great capacity for self-government.

I have been privileged to study a series of reports submitted by Mr. Tom Collins, manager of the Arvin Camp, to his superiors. In addition to being social documents of the first importance, these reports make fascinating reading. To take a sample week, Mr. Collins tells of the arrival in the camp of a woman so filthy that she resembled an animal: She had been living for two months on a vacant lot. The whole camp is excited over the arrival of a baby—the first to be born in the camp. Again, Mr. Collins is busy instructing mothers on the technique of trimming toenails, and the general advisability of the procedure, and the use of toilet paper (many of them had never used toilet paper in their lives). He then has to turn his attention to the Baby Clinic, which is well attended, and to the lectures sponsored by the Good Neighbor Committee for the women living in the camp. The baseball game has to be supervised; the weekly dance organized; and committees must be put to work cutting weeds and painting. He notes with approval that the residents soon change their diet; "the old reliable sow belly" is being replaced by fruit and vegetables. In reading these reports, one can see a whole new community coming into existence as these people, who have suffered untold privation for years, slowly,

DID YOU KNOW?

Tom Collins Explains His Attitudes toward Camp

Every day, the duties become more interesting, more absorbing. The piteous, sordid, and miserable cases of neglect, due to various social and economic displacements, which come to us at camp from time to time, spur me on to better and more intensive work. I have found it possible to make the work, my interest and my pleasure. To effectively do this work, I have followed, what I believe is the best quality—do things cautiously, perform the duties quietly, keep in the background and let the results of the work we are accomplishing, be our best and only justification of the program for the migratory laborers, and to have the migrants themselves in the foreground, with their wonderful response to our program of self community government and the progress they have made through this program based on our slogan—the most successful method for helping a person is to help him help himself. Truly, despite the many times they slip, and thereby forcing us to begin again with them, the success we have obtained to date, is due to the migrants themselves.

Source: Memo from Tom Collins to Omar Mills. May 1, 1936. Farm Security Administration Papers, National Archives, Washington, DC. Quoted in Jackson L. Benson, " 'To Tom, Who Lived It': John Steinbeck and the Man from Weedpatch." *JML*, 5, 2 (April 1976), 170.

begin to rehabilitate themselves. . . . Of the utmost importance is the fact that the workers are permitted in the assembly hall and discuss their problems. No attempt is made to organize the workers, but the managers all recognize that the residents of the camp, as American citizens, are free to join any organization that they desire. It is strictly up to them as individuals, whether they want to join a union or not. Potentially the camps provide the measure of stabilization from which organization will unquestionably develop. While living in the camps, the workers can hold meetings; they cannot be evicted; and a measure of protection against vigilantism exists.

In much of the current writing about the problem of farm labor in California, the migratory camps have been hailed as a solution of the farm-labor problem. But the migratory camps are not a solution. They are merely demonstrations of what might be accomplished. At the present time the camps are wholly inadequate; they provide shelter for only a small portion of the workers involved. It should be pointed out moreover that the camps enable the residents to work at very low wages and, to this extent, they have probably tended to keep farm wages at a sub-subsistence level. The solution of the farm-labor problem can only be achieved through the organization of farm workers. The chief significance of the migratory camps is that they provide an agency through which organization can be achieved. Quite apart from this consideration, however, they are social agencies of great practical importance and they demonstrate that the stabilization of migratory labor can be accomplished. Already it is planned to augment the camps by granting five and ten-acre tracts to the residents at nominal prices. . . .

. . . In 1937 it became increasingly apparent that a basic change had taken place in the character of farm labor in California. Although the change had been taking place for some time, it was suddenly realized in 1937 that the bulk of the state's migratory workers were white Americans and that the foreign racial groups were no longer a dominant factor. . . . [T]he pattern of exploitation has not been altered; it remains exactly the same. The established pattern has been somewhat as follows: to bring in successive minority groups; to exploit them until the advantages of exploitation have been exhausted; and then to expel them in favor of more readily exploitable material. . . . From what source, then, was the latest army being recruited? The answer was soon forthcoming: from the stricken dust-bowl areas, from Oklahoma, Texas, Arkansas. The circumstances of their misery made them admirable recruits. They came in without expense to the growers; they were excellent workers; they brought their families; they were so impoverished that they would work for whatever wage was offered. They came, moreover, in great numbers. The growers naturally seized upon these workers as a providential dispensation. But they failed to perceive that, with the arrival of the dust-bowl refugees, a cycle of exploitation had been brought to a close. These despised "Okies" and "Texicans" were not another minority alien racial group (although they were treated as such) but American citizens that were familiar with the usages of democracy. With the arrival of the dust-bowl refugees a day of reckoning approaches for the California farm industrialists.

SOURCE: Carey McWilliams, *Factories in the Field: The Story of Migratory Farm Labor in California*. Boston, MA: Little, Brown and Company, 1939. Used by permission of Nancy McWilliams, executor, estate of Carey McWilliams.

ANALYSIS

American authors published (or tried to publish) at least three outstanding books about homeless migrant farm workers in 1939. The most well-known and celebrated of them was John Steinbeck who wrote *The Grapes of Wrath*. Since its publication, this novel has received great praise and is always included on lists of the "best American novels." It brought Steinbeck a Pulitzer Prize in 1940 and was cited as one of the major reasons for awarding him the Nobel Prize for literature in 1962.

The second author was Sanora Babb. She wrote a much less well-known novel at the same time as Steinbeck, *Whose Names Are Unknown*. When she finished writing it, she sent the manuscript to a legendary publisher, Bennett Cerf, in New York City. He promptly agreed to publish it, telling Babb that he considered the book "exceptionally fine." But, after *The Grapes of Wrath* appeared, Cerf withdrew his acceptance, telling Babb that there was no market for two books about migrant and homeless farmers. Babb tried to interest other publishers, but they all told her exactly what Cerf had said. Discouraged, Babb stuck the book in a drawer where it remained for 65 years. When she found it again, the University of Oklahoma Press agreed to publish it—to glowing reviews. One of them called the book "a little masterpiece," and several others compared it favorably to *The Grapes of Wrath*.

The third superlative book about homeless people published in 1939 was *Factories in the Field: The Story of Migratory Farm Labor in California* by Carey McWilliams. An unknown lawyer at the time, McWilliams would soon gain fame as an author and editor. *Factories* resembled *Grapes of Wrath* and *Names Are Unknown* in several important ways. Like the two novels, it told the story of migrant laborers in California during the 1930s. Also like those books, it was an impassioned plea for the country to do something about the horrible conditions faced by homeless people.

But, there were also important differences between *Factories* on the one hand and *Grapes* and *Names* on the other. Unlike those books, it was not fiction. McWilliams was not only a writer; he was a journalist and an editor, most prominently for 20 years editor of *The Nation* magazine. He presented stories in ways that did not let a reader dismiss or ignore them because they were "not true" or "made-up." McWilliams insisted that he was telling the truth, and he insisted on *not* being overlooked.

The other important difference among the books is that *Factories in the Field* was much broader in scope. Steinbeck's and Babb's books each told the story of a small group of people and how they interacted with each other and the world around them. The power of the two books derived from their readers' ability to identify with a small group of people and empathize with the conditions of their lives. McWilliams, however, painted a broader stripe. He assumed that the reader was already aware of individual stories. He wanted to put those individual stories into a broader context and to explain why those stories had developed as they had. He wasn't interested in telling just the story of the Joads (the protagonists of *The Grapes of Wrath*). He wanted to explain why California agriculture had developed the way that it had, and to tell the reader why migrant farmworkers had no homes and had to endure such miserable living conditions. He wanted people to understand that agriculture in California bore no resemblance to the family farm that Americans had romanticized and fantasized about for generations.

To present that version of reality, McWilliams narrated what he called a "hidden" chapter in the history of California that "commentators have largely ignored," the history of agriculture and its development in the state. McWilliams summed his story up in the Introduction to the book:

It is, in many respects, a melodramatic history, a story of theft, fraud, violence, and exploitation. It completely belies the sense of peace and lassitude that seems to hover over rural California. It is a story of nearly seventy years' exploitation of minority racial and other groups by a powerful clique of landowners whose power is based on an anachronistic system of landownership dating from the creation, during Spanish rule, of feudalistic patterns of ownership and control. The most remarkable single circumstance pertaining to the entire record is the unbroken continuity of control. The exploitation of farm labor in California, which is one of the ugliest chapters in the history of American industry, is as old as the system of landownership of which it is a part. Time has merely tightened the system of ownership and control and furthered the degradation of farm labor. As far as the vast army of workers who operate these vast tracts are concerned, their plight is nearly as wretched today as it was thirty years ago.

In all America it would be difficult to find a parallel for this strange army in tatters. It numbers 200,000 workers and a motlier crew was never assembled in this country by a great industry. Sources of cheap labor in China, Japan, the Philippine Islands, Puerto Rico, Mexico, the Deep South, and Europe have been generously tapped to recruit in ever-expanding ranks. As one contingent of recruits after the other has been exhausted, or has mutinied, others have been assembled to take their places. Although the army has been made up of different races, as conditions have changed and new circumstances arisen, it has always functioned as an army. It is an army that marches from crop to crop. Its equipment is negligible, a few pots and pans, and its quarters unenviable. It is supported by a vast horde of camp-followers, mostly pregnant women, diseased children, and flea-bitten dogs. Its transport consists of a fleet of ancient and battered Model T Fords and similar equipage. No one has ever been able to fathom the mystery of how this army supports itself or how it has continued to survive.... Today the army has many new faces as recruits have swarmed in from the dust-bowl eager to enlist for the duration of the crops at starvation wages. But, in substance, it is the same army that has followed the crops since 1870.

Throughout *Factories in the Field*, McWilliams tells a bleak story about agricultural development and the wretchedness of the agricultural labor force. The only section of the book that is even remotely positive occurs in the next to last chapter, in a section he called "The Migratory Camps." In some ways, this short section seems out of place and seems to have a tone out of character with the rest of the book. It seems so discordant that one has to wonder why McWilliams wrote it.

The best answer seems to be that he was suggesting a way to escape the terrible situation. He wasn't satisfied with only providing another description of the horrible realities, and not content to explain why such conditions existed. McWilliams wanted to suggest that a solution had already been found. That solution was to follow the model that had already been constructed in a few places: establish camps for migratory laborers that resembled the Arvin Migratory Labor Camp near Bakersfield, California. This was one of the first migrant camps established by an agency of the federal government, the Farm Security Administration.

One can argue that McWilliams overemphasized the positive aspects of this camp. However, it is instructive to realize that the Arvin camp also provided the model camp, called Weedpatch, where Steinbeck finally located his characters in *The Grapes of Wrath*. While it was by no means perfect, and had more than its share of flaws, and would probably have been unacceptable to a large part of the American middle class, it was vastly superior to almost any other place where migrant farm workers could attempt to establish homes for themselves.

FURTHER READING

Benson, Jackson J. " 'To Tom Who Lived It': John Steinbeck and the Man from Weedpatch." *Journal of Modern Literature*, 5, 2 (April 1976), 151–95.

Campbell, Ann M. "Records from Weedpatch, California: The Records of the Farm Security Administration." *Agricultural History*, 48, 3 (Summer 1974), 402–4.

"Camps for Homeless Boys." *The New Republic*, 74 (March 15, 1933), 132.

Cox, Martha Heasley. "Fact into Fiction in *The Grapes of Wrath*: The *Weedpatch* and *Arvin* Camps." *Steinbeck Monograph Series*, 8 (1978), 12–21.

"Five Weeks in a Transient Camp." *Commonweal*, 22 (October 18, 1935), 599–601.

Lovejoy, Owen R. "Prison Camps for Homeless Boys." *The New Republic*, 74 (March 1, 1933), 77.

Nealand, Daniel. "Archival Vintages for the *Grapes of Wrath*." *Prologue*, 40, 4 (Winter 2008), 18–27.

"On the Housing Front: Uncle Sam Houses the Migrant Workers." *Architectural Record*, 82 (July 1937), 26.

Parrish, Wayne William. "Federal Camps Tackle Problem of Transients." *Literary Digest*, 118 (July 7, 1934), 33–34.

"Transient Camps Improved." *The Survey*, 71 (April 1935), 120.

23

HOOVERVILLE

A Shanty City

- *Document:* This document is an account of a typical community of urban homeless men (and a few homeless women) during the Depression. It was written by the unofficial mayor of the Hooverville, located in Seattle, Washington.
- *Date:* The document was published in 1940 but was probably written between 1933 and 1936.
- *Where:* The setting of the story is Seattle, Washington.
- *Significance:* The document describes a number of details about a typical Hooverville. It provides insight into the social and political structures, formal and informal, of these impermanent "neighborhoods." It also, once again, indicates the ability of homeless people to manage their own lives and to overcome great disadvantages with bravery and fortitude.

DOCUMENT

This is a true story of my own personal experiences. I was one of the first twenty to build a shack on the property of the Seattle Port Commission, located upon Seattle's waterfront. This settlement passed through many hardships and grew to a shanty city of six hundred shacks and one thousand inhabitants.

I am a lumberjack. I spent almost a quarter of a century in the woods of the Pacific Northwest. Like most lumberjacks, I made fairly good wages, and being no exception to the rule, I spent most of these wages freely. When the world-wide depression struck the U.S.A. in 1929, I had a small savings account in one of Seattle's savings banks, but as the depression dragged on, my savings were gradually exhausted. In October 1931, my funds were gone, and I was compelled to seek help from a community fund agency. At this time no national or state relief system had been set up so the task of caring for the needy was being attempted in a feeble way by the community fund agencies. [They] were not prepared to handle such a gigantic and unexpected problem, and naturally, the relief given, through no fault of theirs, was pretty bad.

I was registered at a Central Registry for single, homeless men and given a ticket that called for one evening meal at a soup kitchen that resembled pig swill more than it did human food, no morning or noon day meal, and as no beds or bedding had been provided yet, I was allowed to sleep upon the hard floor of the institution at night, using a few newspapers that I had picked up during the day for a bed. These conditions caused me to rebel against such a scheme of things and find a way to get away from the thing. I was not alone—there were many others. One week of this abuse was enough.

Mr. Walter Gifford, the telephone and telegraph executive, headed a fact-finding commission, by appointment from President Herbert Hoover, to look into employment and unemployment conditions in the U.S.A. His first official act was to advise America's unemployed not to run around over the country seeking jobs but to stay stationary in some place, so that they might be better taken care of. We immediately took possession of the nine-acre tract of the vacant property of the Seattle Port Commission and proceeded to settle down. We set in with the resources we found strewn over the property to construct relief shelters of our own. We were among the first to face and taste the bitter realities of a social system that could not provide employment for willing workers to enable them to care for themselves, or humane relief system to relieve their sufferings in a time like this.

It seemed but a few short days until more than fifty shacks were set up, and then our troubles began. Business houses in this district did not know us. They considered us a bunch of ne'er-do-well undesirables and wanted to be rid of us. Seattle officials decided our shacks were unfit for human habitation and a menace to health conditions in the city, and posted official notices on our doors informing us of the fact and giving us seven days in which to vacate them. We had no other place to go and thought that the

DID YOU KNOW?

Hooverville, Seattle

These two letters indicate the city government's attitudes toward homeless people and toward the Hooverville that had been in Seattle.

Letter on letterhead stationery of Housing Authority of the City of Seattle
Signed by G. W. Coplen, Chairman
Dated March 4, 1941
Addressed to the City Council, City of Seattle

Dear Madam and Gentlemen:

In our comprehensive survey of housing conditions in the City of Seattle, we included a special study of shacks and at this time wish to submit to you for your information and possible action our findings and recommendations.

We are interested in the "shack" problem even though our own statutory powers are not broad enough to deal with it directly. If shacks continue to remain or their number grew, it is quite possible, in the light of general conditions, that many families will seek to occupy them. Then we would become directly concerned, as would you, in the accompanying threat to good housing, and in the consequent threat to good housing, and in the consequent hazards to health and safety. We deem our work to be preventive as well as corrective.

We do not, however, suggest the immediate or wholesale elimination of shacks, but rather a less disruptive, more orderly or planned method. Specifically, we wish to make the following recommendations:

(1) That none of the present occupants of shacks be forced to vacate at the present time.
(2) That as soon, however, as any shack is no longer inhabited by its present occupants, the proper departments of the City be authorized and directed to demolish it.
(3) That the proper departments of the City be authorized and directed to demolish immediately all presently vacant shacks.
(4) That these departments be authorized and directed to prevent the building of any additional shacks in the City of Seattle.
(5) That notices of these intentions of the City be given to all occupant of shacks, and public notices posted in concentrated and other shack areas.

(It is not the intention of the Housing Authority of the City of Seattle to seek credit (under the United States

Housing Act of 1937, as amended) for any elimination of shacks made pursuant to the above recommendations.)

We have defined a shack as "a dwelling unit of more or less temporary character, constructed without benefit of formal design or plan, of second-hand, nondescript building materials, and located indiscriminately. (In most instances, shacks violate legal building requirements.)"

A total of 1687 shacks was found in the city....

We shall be glad to co-operate in any way we can to the end that Seattle may become a city without shacks.

Sincerely yours,
G. W. Coplen
Chairman

Source: Housing Authority of the City of Seattle to City Council, March 4, 1941. CF 1801-02, Seattle Municipal Archives.

authorities were bluffing, so we paid no attention to the notices. The authorities were not bluffing. At the expiration of the seven-day notice, at five a.m., just as daylight was breaking, at one of the heaviest downpours of rain that fell in Seattle that fall, a regiment of uniformed officers of law and order swooped down upon us, with cans of kerosene and applied the torch. Amidst the confusion that followed, we salvaged our few belongings, and just as soon as the officers were out of sight, we returned and rebuilt our burned shanties.

One month later this performance was repeated. This time we did not rebuild, but dug instead. With any kind of digging tool we could find, we shoveled the loose sand out of the concrete machinery pits, over the top of which we placed tin for a roof. This time we knew that the authorities would have to find another way to get rid of us.

By this time a heated city election was on, and one of the issues was the destruction of the shacks of Seattle's unemployed. The result was a new city administration....

In June, 1932 the new administration was inaugurated, and a committee of different city departments visited us and called us together. The spokesman for the party told us that we were going to be tolerated until conditions improved, that they were going to lay down a few simple rules and regulations for us to follow and for us to select a board of commissioners from the ranks to write these regulations. The rules laid down were most reasonable. The health Commissioner decreed that we must get some materials and build our shacks on top of the ground and come out of the gopher holes. He laid down a few other simple rules covering sanitation. The Police and Fire Department heads were also reasonable.

... After our conference with the Department heads, we went searching ... [for] materials with which to build more suitable homes. By this time the business houses in this district had become better acquainted with us and their attitude toward us changed and they became more friendly, and contributed ... to our needs, in supplying us with ... building materials and ... foodstuffs as well.

It seemed but a few ... weeks until more than a hundred shacks were under ... construction. The grapevine ... carried the news that it was O.K. to build the shacks here and it was amazing at the number who wanted to squat here. Our numbers increased rapidly.

One evening several of us sat around an open campfire and one of the shanty dwellers remarked that, "We must have a name for this place." ... Another remarked, "This is the era of Hoover; let's call this place 'Hooverville.'" So the name "Hooverville" has clung to the place ever since.

The shacks in Hooverville are built out of every sort of material, and all sorts of architecture is followed.... Some are no bigger than piano boxes and some have five rooms. There is no gas, electricity, or running water. Kerosene lamps are used for lighting and wood stoves are used to cook and heat with. We have no modern home furnishings. The furnishings are either castoffs or hand made. Bunks are made of wood; boxes are used for tables and chairs. We discovered that gas tanks from automobiles make good stoves to cook and heat with when set upon legs and a pipe ... fitted to take care of the smoke. The writer's stove is made from an ice tank once used ... to freeze a cake of ice.... An end is fitted with a door, and a hole is cut to take care of the stovepipe, which is made from a discarded gutter pipe.... Many people ... remark that "you fellows have gone back to pioneering." We apply the hobo term and call it plain, downright "jungling."

A big percentage of the men have built pushcarts, using two automobile wheels, no tires and any old sort of a rod for an axle. They push these carts through the alleys of the business district of the city collecting waste materials, mostly paper that is sorted and baled, and sold to the salvage concerns, thus realizing a little each day. Others have made rowboats and fish in the waters of Elliott Bay for a living. Some catch a few fish each day that are sold in Seattle markets and others fish for driftwood that is ... sold to the fuel companies. There are a few ... men who ply their trades ... such as boat building, shoe repairing, selling daily papers, etc. None of them realize very much ... but they can hold their heads up and say, "I am not on relief." ... [W]hen times have been their worst, never more than one third of us have ever been on the relief rolls at any one time. If former President Hoover could walk through ... the little shanty [town] ... bearing his name ... he would find it is not inhabited by a bunch of ne'er-do-wells, but by ... men who are bending every effort to beat back and regain the place in our social system that once was theirs.

Hooverville is the abode of the forgotten man. Seattle city authorities have decreed that no women or children would be permitted to live here, so no more than a dozen women live here.

The men are past middle age in life. Seldom is any one ... less than thirty years of age.

The population is a sliding population. In midwinter it is at its peak, somewhere near one thousand two hundred, and goes down in midsummer to one-half this number. Every spring a lot of fellows decide to leave and go in search of work ... in Eastern Washington or in ... Montana and the Dakotas. They offer their

DID YOU KNOW?

Letter on letterhead stationery of Housing Authority of the City of Seattle
Signed by Jesse Epstein, Executive Director
Dated May 9, 1941
Addressed to Mrs. Frances F. Powell, City Councilwoman

Dear Mrs. Powell:

Under date of March 4, 1941, we submitted to the City Council the results of our survey of shelters in the City of Seattle, together with the following recommendations:

(1) That none of the present occupants of shacks be forced to vacate at the present time.
(2) That as soon, however, as any shack is no longer inhabited by its present occupants, the proper departments of the City be authorized and directed to demolish it.
(3) That the proper departments of the City be authorized and directed to demolish immediately all presently vacant shacks.
(4) That these departments be authorized and directed to prevent the building of any additional shacks in the City of Seattle.
(5) That notices of these intentions of the City be given to all occupant of shacks, and public notices posted in concentrated and other shack areas.

Following the above report and at your request, representatives of several private social welfare agencies and public departments met with you and other members of the City Council to discuss the possibility the objective outlined under recommendation under No. 2 above. At the meeting, because it appeared that the vacating of shacks might be accelerated by municipal notices to vacate at specified times, the represented agencies offered to extend their services under the supervision of the Seattle Housing Authority to those shack occupants who were given notice to vacate. This offer was made with the understanding that the legal aspects of the situation would be officially initiated and completed by the City before the services by social agencies to shack dwellers who wished assistance in relocating could be instituted.

The function of the social agencies is necessarily limited to direct services to specific individuals and can be offered only after the legal steps have been taken by the City or one of its designated; namely, the posting of notices to vacate, and the determination of the date on which specific shacks are to be vacated. Upon official information by the City, or through one of its designated departments, that this legal action has been taken, social agencies under the supervision of the Seattle Housing Authority would then offer their services directly to those shack dwellers who wished assistance in finding other living quarters.

The Seattle Housing Authority is willing to serve in an advisory capacity if called upon, concerning the determination of the order in which shacks are to be vacated, so that the legal steps to be taken by the City will be effectively coordinated with the capacity of the social agencies to offer their services to the individuals who may wish to have such services in finding other living quarters. The services of the public and private social agencies which will work under the supervision of the Seattle Housing Authority are offered to the City Council as a supplementary activity to the legal action which the City may wish to take with respect to the shacktown problem. In those instances where the programs of the social agencies are not broad enough to cope with any particular relocation problem, the solution must necessarily be found elsewhere.

This proposal is concurred in by the Seattle Welfare Council, King County Welfare Department, Family Society of Seattle, and Travelers Aid Society.

Sincerely yours,
Jesse Epstein
Executive Director

Source: Petition of Seattle Housing Authority regarding demolition of shacks, May 12, 1941. CF 170058. Comptroller Files, 1802-01, Seattle Municipal Archives.

shacks for sale . . . and realize a few dollars . . . to tide them over until they are earning again. The prices vary from $3.00 to $25.00 depending upon the size and condition. . . . The same men often return the next fall . . . and buy back the shack at twice that price and have enough left to "hole up" for the winter.

One of the most perplexing problems we had was the problem of numbering our houses so that it would be easy to find anyone. . . . The houses are not built in line on streets and avenues, but are set up in any old way, leaving barely enough room for pushcarts to pass through. After carefully studying the matter . . . we plotted the town in sections using the pushcart lanes for dividing lines, and numbering each section alphabetically, beginning with A and starting 1-A, 2-A, and so on, until section A was filled, then to B, C, and so on, putting not more than fifty shacks to a section. . . .

Questions often asked are, "Where do the residents of Hooverville come from?" "Who are they?" "How do they like to live in Hooverville?" Most of the men are honorable unemployed seamen, lumberjacks, fishermen, and miners. There are, of course, other craftsmen here. Most of them have service records with some Seattle business firm, showing that at some time or other they had been employed by that firm, and if given an opportunity, would be . . . doing useful work again. . . .

Most grown-ups remember the years . . . when great numbers of men roved around over the West, either walking the highways or riding freight trains, carrying big rolls of blankets over their shoulders. "Bundle stiffs" they were called. They picked up jobs wherever they could find them, sometimes in railroad construction camps, or digging tunnels, or building dams. They never stayed very long in one place, and then drifted on. They . . . wore rough clothing and cooked and ate their meals in the jungle camps and unrolled their blankets and slept either in box cars or out in the open. . . . The police always saw to it that they never stayed very long in one town—"just long enough to cook up and boil up" . . . and if Mr. Bundle Stiff did not voluntarily move on, police pressure was used to force his departure. He was being continually informed of there being plenty of work "right over the hill," and that the best thing he could do would be to go and take on some of it. He was always kept on the move. . . .

Hooverville is five years old. In the years that have passed, it is safe to estimate that more than seven thousand people have lived here. . . .

Our settlement has been publicized by teachers and writers. Once they called us pretty low-brow names; now they speak of us in high-sounding words and phrases—"pioneers," "human driftwood," and one writer . . . calls us "life's steerage passengers." He writes, "We walk through Hooverville. Poverty is rearing its ugly head, . . . but is it poverty? The shacks are neat, clean, and orderly. The men live here to escape the moldy existence of flop houses and transient bureaus that reek with disinfectant. Some have lack-luster eyes and seem saturated with misfortune, but for the most part they are chin-up individuals, traveling through life for the minutes steerage."

"What manner of man is the mayor of Hooverville?" "How did he get his job?" "What are his duties?" "How big is his salary?" These are some of the questions I hear asked quite often. . . .

Really, I am no different than anyone else. At the time the settlement was founded, I was called a "Contact Man," a man to contact the city authorities and business houses, if the need arose. A few months later, I was being called "The Mayor." A few months later, a writer in one of the . . . newspapers wrote . . . a syndicated article with the heading, "Hooverville, Seattle's city of shacks, is ruled by a dictator." All of these titles are wrong. I am just a simple person, living among simple people, whose status in life is the same as theirs, trying to do the best I know how to administer in my poor way to their wants. The men often seek my advice and bring their troubles to me. I advise them on many questions. By interceding at the right time, I am often able to prevent many little rows that might develop into big ones.

> ## DID YOU KNOW?
>
> ### A Description of a Hooverville at the Foot of Henry and Clinton Streets, Brooklyn, New York
>
> An insider's view of the city is provided . . . by two residents, Mr. Blair, an unemployed, middle-age machinist, and Mr. Lyon, a fifty-six-year-old seaman who, like many others in his trade, found himself abandoned and without residency rights in one of the many ports serviced by the now-depressed shipping industry. One of the most striking aspects of the stories they told was the ingenuity shown by the residents. Mr. Blair, for example, originally constructed his home out of the body of a discarded truck and his bed out of two old sailor's bunks. He later added an extra room by joining a second truck body to the first. For cooking and warmth, he constructed a stove out of old pipes, iron bars, and ash cans. Mr. Lyon's place, a two-room cottage furnished with some overstuffed furniture that he salvaged from the garbage heap and repaired, and floored with some old discarded linoleum, was appropriately enough referred to by his neighbors as "The Palace." Topsoil carted from a vacant lot provided the bed for a vegetable garden he cultivated outside his door. Other similarly improvised their own homes and implements and a community grew.
>
> *Source:* Quoted in Henry Miller, *On the Fringe: The Dispossessed in America.* Lexington, MA, and Toronto, Canada: D. C. Heath and Company, 1991, 59.

When there is something to be taken up with the city authorities, that job usually falls on my shoulders. When any one is sick, I am the one called upon to get the doctor and get him to the hospital. When the city authorities find anything wrong in Hooverville, I am the one who gets bawled out. My duties are many and varied. Sometimes I sorely tire of them. It is a bigger job being "Mayor of Hooverville" than one would think.

The fame of Hooverville and its mayor has spread far and wide. Seldom a day passes that the mail does not bring a letter addressed to "the Honorable Mayor of Hooverville," written by some person . . . seeking information about the place. It is sometimes a writer wanting material for history, sometimes a social worker who wishes to know something about the place. The most pathetic of them all are those I receive from some mother, asking me to help locate her runaway boy, or from a wife whose husband is missing. I am sometimes able to find the missing person. . . .

My salary is nothing. I do not feel that I am serving the city or state in any capacity. I am serving a bunch of fellows who are on their uppers, the same as I, and who have nothing to pay; consequently, I am not on any kind of a payroll.

As the Depression worsened, and as more and more people lost both their jobs and their dwellings, the newly homeless began constructing ramshackle huts to provide even minimal shelter. Every U.S. city exhibited an area where people without homes used any material they could find—fabric, wood, paper, clay, scraps of metal—to construct shacks and sheds to provide shelter for themselves. These places became known as Hoovervilles—so-called in "honor" of President Herbert Hoover whose policies came to be seen as a major cause of the economic crisis. The picture illustrates the Hooverville constructed in Central Park—right in the heart of New York, the country's largest city. (Library of Congress)

Pretty near every day brings something new. This is just another shanty town, nine and a half acres of ground, but be it ever so humble, it's home sweet home. You ask something about the political and social life. I had a very interesting letter. It was in June 1935, from a school teacher in Tennessee. She says, "I have just read [about Hooverville in] my local paper—." . . .

I told this school teacher that I think all of these men haven't been used to a better home life than this. All we have been used to in the past quarter century is a very hard and rough life. Most of these men have no interest in politics, but I am the Democratic precinct committeeman. I told her that this is a settlement of forgotten men.

Our women down here are in most cases a bad sort. This teacher wrote back and said. "Where are the families of these men? What are their plans for returning to them? I did not know that the Western men are such hermits." It is a question of living the life that we have had to live for the past quarter century. You might say that we have been living in a man's world. A lot of them perhaps have had no families to leave. There are quite a few brought in here. I have never heard of anybody mistreating any woman who came down here, but it is not a safe place for them. We have about a dozen here now. I don't know how many different walks of life are represented here.

Letters from relatives come less and less frequent. Folks get out of touch, and you don't even know if a fellow is living under his right name. There is one man under sentences that I know of living here. He makes his regular reports to the parole board. We know all about it, but nobody else does. They thought that they were living the life of a black sheep and didn't want anybody to know anything about it.

We had one young fellow come in here a while back. (As a rule we don't have young men). He said he was over twenty-one and I said it was all right for him to stay, but I thought he looked kind of young. I happened to pick up an Oregon paper one day and here was this fellow's picture saying he had left home, and he was only seventeen. I went to him and asked him why he didn't write to his mother, but he said he couldn't go back home, that he was "wanted" back there. I wrote to the police chief and he answered that this boy was only wild, not bad, and wasn't wanted for anything but running away. He has gone back home where he belongs now. Pretty nearly every day we have letters asking, "Can you help me find this one or that one?"

These last few days I have had a lot of foreign-born making application for their first papers. My honest opinion is that the average working man doesn't know what he wants in a political way. I really believe that I can count the Communists on the fingers of my two hands from the state of Washington. Down here in this settlement, I find that they are standing pretty solidly behind Mr. Roosevelt and the present administration. They have tried to hand out a little something to everybody.... The foreign-born is taking out his papers so that he can get on the W.P.A. If you haven't got your papers, they'll look at you and say, "You're a nice fellow, but we can't do anything for you." The boys down here don't blame Mr. Hoover for this mess. It is just one of those things that happen.

In voting here, I think we gave Mr. Roosevelt a vote of about 7 to 1. The foreign-born don't take much stock in politics. We have about 80 percent foreign-born and the other 20 percent native born.

The social outlook of most of the men doesn't amount to a very bright future. We feel that we have lived our life—as I say, we have no young men. The average man feels that he has his life ahead of him. The average age is fifty here, and when a man passes that, he feels that his life is over. We have very few here younger than thirty. All we have ever been used to is camps and jungles, so we are used to rough living. This life is nothing new to us at all. We go around here and chin with one another. ... Most of the boys are friendly. We call them by Shorty and Slim and Fat. We get around and visit a lot. Quite a few of the man have radios. President Roosevelt usually makes a hit when he is on the air.

Everybody goes his way providing he doesn't disturb his neighbor. ... If a man is out of eats, I think his neighbor will share with him. One fellow went up town this afternoon, and one groceryman who was going out of business had sixteen pounds of butter and he gave it to this fellow. He brought it back and divided it up among all of us. I would say it is more of an individualistic life, but we do divide up quite a lot. . . . [B]ut it is more of a settlement of rugged individuals.

In case of sickness, they are sent to Harborview Hospital. Veterans and seamen go to the Marine Hospital. It is up to us to see that our neighbors don't throw out rotten foodstuffs, but the boys do pretty well. Our biggest job now is with the Fire authorities. If a spark should get in, it would be gone just like that. I have found men dead in their shacks. They have just passed away during the night. We have had five or six such cases during the past two years. It is up to us to look through their belongings, etc. The coroner takes care of most of it—and looks up his relations—then we give his shack to someone else.

We draw up a few laws, but most laws are not laid down by us, but for us. The city authorities lay them down. I just go along, and if I see someone doing the wrong thing, I just say, "Now, George, this won't do. Let's respect our neighbor a little bit more than this." Drink is our big trouble. We have some D-horners. The biggest part of these men will work hard, but after they get it [money], that is the question, what are they going to do with it afterwards.

Most of the men are very bitter against war. We have probably two dozen World War veterans. We have some Russians here who were in the Russo-Japanese spree. If you try to talk to the average Russian, they just "don't savvy." All we want down here is to be let alone. Rugged individualism is their creed. One of the reasons we came here was to get away from relief organizations. The Salvation Army did everything they could, but when the band used to come down here to play for the fellows, some of them would say, "We came down here to get away from the Salvation Army." I don't blame the Salvation Army. They did everything they possibly could, but this thing was so big that the community fund organization just couldn't handle it.

You can't come here and do just what you want. You can't live alone. You have to respect your neighbor, and your neighbor must respect you. If a trouble-maker doesn't want to listen to me, we call higher authorities than I am to come and get him. The boys drink a little more than they ought to down here.

A good many of the fellows feel blue and down and out. One time I heard my neighbor crying. I advised him to go east of the mountains to pick some cherries or something. I gave him a token so that he could ride out to Interbay where you can catch the train. All the railroads ask is for us to keep out of the way of the train crew and get out of the way of the moving trains. . . .

I made my own stove out of things I collected. This tank was once used to freeze ice in the Arctic Club. I made a talk up there once. When I had finished, I went out the back way, found three of these tanks, picked them up, and brought them home. The stove legs are part of an iron cot. I sawed off the right length, drilled a hole, and put bolts on. I got this white enameled stove shelf from a restaurant supply house. I picked the gutter pipe out of an alley.

The boys get a lot of junk around here. It just takes a little ingenuity to put it together. Sometimes I don't get any sleep at night so many of the boys will be knocking at the door and asking for different things. Last Sunday and Saturday nights, I didn't get one night's sleep. . . .

When some official says he is going to tear down all these shacks, the men ... get excited. A bunch of the fellows picked blackberries from Beacon Hill and I have made a lot of blackberry jelly.

SOURCE: Jesse Jackson, "The Story of Seattle's Hooverville," in Calvin F. Schmid, *Social Trends in Seattle*. University of Washington Press, 1944. Used by permission of University of Washington Press.

ANALYSIS

Jesse Jackson's reminiscence of Seattle's Hooverville and of his "mayoralty" can be read in several different ways: a personal memoir of Jackson, a description of an urban settlement, or as an indication of the continuity between events in the past and events in the present.

Like many other American men during the Depression, Jackson's sojourn as a homeless man began when he lost his job as a timberman. He went to Seattle where he lived on his savings until they disappeared. He seems to have thought of going tramping until an official of the Hoover Administration told homeless men that they should stay where they were so that they could be found and assisted, whereas if they went roaming around the country, they would not be able to be located.

So, Jackson and others like him retreated to a large piece of land owned by the Seattle Port Authority and began to build shacks from whatever materials were lying around. They soon began to call the encampment "Hooverville" as a sarcastic jibe at the very-disliked President of the United States. According to a census taken in 1934, Seattle's Hooverville had 632 men and 7 women living in 479 shanties. Their ages ranged from 15 to 73. The population of the settlement included 478 Caucasians of whom 292 were foreign-born. In addition, there were 120 Filipinos and a handful of Hispanics from Mexico, Costa Rica, and Chile. There were 29 African Americans, and several American Indians and Eskimos.

If Jackson's account is accurate, the community was just that, a "community," and the men treated each other like members of the same community. In fact, there seems to have been some similarity between Hooverville and the Hobo settlements that had previously dotted the country. Very early on, Jackson consciously uses a word from the hobo vocabulary, *jungling*. He then makes it clear that he does not consider the Hoovervillians to be bums, or vagrants, or subhuman. They were extraordinarily clever at using whatever scrap materials they could find to help them complete their homes—and that word is correct, Jackson does call Hooverville "home sweet home" at one point in his reminiscence.

The men also created institutions that resembled those in the larger American world. This is especially noticeable in the treatment of housing. There was a recognition that some people owned some land and dwellings, there was a mechanism to buy and sell the shacks, and most of the men kept their dwellings "neat, clean, and sharp."

It would be stretching more than a little bit to characterize Hooverville as having a government, but Jackson does mention the existence of some commonly accepted rules that were followed. More important, he mentions a number of different ways in which the men formed a real community. Everyone was expected to respect his neighbors, and when Jackson saw a man who had had too much to drink, he told him that his behavior wouldn't do and that he had to respect his neighbors. He remarked that people generously shared food with others in the camp, and he mentioned that one day he had been helping foreigners fill out the forms needed to get their first papers from the U.S. government. Jackson also referred to men with emotional problems because they were separated from families, and he tried to help them rebuild contact with their families.

Finally, and perhaps most important, he noted that most men did not want to take charity because that would cost them their self-respect. Jackson empathized with the other homeless men and worked to create a community with them. It seems most unlikely that they did not reciprocate his feelings and his behavior.

24

PICKING GRAPES IN LODI

Grape Strike at Fresno and Lodi, September–October, 1933

- **Document:** In 1945, an agency of the U.S. Department of Labor, the Bureau of Labor Statistics (BLS), published a report called *Labor Unionism in American Agriculture*. Before writing its report, the BLS conducted extensive investigations about the attempts of farmworkers to create labor organizations to improve both their working conditions and their wages. These investigations also led the BLS to write at length about conflict between agricultural workers and their employers. This section of its report discusses the Grape Strike in Fresno and Lodi, California, in September and October 1933. This particular strike is significant because most of the grape pickers were white whereas farm laborers working other crops were more likely to be Hispanic or Filipino. This difference raises questions of whether the miserable conditions experienced by all farmworkers, especially their housing, resulted from racism based on skin color or on a broader discrimination against farmworkers by large agricultural interests. One question to think about is whether white farmworkers were, in fact, being stigmatized as another racial minority.

- **Date:** The report was issued in 1945 and, as a whole, concerns events that took place throughout the 1930s across the United States.

- **Where:** The events described in this document took place in Lodi and Fresno, California, in 1933.

- **Significance:** These events typified the conditions that farmworkers confronted across the United States, but especially in California in the 1930s. The prevalence of similar circumstances nationally suggests that organizing and relying on unions to improve their economic situation—and thus their housing—was not likely to succeed. Large farmers simply had too much power and too much control over state and local governments. Conditions were so stark that one almost has to wonder if farmworkers could do anything to improve their economic positions.

DOCUMENT

The C. & A.W.I.U. (Cannery and Agricultural Workers Industrial Union) made an . . . unsuccessful bid for leadership among seasonal workers in the grape harvest in and around Fresno and Lodi during the fall of 1933. This movement was one of the most violent that occurred in California agriculture during the thirties, particularly in the techniques for suppression employed by growers and local law-enforcement authorities.

C. & A.W.I.U. organizers were active . . . by mid-August. On August 21, State Labor Commissioner MacDonald announced publicly that a general strike of workers was impending unless the growers agreed to pay at least 25 cents per hour. . . . The vineyardists refused, offering instead a standard rate of 20 cents per hour. A strike followed in Fresno, during the course of which both growers and workers resorted to direct action. The walk-outs around Fresno and Modesto . . . were broken almost immediately by arrests and imprisonment of the more active leaders.

The union meanwhile was organizing pickers in the Lodi area, and the growers were making counter preparations. On September 7 some 800 vineyardists at a mass meeting agreed upon a standard wage scale. . . . Several hundred workers at a mass meeting on September 13 collectively demanded a flat 50 cents per hour and other conditions.

After fruitless negotiation . . . a strike began on September 27, involving more than 500 pickers employed on 150 ranches. . . .

Local authorities used drastic methods to end the trouble on the second day of the strike. The sheriff moved additional deputies into the Lodi area, and 70 special deputies from a loosely formed vigilance committee were later sworn into office by a local justice, with instructions to use "disturbance of the peace charges whenever trouble appeared."

DID YOU KNOW?

Grape Pickers at Lodi

Most of the Filipinos—27,000 or 60 percent—worked in agriculture. Riding . . . old cars and trucks, they moved from field to field, area to area, following the ripening fruits and vegetables. "We traveled, I mean we moved from camp to camp," a Filipino said. "You start out the year, January . . . you'd find a place and it was usually an asparagus camp. . . . From asparagus season, we would migrate to Fairfield, to Suisun, and there the men worked out in the orchards picking fruit while the women and even children, as long as they could stand on their boxes, worked cutting fruits. Filipino farm laborers were shuttled from one place to another—Salinas, Manteca, Stockton, Lodi, Fresno, Delano, Dinuba, San Luis Obispo, Imperial, Sacramento, cutting spinach here, picking strawberries there, then to Montana, where they topped beets, to Idaho to dig potatoes, to the Yakima Valley in Washington to pick apples, and to Oregon to pick hops. . . .

At six o'clock in the evening, the workers climbed into wagons and were taken away from the field. Always the Filipino workers returned to their camps covered with dirt; their bodies sweaty and itchy, they were hardly able to wait for their baths. But sometimes the wait was a long one. In the agricultural camp, a Filipino recalled, there was only one bathtub, a large individualized galvanized can for the use of one hundred workers. Everyone took a bath each day after working, for it was impossible to sleep and rest without bathing. Some five to ten people took a bath in the same water before it was changed and heated again. "So the job of bathing one hundred boys was an ordeal. It took six hours to heat enough water to wash one hundred dirty men." After dinner the tired men went to bed, but many of them slept restlessly." . . .

Their camps were composed of dilapidated bunkhouses and shacks resembling "chicken houses." "The bunkhouse was made of old pieces of wood," one Pinoy remembered, "and was crowded with men. There was no sewage disposal. When I ate, swarms of flies fought over my plate. . . . I slept on a dirty cot; the blanket was never washed." A Japanese grower told an interviewer in 1930 that he preferred to employ Filipinos because they were single men and could be housed inexpensively. "These Mexicans and Spaniards bring their families with them and I have to fix up houses; but," he said laughingly, "I can put a hundred Filipinos in that barn" (pointing to a large fire trap). Sometimes Filipinos were housed in temporary shelters, a cluster of tents. "We lived in tents with board flooring which was very convenient because when it rained, there was no mud," a Filipino said. "We slept in cot beds. They gave us enough blankets. It got cold at nights." Never did it get so cold back home. "Having just arrived from the Philippines, it was hard to get used to the cooler climate. Oh man, sometimes I had to cover myself with the old mattress to stay warm through the night. It was cold, awful cold, and you could feel the wind blowing through the cracks in the wall." Other Filipino farm laborers had to be even more resourceful. "You made your own house, cooked you own food, you had to make your own stove out of anything. In the field, Filipinos, Oakies, and Mexicans—the famer didn't supply you with shelter or anything." . . .

. . . As Rodrigo and thousands of his *kababayan*, or countrymen, struggled for economic justice, they came to realize how determined they were in their "search for a door into America."

But the door was not open to Filipinos. . . .

Filipino immigrants encountered racial discrimination, often finding themselves identified with the Asian groups that had entered the country earlier. . . .

Finding a place to live was usually a frustrating ordeal. Filipinos were told by landlords and realtors, "Orientals are not allowed here." "Only whites are allowed in this neighborhood." "The reason why Orientals are not allowed to rent a place here is the fear that the place might be over-crowded with other nationalities. You were not the first one to try to rent a place here. I have other Filipinos, as well as Japanese, Chinese, and Mexicans in my office, and always I have to turn them away." Furthermore, Filipinos could not buy land because they, Japanese, Chinese, Koreans, and Asian Indians, were not "white" and thus not eligible to naturalized citizenship. "My folks were not citizens," Terry Rosal said, "so they could not buy a house. They bought the house, but the house was under my name and my brother George, and still is. . . . They could never own a farm. They were just laborers working in the agricultural fields." Not permitted to buy a house in Oakland, Antonio and Angeles Mendoza received special help from their landladies. They had been renting an apartment room from two Irish sisters; concerned about the young Filipino couple, the sisters secretly saved the rent money each month and used it to buy a house for them as a gift. "That's how we got to own a house," explained Angeles Mendoza. "One of the white families tried to circulate a petition demanding we move out of the neighborhood, but no other families would sign it." . . .

Source: Ronald Takaki, *Strangers from a Different Shore: A History of Asian Americans.* New York: Penguin Books, 1989. 318–25. Copyright © 1989, 1998 by Ronald Takaki. By permission of Little, Brown and Company.

To combat the "guerilla picketing" of the strikers, two deputies in cars were assigned to every carload of pickets, with orders to arrest them for "disturbing the peace" whenever they attempted to interfere with harvesting of the crop. Col. Walter E. Garrison, who became prominent as a leader of the Associated Farmers of California, was selected to head this group of volunteer deputies.

Arrests grew in number as the strike began to affect the picking operations. By the end of the second day, 8 pickets had been arrested. A vigilante raid on union headquarters in Lodi netted 6 strike leaders who were held on charges of conspiracy to obstruct the law. By the end of the third day, 28 had been jailed.

. . . The strikers held numerous mass meetings . . . to formulate further demands. They threatened that all picking operations would be stopped "even though it required taking pickers from the vineyards." Approximately 1,000 local townspeople and ranchers held a mass meeting in response to this threat. . . . One Lodi businessman and prominent Legionnaire suggested that "all they [the strikers] have got is mob rule. Let's beat them to it." Colonel Garrison and Sheriff Odell led the "peace faction," cautioning against violence.

The following morning several hundred citizens assembled before the union's strike headquarters in Lodi, from which pickets were regularly dispatched. Led by a prominent shipper and vineyardist who was reported to have shouted, "What are we waiting for? To hell with peace talk! Let's get them moving!" the vigilante mob charged the ranks of the strikers with guns, clubs, and fists, and drove them out of town. Later attempts by strikers to meet and reorganize were reported to have been broken up by vigilantes with fire hoses and tear-gas bombs. As a violent aftermath, a striker shot and killed a ranch foreman and made good his escape.

The strong feeling which the strike had aroused among some elements in the community were indicated in the remarks made by Justice Solkmore of the Municipal Court to strikers brought up before him for trial. These were reported in several newspapers and were published in Hearings before the Committee on Labor in the U.S. House of Representatives:

Several of you have listened to nitwits, half-baked radicals. * * * Some of you, I am afraid, are not intelligent enough to know what it is all about. If you were in the right crowd, I would gamble that many of you would go to work at once. I am not attempting to threaten or coerce you. I am warning you, if you insist on jury trials, and if you should be found guilty, you cannot expect leniency from this court....

On October 6, during the preliminary hearings of one striker, held for trespassing, the justice declared in a dispute with the defendant's attorney that—

... These men are nothing but a bunch of rats, Russian anarchists, cutthroats, and sweepings of creation. This defendant doesn't know when he is well off if he wants a jury trial. In some places, they would take him and his kind and hang them from the town hall.

The attorney interrupted with the comment: "But they wouldn't dare to do that here."

"Don't you be too sure about that. This town may see a few hangings yet."

The attorney insisted: "I want a jury trial."

"Juries be damned," replied the judge. "Juries are reminiscent of medievalism. They are a means of escape for guilty men. If I were innocent, I would rather go before a judge. They usually get twelve boneheads to sit on a jury...."

A change of venue was finally granted the striker defendants, on the ground that they could not obtain a fair trial in the Lodi municipal court.

SOURCE: Stuart Marshall Jamieson, *Labor Unionism in American Agriculture*. United States Department of Labor. Bureau of Labor Statistics. Bulletin 836. Washington, DC: GPO, 1945.

ANALYSIS: MODERN VIGILANTES

In 1939, having seen the unspeakable housing conditions of California's agricultural workers, and also having seen the improvements that had taken place at a migrant camp established by the Farm Security Administration, Carey McWilliams suggested a way to improve the quality of agricultural workers' housing. He recommended establishing similar camps for migrant laborers everywhere, not just for a few thousand workers in California.

Perhaps implementing that idea would have succeeded, but we will never know. We will never know for the simple reason that the idea was never tried.

Several reasons explain the failure of McWilliams's suggestion to get off the ground. Given the economic situation of the country in 1939, the idea was probably not realistic. In 1939, the unemployment rate still hovered at about 19 percent, and it only dropped slightly in 1940, to 17.2 percent. In addition, the federal government was running huge budget deficits, and Washington seemed totally disinclined to begin a major new social program. By that time, the crusading zeal of Roosevelt and his New Dealers had faded noticeably, and the President seemed uninterested in such a monumental project. At its maximum, the model camp so admired by McWilliams and others could house only 1,200 people, and its usual population was about 650. Taking a conservative estimate of 200,000 migrant farm workers in California and a population of 1200 residents per camp, the government would have had to construct about 160 such camps to house all of the migrant farmworkers. If the camps housed only 650 people each, the project would have required nearly twice as many camps. There simply was no money for a project of that magnitude and no strong desire to attempt anything like it.

Also, by 1938 and 1939, foreign affairs were dominating Roosevelt's attention. The rise of Adolf Hitler in Germany, Italy's imperialistic desires, and Japan's growing territorial presence in Asia were troubling events that foretold the outbreak of World War II in 1939. Those international problems weighed much more heavily on Roosevelt's mind than the housing conditions being suffered by migrant farmworkers.

There also would have been a personnel problem if the government had tried to provide so many camps and to house so many people. By all accounts, one important reason for the success of the Arvin Camp in California (the one so admired by McWilliams) was its first director, Tom Collins. An unusual man, Collins possessed the ability to let camp residents make all of the basic decisions for themselves and essentially run the camp. He had no particular interest in "maintaining power" and controlling what happened there. He thought his responsibility went no further than helping the residents build better lives for themselves. Collins was so widely credited with the success of the Arvin Camp that he apparently was asked to leave there and supervise the establishment of several similar camps. It would have been all but impossible to locate enough people with the outlook of Collins to replicate his success in 150 or more additional places.

In trying to understand the failure to replicate the housing success experienced at Arvin, one also has to consider some unpleasant political and social realities of the time. Through no fault of their own, the migrant agricultural workers were not particularly popular. The large California fruit and vegetable growers who employed them cared little about the migrant laborers. They only desired this labor force to produce the highest possible profits; that meant working for minimal wages. The best way of assuring this condition was by keeping laborers powerless and downtrodden. The growers did not want this enormous supply of cheap labor to escape from poverty, begin to think that they had the same rights as everyone else, and begin to challenge the power of industrial agriculture. And, there is no mistaking the fact that major agricultural interests in California were extremely powerful, benefiting from strong ties to the established political parties in the state, especially the Republican Party. They easily could, and often did, use those connections for their own advantage and the workers' disadvantage. Also, the Bum Brigade and the attempt of some politicians to close California's borders to incoming migrants provide ample evidence of the unpopularity of the migrant workers pouring into the state.

Finally, the growers had a powerful ally in the form of public hostility to the farm workers. As McWilliams had said, the general public considered the farmworkers to be no different from powerless non-white immigrants. There had never been a strong inclination in California to think about the interests and well-being of foreign immigrants to the state, and that proclivity wasn't about to develop now. Californians easily marginalized the incoming Americans in the same way that they had previously marginalized Asian and Hispanic immigrants to the state. In essence, Californians looked at the migrants from Oklahoma and the Dust Bowl simply as another inferior ethnic group. With a substantial number of the newcomers arriving from the South or southern plains, speaking with a different accent, and almost having a different religion (evangelical Christianity), Californians considered them to be just another group of immigrants whom they could mistreat and take advantage of.

All of that can be seen easily by looking at labor relations in California during the 1930s. California was like an open battlefield with farm workers on one side and large agricultural interests on the other. There were hundreds of strikes during the decade, and there is no doubt about who possessed more power. Nor is there any doubt about how they maintained their power. Government forces almost never entered the fray; rather, government allowed growers to create their own groups of enforcers—vigilantes—and exercise power through them.

For McWilliams's notion of building a large number of camps with improved housing, it would have been necessary for farm workers to gain enough power to bring about change. This they could not do. And because the workers were unable to gain political power or leverage, they were unable to improve their housing conditions.

FURTHER READING

Jamieson, Stuart Marshall. *Labor Unionism in American Agriculture*. Washington, DC: GPO, 1945.

Jones, Lamar B. "Labor and Management in California Agriculture, 1864–1964." *Labor History*, 11, 1 (1970), 23–40.

McWilliams, Carey. *Factories in the Field: The Story of Migratory Farm Labor in California*. Boston, MA: Little, Brown and Company, 1939.

25

ARTS AND CULTURE

A Picture is Worth a Thousand Words

- *Document:* The documents are photographs taken by Dorothea Lange. A professional photographer in San Francisco before the Depression, Lange was one of an extraordinary group of photographers hired by the Farm Security Administration to record life in the United States during the Great Depression.
- *Date:* Lange took these photographs between 1935 and 1939.
- *Where:* Lange took pictures in many different parts of the country, but she made most of the ones presented here either along Route 66, the main highway from Texas to Bakersfield in the Central Valley of California, or in the Central Valley of California itself.
- *Significance:* These pictures vividly document the housing conditions experienced by millions of homeless migrant farm workers during the 1930s. They are particularly significant because they show not just the housing conditions but also small details that reveal how the residents experienced that housing. The pictures are meant to evoke an emotional response from the viewer—and they do.

DOCUMENT

"Drought refugees from Oklahoma looking for work in the pea fields of California." At first glance, this photo snapped by Dorothea Lange in 1935 seems straightforward and easy to "read." The image depicts two adult women and two small children sitting in or standing next to a car or truck laden with their possessions—furniture, suitcases, and buckets along with many other items. However, even a cursory glance at some related documents reveals that the picture is not as simple as it seems. In her notes to the Resettlement Administration (the federal agency that had hired her to photograph the Depression) Lange referred to the passengers as "migrants . . . camping by the roadside." She also commented that by 3:00 PM on the day she took the picture, 23 carloads and truckloads of people from Arkansas and Oklahoma had already crossed the border between Arizona and California. Paul S. Taylor, one of her associates whom she would marry later that year, could have been describing this picture when he wrote that, "the refugees travel in old automobiles and light trucks, some of them home-made, and frequently with trailers behind. All their worldly possessions are piled on the car and covered with old canvas or ragged bedding, with perhaps bedsprings atop, a small iron cook-stove on the running board, a battered trunk, lantern, and galvanized iron washtub tied on behind. Children, aunts, grandmothers, and a dog are jammed into the car, stretching its capacity incredibly." In another place, Taylor envisioned the future of these migrants and predicted homelessness for them. As he put it, many of them "will mill incessantly through the harvests and live in squatters' camps and rural slums. . . . The refugees are conscious of their present destitution and forced mobility, and grope for help. 'Poor folks has poor ways, you know.'—'There's more or less humiliation living this way, but we can't help it. Our tent's wore out.'—'Can't we have better houses?'—'What bothers us travellin' people most is we can't get no place to stay still.'" After reading Taylor's comments, Lange's initial reference to the people depicted as "refugees" becomes more than an offhand label. (Library of Congress)

"Living conditions for migrant potato pickers. Tulelake, Siskiyou County, California." This 1939 picture recalls the one that Lange took in 1935, and it suggests where some migrants slept on their way to California. Without using any words the picture vividly depicts homelessness. Even more, the two images epitomize her work. While they introduce the subject and give the viewer some information, they raise as many questions as they answer. Although the sleeping gear on the ground seems to suggest that the automobile and the surrounding ground serve as someone's "house," the picture leaves a long list of unanswered questions. How do these "residents" get shelter from the elements? Where do they get food and water? Where are their hygienic and sanitary facilities? How do the people whose homelessness is depicted in Lange's photographs spend their leisure and recreational time? How and where do these people interact with family and friends? Part of the power of Lange's pictures comes from her demand that the viewer acknowledge that none of the basic necessities of daily life exist for these people: shelter, food, water, hygiene, sanitation, free time, family, and society. Once again Paul Taylor turned Lange's pictures into words: "the struggle against unsanitary conditions, flies, and bad water is too much for many people, and they give up. 'I hate to boil the water because then it has so much scum on it,' said a pea-picker who drew his water from the irrigating ditch in the usual manner." (Library of Congress)

"Migrant agricultural worker's family. Seven hungry children. Mother aged thirty-two. Father is native Californian. Nipomo, California." In 1936, while travelling through California's Imperial Valley, Lange chanced upon a migrant woman and four of her seven children. Lange quickly snapped a handful of pictures, and these shots became iconic views of homeless agricultural workers during the Great Depression. The great photographer Edward Steichen once called them "the most remarkable human documents ever rendered in pictures." In his analysis, Steichen was almost certainly referring not just to the poverty and hunger of the family but to the psychological and emotional resilience that Lange captured so forcefully. Forty years after Lange took the pictures, and after the mother figure had been identified as Florence Thompson, one of her daughters, Katherine McIntosh (the girl at the far left), told a reporter that her mother was "a very strong lady." She was "the backbone of our family.... We never had a lot, but she always made sure that we had something. She didn't eat sometimes, but she made sure us children had something. That's one thing she did do." When Thompson herself was interviewed, she expressed irritation not at the horrid conditions of her life but at the fact that Lange had never asked her name, had promised never to sell the pictures but did, and had promised to send her copies of the photos but never did. Both mother and daughter recalled that the pictures made them feel shame at their poverty. The homelessness rendered by their poverty seems to have meant less to them than having it displayed publicly. The psychological impact rendered by their need was more significant than the great need itself. In pictures like these, Lange rendered the abstraction of homelessness into a concrete object that any viewer could understand. (Library of Congress)

"Date picker's home. Coachella Valley, California." In her reports about the housing conditions of agricultural laborers in California, Lange supplemented her photographs with verbal descriptions. One of them could have been describing this shanty. It had no foundation and no floor. Its framework consisted of "rough mesquite or tamarisk poles wired together with baling wire," and its walls were an ersatz muddle of palm leaves, tin, and burlap. Likewise, the roof (perhaps covering would be more apt) consisted of corrugated iron, more palm leaves, pieces of cardboard, and scraps of canvas. Plumbing was non-existent, and kerosene lamps and candles provided the only light. Makeshift stoves provided the only available heat. Although the two waif-like children standing in the doorway make one wonder whether this hovel should be called a "home," one is forced to recognize that Lange never criticized or demeaned her subjects regardless of their age, sex, race, or poverty. When she criticized their housing, she never blamed them or accused them of any transgression, and she affords them the same respect that she would have given any middle-class person who had a more conventional home. (Library of Congress)

"Mexican field laborers' houses. Brawley, Imperial Valley, California." César Estrada Chavez is most often remembered as the labor leader who organized the United Farm Workers during the 1960s and 1970s, but he played a role much greater than that. Perhaps more than anyone else, he led the fight to secure for Mexican Americans the full rights belonging to all Americans. Chavez burned to end discrimination against Mexican Americans, and he has frequently been called the Mexican American Martin Luther King. The son of migrant Mexican agricultural laborers, as a child Chavez and his family occupied housing similar to that which Lange photographed so vividly. One of his biographers tellingly described the house in which Chavez grew up in the 1930s. "The Chavez family was homeless and had to spend the winter living in a tent that was soggy from either rain or fog. They used a 50-gallon can for a stove and tried to keep wood dry inside the tent. The children did odd jobs around town while the adults tried to find work. Moving north to the San Joaquin Valley, they stayed in labor camps where they lived in tiny tarpaper-and-wood cabins without indoor plumbing and with a single electric light. There were no paved streets, and in the winter the ground turned into a slippery quagmire." (Library of Congress)

"Company Housing for Cotton Workers near Corcoran, California." Lange took this picture of houses at a large cotton ranch located near Corcoran, California. On these ranches, migrant laborers were "given" housing in one of the shacks, and the rent was deducted from their pay. The tenants were expected to buy all of their food and other supplies at a store owned and operated by the ranchers. Needless to say, rents were high and so were the prices of goods in these company stores. Agricultural laborers rarely took home anything near the amount that they had earned. Living conditions in shacks like these were truly abysmal. After the National Labor Board investigated conditions, one member wrote that cotton growers were "paying less than a starvation wage." He had seen "a tabulation of the pay checks of 204 pea pickers showing an average daily wage of 56 cents. The earnings were somewhat larger at the peak of the harvest; but never were sufficient to satisfy the most primitive needs." One Los Angeles journalist found that families of 10, all of them working, could clear about $2 a day. As for housing, the National Labor Board found "filth, squalor, and entire absence of sanitation and a crowding of human beings into totally inadequate tents or crude structures built of boards, weeds, and anything that was at hand to give a pitiful semblance of a home at its worst. Words cannot describe some of the conditions" seen by members of the Board. In short, it is not unfair to see similarities between the company houses for agricultural laborers in California during the 1930s and the slave cabins on plantations in the South before the Civil War. It is hard to say which were worse. (Library of Congress)

"Migrant Mexican children in contractor's camp at time of early pea harvest, Nipomo, California." Dorothea Lange was a master artist whose photographs expressed a commitment to democratic values and to social justice. To her, all people were worthy and deserving of respect. She depicted poor Americans as being dignified and not disabled. She depicted women as hard-working and competent, not broken and downtrodden. She even portrayed men in poses usually reserved for Madonna figures, beings able to show as much tenderness for their children as mother figures did in traditional Christian iconography. Lange depicted people of all colors and all races as having the same human characteristics and natures. Lange had similar instincts and insights about children. She showed them with the same dignity and humanity as older people, not as unfinished, imperfect adults. She would often picture an older child in an adult posture, showing great tenderness toward a younger sibling. Only by looking closely at many of these pictures do we see that the poor quality of the housing depicted is a fundamental symbol within Lange's art. But the housing, no matter how miserable and how objectionable, never destroys the humanity of the people in Lange's photographs. In this picture of a young girl and her younger brother, their physical postures vividly depict their affection, and the arrangement of the two small figures standing in front of the canvas tent suggests their dominance over it. In this image, Lange implants within the viewer's mind, almost certainly unconsciously, the image of Mary and Joseph at the inn, with their infant in a manger. One analyst has counted Lange's pictures and determined that about one-third of those taken during the Depression portrayed people of color; at the time, however, those pictures did not match commonly held attitudes toward people of color, and most of them were not printed or distributed. As a result, this aspect of Lange's work has often been overlooked. Likewise, her depiction of children as real people has not been emphasized because children have so often been seen as less-than-fully human who require training and civilizing. Lange's depiction of housing, too, has not been fully comprehended. Her portrayal of housing is not just a background or a setting. It represents a hostile aspect of the elemental environment that all people, including children, are able to overcome and transcend. (Library of Congress)

"Oklahoma potato picker's family encamped on the flats near Shafter, California." This picture of Lange's deserves more attention than it has received. The construction of the scene, and the positioning of the subjects in it, gives the photograph an extraordinary power. In the picture, four siblings are assembled in a tent, really only a frame with a piece of canvas thrown over it. The setting is truly dreadful, not even an abode much less a home. There is one single bed for a family of at least six (these four children and their parents). Some of the family's possessions are scattered haphazardly on the ground; a bucket and a shoe lie in the foreground. The food supply—a bunch of potatoes—lies on the ground under the bed. But, what effect does this misery seem to have on the children? Amazingly, none at all. The girl at the left end of the bed is just lying there, musing and looking at her guitar. The two children at the right end of the bed seem to be playing with each other, with the older entertaining the younger. And the fourth child, sitting or standing in the background, seems to be watching his older siblings. "Yes," we can imagine Lange thinking, "conditions are pretty bad. But, calm down, don't worry about it. These kids will survive." One has to wonder what effect this picture might have had if the picture had been widely circulated and seen. Was Lange depicting the wretched conditions of migrant farmers' housing as a call for action to upgrade it? Or, did she mean to reveal the power of these children to overcome their surroundings and suggest that no remedial action was needed? What would people who saw the picture have thought? Would they have come away from it deploring the wretched physical conditions, or would they have walked away and wondered at the capacity of these children to transcend their environment and their housing? Perhaps, better than anyone else, Lange had the remarkable ability to portray people enduring misery but maintaining their ability to overcome conditions and not become their victims. Lange seems to be saying both that these people will endure and also that they deserve better housing. (Library of Congress)

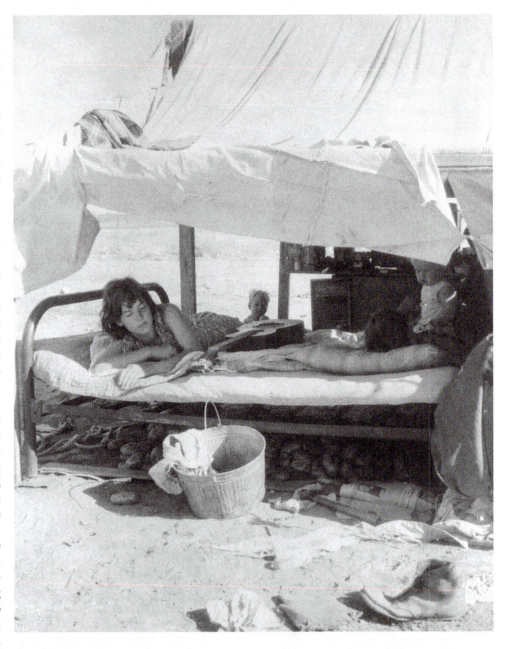

"Texas tenant farmer in Marysville, California, migrant camp during the peach season. 1927 made seven thousand dollars in cotton. 1928 broke even. 1929 went in the hole. 1930 lost everything. 1932 hit the road. 1935 fruit tramp in California." Taken in September 1935, this picture differs from many of Lange's others. Although it depicts a displaced farm family that has experienced hard times, migrated to California, and now lives in substandard housing, this image differs from some of Lange's better-known shots. As Richard Godden, a historian of Southern poverty, has written, "it presents a conventional family group—a little down on their luck, but united." The picture shows a man reaching out to a small child who has grabbed his finger. Next to the man stands his wife, pregnant and holding another small child. She looks down at the first small child. The father also looks at that child who gazes back at him. Godden contends that the shared glances of the family indicate that it was a united group bound closely together. According to Godden, this picture and another, both printed in the *New York Times*, "constituted the type of people deserving of government assistance. The image of the united family addresses the anxieties of small town communities, expressed in urban newspapers, concerning the type of rehabilitation or resettlement client." In the accompanying picture (not shown here), the structure behind the family is revealed to be a large trailer or boxcar, and other details emphasize the family's mobility and the impermanence of their housing. A wheel appears in the background, a license plate lies next to the man, and a tire appears in the foreground. The white triangle to the left of the mother is a large tent. These images confirm that this family is transient. Why then does Lange depict them so differently, as a tightly bound unit and not as a broken family missing one or both parents? The most evident answer surfaces when the location of the picture is recognized. This family was not living in one of the many squatters' camps but had found their way to the new federally sponsored camp in Marysville, California. Whatever its failings, this and the other government camps for migrant workers veered sharply away from the squatters' camps or company camps that preceded them. One state housing inspector wrote that in the squatters' camps he "found filth, squalor and entire absence of sanitation, and a crowding of human beings into totally inadequate tents or crude structures build of boards, weeds, and anything that was found at hand to give a pitiful semblance of a home at its worst. Words cannot describe some of the conditions we saw." He concluded by saying that the squatters' camps "violate all the recognized standards of living." Simon Lubin, another investigator addressed the Commonwealth Club of San Francisco, and he told them that "the workers live in camps . . . the wretchedness of which no photograph and no words possibly could do justice— with filth, disease, and misery on all sides. The muddy drinking water from the ditches is unpalatable and a menace to health." To anyone who had ever endured one of these camps, the federally sponsored camps, whatever their shortcomings, were an improvement and a reason for some satisfaction. In these places, as Lange shows in this picture, a family could survive and overcome its misfortunes together. Even if the physical housing was less than ideal, it was still possible to create a home there. (Library of Congress)

"The Fairbanks family has moved to three different places . . . in one year. Willow Creek Area, Malheur County, Oregon." Lange photographed women much more frequently than men, and some of her pictures of women spring to mind immediately whenever Lange's name is mentioned. She did, however, take pictures of men, and some of them are among her most provocative and insightful. One can only wonder what story she is telling in this picture. It depicts a family of three people living in a tent in Oregon, two parents and a child. But, what are they doing there, and why are they living there, with no sign of any other human life in sight? Why is the man riding away from his wife and their tent, and why does the child seem to be crying? Why does the wife seem to be looking away from the man and child on the horse? The picture only asks, but never answers, these questions. With no other information about the picture available, one can read it as a metaphor for homelessness-poverty, inadequate housing, strained family relations, isolation, abandonment, and no indication of any betterment to come. The land seems bare and desolate, and life seems to have sunk to a level far lower than anyone could endure. The very composition of the picture, with the horse and riders seeming to abandon their world and enter ours suggests the separation that occurred within that world and implies how deeply homeless people want to escape the reality of their lives. At the same time, Lange's most recent biographer, Linda Gordon, also interprets this picture as a reference to the mythic American cowboy image—a man on a horse wearing cowboy boots and a cowboy hat, and who has the ability to take care of himself and his people, no matter how difficult conditions have become. Once again, Lange has been able to show, in a single picture, the horrible conditions of life, especially housing, and also the ability of people to conquer adversity. (Library of Congress)

SOURCE: Library of Congress, Prints & Photographs Division, FSA-OWI Collection.

ANALYSIS

One of the least expected, and one of the few positive, aspects of homelessness in the United States during the Great Depression was its contribution to an extraordinary richness of cultural expression. Homelessness revealed itself in almost every form of art, in both works by homeless people and works about homeless people.

One major example of the artistic representation of homelessness was in literature, especially in the novels of John Steinbeck. The most famous of these was *The Grapes of Wrath*, but he also wrote two other novels in which homelessness played a major role, *Cannery Row* and *Of Mice and Men*. Both of them had important characters who were homeless, and they helped establish Steinbeck's reputation as one of America's foremost novelists.

Although he is the best known, Steinbeck was not the only novelist who used homelessness as an important theme. Sanora Babb wrote many highly regarded short stories as well as her fine novel *Whose Names Are Unknown*. Another relatively unknown woman writer for whom homelessness provided an important plot element was Meridel LeSueur. In 1932, she published the story "Women on the Breadlines" in the magazine *New Masses*, and during the 1930s she, too, like Sanora Babb, wrote a novel, *The Girl*, which remained unpublished for many decades. In it, LeSueur worked out her feelings about how someone could just as easily accept or ignore homelessness.

You can get so you can go on thinking and living in the streets because you got no home. The streets used to be only something you walked through to get someplace else, but now they are home to me, and I walk around, and walk in stores and look at all the people, or I sit in the relief station waiting to see the caseworker, and I sit there close to other women and men, and I look, and I feed off their faces.

Using a different mode of presentation, in 1938 the author and playwright Arthur Arent lifted a powerful phrase from Franklin Roosevelt's Second Inaugural Address and used it as the title for a play that he called "One-third of a Nation." Sponsored by the Federal Theater Project (FTP), it surpassed most of the Project's other offerings and ran in New York for 237 performances. Arent himself was employed by the FTP's Living Newspaper Unit, and he relied almost exclusively on clippings from newspapers and other published works to construct the important dialogue in the play. In episodic form, the story begins in 1924 with the destruction of a ramshackle tenement building in New York City. An unspeakable fire leaves 17 people dead. With those events in the forefront, the play progresses backwards with great realism to 1924 to reveal how such an event could have happened. Although on the surface the story concerns the terrible housing conditions of the past, its power materialized by being an unrestrained attack on housing conditions in U.S. cities in the 1930s.

Housing conditions in the 1930s provoked art forms other than the written word; the spoken word, and especially the harmonic word, matched its significance. In fact, homelessness appeared as a central topic in several musical genres and was especially apparent in popular songs. Some songs about homelessness first appeared in films and then crossed into the sphere of popular music. Some songs were romantic, some satirical, and some were just plain angry.

One of the most famous popular songs about homelessness was called "It's only a Shanty in Old Shanty Town." First performed in a movie, *The Crooner*, in 1932, it became almost the national anthem of homelessness when the highly popular Ted Lewis and his band played the song and recorded it. The message of the song seems to be that homelessness and wealth are not terribly significant and can easily be exchanged for each other. The man singing the song, who says that he is "up in the world," would abandon it all if he could return to his "tumbled down shack by an old railroad track." Waiting there was a queen with "a silvery crown," and that miserable shack was calling him back.

Despite the general popularity of both Ted Lewis and the song, one has to wonder if homeless people, many of them living in abject poverty, responded favorably to a song suggesting that a wealthy man could abandon his fortune so easily and wish it away so willingly. The song must have appealed more to people who had not fallen into homelessness and needed to ease any feelings of discomfort or guilt about their own continued survival while the lives of so many of their fellow citizens had deteriorated so badly.

Other popular songs seem much more likely to have elicited a favorable response from homeless people. Some of the ballads of Woody Guthrie, especially his "Dust Bowl Ballads," spoke much more clearly to, and for, the homeless population. Guthrie himself had been homeless and now sang about his experiences. In doing so, he emerged as one of the loudest voices of homeless people during the 1930s. He also spoke for those Americans who had not yet become homeless but feared such a possibility and worried that they, too, might fall into that condition.

In 1938, Guthrie composed one of his signature songs, "I Ain't Got No Home." He wrote the words as a satirical take-off of a song popularized by the Carter family, "This World Is Not My Home." Their song had begun as a jolly, uplifting Baptist hymn expressing the thought that heaven was really one's home, but when Guthrie heard it, he found it deeply disturbing. He determined that his sentiments came from the song's message—that people should accept their trials on earth while looking forward to their reward in the afterlife. Guthrie decided that people, especially homeless people, needed to hear a different message so he composed a parody. The narrator of the song declared in every stanza that he "ain't got no home in this world anymore." In the first stanza, he explained that he just rambled around, and the police made it hard wherever he went. In the second stanza he related that his siblings were stranded on "a hot and dusty road" and that a rich man had stolen his own home and driven him out of it. In the third stanza, he revealed that he had failed as a farmer, that his income was insufficient to pay his debts, and that his wife "took down and died upon the cabin floor." Finally, in the last stanza, he revealed his view of the "wide and wicked" world. What a "funny place" it was where "the gamblin' man is rich an' the workin' man is poor," and he "ain't got no home in this world anymore."

Other songs about homelessness were sung by homeless people themselves but never became popular favorites, generally not even known to the general public. One of the longest of these was sung in the Arvin Migratory Labor Camp in California that was established by the Farm Security Administration to provide decent housing for transient farm laborers during the Great Depression. We know of the song's existence only because the camp's director, Tom Collins, transcribed the words and reported them in one of his regular reports to the Farm Security Administration.

Eleven Cent Cotton and Forty Cent Meat

Eleven cent cotton and forty cent meat
How in the world can a poor man eat?
Flour up high, cotton down low,
How in the world can you raise the dough?
Clothes worn out, shoes run down,
Old slouch hat with a hole in the crown.
Back nearly broken, fingers all worn,
Cotton going down to raise no more.
Eleven cent cotton, eight bucks pants
Who in the world can have a chance?
Can't buy clothes, can't buy meat
Too much cotton and not enough to eat.
Can't help each other, what shall we do?
Can't solve the problem so it's up to you.
Eleven cent cotton and one dollar hose
Guess we have to go without any clothes.
Eleven cent cotton and forty cent meat,
Cheeks are getting thin because we don't eat.
Try to raise peas, try to raise beans,
All we can raise is turnip greens.
No use talking, any man's weak
With eleven cent cotton and forty cent meat.
Eleven cent cotton and forty cent meat
How in the world can a poor man eat?

Here, in fact, was one homeless man's perception of the world and its problems, expressed as a musical plea for a more just and sympathetic world.

While writers and singers used words to portray homelessness, other artists depicted it visually. Certainly there were painters who articulated their feelings by putting images on canvas or paper. Artists such as Reginald Marsh, Isabel Bishop, and William Gropper focused on life in U.S. cities and developed a highly politicized school of painting known as Social Realism. Some of them became well-known, and their artistic creations received recognition.

However, some visual artists working in a different medium became better known, both then and now. These were the great photographers of the Depression—Walker

Evans, Dorothea Lange, Arnold Rothstein, Ben Shahn, Margaret Bourke-White, and Marion Post Wolcott, among others.

All of these photographers were brought together to photograph the Great Depression in the United States by Roy Stryker. Stryker had been a student of economics at Columbia University where he worked with Rexford Tugwell, a close aide to New York's Governor Franklin D. Roosevelt. After Roosevelt's election as President, he brought Tugwell with him to Washington, and Tugwell asked Stryker to come along, too.

Tugwell appointed Stryker head of the Historical Section (Information Division) of the Resettlement Administration, which was later renamed the Farm Security Administration. Together, Tugwell and Stryker set out to document the country's problems during the 1930s, and Stryker decided that this could best be done by taking photographs.

With the goal of taking thousands of pictures across the country, Stryker hired the finest photographers he could find. He was not especially interested in a photographer's technical knowledge about making photographs; he was much more concerned about finding photographers who could capture the significance of an image and cause the observer intuitively to understand a certain position and point of view about the subject. In an oral interview in 1965, he recounted that the ideal photographers were people who "report[ed] things that they felt and saw based upon past experience, based upon a good deal of investigation. Above all else . . . [they possess] a sincere, passionate love of people, and respect for people. That's the most important thing."

Among the photographers he hired was Dorothea Lange. For many years, Lange had been a successful portrait photographer with a studio in San Francisco. In the first few years of the Depression, she began using her photographic skills to document the severe economic suffering the country was experiencing. Lange said that she had to use her camera to record the effects of the Depression because she "was driven by the fact that [she] was under personal turmoil to do something." She soon gave up portrait photography to devote herself entirely to documenting the social crisis.

Sometime between 1935 and 1937, Stryker saw an exhibition of Lange's Depression pictures and immediately decided to hire her as one of the photographers for the FSA project. Altogether, his unit took more than 150,000 pictures. Among all of these, Lange's stand out and became the best-known. Her images create a certain mood and feeling for time and place, and her pictures have been called "iconic." Her most famous pictures are of people, and she captured their lives with the smallest details of face and gesture. But among her many thousand of photographs, now located in the Library of Congress, are pictures of housing, especially that of migrant agricultural laborers in California. More than any other contemporary evidence, these images convey the quintessence and the reality of homelessness at the time.

FURTHER READING

Blake, Matthew. "Woody Guthrie." *Journalism History*, 35, 4 (Winter 2010), 184–93.

Briley, Ron. "Woody Sez: Woody Guthrie, the 'People's Daily World,' and Indigenous Radicalism" *California History*, 84, 1 (2006), 30–46.

Butler, Martin. *Voices of the Down and Out: The Dust Bowl Migration and the Great Depression in the Songs of Woody Guthrie.* Heidelberg, 2007.

Buttitta, Tony, and Barry Witham. *Uncle Sam Presents: A Memoir of the Federal Theatre Project, 1935–1939.* Philadelphia: University of Pennsylvania Press, 1982.

Casey, Janet Galligani. *The Novel and the American Left: Critical Essays on Depression-Era Fiction.* Iowa City: University of Iowa Press, 2004.

Crist, Elizabeth Bergman. *Music for the Common Man: Aaron Copland during the Depression and War.* New York: Oxford University Press, 2005.

Davis, Keith F. *The Photographs of Dorothea Lange.* Kansas City, MO: Hallmark Cards with H. N. Abrams, 1995.

Federal Writers' Project. *These Are Our Lives: As Told by the People and Written by Members of the Federal Writers' Project of the Works Progress Administration in North Carolina, Tennessee, and Georgia.* Chapel Hill: University of North Carolina Press, 1939.

Finnegan, Cara A. "Social Engineering, Visual Politics, and the New Deal: FSA Photography in Survey Graphic." *Rhetoric and Public Affairs*, 3, 3 (Fall 2000), 333–62.

Flanagan, Hallie. *Arena: The History of the Federal Theatre.* New York: Benjamin Blom, 1940.

Gordon, Linda. *Dorothea Lange, a Life beyond Limits.* London & New York: W. W. Norton &Co., 2009.

Hirsch, Jerrold. *Portrait of America: A Cultural History of the Federal Writers' Project.* Chapel Hill: University of North Carolina Press, 2003.

Lange, Dorothea, and Paul Schuster Taylor. *An American Exodus: A Record of Human Erosion.* New York. Reynal & Hitchcock, 1939.

Lomax, Alan. *Hard-Hitting Songs for Hard-Hit People: [American Folk Songs of the Depression and the Labor Movement of the 1930s].* Notes on the Songs by Woody Guthrie; Music Transcribed and Edited by Pete Seeger. New York: Oak Publications, 1967.

McDonald, William Francis. *Federal Relief Administration and the Arts: The Origins and Administrative History of the Arts Projects of the Works Progress Administration.* Columbus: Ohio State University Press, 1968.

McKinzie, Richard D. *The New Deal for Artists.* Princeton, NJ: Princeton University Press, 1973.

O'Connor, Francis V., ed. *Art for the Millions: Essays from the 1930s by Artists and Administrators of the WPA Federal Art Project.* Greenwich, CT: New York Graphic Society, 1973.

O'Connor, Francis V. *Federal Support for the Visual Arts: The New Deal and Now.* Greenwich, CT: New York Graphic Society, Ltd., 1969.

O'Connor, John, and Lorraine Brown, eds. *Free, Adult, Uncensored: The Living History of the Federal Theatre Project.* Washington, DC: New Republic Books, 1978.

Oral History Interview with Roy Emerson Stryker, 1963–1965. Archives of American Art, Smithsonian Institution.

Penkower, Monty Noam. *The Federal Writers' Project: A Study in Government Patronage of the Arts.* Urbana: University of Illinois Press, 1977.

Remsberg, Rich. *Hard Luck Blues: Roots Music Photographs from the Great Depression.* Urbana: University of Illinois Press, 2010.

Spirn, Anne Whiston. *Daring to Look: Dorothea Lange's Photographs and Reports from the Field.* Chicago, IL: University of Chicago Press, 2008.

Young, William, and Nancy K. Young. *Music of the Great Depression.* Westport, CT, and London: Greenwood Press, 2005.

26

LIQUIDATING THE FEDERAL TRANSIENT PROGRAM

The "Liquidation" of the Federal Transient Service

- *Document:* The document is a "note" published in an important journal for social workers.
- *Date:* The article was published in December 1935.
- *Where:* The journal was published at the University of Chicago.
- *Significance:* The tone of the note indicates how dissatisfied many people were with the way in which the federal government was approaching the problems of homelessness and poverty. The events that the note discusses also raise questions about the willingness or ability of the federal government to decrease the amount of homelessness in the country.

DOCUMENT

On September 6, [1935] the F.E.R.A. notified all state relief offices that no more persons should be accepted for service and relief from special transient funds after September 20. This same ukase announced the "liquidation" of the transient relief program by November 1.

Social workers will recall that the late Senator Bronson Cutting, of New Mexico, introduced a transient relief bill in 1933 and that there was general support for the measure. It was, with his approval and with the approval of social workers who supported his bill, incorporated in the Federal Emergency Relief Act of 1933 . . . that responsibility for nonresident transient and homeless persons was to be a federal responsibility. None of the subsequent acts has restricted the scope of federal responsibility thus acknowledged. Therefore, morally at least, the federal obligation remains unaltered and "liquidation" can be achieved only by reabsorption of the transients into industry or by the substitution of an alternative method of care.

A realistic appraisal of the present outlook for care by either of these two methods discloses the gravity of the situation. Clearly the transients have a bad winter ahead. Many of those unfortunate enough to apply for aid after September 20 have already been forced to resort to begging. Those accepted for care prior to September 20 are at this writing still being carried along on federal funds. The plan is to transfer them to W.P.A. employment. Under date of October 12 the central authority in Washington issued an order to all state Works Progress administrators which said:

Certified heads of transient families and unattached transients not absorbed on other projects must be absorbed in local Works Progress Administration projects in the same way as persons on the local relief rolls. Discrimination against non-residents is definitely contrary to Executive Order No. 7046 . . . and any such policy must therefore be regarded as unauthorized and illegal.

DID YOU KNOW?

Liquidation

Throughout its brief existence, the Transients Bureau was plagued by the familiar and very stubborn conviction, held by the community at large, that transients were dangerous degenerates. Whenever a problem occurred within the camps and shelters and was reported in the local newspapers, there would be a predictable cry of indignation. Most of these incidents revolved around drink: "The arrest of one transient for vagrancy or alcoholism did more to shape community attitudes than the behavior of 100 men working 30 hours a week on community projects." Reports of theft, and every once in a while, more heinous incidents, such as murder or rape, generated frantic outrage. At another level, there was even a touch of jealousy in the critique.

Source: Henry Miller, *On the Fringe: The Dispossessed in America*. Lexington, MA, and Toronto, Canada: D. C. Heath and Company, 1991, 76.

These are admirable sentiments, but the evidence of past experience justifies the fear that they will be widely ignored. A recent news release (November 2, 1935) states that 788,452 individuals are now employed on W.P.A. projects and 172,029 on other federal projects. Thus more than two-and-a-half million additional workers must be assimilated into the new program before the announced goal of "3,500,000 employables at work" is attained.

Many careful students of the relief program think this goal will not be reached. Whether this view is right or wrong, it is certainly clear that a vast majority of resident employables had not been absorbed in W.P.A. when the November 1 deadline arrived and would not be for a considerable period thereafter. While W.P.A. is a federal, not a state, service, certification is left to the state organizations which will undoubtedly reflect the general feeling about transient versus resident unemployed, and it is not to be expected that W.P.A. administrators will be wholly free from it.

The abrupt termination of transient intake on September 20, before any alternative provision for care was in effective operation, violated every tenet not only of community planning but of ordinary fair play. Presumably the shock should fall least heavily on the wealthy and better-organized urban communities. Yet New York has been among the foremost in pleading for a more considered approach to the problem.

The average number of transients under care in New York City each day during September was 6,876. The mayor has declared the municipality will not care for them as they do not have legal residence. Does anyone think that private agencies, even in wealthy New York, can promptly muster the funds to care for this army? The monthly reports of the New York Welfare Council show that not one of the transient family welfare agencies has a total case load half the size of the transient group. A protest issued by the Welfare Council declared that withdrawal of the federal government from transient activities will leave 13,000 individuals stranded in the city.

. . . In certain parts of the country the present plan will mean a return to the deplorable condition of 1932. The number of transients applying for aid each month in some of the towns of New Mexico and Arizona equal or exceed the total population of the community. Senator Cutting knew in 1932 that local funds could not provide even rudimentary physical care for these people. By what miracle local projects in towns of four or five thousand population can assimilate them has not yet been revealed.

The most recently published report of the F.E.R.A. shows roughly 264,000 transients under care in the United States—an increase of 40.2 per cent over the number under care on the corresponding date last year. The service is thus being cut off, not only before W.P.A. is ready to assume the load, but also when the numbers affected by this summary procedure are on the increase.

Has the habit of thinking in terms of millions of cases warped the Washington perspective? In the old days, 264,000 individuals would have been considered a load of catastrophic proportions. The total number of cases assisted by all agencies, both public and private, in the group included in the Registration of Social Statistics in 1928 was only 33,000. In those days a proposal to close up all agencies and throw 33,000 clients onto the street would have seemed preposterous. Now eight times that number—264,000—seems small in comparison with the total case load of 20,000,000 individuals; so small in fact that it has seemed feasible in Washington to turn them back to the mercies of local officials without any valid guarantee that they can be or will be taken care of.

A transient program financed by federal funds has been needed in this country for many years. The need existed in the boom days prior to 1929 and will continue long after prosperity has been restored. The bitter truth is that some of the basic crops and industries of the nation have been and still are dependent upon migratory labor. The unorganized state of the labor market makes possible a ruthless exploitation of these workers. Seldom is their total annual wage sufficient to maintain them throughout the year. Conflicting laws of legal settlement have hitherto left many of them stranded at various seasons in communities where there was no orderly provision to assist them. The federal transient service thus met a need that had long been acute. Because of the depression and the consequent curtailment of employment opportunities, it has not been possible to make constructive plans for these men. But in the future a national transient bureau, working in co-operation with the United States Employment Service, should be able to disentangle this whole problem of seasonal migratory labor. No local or state agency can. Local communities cannot and will not foot the bill which the national demand for a mobile labor supply fosters.

SOURCE: "The 'Liquidation' of the Federal Transient Service," *The Social Service Review*, IX, 4 (December 1935), 765. Used by permission of University of Chicago Press.

ANALYSIS

Despite their many supporters, the Federal Emergency Relief Act (FERA) and the Federal Transient Program (FTP) ended abruptly in the fall of 1935. Many factors accounted for this unexpected development. To many of the agencies' detractors, questions about the proper role of the federal government relative to state and local governments loomed large. They especially took offense that transients accepted into the federal program sometimes received greater benefits than those assisted by state agencies. Others claimed that the programs encouraged transiency by giving benefits to individuals who did not work for them. Still others believed that terminology damaged the ability of the program to gain public acceptance—the use of the word *transient* seemed to imply that that program benefited unstable, wandering, unemployed individuals. Additionally, many in Washington also began to wonder if it would not be more effective to create and fund programs that would provide long-term economic security for many Americans rather than providing short-term assistance to people who were momentarily (hopefully) suffering from temporary (hopefully) economic dislocation.

By the fall of 1935, many members of the administration in Washington had begun to think about economic security for older Americans. While some of the President's advisers undoubtedly thought about this topic independently, the well-publicized political actions of Father Charles Coughlin in Detroit, Huey Long in Louisiana, and Upton Sinclair in California placed the economic condition of older Americans right at the center of public attention. Coughlin's National Union of Social Justice, Long's Share our Wealth Program, and Sinclair's slogan, EPIC, End Poverty in California, all suggested to Roosevelt and his advisers that improving the well-being of transients would not generate the same political gains as devising programs that would benefit a larger percentage of the population.

In mid-1935 the Roosevelt administration began to redesign the federal government's role in providing relief. The federal government continued to provide work relief for the unemployed who were "employable" through the Works Progress Administration (WPA), but it returned much of the responsibility for direct relief of "unemployables" to state and local governments. Meanwhile, under the Social Security Act of 1935 the federal government began assisting individual states to help them provide aid to several groups of disadvantaged citizens: dependent children, the blind, and the elderly poor. Another part of the administration's attempt to restructure aid was to reorganize government agencies to provide work for a much larger number of needy Americans than the FTP—the Rural Rehabilitation Administration (later called the Farm Security Administration), the National Youth Administration (NYA), an expanded Civilian Conservation Corps (CCC), and the Works Progress Administration (WPA). The Rural Rehabilitation Administration would deal with farm problems, and the NYA would assume the educational responsibilities of FERA's programs. The expanded CCC would accept army veterans and more youth into its camps, and the WPA would provide jobs in programs established and supervised by the national government. Nowhere, however, was any consideration given to the plight of destitute and homeless migrants. None of the new federal programs included them, and, because most migrants had not resided continuously for one year in a state, they were ineligible for assistance by state programs.

All that fall, social workers, especially advocates for homeless people, protested the new government policies. Dr. Ellen Potter, chair of the National Committee on Care of Transient and Homeless, testified before the Senate Finance Committee and criticized the new legislation and administrative reorganization strenuously. She especially criticized President Roosevelt, saying that "if we take" him "at his word, that groups of this sort [transients and homeless people] are to be handled by the States and local communities as they were previously, we go back to a system of handling that was of neglect, cruel, and sometimes punitive to these individuals, because local communities, particularly since the depression has become so long and so acute, feel that they have wanted to maintain their own people and did not welcome at all the stranger, even though the stranger came looking for work."

Later that year, in an unsigned note, *The Social Service Review*, a professional journal published at the University of Chicago, agreed entirely with Potter in the document presented above. The dismembering of the FERA and the FTP ended federal government intervention in providing housing for many decades to come.

FURTHER READING

Charles, Searle F. *Minister of Relief: Harry Hopkins and the Depression*. Syracuse, NY: Syracuse University Press, 1963.

Hopkins, Harry L. *Spending to Save: The Complete Story of Relief*. New York: W. W. Norton & Company, Inc., 1936.

Stein, Walter J. "A New Deal Experiment with Guided Democracy: The FSA Migrant Camps in California." *Canadian Historical Association Historical Papers*, 1970, 132–46.

Wickenden, Elizabeth. "Reminiscences of the Program for Transients and Homeless in the Thirties." In *On Being Homeless: Historical Perspectives*. Ed. Rick Beard. New York: Museum of the City of New York, 1987.

Williams, Edward Ainsworth. *Federal Aid for Relief*. New York: Columbia University Press, 1939.

Part IV

STREET PEOPLE, BAG LADIES, AND HOMELESS PEOPLE

The outbreak of World War II in Europe in September 1939, and the entrance of the United States into the war a little more than two years later, ended the Depression. The events also ended homelessness in the United States, at least for the rest of the war.

Once England and France committed themselves to military action against Germany and its allies, the demand for U.S. goods soared, and factory production that had been sluggish for years suddenly became vigorous as U.S. industry attempted to manufacture what England and France could no longer make for themselves. As factory production tooled up, plants suddenly had huge demands for workers, and the unemployment rate began to slip—at first tentatively but with increasing momentum over time.

The entrance of the United States into the war after December 7, 1941, was the final blow against unemployment. This was largely due to the fact that, by the end of the war, 16 million people had served in the Armed Forces of the United States—16 million looking for neither jobs nor places to live.

After the end of the war in 1945, unemployment continued to stay low and did not emerge as an issue of public concern. This occurred, in part, because U.S. factories now began to make once again all of the products that could not be made during the war because of shortages of basic raw materials. In addition, the government had placed restrictions on how other raw materials could be used, another limitation on production. Also, at the end of the war, the United States was unquestionably both the richest and also the most powerful nation in the world. The country felt confident about its position in the world, and most Americans preferred to think about the postwar prosperity rather than the prewar Depression.

During the 1950s, the U.S. economy continued to thrive, and unemployment never reached levels anything like those of the 1930s. The country experienced general prosperity, and Americans believed that conditions like those of the 1930s would never reappear. Certainly there was still poverty in the country, and certainly there were people who could have been considered homeless, but, at that time, these did not seem significant to the prospering middle class.

But poverty and the amount of substandard housing became more evident as the 1950s wore on. The escalating racial conflict nightly crept into the homes of everyone who had a television, and while much of the reporting focused on current events and what was happening right then, investigative journalists trying to give context to their stories could not avoid commenting on the social and economic conditions of black life in U.S. cities—conditions that many white Americans had never perceived or had deliberately, if not consciously, ignored.

After the white public was compelled to see conditions in African-American ghettos, the idea began developing that civil rights meant more than being allowed to attend a particular school or being allowed to vote. Rather, civil rights also included issues of economic justice and economic equality. Over time, gaining economic equality became one of the primary goals of the civil rights movement.

Although leaders of the civil rights movement were more and more seeing economics and poverty as some of the fundamental problems facing the black community, and while many white Americans began to understand job discrimination, homelessness never became a central issue to them. It took another two decades, until the early 1980s, for homelessness to become a subject that could no longer be ignored.

This happened as the great U.S. cities—New York, Chicago, and Los Angeles, among others—all witnessed regular scenes of urban homelessness. Men and women huddled on, or even slept on, street grates to gain a bit of warmth. Every night during the fall and winter seasons, homeless Americans built bonfires on street corners to combat the cold. Rest rooms of public libraries and other city facilities were overrun by homeless people using them for all of their hygienic and sanitary needs, and situations developed like the one in San Francisco where the Civic Plaza was literally turned into a "homeless jungle." Moreover, white Americans began to see that African Americans were only one of many groups confronting poverty and homelessness.

The undeniable presence of unknown numbers of homeless people in the country raised serious questions about social policy. Perhaps the first was, simply, "What is a homeless person?" Were people called "homeless" simply malingerers who chose not to work because of laziness and were too indolent to support themselves? Or, were they people who had somehow been injured by conditions over which they had no control, a disease such as tuberculosis or a social disorder such as racism. And these questions inevitably generated more: Why did homelessness occur? Was homelessness the result of some personal failing such as laziness, or drug abuse, or alcoholism? Or, did it result from some disorder or failing in the larger society: racism, a weak economy, or the desire of the construction industry to build buildings that would appeal more to members of the middle class than the working class or poverty-stricken Americans.

The ongoing discussions of the definition of homelessness, and of the causes of homelessness, soon incorporated the question of how many people were experiencing homelessness. These questions have pervaded every discussion or debate about homelessness for the past three decades—the ones that took place on the floors of Congress, in newspaper columns, and in the visual media. Only within the last few years has a wide consensus begun to emerge about their answers. A broad agreement has slowly developed that all homeless people are not the same, that different groups of homeless people have become homeless for different reasons, that they have experienced homelessness in different ways, and that different groups would benefit from different kinds of programs.

At the same time, it has become generally agreed that all homeless people share two fundamental characteristics. First, they do not possess what most of us would define as a "normal" or "typical" home, that is, a flat, house, apartment, or condo in decent condition that an individual owns or rents, which he or she uses for sleeping on a regular basis, and which he or she generally controls. Second, most homeless people, whatever else they might be, are to some extent poor, ranging from "plain" poor to very poor to extremely poor—but poor enough that, at worst, they can afford no housing at all or, at best, are so poor that they are always at risk of losing the home that they currently have.

And that realization leads to the discussion of another dimension of homelessness—Does homelessness exist because some people do not have enough money to acquire homes? Or does it exist because society has not provided enough affordable housing? Has society allowed a deficiency of housing to develop that is so severe that some people can't afford to acquire it?

However you answer these last questions, there are two possible solutions. One is to make sure that everyone has adequate resources to acquire decent housing; do that by making sure that everyone has enough income. We might say that this is fixing the "demand" side of the demand/supply equation by giving people the resources to be able to demand housing that they can afford to acquire. The other solution is to make sure that the supply of affordable housing is increased to the point that the price of housing decreases and more people can afford to acquire some of it at their current levels of income and wealth. This would be fixing the supply side of the equation.

This latter solution, too, could be done in several ways. One avenue would be to lower the costs of land, materials, and construction labor. That solution, however, seems not to be possible given the nature of our economic system and the unwillingness of some players to have their own resources diminished.

The other tactic to provide housing is to make provisions to subsidize its costs. It seems to be generally accepted that, under ideal circumstances, low-income individuals should spend no more than 30 percent of their monthly income on housing. Therefore the strategy (and this is being tried in various cities) is to have individuals locate for themselves decent, acceptable housing, determine 30 percent of their income, and allocate that sum to pay part of the rental cost. Public subsidies would then pay the rest of the fair market price and the government would subsidize the remainder.

This strategy for dealing with homelessness has been tried in several cities and has met with some success. However, in discussions of this proposal, the same issues that have appeared over and over again for decades still show up. Should the government provide direct assistance to individuals to acquire housing, or is it individuals' responsibility to provide for themselves? How much responsibility does society, in the form of local, state, or federal government, have for protecting and defending the social well-being of our citizens? Does government have any responsibility to make sure that every American has a decent home? Is decent housing a basic human right?

The latest scene of this long-running drama is being acted out right now, and the play will not end until the year 2020. Within the last six months, the president and the secretaries of the major federal departments have made it a national goal to end homelessness in the United States within the next 10 years—more precisely, to end the homelessness of military veterans and children within five years and homelessness for everyone else within 10 years.

This highly commendable goal has received both great acclaim and intense criticism. Some, many of them advocates of homeless people, have said that the goal is praiseworthy and the strongest statement ever made about the government's responsibility to guarantee the quality of life of all Americans. Some of those who applaud the goal also say that the plan is too vague and imprecise. They complain that the government has not gone far enough to guarantee the right of decent housing for all Americans and would prefer a plan that goes further.

At the other end of the political spectrum, there is some agreement that the goal is commendable, and even more agreement that the plan is too vague and lacks real specifics. But the real complaint made by the critics is that government lacks the money to pay for the proposal. These critics also imply that, even if government did have enough money, it would be overstepping its proper boundaries and getting into matters that are not its concern.

There is no way of knowing for at least five years what the outcome of this controversy is likely to be, but the subject will certainly appear and reappear during that time, just as it has for the last century.

27

CHARLES DICKENS COINS
THE WORD

A New Word

- *Document:* The first document is a selection from the *Oxford English Dictionary*. It defines the word *homelessness* and gives some information about its etymology. The second selection is from a novel that Charles Dickens published in 1848. It is from *Dombey and Son*, and it is generally thought to have been the first time the word *homelessness* appeared in a written English document.
- *Date:* *Dombey and Son* was published in 1848.
- *Where:* The novel was published in London.
- *Significance:* Dickens's description of Florence's condition, her feelings, and her actions clearly reveal the ambiguities that the word has signified ever since. Does homelessness mean "being without a permanent residence," or does it also suggest "a feeling of personal loss"?

DOCUMENTS

Homeless, a. . . . 2. Affording no home or dwelling-place.
1797 MRS. RADCLIFFE *Italian* vi, Going forth into a new and homeless world.
1812 J. WILSON *Isle of Palms* II. 455 Thus left by herself on the homeless sea.
Hence **homelessly** *adv.*, in a homeless condition, without a home. homelessness, homeless condition.

1829 *Blackw. Mag.* XXVI. 286 Who o'er this scene of clay Once wandered homelessly. **1848** DICKENS *Dombey* xlviii, Forgetful of her homelessness. **1862** R. VAUGHAN *Eng. Nonconf.* 41 His life of poverty and homelessness.

SOURCE: "homeless," *The Oxford English Dictionary.* 2nd ed., 1989. OED Online. (Oxford: Oxford University Press, 1989), passim. Available online at http://dictionary.oed.com. Used by permission.

* * *

In the wildness of her sorrow, shame, and terror, the forlorn girl hurried through the sunshine of a bright morning as if it were the darkness of a winter night. Wringing her hands and weeping bitterly, insensible to everything but the deep wound in her breast, stunned by the loss of all she loved. Left like the sole survivor on a lonely shore from the wreck of a great vessel, she fled without a thought, without a hope, without a purpose, but to fly somewhere—anywhere.

The cheerful vista of the long street, burnished by the morning light, the sight of the blue sky and airy clouds, the vigorous freshness of the day, so flushed and rosy in its conquest of the night, wakened no responsive feelings in her so hurt bosom. Somewhere, anywhere, to hide her head! Somewhere, anywhere, for refuge, never more to look upon the place from which she fled

... Where to go? Still somewhere, anywhere! Still going on; but where! She thought of the only other time she had been lost in the wild wilderness of *London*— though not lost as now—and went that way. To the home of Walter's uncle.

Checking her sobs, and drying her swollen eyes, and endeavouring to calm the agitation of her manner . . . a familiar little shadow darted past upon the sunny pavement, stopped short, wheeled about, came close to her, made off again, bounded round and round about her, when Diogenes, panting for breath, and yet making the street ring with his glad bark, was at her feet.

"Oh, Di! Oh, dear, true, faithful Di. How did you come here? How could I ever leave you, Di, who would never leave me?"

Florence bent down on the pavement, and laid his rough, old, loving, foolish head upon her breast, and they . . . went on together. Di more off the ground than on it, endeavoring to kiss his mistress, flying, tumbling over and getting up again without the least concern.

. . . Florence, who had again quickened her pace, as she approached the end of her journey, ran across the road . . . ran in, and sank upon the threshold of the well-remembered little parlor.

The Captain, in his glazed hat, was standing over the fire, making his morning's cocoa. . . . Hearing a footstep and the rustle of a dress, the Captain turned . . . at the instant when Florence made a motion with her hand towards him, reeled and fell upon the floor.

. . . "Captain Cuttle! Is it you?" exclaimed Florence, raising herself a little.

"Yes, yes, my lady lass," said the Captain.

. . . "Do you live here?" asked Florence . . .

"Yes, my lady lass," returned the Captain. . . .

"Oh, Captain Cuttle!" cried Florence, putting her hands together, and speaking wildly. "Save me! keep me here! Let no one know where I am! I'll tell you what has happened by-and-by, when I can. I have no one in the world to go to. Do not send me away !"

"Send you away, my lady lass!" exclaimed the Captain. "*You*, my Heart's Delight! Stay a bit!"

. . . Florence could do but one thing more to thank him, and to show him how she trusted in him; and she did it. Clinging to this rough creature as the last asylum of her bleeding heart, she laid her head upon his honest shoulder, and clasped him round his neck, and would have kneeled down to bless him, but that he divined her purpose, and held her up like a true man.

. . . "My, lady lass!!" said the Captain, "you're as safe here as if you was at the top of St. Paul's Cathedral, with the ladder cast off. Sleep is what you want afore all other things, and may you be able to show yourself smart with that there balsam for the still small voice of a wounded mind!"

. . . Florence slept upon her couch, forgetful of her homelessness and orphanage, and Captain Cuttle watched upon the stairs. A louder sob or moan than usual brought him sometimes to her door; but by degrees she slept more peacefully, and the Captain's watch was undisturbed.

SOURCE: Charles Dickens, *Dombey and Son*. London and New York: MacMillan and Co., 1900.

ANALYSIS

Homelessness is a relatively new word in the English language. According to the *Oxford English Dictionary*, the authority on the history of English words, *homelessness* had never appeared in print before 1848. Then, Charles Dickens coined it when he was writing the novel *Dombey and Son*. This was rather daring of Dickens. He was exposing himself to criticism for using a word (*homeless*) incorrectly or for using a word (*homelessness*) that no one had ever heard of and that, possibly, no one could understand.

In fact, a close examination of the text suggests that Dickens had two meanings in mind when he used the word. Both of them are consistent with the story that Dickens is telling, and they are clearly present in this selection from the novel.

At the beginning of the selection, Dickens describes Florence as sad, ashamed, and terrified. She is "weeping bitterly" and feels like the sole survivor of a shipwreck. She is quite alone, wanting to "fly somewhere—anywhere." The meaning of this paragraph is developed throughout the chapter (and the entire novel) as Dickens discloses that Florence has nowhere to go—that she has no home.

But Dickens wove another meaning into the story. Florence's misery results not just from the lack of a residence (abode, residence, address). Her depressed state of mind also emerges from the absence of those fundamental qualities that have the power to transform a house into a home. Her demeanor changes noticeably when the dog, Diogenes, suddenly and unexpectedly appears and lavishes affection on her. Also, the warm, demonstrative greeting that she receives from Captain Cuttle and his response to her plea that he let her stay because she has "no one in the world to go to" strongly suggest that her distress results as much from the lack of warmth and affection from any creature as from not having a physical place that is her abode. Because of the dog's devotion and because of Captain Cuttle's boundless welcome, she is able to sleep soundly, "forgetful of her homelessness and orphanage."

In Florence and in *Dombey and Son*, Dickens has intertwined two different ideas into his use of the word *homelessness*. In the context of the novel, Florence's homelessness is both the condition of not having a permanent place of residence and also not having a place where she receives the kind of love that one is supposed to get at home—the sense that one is so bound up in a place that there is an emotional and inseparable connection between person and place.

While the dual meaning of *homelessness* still exists and people use the word to convey both meanings simultaneously, the word can also be used to express only one of those thoughts, When the word *homelessness* is used as Dickens did, to express both of these ideas simultaneously, a person hearing or reading the word has little trouble understanding what the speaker or writer is saying. But a serious problem can arise if the person using the word, and the person receiving the word, are defining the word *homelessness* differently—if one of them means "not having a permanent abode" and the other means "not receiving the kinds of emotional attachments" so often connected with a home.

If this situation occurs, it can have serious social and political consequences. If one of an author's goals is to end "homelessness," that cannot be accomplished if he or she defines the word *home* as a place that is unmistakably affordable, decent housing, but the audience thinks of *home* as a place where a person obtains the kinds of emotional and psychological connections that the poet Robert Frost meant when he wrote,

Home is the place where,
when you have to go there,
They have to take you in.

To those who define *homelessness* as simply the absence of an appropriate living space, there is one obvious solution—simply provide it or make it possible for a homeless individual to obtain decent housing. And this can be done either by increasing the supply of such housing to make it more available, or it can be done by increasing the amount of resources that a homeless individual has to acquire a home. However, if one defines *homelessness* in the broader sense of being absent love, affection, and identity, there is no such "easy" solution. Unlike real estate, these are intangible, abstract feelings and emotions that cannot be bought.

28

CONGRESS DEFINES
HOMELESS

United States Code

- **Document:** In the Homeless Assistance Act of 1987, Congress defined *homeless* and *homeless individual*. Frequently referred to as the McKinney Homeless Assistance Act or the McKinley-Vento Homeless Assistance Act, this was the first major legislative attempt by the federal government to assume responsibility for the problem. Even so, the document's definition is ambiguous about which definition is meant—the narrower one meaning no permanent physical abode or the larger one also referring to the absence of an emotional attachment to a particular place.
- **Date:** Congress passed this law in 1987.
- **Where:** The law was enacted in Washington, DC.
- **Significance:** This was the first major legislation that Congress has taken with regard to ameliorating homelessness in the United States. Although the law was certainly a step in the right direction, it also defined *homelessness* so narrowly that it excluded many thousands of people who could be called "homeless" using either definition of the word. Also, it is important to note that the use of the word in the law seems to make poverty an essential element of homelessness.

DOCUMENT

Title 42, Chapter 119, Subchapter 1

§ 11301. Findings and Purpose

(a) **Findings**

The Congress finds that—

(1) the Nation faces an immediate and unprecedented crisis due to the lack of shelter for a growing number of individuals and families, including elderly persons, handicapped persons, families with children, Native Americans, and veterans;

(2) the problem of homelessness has become more severe and, in the absence of more effective efforts, is expected to become dramatically worse, endangering the lives and safety of the homeless;

(3) the causes of homelessness are many and complex, and homeless individuals have diverse needs;

(4) there is no single, simple solution to the problem of homelessness because of the different subpopulations of the homeless, the different causes of and reasons for homelessness, and the different needs of homeless individuals;

(5) due to the record increase in homelessness, States, units of local government, and private voluntary organizations have been unable to meet the basic human needs of all the homeless and, in the absence of greater Federal assistance, will be unable to protect the lives and safety of all the homeless in need of assistance; and

(6) the Federal Government has a clear responsibility and an existing capacity to fulfill a more effective and responsible role to meet the basic human needs and to engender respect for the human dignity of the homeless.

(b) **Purpose**

It is the purpose of this chapter—

(1) to establish the United States Interagency Council on Homelessness;

(2) to use public resources and programs in a more coordinated manner to meet the critically urgent needs of the homeless of the Nation; and

(3) to provide funds for programs to assist the homeless, with special emphasis on elderly persons, handicapped persons, families with children, Native Americans, and veterans.

DID YOU KNOW?

Another Way of Conceiving Homelessness

The lack of a single term to describe those who worked in seasonal industries suggests the difficulty of relating their history. Examining late-nineteenth and early-twentieth-century commentaries and investigations, and later historical and sociological interpretations, one finds a vast array of names for these people. In addition to the myriad occupation-specific titles *harvest hand, gandy dancer* (railroad worker), and *lumberjack*, there are the general terms: *hoboes, tramps, bums, homeless men, vagrants, transients,* or *mendicants; migratory, casual, floating, unskilled,* and *seasonal workers* or *laborers; rounders, go-abouts, down-and-outers, the underclass, the working poor, the unemployed,* and, of course, *the working class.*

Source: Sophie Watson with Helen Austerberry. *Housing and Homelessness: A Feminist Perspective.* London and Boston, MA: Routledge, & Kegan Paul, 1986.

Title 42, Chapter 119, Subchapter 1

§ 11302. General definition of homeless individual

(a) **In general**

For purposes of this chapter, the term "homeless" or "homeless individual or homeless person" includes—

(1) an individual who lacks a fixed, regular, and adequate nighttime residence; and

(2) an individual who has a primary nighttime residence that is—

(A) a supervised publicly or privately operated shelter designed to provide temporary living accommodations (including welfare hotels, congregate shelters, and transitional housing for the mentally ill);

(B) an institution that provides a temporary residence for individuals intended to be institutionalized; or

(C) a public or private place not designed for, or ordinarily used as, a regular sleeping accommodation for human beings.

(b) **Income eligibility**

(1) **In general**

A homeless individual shall be eligible for assistance under any program provided by this chapter, only if the individual complies with the income eligibility requirements otherwise applicable to such program.

(2) **Exception**

Notwithstanding paragraph (1), a homeless individual shall be eligible for assistance under Title I of the Workforce Investment Act of 1998 [29 U.S.C. 2801 et seq.].

(c) **Exclusion**

For purposes of this chapter, the term "homeless" or "homeless individual" does not include any individual imprisoned or otherwise detained pursuant to an Act of the Congress or a State law.

SOURCE: 101 Stat. 482, 42 U.S.C. § 11301 et seq.

ANALYSIS

At the beginning of Ronald Reagan's first term as President in 1981, every program in the country meant to address problems associated with homelessness was created, funded, and administered at the state or local level. In the view of the newly inaugurated administration, this was appropriate—states and local jurisdictions were best equipped to handle their own homeless problems, and not the federal government.

However, as homelessness became a more evident public problem, pressure grew for the federal government to address homelessness in a visible way. And, as that happened, some argued that the federal government should be an active participant in addressing the needs of homeless people. In 1986, a Homeless Person's Survival Act was introduced in Congress, but it was never considered or discussed in the appropriate committees of the House of Representatives.

Later that same year, legislation containing parts of the Homeless Person's Survival Act was introduced as the Urgent Relief for the Homeless Act. This proposed legislation included emergency relief provisions for shelter, food, mobile health care, and transitional housing. After an intensive advocacy campaign by advocates for homeless people, the legislation was passed in both houses of Congress in 1987 by large bipartisan majorities. After the death of its chief Republican sponsor, Representative Stewart B. McKinney of Connecticut, the act was renamed the McKinney-Vento Homeless Assistance Act. Somewhat reluctantly, President Ronald Reagan signed it into law on July 22, 1987.

The McKinney Act originally consisted of 15 programs providing a range of services to homeless people, including the Continuum of Care Programs: the Supportive Housing Program, the Shelter Plus Care Program, and the Single Room Occupancy Program, as well as the Emergency Shelter Grant Program. These programs are all included within Title IV of the McKinney-Vento Act.

At the beginning of the law, in Title I, there is a detailed statement of the circumstances that justify the act. It specifies six findings that have persuaded Congress to act. Immediately after this section, the bill provides a definition of *homelessness*. At that point, Congress, at least theoretically, could have defined *homelessness* in any way that it wanted. No dictionary, no social worker, no advocate for the homeless, and no opponent of the homeless could force any particular definition on Congress; it had total discretion. At the least, the legislature certainly could have defined the term broadly to include a wide range of situations from "not having a large enough house" to "being part of a dysfunctional family." Sociologists, demographers, and other social scientists had provided a number of possible ways of thinking about the subject. However, Congress did not accept these options. It chose to provide an extremely limited definition for *homelessness*, focusing almost exclusively on where people lived and especially on where they slept. Putting it another way, Congress basically defined *homelessness* as house*lessness*. In fact, the only other qualification that Congress gave to the definition of *homelessness* was to establish an income limitation; no one whose income surpassed a certain sum could be considered homeless. Congress had clearly come down on the side of the minimalists.

DID YOU KNOW?

Social Construction of Homelessness

[Still another Way of Conceiving Homelessness]

Homelessness is an historically and culturally specific concept. Like poverty … it is a relative concept: people make judgments about their own level of deprivation on the basis of what they see around them. Thus, in a society where mud huts are the most prevalent form of housing, and hence the norm, it is probable that their inhabitants would not, in isolation, consider themselves homeless. If, however, the mud hut dwellers were to compare themselves with those living in wealthier societies, or were themselves to live in a mud hut in one of those societies, the situation could be quite different. Subjectively, they might suddenly begin to see themselves as homeless.

Source: Frank Tobias Higbie. *Indispensable Outcasts: Hobo Workers and Community in the American Midwest, 1880–1930.* Urbana and Chicago, IL: University of Illinois Press, 2003.

FURTHER READING

Lee, Barrett A., Kimberly A. Tyler, and James D. Wright. "The New Homelessness Revisited." *Annual Review of Sociology*, 36 (August 2010), 501–21.

29

MITCH SNYDER CLAIMS "MILLIONS"

Statement of Mitch Snyder, Community for Creative Non-violence, Washington, D.C., Accompanied by Mary Ellen Hombs And John Doe

- *Document:* Mitch Snyder was a totally committed advocate for homeless people. As such, he testified before several House and Senate Committees. This document is several short selections from Mitch Snyder's testimony before congressional committees and a selection from a book that he coauthored. They all concern Snyder's estimation of the number of homeless people in the United States.
- *Date:* Snyder's testimony and the book were given or published between 1980 and 1984.
- *Where:* Snyder's testimony was given before the U.S. Congress in Washington, DC, and the book was published in Washington.
- *Significance:* In the 1980s, Mitch Snyder played a critical role in bringing homelessness to public attention and fighting for the rights of homeless people. In these selections, he especially voices a strong statement about the number of homeless people in the country.

DOCUMENTS

How many people in the District of Columbia are homeless? Thousands. How many nationally? Millions. Of that we are certain.

Precisely how many? Who knows? Certainly not the government. Nor the professionals. Not the business community. Not even those who work with the homeless know for sure.

We have been told that in Chicago there are approximately 1,000 homeless people. We have also been told that in Chicago there are nearly a quarter of a million homeless people. What do the experts say? Those are the experts.

In Manhattan, some claim there are less than 10,000, while others estimate more than 75,000.

In Baltimore, take your choice: 320—or, 8,000 depending on who you ask.

Those who most directly serve District of Columbia's street people were asked, "How many?" Their estimates range from 300 to 15,000.

There is, however, agreement in one area: the number of people on the street has increased dramatically.

Do you get the picture? The picture is there is no picture.

We will discover how many people there were on the street, only after they have come in.

District [of Columbia] officials acknowledge the existence of a few hundred hard-core street people. "Hundreds," they say. "What's all this nonsense about thousands?" they say. "Exaggeration! Rhetoric! Hyperbole!"—they say. But they also say, in hushed tones and only when talking to each other, that more than 12,000 homeless men have passed through the city-operated and funded shelters in 26 months.

Why the reluctance on the part of Government to acknowledge the dimensions, or, in some cases, the very existence of the problem? Simple: who's going to pay for the solution? Besides, as a local judge once commented, the issue lacks sex appeal. Who cares? Who's shocked? Incensed? Where's the advocacy? The outcry? Then, too, the homeless themselves lack any semblance of power: they don't vote, or consume, they aren't organized; statistically, they don't even exist.

SOURCE: U.S. Congress, House. Committee on the District of Columbia. *Problems in Urban Centers.* 96th Cong. 2nd sess., 1980. Serial No. 96-16A, 29–30.

* * * *

Statement of Mitch Snyder, Member, Community for Creative Nonviolence

... There are now more people homeless and destitute in our Nation than we have ever seen before. And we believe that includes the Great Depression years because we have so many more people in this Nation.

Between 2 million and 3 million Americans right now are down and out; they are criss-crossing this country looking for work, begging for jobs. They are living in their cars and tents. They are living in abandoned buildings. They are scrambling and

---

DID YOU KNOW?

Homelessness in Australia

The Supported Accommodation Assistance Program Act of 1994 defines a "homeless person" as follows:

> For the purposes of this Act, a person is homeless if, and only if, he or she has inadequate access to safe and secure housing. (Section 4)

The Act goes on to define "inadequate access to safe and secure housing."

> For the purposes of this Act, a person is taken to have inadequate access to safe and secure housing if the only housing to which the person has access:
>
> a. damages, or is likely to damage, the person's health; or
> b. threatens the person's safety; or
> c. marginalizes the person through failing to provide access to:
>   i. adequate personal amenities; or
>   ii. the economic and social supports that a home normally affords; or
> d. places the person in circumstances which threaten or adversely affect the adequacy, safety, security and affordability of that housing.

Source: Supported Accommodation Assistance Act 1994—Sect 4. Available at http://www.austlii.edu.au/au/legis/cth/consol_act/saaa1994359/s4.html.

As the country's leading spokesperson for homeless people, Mitch Snyder attracted attention during the 1980s with a long series of provocative acts. In 1980, he told a congressional committee that there were far more homeless people in the country than had ever been imagined. In 1985, he forced President Ronald Reagan to allow an abandoned federal building to be used as a homeless shelter. And in 1989, he commissioned a statue of the holy family that depicted them as homeless people that he displayed on the steps of the United States Supreme Court. (AP/Wide World Photos)

scraping as best they can to hold their families and themselves together, and they are not doing a very good job of it.

SOURCE: U.S. Congress, House, Comm. on Banking, Finance, and Urban Affairs, Subcommittee on Housing and Community Development, *Homelessness in America*, 97th Cong., 2nd sess., 1982. Serial No. 97-100, 16–17.

* * * *

Selection from *Homelessness in America* by Mary Ellen Hombs and Mitch Snyder

We must work from a single point: this is America, 1982. Homelessness is a problem of massive and increasing proportions, affecting at least 2 million people.*

*No one can say with certainty how many people in this nation are homeless. Not until they come inside will we know for certain how many there are. However, in 1980, we *prepared a report, for a Congressional committee, on the national dimensions of the problem. At that time, we concluded that approximately 1 percent of the population, or 2.2 million people, lacked shelter. We arrived at that conclusion on the basis of information received from more than 100 agencies and organizations in 25 cities and states. That figure has since been widely used by the media, politicos, and organizers. It is as accurate an estimate as anyone in the country could offer, yet it lacks absolute statistical certainty.*

In gathering information for this book, we have learned nothing that would cause us to lower our original estimate. In fact, we would increase it, since we are convinced that the number of homeless people in the United States could reach 3 million or more during 1983. [Italics in original]

SOURCE: Mary Ellen Hombs and Mitch Snyder, HOMELESSNESS IN AMERICA: A Forced March to Nowhere. Washington, DC: Community for Creative Nonviolence, 1982. xvi.

ANALYSIS

Since the middle of the 1980s, the study of homelessness has taken new directions and has been studied in different ways. The kind of participant observation practiced by Nels Anderson, Josiah Flynt, or Jack London no longer satisfies most of the scholars, authors, and journalists interested in understanding and improving social situations and social conditions. The emotion-laden photographs made by Dorothea Lange and other photographers are often considered "soft." The pictures are not considered to be "scientific" evidence about the nature or consequences of homelessness, and there is a strong demand for "real" evidence.

Chief among those insisting on precise information about the number of homeless people (and many other subjects, too) are government officials responsible for developing and implementing policies. As government, and especially the federal government, has assumed a greater role in developing policies to improve social conditions and solve social problems, government officials have demanded (and have sometimes obtained) what they consider to be "hard evidence" about social conditions. They want "proof" that certain policies will produce certain outcomes. For example, if Congress considers legislation to provide publicly financed drugs to people suffering from certain fatal diseases, it would surely want "proof" that those drugs are highly effective. Senators and Representatives would not be satisfied with impressionistic statements such as "three of my best friends all recovered from cancer when they took large doses of that drug" or "I have heard about many people who recovered from small-pox after they took that medicine." Government officers would demand unquestionable statistics showing that people who took a certain drug recovered in much higher percentages than people who did not take it. This is exactly the procedure followed by the Food and Drug Administration when it is considering whether to license a new drug.

To move this discussion back into the context of homelessness, it is only since the end of World War II that this kind of statistical information has been gathered and analyzed. The statistical methodologies involved in determining relationships, for example, among homelessness, poverty, alcoholism, drug abuse, religion, and family dysfunction in a large population such as that of the United States, or even a large state such as California, or a large city such as Houston, Texas, are so complex that they could not have been performed previously with any reasonable speed or accuracy without spending prohibitive amounts of human time and effort.

The development of modern supercomputers, available at a reasonable cost, made this kind of analysis possible and practical only within the past half century. Remember, it was only in 1952 that the first commercial computer was able to predict the outcome of the presidential election accurately when only one percent of the total votes had been counted, and it was not until the mid-1970s that the first personal computers became available. When thinking about the development of computers and computing power, it is important to remember that some of the earliest personal computers possessed more computing power than the Univac that predicted Dwight Eisenhower's election at such an early hour. Even more amazingly, the Windows operating system, which most people now take for granted, did not appear until 1985, only a quarter of a century ago.

The widespread availability, relatively low price, and extraordinary power of current computers have made it possible for researchers, investigators, and government officials to ask more complicated questions and to demand more exact answers than have ever before been asked and answered. Suddenly, someone examining homelessness had the ability to find an answer to the question of whether significant relationships exist among homelessness, poverty, occupation, sex, age, and family dysfunction as well as to consider if there was a statistical likelihood that one of those topics had caused any of the others and which of the variables were independent and which were dependent—that is, did poverty cause homelessness (did people become homeless because they had insufficient money)? Or, did homelessness cause poverty (did people lack money because they were unable to groom themselves appropriately because they did not have a place to clean themselves and maintain a wardrobe)?

The federal government's assumption of greater responsibility for solving social problems since the Depression of the 1930s, along with the fact that the relevant, necessary data can now be gathered and analyzed, have had a huge affect on the analysis of demographic and population data. As the federal government tried to improve social and economic conditions in the country, it could now reasonably demand that hard evidence be provided to show that a certain policy or program would have the desired outcome. And, the more expensive the policy or program, the more clear-cut government officials wanted that evidence to be.

The question, then, clearly, becomes how that information can be provided. Part of the answer is to acquire the numbers that will allow a computer to make the statistical calculations needed to justify a statement. If one wanted to demonstrate that there is a causal relationship between the amount of homelessness in a society and the amount of poverty in that society, one would have to punch a number of different pieces of information into the computer: the total number of people in the society, the number of homeless people in the society, the number of poor people in the society, the number of homeless people in the society who are poor, and the number of poor people in the society who are homeless. And, after all of that information has been submitted to the computer and analyzed, the results can still be questioned or challenged. Did the researcher consider other important relationships and reject them, for example, alcoholism. Had the researcher considered whether alcoholics were more likely to be homeless or poor than were non-alcoholics? And, what was the nature of the relationship? Did alcoholism cause people to become homeless because buying alcohol diverted their resources away from the provision of homes? Or, did homelessness cause people to become alcoholics because their lives were so miserable and they wanted to escape?

Questions about the meaning and interpretation of homelessness statistics were asked at just about the same time that the United States became increasingly aware of the existence of homelessness. The recognition of homelessness was intensified by the greater frequency with which Americans encountered unkempt, scruffy-looking people sitting or lying on sidewalks and surrounded by bags containing all of their possessions. The increased perception of homelessness also stemmed from the amount of attention garnered by advocates for homeless people and by the media, both print and broadcast. One social scientist has shown that in 1981 the *Reader's Guide to Periodical Literature*, the most important cumulative index to popular magazines published in the United States, contained fewer than 10 references to homelessness. By 1989 the number of citations in the *Reader's Guide* had reached nearly 100. Likewise, in 1981 the annual index to the *New York Times* contained 11 references to homelessness. By the end of the decade, in 1989, the index contained 427 citations.

Perhaps no single individual contributed more to the national awareness of homelessness than Mitch Snyder, a man revered and reviled at the same time. Snyder had grown up in Brooklyn, New York, where he married and had several children. However, he left his family, began hitchhiking west, and was arrested for grand auto theft. He spent several years in a federal penitentiary where he met and was deeply influenced by two Roman Catholic priests, the Berrigan brothers, Philip and Daniel, who were strong social activists and vigorous protestors against U.S. involvement in Vietnam.

After being released from prison, Snyder returned to his family but left again after about a year. This time, he went to Washington, DC, where he became an active member of the Community for Creative NonViolence (CCNV), an organization that was assisting poor people obtain medical care, legal services, food, and shelter.

Snyder quickly became one of the driving forces at CCNV, and he pulled the organization to devote more of its time and effort to easing conditions among the city's homeless population. As time passed and homelessness received more public attention, Snyder became the most publicly visible person in the country working on their behalf. He and his activities received widespread national attention, and when Congress decided to investigate homelessness in the United States, Snyder was one of the first people asked to testify before congressional committees. He testified several times during the early1980s, and, during that time, he also coauthored a book about contemporary homeless with one of his colleagues, Mary Ellen Hombs.

Throughout the 1980s, Snyder continued working tirelessly on behalf of homeless people in highly noticeable and provocative ways. He almost single-handedly forced the federal government to turn an abandoned federal building in Washington, DC, into a shelter for homeless people. He made his demands highly visibly and dramatically. On several occasions, he and some of his associates went on extended hunger strikes and continued them until the government capitulated or they themselves came to the brink of death.

The documents provided here are all taken from some of Snyder's earliest testimony before Congress and from the book he wrote with Mary Ellen Hombs. They reveal some of his passion about homelessness and also point to one of his most well-known claims about the number of homeless people in the United States. Snyder's recurring assertions about the extent of homelessness were widely accepted and quickly became one of the most contentious questions about homelessness facing the government because of its potentially tremendous impact on the amount of resources that would be needed to end the problem.

30

HUD DISAGREES SHARPLY

How to Count

- *Document:* The document is taken from the 1984 Report on Homelessness issued by the Department of Housing and Urban Development.
- *Date:* The report was issued in 1984.
- *Where:* The report was released in Washington, DC.
- *Significance:* This report presents a different estimate of the number of homeless people in the United States from the one presented by Mitch Snyder. The report also emphasizes how controversial numbers and their interpretation can be, illustrates the necessity of having clear definitions, and shows how a social issue can quickly become politicized.

DOCUMENT

No one has done a thorough census of the homeless population in the United States. In the absence of one, some observers have claimed that the national total is as high as two or three million persons, and this estimate has received fairly wide circulation. Lower estimates such as 250,000 to 500,000 have also been given, but the two million figure has been cited more frequently by the media, by estimates at Congressional hearings, and by various organizations. The estimate originated in testimony by the Washington, D.C.–based Coalition for Creative NonViolence for the House [of Representatives] Committee on the District of Columbia on July 31, 1980.

However, while the testimony by the CCNV contains information on the homeless situation in several localities, nowhere does the CCNV actually give a figure of one percent [of the total population] or 2.2 million. What is actually said is "How many people in the District of Columbia are homeless? Thousands. How many nationally? Millions. Of that we are certain. Precisely how many? Who knows?"

There is a clear need for more systematic evidence to help in assessing existing estimates. In order to evaluate their validity, four approaches which rely on a variety of information sources and procedures are presented. The use of more than one approach to arrive at a national estimate helps to ensure the reliability of the results, given the difficulty of assessing the size of a population as fluid and often hidden as the homeless. While each approach, in and of itself, has strengths and weaknesses, when combined they tap many different information sources and extrapolation procedures. The approaches include: (1) published local estimates; (2) interviews with local observers in a national sample of 6 Metropolitan areas; (3) interviews with a national sample of shelter managers; and, (4) a combination of shelter and street counts.

The first procedure uses the highest local estimates available but makes no assessment of their reliability in order to see whether extrapolating them to the nation would produce a figure close to the highest existing national estimate. A second approach involves systematically collecting estimates, and assessing their quality, from a range of informants in a random national sample of metropolitan areas. A third approach is a variant of the second; estimates are gathered from one "front-line" group; the managers of shelters for the homeless. A fourth method differs from the first three in that it is based on actual counts of those in shelters or on the streets. The shelter population is based on a nationally representative probability sample of shelters; the street count was done by the U.S. Bureau of the Census, as part of the 1980 decennial census, in a non-random sample of cities.

... As best as can be determined from all available data, the most reliable range is 250,000 to 350,000 homeless persons. This represents the total number of people, nationally, who were homeless on an average night in December 1983 or January 1984, and includes anyone who meets the criteria for homeless adopted in this study. It is important to note that this group consists of people who have been chronically homeless and those who are temporarily without shelter.

SOURCE: U.S. Department of Housing and Urban Development, Office of Policy Development and Research, *A Report to the Secretary on the Homeless and Emergency Shelters*. Washington, DC: GPO, 1984. Reprinted in U.S. Congress, 98th Cong., 2nd sess., House, Committee on Banking, Finance and Urban Affairs, Subcommittee on Housing and Community Development and Committee on Government Operations, *HUD Report on Homelessness*, Banking Committee Serial No. 98-91. May 24, 1984, 338–40, 348.

ANALYSIS

According to the Foreword and Introduction to this report issued by the Department of Housing and Urban Development, Samuel Pierce, the secretary of HUD, asked the Office of Policy Development and Research to provide him with "data and information on homelessness and emergency shelters in America." While the report does not say so explicitly, reading it makes it clear that Secretary Pierce intended to discredit the Community on Creative NonViolence and its estimate that the number of homeless people in the United States exceeded two million. This document overtly criticizes the testimony (of Mitch Snyder) in Congressional hearings and questions whether the CCNV had actual numbers to support their claim about the number of homeless people that had been so widely accepted.

Snyder and his supporters eagerly accepted the challenge of the HUD Report, and Snyder once again testified to a House Committee, this time to a joint meeting of subcommittees of the Committee on Banking, Finance and Urban Affairs and the Committee on Government Operations. In his oral testimony, and especially in his Written Statement to the Committee, Snyder said that he strenuously "object [ed]" to HUD's report. He criticized the way in which its authors had gathered information, the kinds of questions they had asked, the people and organizations they had interviewed, and the way in which they had interpreted information. He said that he had traced down some of the Office's informants and that "not once" did he "encounter anyone of whom HUD had asked the question 'How many homeless people are there in your city, on any given night, including in your estimate those on the street, in the shelters, and in the jails and hospitals who were homeless when they went in and will be homeless when they come out?' Everyone to whom he spoke told him that, had they been asked *that* question, in *that* way, their answers would have been *very* different and much higher."

This open disagreement between Snyder and his supporters on one side, and HUD and its supporters on the other, reveals the difficulty of determining the number of homeless people in the country. It is not the problem of defining *homeless* that was discussed earlier in this book. Rather, it is also the question of how one structures a study, including who conducts the study, who interprets the evidence collected, and who interprets and reports the results.

31

MAKING SENSE OF THE CONFLICT

It's All in the Method

- *Document:* This article attempts to explain why discrepancies such as those between the estimates of Mitch Snyder and the Department of Housing and Urban Development existed.
- *Date:* The article was published in 1996.
- *Where:* The research and analysis contained in the article were conducted at the University of Maryland.
- *Significance:* This article uses several different methodologies to estimate the number of homeless people in the United States. Its purpose was to try to reconcile the disagreements and come up with a more accurate assessment of the amount of homelessness in the United States.

DOCUMENT

The HUD estimate was attacked ferociously by the advocates of the homeless on two main grounds. First, it was argued that HUD had pressured its staff and consultants to keep the local estimates low. . . . In fact, most city estimates used by HUD were very similar to those quoted by the advocates [for the homeless] and sometimes were higher. The second objection was more plausible. It was claimed that while local experts had given estimates for their city, HUD had calculated the homeless rate as though the estimates applied to the whole metropolitan area.

A 1987 study done for the Committee for Food and Shelter by ICF Inc. assumed that this latter criticism was valid and adjusted the HUD figures upward by adding an additional percentage for the suburban homeless. . . . The ICF study, by making these generous assumptions, resulted in the highest total produced by using social science procedures. Their estimate was 735,000 on any one night and as many as two million over the course of a year.

... Three years later ... a study for the National Bureau of Economic Research used an ingenious procedure for estimating the size of the street population. Because most individuals move *from* the street and *back to it again*, if one questions the shelter population about the frequency of their shelter usage, one can calculate the number outside the shelters. ... [The authors] questioned a New York City shelter sample about their shelter usage and, extrapolating from this, calculated that in 1983 there were 279,000 homeless, while by 1985 the number had grown to between 343,000 and 363,000. The accuracy of these estimates depends on the New York sample being representative of the homeless population nationwide. ...

However, in a recently published book Christopher Jencks [a sociologist] used data from a national sample of homeless persons to calculate shelter usage for different categories of the homeless (single adults, couples, etc.). He concludes that "about 50,000 Americans were homeless during March 1987. That figure clearly has a large margin for error. Any figure between 300,000 and 400,000 would be easy to defend. Estimates above 500,000 are considerably harder to reconcile with the available evidence."

Three studies have counted the homeless and used their data as the basis for national estimates. In 1988, Martha R. Burt and Barbara E. Cohen of the Urban Institute surveyed soup kitchens and homeless shelters in large cities and concluded that the number of homeless in these areas was 229,000. From this, they projected that the national total was between 567,000 and 600,000. A year later, Peter H. Rossi [another sociologist] ... argued that "the most believable national estimate is that at least 300,000 people are homeless each night in this country, and possibly as many as 400,000 to 500,000. ... This estimate was an extrapolation for his rigorous count of the homeless in Chicago. In the 1990 census a special effort was made to count the homeless with 15,000 enumerators going to locations frequented by homeless persons. This produced a total of 228,621 homeless persons on March 20. ... This figure is obviously a minimum because it does not include any adjustment for persons missed by the census takers of living in locations not targeted by the census count. ..."

It is striking that most of the social science estimates, although based on different procedures, cluster around the 300,000 to 400,000 figure. The range between the highest and lowest estimates is surprisingly small, from just under 300,000 to just over 700,000. Because most studies used rather generous assumptions about the inaccuracies of the counting procedures, it is possible that the true number is to be found in the low, rather than the high, end of the range. ... However, given the difficulties involved in estimating the number of street people, one can make a plausible case for even the 600,000 to 700,000 figures. What one cannot do is to argue that there are 2–3 million homeless on any one night. Even the National Coalition for the Homeless apparently accepts this.

SOURCE: Christopher Hewitt, "Estimating the Number of Homeless: Media Misrepresentation of an Urban Problem," *Journal of Urban Affairs*, 18, 4 (1996), 431–47. Used by permission of John Wiley and Sons.

ANALYSIS

The huge disparity between the CCNV's estimate of the number of homeless people in the United States and the number given in the HUD Report generated ongoing controversy that many analysts tried to resolve. The issue was important for many reasons, but none was more significant than that the count would determine the amount of money allocated to assist homeless people and even to end homelessness, not to mention its possible effect on the reapportionment of the House of Representatives.

Some analysts attributed the discrepancy to politics. They pointed out that advocates for the homeless preferred the number to be as high as possible to justify their demand for the largest possible amount of government assistance for the homeless. Others argued just the opposite. They wanted the number to be as small as possible to demonstrate the health of the country and to show that presidential and congressional budget cuts to homeless programs were both defensible and also appropriate.

Others who studied homelessness criticized the methodologies and assumptions used to reach both counts, and many others, too. But all of them did agree that it was not possible, for a number of reasons, to reach a precise number of homeless people. One reason was that different researchers used different definitions of homelessness. Another was the impossibility of locating all of the homeless. As Mitch Snyder said, homeless people deliberately tried to remain hidden to avoid being hassled by people who had negative or hostile attitudes toward them. They particularly worried about government officials and law enforcement officers.

In this article, Christopher Hewitt, a sociologist at the University of Maryland, Baltimore County, recognized the impossibility of determining the exact number of homeless people. Instead, he compared a number of homeless counts to see if there was enough consistency to allow students of homelessness to have, at least, a roughly accurate estimate of the extent of homelessness. In particular, he wanted to know if either of the two studies presented here was clearly more accurate than the other. He discovered that, taken together, all of the studies showed that the number of homeless people in the country was much closer to the estimate of HUD than it was to the estimate of Snyder and other advocates for the homeless. The number that Hewitt finally set forth was larger than that proposed by HUD but substantially lower than the estimates of the CCNV.

FURTHER READING

Hewitt, Christopher. "Estimating the Number of Homeless: Media Misrepresentation of an Urban Problem." *Journal of Urban Affairs*, 18, 3 (1996), 431–37.

32

THE NUMBER OF HOMELESS

Executive Summary

- *Document:* This document and the next are different selections from the Executive Summary that begins the most recent *Annual Homeless Assessment Report* prepared by the Department of Housing and Urban Development (HUD). The documents present information about two aspects of the homeless population.
- *Date:* The report was published in 2010 on the basis of information gathered in 2009.
- *Where:* The document was published in Washington, DC, by the Government Printing Office.
- *Significance:* The document began to satisfy the desire to have information about homelessness more reliable than preceding reports and estimates. Its conclusions (especially about the total number of homeless people) have generated less controversy than previous reports or estimates about the number of homeless people.

DOCUMENT

The U.S. Department of Housing and Urban Development (HUD) is pleased to present the 2009 Annual Homeless Assessment Report (AHAR).

The AHAR reports provide the latest counts of homelessness nationwide—including counts of individuals, persons in families, and special population groups such as veterans and chronically homeless people. The report also covers the types of locations where people use emergency shelter and transitional housing; where people were just before they entered a residential program; how much time they spend in shelters over the course of a year; and the size and use of U.S. inventory of residential programs for homeless people.

With the 2009 AHAR, we now have three complete years of data on the number and characteristics of sheltered homeless people, how they become homeless, and how they used the homeless services system. This is important, because we can begin to see discernible trends in homelessness, including the effects of the recession and of changes over time to the homeless services system.

The 2009 AHAR also marks continued improvement in both sources of estimates of homelessness used in the reports. A larger number of communities are reporting Homeless Management Information System (HMIS) data to the AHAR, which is used in the analysis of patterns of homelessness over a year's time. In 2009, 334 communities—representing 2,988 counties and 1,056 cities—reported reliable HMIS data to the report, a sizable increase from last year's report (222 communities). At the same time, the point-in-time (PIT) counts essential for estimating the numbers and characteristics of *all* homeless people, both sheltered and unsheltered, are improving as communities use more rigorous methodologies for conducting the counts.

For the first time, this 2009 AHAR includes information from in-person interviews with local service providers located in nine communities nationwide. This qualitative information provides a contextual backdrop for understanding how homelessness is changing.

Point-in-Time Estimates of Homeless People

On a single night in January 2009, there were an estimated 343,067 sheltered and unsheltered homeless people nationwide. More than 6 in 10 people who were homeless at a single point-in-time were in emergency shelters or transitional homeless programs, while 37 percent were unsheltered on the "street" or in other places not meant for human habitation. The total number of people homeless on a single night has remained fairly stable from year to year, but over time a smaller share of all homeless people is unsheltered, and a larger share is found in emergency shelters or transitional housing. This may, in part, reflect better "street counts," but it probably also reflects community success in getting people off the streets and into shelters or housing.

DID YOU KNOW?

How Many People Experience Homelessness?

[Is it even the Right Question?]

Many people call or write the National Coalition for the Homeless to ask about the number of homeless people in the United States. There is no easy answer to this question, and, in fact, the question itself is misleading. In most cases, homelessness is a temporary circumstance—not a permanent condition. A more appropriate measure of the magnitude of homelessness is the number of people who experience homelessness over time, not the number of "homeless people."

Source: National Coalition for the Homeless, "How Many People Experience Homelessness," NCH Fact Sheet #2. June 2008. Used by permission of the National Coalition for the Homeless.

DID YOU KNOW?

Question
Will the Census Bureau collect information on people experiencing homelessness?

Answer
Yes, we will conduct an enumeration of people experiencing homelessness in an operation called Service-Based Enumeration (SBE). The SBE was designed to provide an opportunity for people experiencing homelessness to be included in the census, by counting them at service-based locations who might not be included through other enumeration methods. Service-based locations include: emergency and transitional shelters for people experiencing homelessness, soup kitchens, regularly scheduled mobile food vans, and pre-identified non-sheltered outdoor locations.

Source: U.S. Census Bureau. Question & Answer Center. "2010 Census: Counting People with No Fixed Address." Washington, DC: U.S. Census Bureau, August 13, 2008. available online at https://ask.census.gov/cgi-bin/askcensus.cfg/php/enduser/std_adp .php?p_faqid=7318&p_created=1

DID YOU KNOW?

S. F. Homeless Count Is a Farce—and I Know This Because I Volunteered

[How Valid are the Counts?]

...[O]ne small and inconvenient fact for everyone involved: The homeless count is a meaningless charade. Anybody who participated (who is not in denial or incredibly stupid) knows that.

Take the volunteer instructions, for example. We were to automatically count people sleeping outside; vehicles with covered windows; and makeshift structures such as tents and boxes. We were *not* to automatically count people leaving bars or waiting for buses. And finally, we were to take factors like loitering, panhandling, shopping-cart pushing, recycling, inebriation, and dishevelry (yeah, I know, not a word, but it should be) into consideration when deciding who was and wasn't homeless. Talk about subjective. Oh, and under no circumstance were we to actually ask a person whether or not they lived in a house. Perhaps that would make the survey a little too accurate?

When asked why volunteers should rely on their own arbitrary judgments rather than simply asking people if they lived in a home, Daryl Higashi, the city's supportive finance director, explained that there would be a follow-up survey of 500 homeless people that would apparently provide all the necessary information. He also emphasized that the volunteers not ... disturb anyone's privacy —but that seems strange to me. Getting people off the streets involves communicating with them at some point. So why not now?

Source: Ashley Harrell. "S. F. Homeless Count Is a Farce—and I Know This Because I Volunteered." *San Francisco News.* January 28, 2009. Available at http://blogs.sfweekly.com/thesnitch/2009/01/the_homeless_count_is_a_farce.php.

Data Sources Used in the AHAR
The AHAR is based on two sources.

1. **Continuum of Care applications are submitted to HUD annually** as part of the competition funding process and provide one-night Point-in-Time (PIT) counts of both sheltered and unsheltered homeless populations. The PIT counts are based on the number of homeless persons on a single night during the last week in January, and the most recent PIT counts for which data are available nationally were conducted in January 2009.

2. **Homeless Management Information System (HMIS)** are electronic administrative databases that are designed to record and store client-level information on the characteristics and service needs of homeless people. HMIS data is used to produce counts of the sheltered homeless population over a full year—that is, people who used emergency shelter or transitional housing programs at some time during the course of a year. The 2009 AHAR uses HMIS data for the most recent one-year reporting period and compares these data to previous HMIS-based findings.

One-Year Estimates of Sheltered Homeless People

Nearly 1.56 million people used an emergency shelter or a transitional housing program during the 12-month period (October 1, 2008 through September 30, 2009). Two-thirds were homeless as individuals, and one-third were homeless as members of families.

For the second straight year, the number of sheltered homeless families increased, while the number of sheltered homeless individuals dropped. In 2009, approximately 1,035,000 individuals used sheltered or transitional housing at some time during the year, as did 535,000 people who were there as part of a family. A family is a household that includes an adult, 18 years of age or older, and at least one child. All other sheltered homeless people are considered individuals. Considered as households rather than separate people, slightly more than 170,000 families were sheltered in 2009, about a 30 percent increase since 2007. . . .

Trends in Sheltered Homelessness, 2007–2009

The overall number of sheltered homeless people increased slightly between 2007 and 2008 before dropping slightly—by about 2 percent or 35,000 people—between 2008 and 2009. The continued rise in family homelessness across the three years, from 131,000 families in 2007 to 170,000 families in 2009, is almost certainly related to the recession. However, the increase was more pronounced between 2007 and 2008, even though unemployment rates remained high during the 2009 reporting period (October 2008 through September 2009).

SOURCE: U.S. Department of Housing and Urban Development. Office of Community Planning and Development. *The 2009 Annual Homeless Assessment Report.* Washington, DC, 2009.

ANALYSIS

Christopher Hewitt tried to reconcile two vastly different and contradictory estimates of the number of homeless people in the United States by using logical argument and rational analysis, but the participants in the debate remained unsatisfied. Homeless people and their advocates maintained that the HUD estimates were far too low while representatives of the federal government and their allies contended that no figures supported the large numbers that Mitch Snyder and advocates for the homeless presented.

As a result, the dispute about the number of homeless people continued after 1996, and other individuals and organizations offered their own carefully calculated estimations. Among them were Peter Rossi, Christopher Jencks, and Martha Burt—all sociologists and eminent scholars of homelessness. In 2001, they were joined by the U.S. Census Bureau, which issued a report on the *Emergency and Transitional Shelter Population 2000.* Later in the decade, the U.S. Conference of Mayors several published several reports about homelessness.

DID YOU KNOW?

Doing the Math to Reduce Homelessness

THE MONITOR'S VIEW

From New York to San Francisco, the nation has arrived at a collective aha moment about how to reduce chronic homelessness. Instead of just trying to manage this entrenched problem, cities are aiming to end it, and they're making laudable headway.

People who may live for years on and off the street are not the largest part of the homeless population; they are only about 10 percent. But they are far more expensive and difficult to deal with than other kinds of homeless. Often mentally ill or addicted to drugs, the long-term homeless shuffle between the street, shelters, detox centers, jails, and emergency rooms.

What cities are discovering is that it's more costefficient—and humane—to provide these individuals a long-term residence up front and assign them visiting caseworkers, rather than allowing them to rack up hefty tabs as "frequent flyers" to city and private services.

Dayton, Ohio, for instance has found that on the street one group of mentally ill homeless individuals cost taxpayers $203 a day. But when they were moved into a 10-unit apartment building with supportive services, that cost dropped to $85 a day.

... Early returns show that the "housing first" approach to chronic homelessness is having an impact. In total, 30 of the 200-plus jurisdictions have reported homeless declines.... Since success breeds success, this should encourage cities to stick to their plans. It won't be easy to actually realize the savings because government agencies are loath to give up budget dollars even ones they no longer need.

At the same time, these cities, as well as the federal government, should redouble efforts for the remaining 90 percent of the homeless. Two of the fastest growing homeless groups are the working poor and women with children (now, sadly, children make up a quarter of that vulnerable population).

Source: "Doing the Math to Reduce Homelessness," by *The Christian Science Monitor* Editorial Board. Reprinted with permission from the June 19, 2006, issue of *The Christian Science Monitor.* © 2006 The Christian Science Monitor (www.CSMonitor .com).

DID YOU KNOW?

[Executive Summary. 2009 Greater Los Angeles Homeless Count Report]

The 42,694 persons counted within the Los Angeles C[ontinuum] of C[are] includes 4,885 individuals that are members of families. Additionally, of the total number, 24,915 or 58% were counted within the City of Los Angeles.

... The 42,694 persons counted in 2009 represents a decrease of 38% when compared to the total number of homeless persons included in the 2007 Homeless Count. This marks a significant decrease in the number of homeless persons in the Continuum of Care.... While many factors likely contributed to this decline, it is important to acknowledge new and expanded programs implemented by the Los Angeles CoC network of housing and service providers. Many of these new programs are funded by the County and City of Los Angeles, including the County's $100 million Homeless Prevention Initiative, the City Permanent Supportive Housing Program, and the ... voucher programs that specifically target homeless individuals and families. Most importantly, local housing and service providers are making an important paradigm shift—now more than ever, programs are centered on housing placement of homeless families and individuals and providing the tools and skills they need to stay housed.

Source: Los Angeles Homeless Services Authority (LAHSA), *2009 Greater Los Angeles Homeless Count Report* (Los Angeles, CA: LAHSA, 2009), 1.

All of these reports had both positive and negative aspects, and each report received both praise and criticism.

The report of the Census Bureau estimated that 178,638 homeless people had lived in shelters and transitional housing in1990. It also claimed that this number had *declined* by about 4.45 percent in 2000, to 170,796. Most importantly, this report distinguished between homeless people who lived in shelters (the "sheltered" or "housed") and those who lived outdoors—on streets, sidewalks, or shrubbery (the "unsheltered" or "unhoused"). Although the report never directly said that locating, counting, and reporting people with no address was much more difficult than discovering people living in a place meant for human habitation, the point was implicit. It expressed this idea by reporting only the number of people who had lived in any kind of shelter. It emphasized the point by explicitly acknowledging that the report did "not provide a count of the population experiencing homelessness." It was only a count of the number of people who had received services from recognizable shelters, soup kitchens, mobile food trucks, and so on. This distinction is crucial and has since become necessary if any attempt to count the number of homeless is to be considered credible and taken seriously.

The report was criticized on several grounds. Most important, it took no account of the people who suffered the greatest degree of homelessness—those without even temporary shelter who spent their nights in alleys, doorways, sidewalks, shrubbery, or on the street. These people were widely understood to constitute a sizeable part of the homeless population, and any estimate that excluded or overlooked them was given little credence. Critics also argued that counting only the number of persons who had used services meant for the homeless did not consider the total homeless population. Because all homeless people did not take advantage of these services, counting only the "serviced" left out a large number of homeless people.

The reports issued by the U.S. Conference of Mayors, *Hunger and Homelessness Survey: A Status Report on Hunger and Homelessness in American Cities, 2007* and *2008*, also had both admirers and detractors. Probably constructed more carefully than any previous similar reports, these explicitly explained, in a sophisticated statistical way, the causes of homelessness and also the social demographics of homelessness and what sorts of people became homeless.

Several criticisms of the reports balanced these positive characteristics. The benefits of the reports were diminished by corresponding disadvantages. First, the reports of the Mayors' Conferences did not analyze only homelessness. They also considered hunger. While hunger was clearly related to homelessness, it was not exactly the same. Moreover, in the structure of the reports, hunger received as much attention as homelessness, seeming to indicate that it had equal importance. This notion might have been strengthened by the fact that the section concerning hunger preceded the section about homelessness in each of the reports. Because of the structure of these reports, the importance of homelessness seemed to have been diminished and the importance of hunger magnified.

Second, these reports did not include or report data concerning homelessness for the entire nation. They provided information only about individual cities. The report issued in December 2007 contained information about 23 cities, and the following year's report considered only 25. Because of this, the total number of cases of homelessness nationally could not be estimated. Aggregate data from the selected cities could be combined and percentages determined for that group of cities, but not the entire country. Some analysts even wondered if the generalizations so derived could be applied accurately to the entire urban system.

As homelessness continued to be a problem during the 1990s, Congress felt the need for more, and better, information about the extent of homelessness, the characteristics of the homeless population, and more understanding of the reasons for homelessness. Therefore, in the Appropriations Act for HUD in fiscal year 1999, HUD was directed to gather certain information in certain specified ways. Congress specified these requirements in "House Report 105-610—Departments of Veterans Affairs and Housing and Urban Development, and Independent Agencies Appropriations Bill, 1999."

> HUD is directed ... to collect, at a minimum, the following data: the unduplicated count of clients served; client characteristics such as age, race, sex disability status; units (days) and type of housing received (shelter, transitional, permanent); and services rendered. Outcome information such as housing stability, income and health status should be collected as well. Armed with information like this, HUD's

DID YOU KNOW?

Rev. Andy Bales, CEO of the Union Rescue Mission in Los Angeles, responds to the LAHSA [Los Angeles Homeless Assistance Authority] Report

I must admit that I was astounded by the results of the 2009 LAHSA [Los Angeles Homeless Assistance Authority] Count. I was especially confounded by the reported 70% reduction in homeless families with children! Our experience for the last 2 years, especially the last 13 months at Union Rescue Mission has us accurately reporting the greatest Tsunami of families with children that we have ever faced in our 118 year history, including the Great Depression. Of the more than 224 families who came to our doors in the last 8 months, 53% reported that they were homeless for the first time. We had to scramble to open up an entire wing for 2 parent families and single dads with children, to add to our already entire 4th floor filled with single moms and children. . . . We opened up our community rooms, our day rooms, and even our chapel to accommodate every family. Families and children at Union Rescue Mission are up 97% since 2007 and our meals each day are up 46%. Emergency calls to the LA county wide 211 hot line from families made homeless by unemployment, eviction and foreclosure doubled during the time and Union Rescue became one of the few places of last resort. . . . What is most amazing is that LAHSA was a big responder to this crisis. They helped U[nion]R[escue]M/[ission]Eimago secure hotel vouchers for the dozens of families representing a 600% increase over the previous year arriving at our LA County wide Winter Shelters sponsored by LAHSA. LAHSA played a key role in providing services, strategy, and resources to address the challenge, and LAHSA deployed Federal Stimulus funds for Rapid Re-housing to area agencies to deal with the crisis of this new face of homelessness, first time, low barrier families. . . . There is hard evidence that what Union Rescue Mission and other agencies assisting homeless families [did] was well documented by the Los Angeles Department of Social Services. This concrete evidence shows that at least 8100 families, possibly 20,000 to 24,000 individuals, are . . . experiencing homelessness, yet the LAHSA Count only documents less than 5,000 individuals as part of families experiencing homelessness? As homelessness lags behind unemployment, the number of homeless families is estimated to reach 10,000 and we need to prepare for that, but instead we get a report that says that homelessness among families has dropped by 70%? As a friend of mine suggested, this is like getting in your car, punching in data in the navigation system to travel somewhere near Mid Wilshire, West [Los Angeles] and instead your systems tells you to go South toward Long Beach [California]. Almost all of us would know that something was wrong with the data before we left our driveway. Yet, LAHSA not only left the driveway, but published the results, and patted themselves on the back for helping to make these results happen, and then had some local economists mention that "though it seemed counter-intuitive, the results are accurate!" I must say that these results are not only counter-intuitive, but absolutely wrong.

Source: Rev. Andy's Blog, "A Long Way from Home," *Union Rescue Mission: The Way Home* (Los Angeles, CA: Union Rescue Mission, 2009). Used by permission.

ability to assess the success of homeless programs and grantees will be vastly improved.

Although HUD gathered some of the information specified and made it available earlier, it was not until 2007 that HUD was able to provide a complete report that satisfied the congressional directive. Called the *Annual Homeless Assessment Report to Congress* (AHAR), it was based on data gathered in 2005. In presenting its first AHAR, HUD tried to address many of the criticisms that had been leveled at earlier attempts to count and describe the homeless population. In the first chapter, the report "Defin[ed] the Scope of Homelessness" and described the "Evolution in Techniques for Measuring Homelessness." The second chapter clearly explained how the information had been gathered at the local level, and it explained two institutions that had been created, at least in part, to provide the requested information—the Homeless Management Information System (HMIS) and local Continuums of Care (CofCs), both of which had been established precisely to gather the required information.

In its third chapter, the *Annual Homeless Assessment Report* (AHAR) described "The Number and Characteristics of Sheltered Homeless Persons," and, in doing so, it explicitly distinguished between homeless people who received assistance in shelters and those who remained without any shelter. It also distinguished between temporary or short-term homelessness and chronic or long-term homelessness. Finally, it explained procedures that had been used for some time to count homeless people. One was the "point-in-time count" technique whose object was determining how many persons were homeless on a single day; in 2005, that day was April 30. The other way of estimating the number of homeless people was not by trying to determine the number of people who had been homeless on one specific day, but rather to determine the number of individuals who had been homeless at any moment during a specified time period. In 2005, that period was February 1 to April 30. That the numbers produced by each technique differed greatly from each other emerges from the fact that people moved into and out of homelessness over time; so if 20,000 people were homeless on February 23 and 20,000 different people were homeless on April 30, the result given by the point-in-time method of counting would be 20,000, but the result of the second method would have been 40,000 because there was no overlap in the two groups of homeless people.

Since it issued the first AHAR, the Department of Housing and Urban Development has issued four more, the most recent in June 2010. Each of these has contained more information than the previous and has reported it more fully. More than that, these reports, unlike others, have received relatively little criticism and have been generally accepted by Congress, the homeless community, and advocates for the homeless—including their critics and foes—as accurate descriptions of reality. One week after the latest AHAR was released, the National Alliance to End Homelessness, one of the most important advocacy groups for the homeless, issued

Since 2003, the Department of Housing and Urban Development has required all applicants for federal homeless assistance to conduct a census of homeless people every two years. This census is supposed to be taken on the last Wednesday in January. The regulation was meant to provide accurate information about the number of homeless people in a certain district and therefore serve as an indication of whether a particular district qualified to receive federal assistance. As the picture shows, it was much easier to establish the regulation than it was to satisfy it. The New Jersey census-taker shown here was able to locate a makeshift encampment, but that didn't necessarily enable him to find the people who lived there. (AP/Wide World Photos)

a press release responding to it. This statement contained no criticisms of HUD's report and presented its major findings as being correct and accurate.

FURTHER READING

Burt, Martha R. "Homelessness: Definitions and Counts." In Jim Bauhmohl (ed.), *Homelessness in America*. Phoenix, AZ: Oryx Press, 1996.

Culhane, Dennis P., and S. P. Hornburg. "Defining, Tracking, and Counting the Homeless." *Understanding Homelessness: New Policy and Research Perspectives*. Washington, DC: Fannie Mae Foundation, 1997.

Hopper, Kim. "Definitional Quandaries and Other Hazards in Counting the Homeless: An Invited Commentary." *American Journal of Orthopsychiatry*, 65, 3 (July 1995), 340–46.

Hopper, Kim. "Homelessness Old and New: The Matter of Definition." *Housing Policy Debate*, 2, 3 (1991), 757–813.

Peroff, Kathleen, "Who Are the Homeless and How Many Are There?" In Richard D. Bingham, Roy E. Green, and Sammis B. White, *The Homeless in Contemporary Society*. Newbury Park, CA and London: Sage Publications, 1989, 16–32.

33

AN OVERVIEW OF THE HOMELESS POPULATION TODAY

Executive Summary

- *Document:* This document and the one preceding it are different selections from the Executive Summary at the beginning of the most recent *Annual Homeless Assessment Report* prepared by the Department of Housing and Urban Development. The documents present information about two aspects of the homeless population.
- *Date:* The report was published in 2010 on the basis of information gathered in 2009.
- *Where:* The document was published in Washington, DC, by the Government Printing Office.
- *Significance:* The document satisfied the desire for more complete and accurate information about the characteristics of homeless people than any preceding report. Its conclusions (especially about the number of homeless people) generated less controversy than earlier estimates.

DOCUMENT

[The first three paragraphs of the document in Chapter 32 will remind you about the Annual Homeless Assistance Report.]

Point-in-Time Estimates of Homeless People

... Nearly two-thirds of the people homeless on a single night were homeless as individuals (63 percent), while more than a third (37 percent) were homeless as part of a family. Only 21 percent of all homeless family members were unsheltered on the night of the point-in-time count, while about half of homeless individuals were unsheltered.

Information from CofC applications includes counts of particular homeless subpopulations, including people whose homelessness is chronic—that is, individuals with disabilities and long or frequent patterns of homelessness. . . . The January 2009 PIT estimate of chronic homelessness is 110.917 people, more than a 10 percent drop from the PIT count of 124,135 chronically homeless people. While measuring the scope of chronic homelessness remains challenging, a majority of CofCs (53 percent) reported a decrease in chronic homelessness between 2008 and 2009.

Homelessness is heavily concentrated in large coastal states, with California, New York, and Florida accounting for 30 percent of the PIT count in 2009. On a single night in January 2009, the states with the highest concentration of homeless people were Nevada, where 0.85 percent of the total population was homeless, followed by Oregon, Hawaii, California, and Washington. Kansas, South Dakota and West Virginia had the nation's lowest concentrations of homeless persons.

One-Year Estimates of Sheltered Homeless People

Nearly 1.56 million [different] *people used an emergency shelter or a transitional housing program during the 12-month period (October 1, 2008 through September 30, 2009)*. Two-thirds were homeless as individuals, and one-third were homeless as members of a family.

For the second straight year, the number of sheltered homeless families increased, while the number of sheltered homeless individuals dropped. In 2009, approximately 1,035,000 individuals used sheltered or transitional housing at some time during the year, as did 535,000 people who were there as part of a family. A family is a household that includes an adult, 18 years of age or older, and at least one child. All other sheltered homeless people are considered individuals. Considered as households rather than separate people, slightly more than 170,000 families were sheltered in 2009, about a 30 percent increase since 2007.

Sheltered Homeless People in 2009

A typical sheltered homeless person in 2009 was an adult male, a member of a minority group, middle-aged and alone. Men are overrepresented in the sheltered

---

DID YOU KNOW?

Conditions in Illinois and Chicago

[What Do We Know about Homeless People]

- In Chicago, fair market rent is $935 for a two-bedroom unit. To afford housing and stay within 30 percent of income, a renter must earn either $17.98 an hour or work 111 hours per week at minimum wage.
- The majority of new jobs through 1912 are expected to pay far blow the current state median household income of $48,008. In Illinois, an estimated 50,000 working families do not make enough to cover basic living costs. A family of four requires a minimum annual income of $36,408 to meet basic living expenses in rural Illinois, and at least $43,704 in Chicago.
- Over the last 15 years, the ethnic wage gap in the state worsened greatly—by 24 percent between whites and Latinos, by 162 percent between whites and blacks.
- Chicago's poverty rate is 21.1 percent, an increase of 2 percentage points in a year.
- Nearly two-thirds of all jobs require more than a high school diploma. In Illinois, more than 594,000 people, ages 25 to 54 have no high school diploma or GED certificate
- At any given time, more people with untreated severe psychiatric illnesses are living on the streets than are receiving care in hospitals.
- Approximately 20 to 25 percent of the single-adult homeless population suffers from some form of severe and persistent mental illness.
- According to the U.S. Conference of Mayors, approximately 26 percent of the homeless population is dealing with issues of substance abuse.
- The U.S. Conference of Mayors—in its hunger and homelessness survey of 23 cities, including Chicago—found that 29 percent of families requesting emergency shelter were turned away in 2006.

Source: "Homelessness: Facts & Figures." The Facts Behind the Faces: A Fact Sheet from the Chicago Coalition for the Homeless. Homeless Report." Spring 2008. Available online at http://www.chicagohomeless.org/files/images/Fact_Sheet_o.pdf.

Determining the number of homeless people in the United States at any particular time has been challenging for states, the federal government, and private organizations and agencies. To try to gain more accurate information about the number of homeless people, extraordinary measures have sometimes been taken. For example, in 2007, at the YMCA in Trenton, New Jersey, homeless men could receive free haircuts, free dental checkups, and free assistance applying for food stamps. The objective was to draw homeless people into places where they could be counted and included in statistical tabulations of the total homeless population. (AP/Wide World Photos)

homeless population—63.7 percent of homeless adults are men, compared to 40.5 percent of adults in poverty. African Americans make up 38.7 percent of the sheltered homeless population, about 1.5 times their share in the poverty population. Only 2.8 percent of the sheltered homeless population is 62 years or older. Homeless people have higher rates of disability than either the poverty population or the total U.S. population; slightly over two-thirds of sheltered homeless adults have a disability, according to HMIS data.

People who are homeless by themselves are very different from those who are homeless with children. Sheltered individuals are overwhelmingly male. More than three quarters are over 30, more than 10 percent are veterans, and more than 40 percent have a disability. In contrast, adults in sheltered homeless families are overwhelmingly female, most are under age 31, and very few are veterans or have a disability. Three-fifths of the people in homeless families are children, and more than half of the children are under age 6.

The geographic distribution of homelessness is markedly different from the distribution of the nation's poverty and total population. The share of sheltered homeless people in principal cities in 2009 is nearly twice the share of the poverty population in these areas, 68.2 vs. 35.6 percent. Homeless individuals are particularly likely to be in urban areas. Nearly three quarters of all sheltered individuals (72.2 percent) accessed a homeless residential program in a principal city, compared with 61.2 percent of persons in families.

Almost two fifths of people entering an emergency shelter or transitional housing program during 2009 came from another homeless situation. Among those already homeless, almost two thirds were in shelter rather than in a place not meant for human habitation.

Another two fifths of people who entered shelter in 2009 came from a housed situation (in their own or someone else's home), and the remaining one fifth were split between institutional settings or other situations such as hotels or motels. Families were particularly likely to be housed the night before becoming homeless: more than 6 in 10 were either in their own housing unit (20 percent), staying with family (29 percent), or staying with friends (14 percent).

Trends in Sheltered Homelessness, 2007–2009

...The continued rise in family homelessness across the three years, from 131,000 families in 2007 to 170,000 families in 2009 is almost certainly related to the recession. However, the increase was more pronounced between 2007 and 2008, even though unemployment rates remained high during the 2009 reporting period (October 2008 through September 2009). It may be that many families already at risk of becoming homeless lacked sufficient support networks and became homeless almost immediately after the economy turned down. A much larger group turned to family and friends and may be doubled up and still at great risk of becoming homeless. The percentage of adults in families who reported that they had been staying with families before entering shelter increased steadily over the three-year period, from 24.2 percent in 2007 to 29.4 percent in 2009, as did the total percentage reporting that they had been in some sort of "housed" situation before becoming homeless, reaching 62.5 percent in 2009.

. . . More individuals—adults entering shelter by themselves—reported that their previous living situation was a place not meant for human habitation in 2009 compared with 2008. This may suggest that communities are having some success in getting people off the "street" and into shelter or other forms of housing, especially since the overall number of number of unsheltered homeless individuals reported by communities in the PIT count did not go up.

Few changes occurred in the demographic characteristics of sheltered homeless people. A slight aging of the adult homeless population (more people over 50) is consistent with other research that points to the aging of a cohort of people who became susceptible to homelessness when they were younger. Both families and individuals identifying themselves as African-American have dropped steadily, from a high starting point. Adults in unsheltered homeless families were more likely in 2009 to be men (20.4 percent) than they were in 2007 (18.9 percent). This likely reflects the pressures of the recession and is consistent with reports from the in-person interviews with providers conducted for this report.

SOURCE: U.S. Department of Housing and Urban Development. Office of Community Planning and Development. *The 2009 Annual Homeless Assessment Report.* Washington, DC, 2009.

ANALYSIS

The document in this chapter is another selection from the Executive Summary at the beginning of the 2009 *Annual Homeless Assessment Report* (AHAR). In fact, this document overlaps the document in the previous chapter and is simply a different editing of the same text. However, the selection presented here contains largely different information and has a different emphasis. Whereas the selection in the last chapter focuses only on the total number of homeless people, the selection in this chapter also tries to report the characteristics of the contemporary homeless population.

Although earlier studies also attempted to characterize and analyze the homeless population, those studies had been largely impressionistic or had analyzed limited geographic areas (only certain cities or states) rather than the entire United States. And, even though pre-*AHAR* analyses strongly suggested that the homeless population at the end of the twentieth century differed from earlier homeless populations, the earlier studies were not conclusive or beyond question.

In contrast, the *AHAR* never received the withering criticism aimed at earlier reports. It attempted to identify and characterize the characteristics of the homeless population in more sophisticated, complex, and convincing ways. When HUD's *Reports* throughout the years from 2005 to 2010 maintained that the contemporary homeless population differed substantially from previous homeless populations, its assertions provoked little skepticism.

The conclusions of the 2009 *Report* confirmed many of the ideas that students of homelessness had been developing since the early 1990s. The 2009 *Report* revealed that more than one-third of the homeless population at the beginning of the twenty-first century were members of families rather than solitary individuals. While the largest number of homeless individuals were white men, if one considers percentages rather than absolute numbers, women and members of minority groups (especially African Americans) were extremely disproportionately represented in the homeless population. The homeless population also contained a disproportionate number of children under 10; and, while more than three-quarters of homeless men were older than 30, a majority of homeless women were younger than 30. When these and other discoveries about homelessness attracted public attention, Americans' perceptions of homelessness began to change significantly. These revelations also began to change the ways in which students of homelessness asked their questions and allowed them to see the homeless population in new ways.

FURTHER READING

Jahiel, Rene I. "The Situation of Homelessness." In Richard D. Bingham, Roy E. Green and Sammis B. White, *The Homeless in Contemporary Society*. Newbury Park, CA, and London: Sage Publications, 1989, 99–118.

VanderStaay, Steven. *Street Lives: An Oral History of Homeless Americans*. Philadelphia, PA, and Gabriola Island, BC: New Society Publishers, 1992.

34

SPECIAL POPULATIONS OF HOMELESS PEOPLE

The Diversity of Homeless Americans

- *Document:* This document is taken from a report presented to a National Symposium on Homelessness Research that was held in 1998. The Department of Health and Human Services and the Department of Housing and Urban Affairs sponsored the conference.
- *Date:* The Symposium was held on October 29 and October 30, 1998.
- *Where:* The Symposium was held in Arlington, Virginia, across the Potomac River from Washington, DC.
- *Significance:* The papers presented at this symposium reported the latest research about homelessness and provided the latest available information about the demographic, social, and economic characteristics of the homeless population.

DOCUMENT

Abstract

Surveys conducted over the past two decades have demonstrated that homeless Americans are exceptionally diverse and include representatives from all segments of society—the old and young; men and women; single people and families; city dwellers and rural residents; whites and people of color; and able-bodied workers and people with serious health problems. Veterans . . . appear in substantial numbers among the homeless as do former criminal offenders and illegal immigrants. Each of these groups experiences distinctive forms of adversity resulting from both societal structures and personal vulnerabilities, and has unique service delivery needs. All, however, experience extreme poverty, lack of housing, and a mixture of internally impaired or externally inhibited functional capabilities. Attention to the distinctive characteristics of subgroups of the homeless is important in facilitating service delivery and program planning, but may also diffuse attention away from shared fundamental needs, and general unproductive policy debate about deserving vs. undeserving homeless people.

. . . In contrast to the diversity, two characteristics are remarkably consistent across subgroups of homeless people; a lack of decent affordable housing and a lack of adequate income. In view of the homogeneity of homeless people with respect to these characteristics, and the obvious relationship of poverty to homelessness, their diversity is striking and deserving of review. . . .

Commonalities: The Need for Adequate Housing and Income Support

Before we consider research on subgroup-specific needs of homeless people, it is important to briefly review the critical impact of policies and interventions that directly address housing and income needs of all types of homeless people.

- During the Great Depression of the 1930s, large numbers of able bodied men were forced into homelessness due to unemployment rates that approached 25 percent. With the outbreak of World War II, however, the federal government provided employment for almost 18 million men and many millions of women, and virtually eliminated homelessness from the American landscape. . . .
- During the early 1950s, homelessness in skid rows was largely a problem of older alcoholic men. With the advent of social security and disability benefits, poverty among the elderly declined from 50 percent in 1955 to 11 percent in 1975, and the risk of homelessness for older Americans was vastly reduced. . . .
- A study comparing homeless and non-homeless people who used the same soup kitchens in Chicago documented that the major difference between these two groups was that those who were not homeless were receiving income through supplemental income (SSI). . . .
- A prospective study of homeless mentally ill applicants for social security disability benefits found that among those who received benefits, 50 percent exited from homelessness within three months of the initial disability determination as compared to only 20 percent among those who were turned down for benefits. . . .
- A study of housing vouchers and intensive case management for homeless people with chronic mental illness found that vouchers, but not intensive case management, improved housing outcomes and that neither intervention affected clinical outcomes. . . .
- A recent epidemiologic study of risk and protective factors for family homelessness indicated that factors compromising a family's economic and social resources were associated with increased vulnerability to homelessness. Specifically, being a primary tenant, receiving a housing subsidy or cash assistance, and graduating from high school were protective against family homelessness. . . .

One of the common misconceptions about homeless people is that they form a homogeneous group and share common characteristics of age, gender, family structure, and ethnicity or race. In fact, the homeless population is remarkably heterogeneous and includes many people who do not fit the typical stereotype. One of the most rapidly growing groups of homeless people is families who have lost their homes. This photograph shows a family who lost their house. They took refuge in a campground for homeless people because they wanted to avoid shelters, stay off the streets, and keep their whole family together. (AP/Wide World Photos)

. . . In each of these cases, in spite of the heterogeneity of the populations, income or employment support substantially contributed to resolving the problem of homelessness. In the sections that follow we consider empirical evidence on the background and needs of specific subgroups of homeless people. We conclude by reconsidering the relative importance of homogeneity vs. heterogeneity in policy development and service planning for homeless people.

Subgroups of Homeless People

People who are homeless can be differentiated along six dimensions: (1) developmental phase of life (age); (2) gender; (3) social unit (families vs. single individuals);

(4) racial or ethno-cultural groups; (5) health status (psychiatric illness, substance abuse, HIV/AIDS, and the multiply diagnosed); (6) social status (veteran vs. citizen vs. criminal vs. illegal immigrant....)

Developmentally Differentiated Groups: Children, Youth, and the Elderly

The loss of "home"—a place that nurtures development and provides safety across the lifespan—is especially troubling to homeless children, youth, and elderly persons. Being without a home challenges the unique developmental tasks of each age group. In addition, all these subgroups are particularly vulnerable to the exigencies of shelter or street life because of their age, frailty, and dependence on others.

Children

... In general, studies show that persistent rather than transient poverty is more detrimental to children, and that children experiencing either type of poverty do less well in school achievement, cognitive functioning, and socio-emotional measures than children who have never been poor....

Homeless children are among the poorest children nationally.... Researchers have noted the similarities between homeless and poor housed children; homeless children look worse on only some parameters.... These findings suggest that homelessness may be only one stressor among many in the lives of poor children and that cumulative effects of multiple stressors may be more detrimental.... One recent study of sheltered homeless and poor housed (never homeless) children and families ... found that the most powerful independent predictor of emotional and behavioral problems in both the homeless and housed poor children was their mother's level of emotional distress.... Clearly, interventions that support the healthy development of poor children must address the well-being of their mothers as well.

Homeless children are generally young children.... The typical homeless family is comprised of a single mother, 30 years of age, with two children under the age of five years.... Research indicates that homeless children have high rates of both acute and chronic health problems.... They also have high rates of developmental delays ... and emotional and behavioral difficulties....

Homeless, more than poor housed children, face the formidable challenges associated with residential instability and related family and school disruptions. Children who have moved three or more times are more likely to have emotional and behavioral problems, be expelled from school, or be retained in the same grade for more than one year....

... Children spending time during their developmental years without the safety and stability of a permanent home are at risk for various negative outcomes. Whether they are victims or witnesses to violence, have learning disabilities, or struggle with asthma or other health conditions, these children need to gain access to developmentally appropriate services. In addition, permanent housing and adequate incomes for their families are critical. An integrated approach toward designing as comprehensive a system of care that serves the well-being of the family is crucial.

Youth

Consolidation of one's identity, separation from one's parents and preparation for independence are key developmental tasks of adolescence and critical for becoming a well-functioning adult in our society. Most adolescents prepare for this transition to adulthood in their homes and schools. However, a growing segment of young people leave their families prematurely, joining the ranks of homeless and runaway youth. . . . Whether by choice or forced to leave, these adolescents are generally ill-equipped for independent living and many become easy prey for predators on the streets.

Despite increasing numbers of homeless youth and their growing proportion among the overall homeless population . . . this subgroup was considered among the most understudied and undeserved until relatively recently. . . . Although empirical studies have been methodologically limited, the growing literature suggests that homeless youth are a special population that require innovative programmatic and policy solutions. . . .

Pathways onto the streets are multiple and complex and include: (1) strained family relationships . . . (2) economic crisis and family dissolution; and (3) instability of residential placements like foster care, psychiatric hospitalization, juvenile detention, and residential schools. . . . [T]he essential distinction between homeless and runaway youth appears to rest on assumptions about choice in leaving home, access to the home of origin or an alternative home, and time away from home. Distinctions like these can be problematic because of presumptions about motives and options. Most definitions of homeless youth refer to unaccompanied young people under age 18; the legal status of minor distinguishes them in terms of access to services, employment, housing, and many other resources. . . .

To survive, many homeless youth resort to drug trafficking, prostitution, and other forms of criminal activity. . . . Homeless youth are at risk for health and mental health problems, including substance abuse . . . HIV/AIDS . . . pregnancy . . . and suicidal behaviors. . . . Their high rates of exposure to various forms of violence . . . increase the likelihood of developing post-traumatic stress disorder. . . .

Limited shelter placements, fear of providers and shelters, and distrust of highly structured, rule-bound programs, present unique challenges to service delivery [to youth]. Street life makes it particularly difficult for youth to access health and mental health services as well as educational programs.

Elderly Homeless

Although the proportion of older persons in the total homeless population has declined in recent years, the numbers of homeless elders, age fifty and older, have grown. . . . While still a relatively small subpopulation, their numbers are likely to escalate as homelessness continues unabated, increasing numbers of baby-boomers reach older adulthood, and the demand for affordable housing continues to outstrip supply. . . .

Elderly homeless persons are of special concern because of their vulnerability to victimization both in shelters and on the streets, their frailty due to poor mental and physical health, and the reluctance of traditional senior service systems to incorporate them into ongoing programs. . . . Homelessness uniquely challenges elderly persons. Not only does their vulnerability make meeting basic human needs for food, shelter, and safety more problematic, but it interferes with resolving the later developmental tasks of the lifecycle: the opportunities to reflect on one's life, consolidate personal integrity, and experience completeness rather than despair. . . .

The research on homeless elders remains limited. . . . With the declining age of the homeless population, studies have primarily addressed the needs of younger individuals and families. Earlier research that contained samples of older men among the single adult population focused on alcoholism or "skid row" lifestyles rather than their age or life-cycle challenges. In addition, declining rates of poverty among the elderly and a federally mandated system of targeted benefits and programs for older Americans, coupled with the stigmatization of this subgroup has made the elderly of limited concern to policy makers.

. . . Factors that have been identified as contributing to the presence of elderly persons among the homeless include deinstitutionalization . . . poverty, especially among elderly women . . . and the lack of affordable housing. . . . Limited access to affordable housing and supportive services is especially problematic for minority elders. . . . While elderly homeless are generally thought to have more consistent incomes from pensions or social security than younger homeless individuals, poor older women who have never worked, individuals with very limited benefits, and elders whose meager incomes have been exploited by others, are still too poor to support themselves in stable housing. . . .

Older homeless adults experience various health and mental health problems, are more likely targets for victimization and consequent injury, and lack networks of relatives or friends that could provide emotional or material support. . . .

Elder homeless need a complex and coordinated system of care that includes: specialized outreach, help in meeting basic needs and sometimes routine activities of daily living, 24-hour crisis assistance, health and mental health care, transportation services, assistance with the development of social relationships and social ties, and a range of housing options with easy access to services. . . . For homeless elders in hospitals, drug treatment programs, or nursing homes, policies must ensure that they are discharged only when adequate residential services are secured and that they are never discharged to shelters or the street. In addition, cost reimbursement policies should not encourage premature discharge or discharge without housing in place. . . .

Gender Issues

Since the 1980s, many more women have become homeless with the ratio of men to women approaching 3:2. Women now comprise more than one-fifth of the overall homeless population. . . . The rapidly growing numbers of homeless mothers (i.e., families with children in tow) and homeless women alone ("singles") account for these numbers. Although the majority of "single" women have children, they reside in shelters without them. In contrast only an estimated 40 percent of single men are fathers who are less likely to have been married and are not active caretakers. . . . [Two researchers] concluded that "women bring their gender responsibilities into the homeless situation." . . . As a result, many authors have called for programming to meet their unique needs. . . .

In part, the transformation of homelessness by women reflects the feminization of poverty. Many extremely poor women have limited earning power, job skills, and education and are overwhelmed by childcare responsibilities. If they are raising children alone, these burdens are compounded. Female-headed families are generally poorer than two-parent families because of the presence of a single income and the cost of child care. . . .

For women with limited education and job skills, the picture is even bleaker. Improved technology coupled with competition from third world countries have led to reduced wages and higher unemployment for these women. The availability of fewer jobs paying decent wages has particularly affected the standard of living of young adults and minority group members. . . . Many homeless mothers have worked sporadically at low-paying service jobs . . . but generally not in the year before becoming homeless. Even if a woman were working full-time and was able to arrange free child-care, her housing expenses are likely to comprise an inordinate proportion of her income—far more than the 30 percent allotment that is considered feasible; women comprise a disproportionate percentage of households who are "cost-burdened." . . .

. . . Motherhood (in particular, pregnancy and the recent birth of a baby), especially when parenting alone, may jeopardize a woman's ability to maintain her home. . . . Women must juggle many roles—worker, homemaker, and mother—often without adequate resources and social support. Raising children is a financial burden and without government-sponsored childcare and enforceable child support laws, it further constrains a mother's already limited job possibilities and earning power. Poor women who manage to work are often on the edge of a precipice: a missed paycheck, medical emergency, unreliable childcare, or other complication, may lead to job loss, eviction, and homelessness.

Although eviction and housing-related problems are a common precipitant of homelessness, domestic violence is also a major factor. The risk of victimization is heightened in neighborhoods plagued by extreme poverty, in situations where women are alone and lack protection, and in relationships with men who suffer addictions. . . .

Not surprisingly, many homeless people have various personal difficulties as well. Both single women and men are far more likely to have histories of mental disorders, hospitalization, and suicide attempts than women with children in tow. . . . As a result, many single women have had their children placed in foster care or other out-of-home placements. With regard to substance use disorders, single men have double the rate of single women who have double the rate of mothers with children. It is also more likely that men are on the streets because of substance abuse problems and involvement with the criminal justice system. . . .

In sum, although pathways into homelessness may be different for homeless men and women, each has unique service needs that require innovative programming. "Homeless women suffer disproportionately from every catastrophe specific to their genre and race. The problems they experience mirror those of low-income women and are further compounded for women of color. . . . Homelessness specifically demonstrates how gender-related inequalities in large measure shape women's experiences." . . .

Social Units: Homeless Families

Family homelessness is a relatively new American social problem. Not since the Great Depression have significant numbers of families and children been on the streets. Beginning in the early 1980s, families with young children in tow have become one of the fastest growing segments of the homeless population and now comprise approximately 36 percent of the overall numbers. . . .

The rapidly increasing gap between the incomes of rich and poor in America has jeopardized the stability of large numbers of families. With limited education, job skills, child support and child care, their only options for survival are low wage jobs or public assistance, neither of which provide sufficient resources to keep a family stably housed. Often employed at minimum wage jobs, these families tend to pay an inordinate percentage of their income on housing, thus increasing the pool of families at risk for losing their homes. . . . Homelessness is a devastating experience. Losing one's home is a metaphor for disconnection from family, friends, and community. Not only have homeless people lost their dwelling, but they have also lost safety, privacy, control, and domestic comfort. . . . Homelessness disrupts every aspect of family life, damaging the physical and emotional health of parents and children and sometimes threatening the intactness of the family unit. For example, many family shelters exclude men and adolescent boys. To avoid the stress of homelessness, some parents voluntarily place their children with family, friends, or even in foster care. Others lose their children to the foster care system just because they are homeless. . . .

. . . Who are homeless families and what are their needs? Most are headed by women in their late 20s with approximately 2 children, the majority of whom are less than 6 years old. Their race/ethnicity reflects the composition of the city in which they reside, with minority groups disproportionately represented. The majority of mothers did not graduate from high school and were not currently working. However, most had some work experience. Not surprisingly, homeless families were extremely poor, with incomes significantly below the federal poverty level.

. . . In addition to [their] basic needs, other aspects of these families' lives must be addressed. Interpersonal violence may well be the subtext of family homelessness. Abuse and assault seem to be the salient feature of homeless mother's childhood and adult experiences. Women suffer its devastating medical and emotional consequences for the rest of their lives. . . . Many women are fleeing violent relationships when they enter shelter. Others are unable to leave these relationships without extensive support and as a result are unable to maintain jobs. To be effective, policy makers must account for the pervasiveness of interpersonal violence in program planning.

. . . Why do some very low-income families become homeless while others do not? . . . Researchers in New York City . . . Los Angeles . . . and Boston . . . have examined variables, such as social support, violence, and mental health, which may account for a family's increased risk of becoming homeless. . . .

In response to the growing crisis of family homelessness, a safety net of family shelters and transitional housing facilities has sprung up in the United States. Based on the latest HUD shelter survey (1989), conducted in areas with populations greater than 25,000, the number of family shelters had doubled between 1984 and 1988—from 1900 to 5000.... In addition to housing assistance, most programs provide a broad array of programs including social services ... and life skill training.... Rarely, permanent service-enriched housing is also available, but these programs tend to target families already living in subsidized housing who need additional services to become self-supporting.... Although this continuum of care is a good beginning, the data indicate that the emphasis in program planning should be on permanent housing with services and supports available to families who chose them. ...Until more comprehensive programming is accomplished, the well-being of these families will continue to be compromised.

Racial and Ethno-cultural Subgroups

Racial and ethno-cultural minorities have long been at a serious disadvantage in the United States.... [Perhaps this] has contributed to our inattention of homelessness among minority groups....Thus, although minorities are at dramatically greater risk for homelessness than other Americans, there has been virtually no specific study of minority pathways into homelessness. Surveys that address minority issues have been, almost exclusively, sub-analyses of other, more general surveys....

Blacks and Latinos in America are far more likely than other Americans to be poor and therefore more likely to be homeless. In 1980, as the numbers of homeless began to grow, 30 percent of African Americans lived in poverty and 23 percent of Hispanics, as compared to only 8 percent of non-Hispanic whites....

Consistent with these income statistics, surveys conducted in the 1980s all showed that about half of all homeless people were black, almost five times their representation in the general population.... Hispanics, paradoxically, were not over-represented among the homeless in most localities and were under-represented in some.

Homelessness among African Americans

It is important to note ... that poverty alone does not account for the high risk of homelessness among blacks. A systematic comparison of the proportion of blacks among the homeless and among domiciled people living in poverty in U.S. cities with populations of 100,000 or more, showed that poor blacks living in urban settings were twice as likely to be homeless as poor whites in the same cities.... Several factors may explain this ... difference: (1) wealth is likely to be more important than income in the etiology of homelessness, (2) white flight and the departure of middle class blacks to the suburbs have left pockets of concentrated poverty and reduced job opportunities in urban areas, and (3) extreme desegregation of housing by race and class seriously augments the adverse effects of other types of economic disadvantage.

First, the gap in wealth between whites and blacks is considerable....

Racial differences in wealth are important because, while income reflects resource availability in an average week or month, wealth (savings) is what allows people to survive periods of adversity such as job loss or recession. Thus, the much larger gap between blacks and whites in wealth can be expected to result in far greater vulnerability among blacks to residential displacement during economic downturns and lower levels of resource buffering capacity in their social networks.

Second ... the loss of jobs in inner cities has dramatically reduced employment opportunities for black men. This loss has been compounded as upwardly mobile blacks have followed whites to more prosperous communities in the suburbs. Thus, many inner city communities have lost their internal cultural strength.

Third, housing segregation has contributed substantially to the exceptionally high risk of homelessness among blacks.... "Redlining" [was] the official government policy during the 1930s that kept blacks from moving into white neighborhoods, and continuing patterns of *de facto* segregation have kept blacks and whites separate. The separation is increasing, and it seriously compounds problems associated with poverty and limited economic opportunity.... In segregated communities, when poor people experience an economic downturn or a reduction in public support, their communities suffer devastating losses of material resources, infrastructure, and institutional capital.... Factors operating at the community level are likely to account substantially for the increased risk for homelessness among blacks beyond income differences....

Homelessness among Latinos

The under-representation of Latinos among homeless people in spite of their high poverty levels has been deftly explained by Susan Gonzalez Baker ... who coined the phrase "The Latino Paradox." She suggested four possible explanations for the low numbers of Latinos among the homeless: (1) survey methods may systematically undercount Latinos in homeless samples, (2) Latinos may have lower levels of personal risk factors such as psychiatric or substance abuse disorders that reduce their risk of homelessness, (3) Latinos may face fewer social disadvantages than other groups, particularly compared to blacks and (4) exceptionally strong traditions of mutual familial support may be protective against homelessness.... Although not definitive, available data most strongly suggest that Latinos may be subject of less housing and job discrimination than blacks, and that they are more likely to incorporate additional family members in a single household....

In the brief period since Baker's study, considerable attention has been focused on the large and growing number of Hispanic immigrants in this country.... Studies of the new immigrants have documented several characteristics that may affect their risk for homelessness. (1) Immigrants from the same towns in Latin America are tightly bound to one another and are deeply committed to mutual protection.... (2) They are often apprehensive about using conventional governmental services for fear of being identified as illegal residents.... Finally, epidemiologic studies suggest that recent migrants, especially those to the Southwest have fewer health problems....

A recent study from the Northeast, however, also found that Puerto Rican single mothers who were poor had experienced less violence and had fewer mental health problems (with the exception of major depression) than whites.... Each of these factors could result in a reduced risk of homelessness among recent immigrants and among less acculturated Latinos. Little is known about the specific risk of homelessness among recent immigrants. The possibility that the Latino paradox may reflect specific conditions faced by more recent immigrants will hopefully generate additional discussion and research. . . .

Homelessness and Health: Psychiatric, Substance Abuse and Medical Disorders

. . . The prevalence of psychiatric and addictive disorders among homeless people has probably been studied more intensively and more rigorously than any other problem. Early accounts suggested that as many as 90 percent of homeless people might be suffering from mental illnesses—including many with severe illnesses such as schizophrenia and other psychoses. . . . Many critics quickly identified the deinstitutionalization of people with mental illness from state hospitals as a major "cause" of homelessness in the 1980s. . . .

In the mid-1980s the National Institutes of Mental Health funded a series of rigorous epidemiological studies. . . . These studies demonstrated that 20–25 percent of homeless single adults had lifetime histories of serious mental illness, about half had histories of alcohol abuse or dependence; and about one-third had histories of drug abuse or dependence. . . . While these rates of lifetime mental illness were 3–5 times greater than rates in the general population, these studies demonstrated that most homeless people did not have serious mental illnesses, and that less than 15 percent had suffered from schizophrenia. . . . Although far more modest than rates reported in previous studies, these data clearly showed that severely mentally ill people were at much higher risk for homelessness than others and that they endured homelessness for greater periods of time. Because the public believed that the needs of people with serious mental illness had not been adequately addressed by the community mental health movement, and because it was more widely accepted that people with serious mental illness "can't help themselves," the public has been willing to support outreach programs to facilitate the entry of distrustful homeless people with mental illness into programs.

Alcoholism has long been identified as a central feature of the lives of homeless people and an explanation for their homelessness. . . . However, among the homeless people who became visible during the 1980s, alcohol addiction was often found in younger members of minority groups . . . and among people with concomitant mental illness. About half of those with serious mental illness also had substance abuse disorders—the so-called dually diagnosed. . . . Alcohol abuse and dependence were often combined with the use of illicit drugs, especially crack cocaine. . . . Because crack cocaine was much cheaper than other drugs and other forms of cocaine, it was widely used by low income people during the years after 1984.

The high level of addictiveness of crack cocaine resulted in sustained, widespread use; one survey found 66 percent of anonymous urines collected in a New York City homeless shelter were positive for crack cocaine. . . . While the path from alcoholism to homelessness was not a new one, the path from crack cocaine to homelessness was new, and was markedly facilitated by the low cost of the drug. Here, too, it affected the poor, infirm, and disadvantaged with special harshness.

In addition to the high rates of alcohol, drug, and mental disorders, homeless people also suffer from serious medical infirmities and experience mortality rates as much as twice as great as those of poor, domiciled people with mental illness. . . . The rate of HIV infection is especially high among homeless people. . . .

Homelessness is thus both an effect and a cause of serious mental and physical health care problems. On the one hand, survey data strongly suggested that people with physical and mental infirmities are far more likely to become homeless than others. On the other hand, the exposure to the elements, poor nutrition, and lack of basic comforts experienced by homeless people worsens their already compromised health status. There is little question that homeless people need health services well beyond those they receive through conventional channels.

Homeless People with Special Status in Society

Homeless Veterans

. . . Surveys conducted during the 1980s indicated that as many as half of homeless veterans served during the Vietnam era compared to only one-third of veterans in the general population. These estimates led many to suggest that homelessness among veterans might be yet another consequence of military service during the Vietnam War and, more specifically, of combat-related post-traumatic stress disorder (PTSD). . . . Although studies have clearly shown that some Vietnam veterans have suffered prolonged psychological problems related to their military service, the assumption that homelessness among veterans is primarily related to Vietnam service is not supported by available evidence.

A systematic synthesis of survey data indicated that 40 percent of homeless men report past military service, as compared to 34 percent in the general adult male population, . . . a modest increase in risk. Further studies using numerous, diverse data sets show that homeless veterans are not more likely to have served during wartime or in combat than age-matched peers who were not homeless, and were no more likely to have war-related post-traumatic stress disorder than non-homeless low income veterans. . . . In fact, the subgroup of veterans at greatest risk of homelessness as compared to their non-veteran peers are those who served after the Vietnam War, during the initial period of the All Volunteer Army, when the military was unpopular, paid low salaries, and was forced to admit many poorly adjusted recruits. . . .

Studies conducted during the 1980s consistently reported that homeless veterans were older and are more likely to be white than other homeless men. . . . Some of these studies also reported that homeless veterans had more often been in jail than homeless non-veterans; more likely to be white; better educated; and more often previously or currently married, but were not different on indicators of residential instability, current social functioning, physical health, mental illness or substance abuse. . . . Thus, it appears that the personal risk of homelessness among veterans was due primarily to the same factors as homelessness among other Americans—poverty, joblessness, mental illness and substance abuse.

However, homeless veterans have received considerable special attention and . . . because of their past service to society. . . . Secretary of Veterans Affairs, Jesse Brown told the Congress that homelessness among veterans "is an American tragedy.... The way a society treats its veterans is an indication of who we are as a nation." It is unlikely that any other cabinet officer has spoken as feelingly or as convincingly about a particular subgroup of the homeless.

Criminal Justice System Users

In dramatic contrast to the public's view of veterans are the feelings about the large number of homeless persons who have past histories of involvement in the criminal justice system.... An estimated 20 percent to 66 percent of homeless people have been arrested or incarcerated in the past as compared to only 22 percent of men and 6 percent of women in the general population.... These high rates may reflect one of four distinct personal configurations: (1) long-term deviant life-styles (people who are deeply involved in crime and antisocial behavior as a way of life, including drug abuse); (2) subsistence (the need to commit crimes for material sustenance); (3) adaptation (criminal behavior as a necessary part of adjusting to life on the street; or (4) diminished capacity (crime resulting from the inability to tell right from wrong due to mental illness). Reliable estimates of the relative importance of these four patterns among homeless people are not available, although they have different implications for social policy. Long term deviant life styles, for example, might suggest the need for increased incarceration while the diminished capacity explanation suggests targeting additional treatment resources to the homeless.

Illegal Immigrants

[This is] a subgroup of homeless people whom nothing has been written about. While this population has been growing rapidly and has provoked a harsh backlash reflected in the passage of Proposition 187 in California in 1994,... we know of only clinical anecdotes revealing the presence of such people among the homeless. Little is known about this population for the following reasons: (1) they may not be very numerous; (2) they may be unwilling to identify themselves for fear of being deported; and (3) they receive little attention because they have the least claim on our sympathies (a point deeply underscored by the passage of Proposition 187). To better serve this group, additional information about their needs is necessary.

Summary: Heroes, Deviants, and the Invisible

In this brief discussion of homelessness among veterans, users of the criminal justice system, and illegal immigrants, we have described three subgroups that cross social status levels: from some of the most idealized members of society, to some of the most despised; to the largely ignored. And yet survey data suggest that the boundaries among these groups may be much clearer in the public imagination than in reality. In a sample of over 10,000 homeless mentally ill veterans seen in a national Congressionally funded VA program, one-third of whom had served the nation in combat, over 50 percent of the sample had significant criminal justice histories; ... in fact they differed little from other homeless men in this or any other respect.... In our reflection on homelessness among these three subgroups we confront most dramatically the tension between attending to each subgroup in order to better understand and respond to their needs—or to differentiate among them to best decide who are deserving of public provision and who are not.

Discussion

In this discussion we have reviewed research on the diverse needs of various subgroups of homeless people. While we have discussed the distinct needs of each subgroup, we have also provided evidence indicating that the most effective way of preventing homelessness is to directly provide residential services and adequate income support. Although many homeless subgroups, especially the young and the mentally ill, need personal support and re-moralization to take full advantage of expanded opportunities, the late 1970s and early 1980s was not a time of epidemic demoralization but of structural change in our society.

. . . While other industrial nations have maintained a broad commitment to social provision for their citizens . . . the United States has long questioned the motives and deservingness of its poor. . . . In fact, Americans have reduced their national commitment through various welfare reform measures and retrenchments. . . . The American approach to public assistance has traditionally been based on a critical evaluation of deservingness, rather than on a broad commitment to assisting the economically disadvantaged. The current withdrawal of public support has occurred in the face of compelling evidence that the distribution of income has become increasingly inequitable since the mid-1970s and that earning opportunities for unskilled workers continue to diminish. . . .

It is not surprising that within this context the differential composition of the homeless population in America receives so much attention. While in other wealthy industrial countries, the mere fact of homelessness justifies a public response, the traditions of social provision in this country demand further justification of the claim for public sympathy and support for each specific subgroup of homeless people. In a broad empirical review of the performance of the U.S. Government, former President of Harvard University, Derek Bok, concluded that while our country excels above all others in its productivity and high standard of living, and that our government is both effective and efficient, it does less well than other countries at protecting its citizens and assuring their personal security.

Convincing others that people are deserving of assistance requires that researchers specializing in the problems of each subgroup advocate for the legitimacy of their needs. This also may explain why so much scholarly attention is directed at subgroups of the homeless who are regarded as "deserving": families, children, the mentally ill, and veterans. Little emphasis is placed on other subgroup characteristics such as extreme poverty, minority status, or being an illegal immigrant.

We do not mean to underplay the importance of addressing the pressing needs of subgroups of the homeless. . . . All the disadvantaged need encouragement and support. . . . But the studies we have reviewed suggest that as important as these specialized services are, they are not the most effective way out of homelessness. That data strongly indicate that all services must be targeted to the specific needs of individual clients, and that emphasizing subgroup characteristics and needs should in no way imply a *de facto* acceptance of homelessness. Since we as a people are not committing the funds to provide subsistence resources for the poor, we understand that there will continue to be hundreds of thousands of homeless persons on any given night, and we are resigned to providing for their educational, health care and job training needs within that context. To do so is certainly preferable to neglecting those needs. However, it is imperative that policy makers understand that such a response may reflect capitulation to an outcome that is not inevitable. If the political will were present, homelessness could be eradicated, or at the very least, very markedly reduced.

SOURCE: Robert Rosenheck, Ellen Bassuk, and Amy Salomon, "Special Populations of Homeless Americans," *Practical Lessons: The 1998 National Symposium on Homeless Research*, ed. by Linda B. Fosburg and Deborah L. Dennis. Washington, DC: U.S. Department of Health and Human Services, U.S. Department of Housing and Urban Development, Interagency Council on the Homeless, 1999.

ANALYSIS

The growing concern during the 1980s and 1990s about homelessness, and the desire for more accurate information on which to base programs and policies, produced a literal flood of publications. Some were written by individual researchers, others by government or quasi-governmental organizations, and still others by private philanthropic associations. Some of the studies were compilations and analyses of recent literature about homelessness, and they were intended to highlight new insights into homelessness and help shape more effective policies and programs in the future. Others were meant to report information about homeless people themselves and also the programs that served them.

One of the most important of this latter group was the 1996 *National Survey of Homeless Assistance Providers and Programs*. It "was designed to provide updated information about the providers of homeless assistance and also the characteristics of homeless persons who use services." The survey was "based on a statistical sample of 76 metropolitan and nonmetropolitan areas, including small cities and rural areas." Twelve federal agencies (including 10 cabinet-level departments, the Social Security Administration, and the Federal Emergency Management Agency) worked together under the guidance of the Interagency Council on the Homeless to design and fund the report. The U.S. Bureau of the Census collected the data for the report, and the Urban Institute analyzed it. During the whole process, "a panel comprised of public interest groups, nationally recognized researchers, and other experts on issues related to homelessness reviewed and commented on the analysis, plan, and draft reports."

The Preface to this report clearly expressed its intent and also what it was *not* intended to do. "The survey was not designed to provide a national count of the number of homeless people," nor did it "include information on client characteristics at the regional or local levels." It *was* designed to provide up-to-date information about the providers of assistance to homeless people, the characteristics of those who use services that focus on homeless people, and how this population has changed in metropolitan areas since 1987. In addition to analyzing the service providers, the report also contained, but was "not limited to, [information about] such characteristics as age, race/ethnicity, sex, family status, history of homelessness, employment, education, veteran status, and use of services and benefits."

A different kind of report was also published in 1999. Written by three distinguished scholars, it did not present new data about homeless people themselves. Rather, it reviewed some of the enormous literature about homelessness that had been published during the previous two decades. In doing so, it evaluated many of those articles and books, pointed out the new directions being taken by students of homelessness, and presented the perspectives on homelessness held by the authors of this article. In the conclusion to the article, the authors clearly express the point of view that, while it is important to recognize and respond to the many subgroups of homeless people, a more satisfactory and effective way of responding to homelessness would be to recognize that all homeless people shared two important traits—they lack decent housing and they lack adequate incomes. Supplying them with adequate economic means to acquire suitable housing would do more than anything else to reduce, or even eradicate, homelessness.

In reading the excerpt from the article presented here, keep in mind that each generalization about homelessness is immediately followed by a reference telling the source of the statement (in the original printed version).

FURTHER READING

Baumohl, Jim, and R. Huebner. "Alcohol and Other Drug Problems among the Homeless." *Housing Policy Debate*, 2 (1991), 837–65.

Cohen, C., and J. Sokolowsky. *Old Men of the Bowery: Strategies for Survival among the Homeless*. New York: Guildford Press, 1989.

Currie, E. *Reckoning: Drugs, the Cities, and the American Future*. New York: Hill and Wang, 1993.

Johnson, T., and S. Freels. "Substance Abuse and Homelessness: Social Selection or Social Adaptation." *Addiction*, 92 (1997), 437–45.

Lehman, A. F., and D. S. Cordray. "Prevalence of Alcohol, Drug, and Mental Disorders among the Homeless: One More Time." *Contemporary Drug Problems*, 20 (1993), 355–83.

Oakley, D., and D. L., "Responding to the Needs of Homeless People with Alcohol, Drug, and/or Mental Disorders." In Jim Baumohl (ed.), *Homelessness in America*. Phoenix, AZ: Oryx Press, 1996, 179–86.

35

HOMELESS CHILDREN AND THEIR FAMILIES

Testimony of Ellen L. Bassuk before the Subcommittee on Housing and Community Opportunity of the Finance Committee of the House of Representatives, October 16, 2007

- **Document:** The document presents the testimony of Ellen Bassuk, a prominent analyst of child homelessness, before a Congressional Committee. In her testimony, she explains the condition of homeless children and suggests how some of their problems can be solved.
- **Date:** Dr. Bassuk gave her testimony to the Subcommittee on October 16, 2007.
- **Place:** The hearings were held in the U.S. Capitol in Washington, DC.
- **Significance:** Dr. Bassuk presents shocking statistics about the condition of homeless children in the United States. The information that she gave the Committee was generally unknown before her testimony. Most people are still unaware of either the extent of child homelessness or of how the condition affects children. While giving her testimony, Dr. Bassuk implored the Committee to maintain funding for programs to assist children without proper homes.

DOCUMENT

For the first time in the history of the United States, with the exception of the Great Depression, homeless children and their families have joined the ranks of the homeless population. ... While the numbers of families and children in the mid-1980s were negligible, they now comprise 35–40% of the overall homeless population. ... It is astounding to consider that 1.8% of all families and 8% of poor families in the United States experience homelessness annually. ... We know these numbers underestimate assistance services. Local reports suggest that family homelessness is now increasing significantly. For example, Massachusetts has seen a 29% increase in family homelessness in a little over a year.

Homelessness for a child is more than the loss of a house. It disrupts every aspect of life. It separates children from their belongings, beloved pets, reassuring routines, friends, and community. At a time when children should be developing a sense of safety and security, trust in their caregivers, and freedom to explore the world, they are severely challenged and limited by unpredictability, dislocation, and chaos. They begin to learn that the world is in fact unsafe, that their parents are understandably stressed and preoccupied, and that scary and often violent things happen around them. These experiences are not lost on children—even the youngest. Ongoing, chronic stress can have profound and lasting effects that may still be manifested in adulthood.

Based on a . . . study we conducted, The National Center on Family Homelessness has documented that residential instability, interpersonal violence, and family separation are inextricably linked. Ninety-seven percent of homeless families move, many up to three times, in the year before entering shelter. . . . These moves are not positive: 26% of homeless families have been evicted from their homes; 89% had been doubled-up where they were faced with overcrowding, friends and family who resented their presence, and significant risk of physical and sexual abuse. . . .

Perhaps the most striking finding from our research is the astoundingly high rates of interpersonal and community violence in the lives of these families. . . . The pervasiveness of victimization in the lives of homeless mothers is staggering.

- 92% of homeless mothers have been severely physically or sexually assaulted during their lives—and their average age is 27 years.
- 63% of homeless mothers have been violently abused by a male partner with 27% requiring medical treatment.
- 25% of homeless mothers have been victims of random violence.

These findings are particularly pertinent considering that a mother's emotional status is often the most important mediating factor determining the outcomes for her children—especially younger children.

Homeless children are also exposed to extreme levels of violence. For example, although difficult to document accurately due to under-reporting, we know from a recent study of homeless children aged 8 to 17 years

- 62% have been exposed to at least one form of severe violence; 37% reported two or more events, and 23% reported three or more.
- 13% reported that grown-ups at home had hit each other.

DID YOU KNOW?

Homeless Adolescents

Homelessness is a widespread challenge in the United States with 12% of the homeless population consisting of adolescents. . . . According to one representative survey, the annual prevalence of homelessness among adolescents in 7.6% . . . making adolescents the single most susceptible age group to experience homelessness. . . . Compared to housed youth, high rates of substance use, mental health problems, teen pregnancy, suicide and high-risk behaviors among homeless youth have been amply noted by researchers.

Source: Slesnick, Natasha, et al. "Predictors of Homelessness among Street Living Youth." *Journal of Youth and Adolescence,* 37, 4 (2008), 465–74.

DID YOU KNOW?

Is Homelessness the Most Appropriate Word?

The study of rural child and family homelessness requires that a different definition be used to describe their experience for four reasons: (1) the word *homelessness* carries too many urban stereotypes to be useful in understanding those who are homeless in small towns and their experience. (2) The term does not readily convey the *process* by which children and families come to lose housing in small towns. (3) While the rural homeless may have a roof over their head, shelter alone does not give one a sense of home. Psychological homelessness is as much a threat to one's well-being as physical homelessness. (4) The term *homelessness* has no positive attributes. Yet the rural displaced have integrity. They are not generally lazy, substance-abusing, mentally ill misfits. The rural homeless are folks who largely have fallen on hard times that got the better of them. Therefore, rural homelessness is defined . . . as the lack of a consistent, safe, physical structure and the emotional deprivation that occurs as a result. The lack of housing denies children a secure sense of psychological belongingness in a community where other people have access to regular homes.

Source: Vissing, Yvonne M., *Out of Sight, Out of Mind: Homeless Children and Families in Small-Town America.* Lexington: University of Kentucky Press, 1996.

- 53% reported hearing gunshots, 17% said they had seen someone shot, and 17% said they had seen a dead body.
- 8% reported that someone had threatened to kill them.

This exposure to violence was a salient predictor of children's mental health over and above other explanatory factors. . . .

Homelessness is also marked by family separations and disruptions. . . . Homeless children are at high risk for out-of-home placement: 22% live away from their immediate family at some point, 12% are placed in foster care, compared to just over 1% of other children. . . . The impact of family separation is significant. Caring attachments between adults and children are fundamental to human development. When a child's bond with her mother or mother figure is precipitously disrupted or inconsistent, the child is likely to suffer long-term negative effects such as behavioral difficulties and an inability to form supportive trusting relationships that may extend into adulthood.

Understandably, given their circumstances and the unrelenting stresses they experience, including the stress of homelessness itself, many homeless children face physical, emotional, behavioral, and cognitive development issues. . . . Compared to their housed counterparts, homeless children have more acute and chronic medical problems, four times the rate of development delays, three times the rate of anxiety, depression and behavioral difficulties, and twice the rate of learning disabilities. By age 8 years, approximately one in three homeless children has at least one major psychiatric disorder. It is not surprising that they struggle in school and have difficulty learning. Almost three-quarters perform below grade level in reading and spelling. An estimated one-third have repeated a grade. Despite their extensive needs, most are not receiving appropriate special educational services or treatment when needed. . . .

It is important to add a hopeful caveat to this dire picture. We have data that strongly suggest that many homeless children are resilient and do well with adequate supports and clinical treatment when needed. . . . Stable permanent housing is the critical foundation for achieving these positive outcomes.

Homelessness is traumatic for children and its effects can last a lifetime. . . . It is not just the children who lose out. Our society as a whole faces a profound moral dilemma and pays a high economic price for this tragedy. Efforts must be made to strengthen the federal response to family homelessness before the homeless children of today become the chronically homeless adults of tomorrow. Permanent housing with transitional supports is the basis for the solution and can pave the way to ending homelessness. With children in such dire circumstances, we either pay now or pay later.

. . . [W]e [The National Council on Family Homelessness] offer various suggestions [about what to do].

First, we urge aligning the HUD definition of homelessness with those used by the Departments of Education, Health and Human Services, and Justice. Families, children, and youth who are doubled up or living in hotels or motels and do not have a fixed, regular and adequate living situation are homeless. These families live in overcrowded, unsafe, and unstable living situations with entire families often having to live in a single room with no access to cooking facilities or play spaces. Not only are these situations emotionally damaging for children they also can be physically damaging as children in these situations are at increased risk for physical and sexual abuse. These families are homeless and in need of services and safe, stable housing.

Second, we support provisions in the HEARTH (Homeless Emergency and Rapid Transition to Housing) Act that allow communities the flexibility to implement a range of housing and service options based on local needs. These strategies are more likely to be responsive to local needs and allow the possibility of supporting preventive services. . . .

Finally, if there is to be a set aside for permanent supportive housing, it is essential that the definition is expanded to include the needs of homeless families and children. Homeless families and children have different mental health needs than those of homeless single adults. . . . Some family members have serious physical and/or mental health needs that are disabling enough to warrant ongoing community services and treatment, including placement in permanent supportive housing. Because research data on this remain limited, there has been disagreement about the percentage of families in this category. Many family members have problems such as post-traumatic stress disorder (PTSD) and clinical depression which are often under-recognized and under-treated. . . . Among the mothers, these conditions when untreated, often lead to difficulties accessing critical services, becoming self-supporting and

---

DID YOU KNOW?

Homeless Infants

At 5 weeks old, with a crown of dark hair and big blue eyes, Anastasia Garcia is one of the newest faces of the economic crisis. She was born homeless.

"When we are lucky enough to be settled, we will tell her that things were not always as easy as you may think," said Angela Garcia, 26, laying the infant down in a crib crammed into the corner of a small room at the Broward Outreach Center in Pompano Beach she shares with her husband David Henson and their two older daughters, ages 2 and 6.

In Fort Lauderdale, Demali Staple's youngest child, 4-month-old Jabari, is another recession baby, entering a world gripped by the worst economy in more than a generation. When Staple finishes work as a landscaper for the city of Oakland Park, she picks up her infant son and his brother Alvash, 3, at a day care center and they return to a room at Covenant House, a shelter for runaways and homeless youth.

"There are days when I want to give up," said Staple, 21, a single mother. "But I don't want my boys to go through what I went through. So I push myself."

Throughout South Florida, social service agencies report sharp increases in the number of infants and very young children being sheltered in homeless facilities.

In Palm Beach County, Center for Family Services Executive Director Dorla Leslie said her nonprofit organization has been "deluged over the past several months, and a majority are single mothers with young children, some with infants."

All 18 rooms of a West Palm Beach apartment complex that the center runs are full, with about 65 people, said Leslie, while another half-dozen families are being housed in motels.

At Covenant House, Executive Director Jim Gress said, "Moms and babies have been the largest proportion of our population lately."

The reasons for a surge in homeless infants and young children may be no more complicated than the sagging economy. As jobs disappear, intact families and single moms who were once able to provide for their children no longer can.

A recent study by the National Center on Family Homelessness found that 1 in 50 American children is homeless. Florida's population of homeless children is estimated to be 50,000.

For pregnant women and newborns, health concerns are magnified by poverty and homelessness. Studies show

---

that homeless children are more likely than other children to have asthma and ear infections, and suffer from emotional and behavior problems.

"It is not ideal in any way, shape or form to have baby in a shelter," said Patricia Mantis of the Broward County's Coalition to End Homelessness.

Priscilla Garrett, 25, lived with her mother in Delray Beach until family problems led her to the Broward Outreach Center four months ago. On June 18 she gave birth to an 8-pound, 2-ounce girl, and she and her daughter returned to the shelter this week.

"I see myself as going through a transitional phase right now," said Garrett, whose last job was as a Family Dollar store clerk. Years from now, she said, she would explain to her child her personal history: "You were born in a place where friends were, with people who helped you and me."

For struggling parents such as Garcia and Henson, shelter living with an infant means access to free diapers, some clothing and even a stroller. They also benefit from counsel supplied their Broward Outreach Center caseworker Shirley Favali.

Less than ideal are extremely tight quarters, sharing a bathroom with dozens of others, and none of the extended family support that many young parents rely on.

During weekdays, Alisa, 6, goes to camp while Garcia stays in the shelter's family wing with her baby and Alexis, irrepressibly active. If Garcia can find day care for Alexis and the baby in the next few days, she plans to begin looking for a job.

"We never thought this would happen," said Henson, 31, of the couple's spiral into homelessness that accelerated when he lost his construction job in January. "Really, I am shocked that I let us get this far down."

Together for seven years, Garcia and Henson grew up in Hollywood and lived there in a rented apartment. When they could no longer afford it, they moved in with Garcia's mother. He worked day jobs through labor pools.

After a fruitless bus trip to find work in Texas, where Garcia's father lives, the couple returned to Broward County this spring, completely broke.

Henson recently found a job in a Home Depot warehouse, and Favali said the couple are on track to qualify for a move to transitional housing, where they can stay rent-free for up to 18 months. "I think they are really trying," said Favali. "They are motivated."

Staple is also trying. Born in Jamaica, she attended Piper High School in Sunrise until she became pregnant with Alvash. She was taking technical school courses and staying with her father until earlier this year.

Her second child was born after she found a space at Covenant House, a private Christian ministry that operates youth shelters in several U.S. cities.

parenting effectively. If substance abuse is added to the equation, their challenges are even greater. Homeless disabilities must also be included within such a set aside. A significant number of these children suffer from disabilities that place increased demands on their families and can limit a parent/caretaker's ability to exit homelessness.

... There are two generations within homeless families, parent/caretaker and child(ren) and a significant percentage of these children are under 6. The impact of homelessness is very different for children; experiencing homelessness for even one or two months (much less a year or more or four times in a three year period) may have a devastating impact on their healthy growth and development....

Homeless children do not become homeless by themselves. We cannot expect them to stabilize their lives alone. As the society which has fashioned their condition, we have a moral responsibility to devise their rescue.... The knowledge and strategies to end family homelessness exist. We now need the desire to ensure a decent life for all children and the will to make it happen.

SOURCE: U.S. Congress. House. Committee on Financial Services. *Reauthorization of the McKinney-Vento Homeless Assistance Act, Part II. Hearing before the Subcommittee on Housing and Equal Community Opportunity.* 110th Cong., 1st sess., 16 October 2007.

ANALYSIS

The "rediscovery" of homeless families could not have taken place without observers also recognizing that women and children are part of the homeless population. It had always been known that there were a small number of homeless women and children, but analysts rarely included them among the "mainstream" homeless, considering them to be anomalies and outside the usual categorizations. They frequently thought that all homeless women resembled Boxcar Bertha, a fictional creation of Ben Reitman, who "edited" her autobiography. Reitman presented her as a rough, tough woman who knew how to take care of herself, did what she wanted when she wanted, and could battle equally with any man at any time. In fact, although Reitman presented her as being clearly female and even alluded to her sex life, he actually portrayed her in ways reminiscent of the stereotype of young male hoboes filled with wanderlust and eager for adventure. Although he did not present young men and women in exactly the same way, and presented the reasons why they chose to leave or were forced to leave their homes, in his 1934 book about the *Boy and Girl Tramps of America* Thomas Minehan conveyed the attitude that these children and youth were abnormalities and should be looked at somewhat askance.

"I am saving all the money I can," said Staple, who catches a 7 a.m. bus so she can drop the kids off at day care before and get to work by 8.

With the baby in her arms, and Alvash bouncing on a couch, Staple looked around a lounge-like play room in the former motel that Covenant House runs as a family center. "This is not the life I imagined, being in this position," she said. "I'd still like to be a nurse, or get my GED and go into the military.

"But, look, I'm here now."

Source: Clary, Mike. "Number of Babies in Homeless Shelters Increasing." *South Florida Sun-Sentinel,* July 13, 2009. Reprinted with permission from the *Sun Sentinel.*

During the 1980s and 1990s, as homelessness became more common, and more commonly perceived in the United States, government officials and social scientists who had gathered more and more accurate information about homelessness and the nature of the homeless population began to recognize that the contemporary homeless population differed in important ways from the homeless people of the past. They discovered that the contemporary homeless population was not nearly as white, or as male, or as aged as the homeless population of the past. And, as they collected data to study the "new homeless," they began asking a whole range of new questions that they hoped their data would allow them to answer.

While they asked questions that now seem all too obvious—questions about age, race/ethnicity, sex, place of birth, and so on—their developing understanding of homelessness as an aspect of U.S. society pushed them into asking much more complex questions—questions about the causes of homelessness and also its consequences. They wondered if different kinds of homelessness could be identified, and they speculated about whether the homeless could be studied as a single group or if different groups of homeless people actually had different demographic and social characteristics. They also conjectured about whether an individual's homeless state resulted from the circumstances of that person's character and status in life or if it resulted from a social and economic context over which the individual had little control.

Much of the information to answer these questions was gathered by agencies of the federal government concerned with homelessness—the Department of Health and Human Services, and the Department of Housing and Urban Development, and the Department of Education, for example. Much of the data and the information about homelessness emerged from investigations conducted by nonprofit organizations and quasigovernmental agencies working to alleviate the condition and the severity of homelessness—groups such as the National Coalition for the Homeless, National Center on Family Homelessness, and the United States Interagency Council on Homelessness, just to mention a few.

There has also been a handful of extremely important individuals who are difficult to place in a single basket. Their concerns about homelessness cross the usual

DID YOU KNOW?

Survival Strategies

This is how Shiv and I found the Clubhouse. One night about 2 AM we were walking around looking for a place to sleep. The station was closed, so we couldn't go there. . . . We were heading to this park over on First Avenue, and we passed a bunch of empty boxes stacked in front of an apartment building.

"Let's take some cardboard to sleep on," Shiv said. I started to rip up a box but Shiv told me wait a minute. "We gotta take this one," he said. It was an enormous box, the kind refrigerators come in. "Help me carry it," he said. "Carry it where?" He said back to Grand Central [Station]. "For what? Grand Central's closed."

He told me hush up, he said, "Don't I always know what I'm doing?" So we lugged the damn thing six or seven blocks. . . .

We carried the box up the ramp to the elevated street that circles Grand Central, which put it alongside the second floor of the station. There's an entrance up there, it's mainly for the cops because it's right next to their precinct in the station's balcony. Near that entrance is a big tool-shed, six or seven high, and behind the toolshed is a ledge about four feet off the ground. And that's where we put the box. Shiv . . . laid the box on its side, and you could hardly see it because of the toolshed.

"Brilliant, huh?" he said. "Now we got our own private little house." . . . [S]ince we were outside the station, we couldn't get arrested for criminal trespass. It was just squatting, which didn't carry any charges.

The second night, it rained, and Shiv got a plastic tarp to put over the box to keep it dry. When it was getting chilly, because it was late September already, he snuck into a moving van, stole one of those big quilted blankets that movers use, put that underneath the plastic tarp. It wrapped the whole box up and insulated it. Later, in October, Shiv brought some wooden planks to lay on the roof to make it stronger and warmer. We had blankets and also we started keeping clothes in there, and the shampoo and toothpaste and stuff for when Shiv took me to the Y.

Source: Bolnick, Tina S., and Jamie Pastor. *Living at the Edge of the World: A Teenager's Survival in the Tunnels of Grand Central Station.* New York: St. Martin's Press, 2000, 179–80.

boundaries. They care about homelessness as an intellectual problem, so they do research, and many of them teach at colleges and universities in Departments of Sociology, or Urban Affairs, or Public Health, or Social Welfare. But many of these individuals are also activists who see their research as an enterprise that has the practical value of determining the causes of homelessness and its eradication. Some of these people are also closely identified with the organizations devoted to solving the problems associated with homelessness, like the ones mentioned a few sentences previously.

A few of the more prominent individuals whose careers cross over the individual boundaries are Ellen Bassuk, Jim Baumohl, Martha Burt, Kim Hopper, Dennis Kulhane, and Marybeth Shinn, just to mention a few of the most eminent. All of these individuals have written extensively about homelessness, all of them have been closely involved with organizations that study homelessness and are dedicated to alleviating or eradicating it, and all of them have either consulted with government agencies, testified before Congress or congressional committees about homelessness, and many of them have collaborated with one or more of the others in writing about various aspects of homelessness.

On October 16, 2007, Ellen L. Bassuk, MD, testified before the Subcommittee on Housing and Community Opportunity of the House of Representatives Financial Services Committee. Dr. Bassuk was an Associate Professor of Psychiatry at the Harvard University Medical School and the founder and President of the National Council on Family Homelessness. She had also written dozens of articles and several books about homelessness, especially homeless women, children, and families. At the beginning of her testimony before the Subcommittee, Dr. Bassuk described the work of the National Council and also, implicitly, her own goals.

[T]he National Center on Family Homelessness is a mission-driven, non-profit organization committed to family homelessness by understanding the needs of homeless families and children, developing and refining responsive programs, and delivering technical assistance to communities and service providers. We have conducted dozens of research, evaluation, and technical assistance programs and policies across the country, including some of the first studies of homeless families in the early 1980s that helped put that issue on the nation's program and policy agenda. We currently work in 47 states across the nation.

As she presented the rest of her testimony, Dr. Bassuk disclosed a great deal about what she and other researchers had learned in the last few years about homeless children and homeless families.

DID YOU KNOW?

... [T]he scariest finding to emerge from our study is the extraordinary number of poor people in New York City who are badly housed and therefore at risk of becoming homeless. For example, we know that some 13% of families on the city's welfare caseload don't have their own apartment and are living doubled up with families. And we know that doubling up—always a fragile social arrangement—often precedes entry into the shelter system. Under these conditions, our results suggest, family homelessness will endure.

Source: "NYU Study Says Affordable Housing Is Best Cure for Family Homelessness," New York University Press Release, November 1, 1998. Available online at http://www.nyu.edu/publicaffairs/newsreleases/b_NYU_S5.shtml.

FURTHER READING

Karlen, Neal, et al. "Homeless Kids: 'Forgotten Facts.'" *Newsweek*, January 6, 1986, p. 20.

Rafferty, Y., and M. Shinn. "The Impact of Homelessness on Children." *American Psychologist*, 46 (1991), 1170–79.

Robertson, Marjorie J., and P. A. Toro. "Homeless Youth: Research, Intervention and Policy." In L. Fosburg and D. Dennis (eds.), *Practical Lessons: The 1998 National Symposium on Homelessness Research*. Washington, DC: Department of Housing and Urban Development and Department of Health and Human Services, 1999.

"Runaway and Homeless Youth" and "Families." In Steven VanderStaay, *Street Lives: An Oral History of Homeless Americans*. Philadelphia, PA, and Gabriola Island, BC: New Society Publishers, 1992, 81–98, 1578–82.

Sullivan, Patricia A., and Shirley P. Damrosch. "Homeless Women and Children." In Richard D. Bingham, Roy E. Green, and Sammis B. White, *The Homeless in Contemporary Society*. Newbury Park, CA, and London: Sage Publications, 1989, 82–98.

United States Department of Housing and Urban Development. *Rental Housing Assistance: A Report to Congress on Worst Case Housing Needs*. Available at http://www.huduser.org/Publications/AFFHSG/WORSTCASE00/worstcase00.pdf.

United States General Accounting Office. *Children and Youths: About 68,000 Homeless and 186,000 in Shared Housing at Any Given Time*. Washington, DC: GAO, 1989.

Uys, Errol Lincoln. *Riding the Rails: Teenagers on the Move during the Great Depression*. New York: Routledge, 2003.

36

HOMELESS VETERANS

The Report of the Congressional Research Service to Congress about Veterans and Homelessness, 2007

- *Document:* The document is selected from a report about homelessness among veterans prepared for Congress by the Congressional Research Service.
- *Date:* The report is dated May 31, 2007.
- *Where:* The report was issued in Washington, DC.
- *Significance:* The report informed Congress about the growth and nature of homelessness among veterans between about 1980 and 2005. It was influential in shaping the attitude of Congress toward developing more programs and providing more funds to care for and assist homeless veterans. It was especially important in informing them about homeless veterans from the wars in Iraq and Afghanistan.

DOCUMENT

Overview of Veterans and Homelessness

Homeless veterans began to come to the attention of the public at the same time that homelessness generally was becoming more common. News accounts chronicled the life of veterans who had served their country but were living (and dying) on the street. The commonly-held notion that the military experience provides young people with job training, educational and other benefits, as well as the maturity needed for a productive life, conflicted with the presence of veterans among the homeless.

Characteristics of Homeless Veterans

Homeless male veterans differ from homeless men who are non-veterans in a variety of ways. According to data from several studies during the 1980s, homeless male veterans were more likely to be older and better educated than the general population of homeless men. However, they were found to have more health problems than non-veteran homeless men, including AIDS, cancer, and hypertension. A study published in 2002 found similar results regarding age and education. Homeless male veterans tended to be older, on average, than non-veteran homeless men. Homeless veterans were also different in that they had reached higher levels of education than their non-veteran counterparts and were more likely to be working for pay. They were more likely to have been homeless for more than one year, and more likely to be dependent on or abuse alcohol. Family backgrounds among homeless veterans tended to be more stable, with veterans experiencing less family instability and fewer incidents of conduct disorder, while also being less likely to have never married than non-veteran homeless men.

Homeless women veterans have also been found to have different characteristics than non-veteran homeless women. . . . Female veterans, like male veterans, were found to have reached higher levels of education than non-veteran homeless women, and also more likely to have been employed in the 30 days prior to being surveyed. They also had more stable family backgrounds, and lower rates of conduct disorder as children.

Overrepresentation of Veterans in the Homeless Population

Research . . . beginning in the 1980s has found that both male and female veterans are overrepresented among the homeless, and that, overall, veterans are more likely to be homeless than their non-veteran counterparts. This has not always been the case, however. Although veterans have always been present among the homeless, the birth cohorts that served in the military more recently, from the Vietnam and post-Vietnam eras, have been found to be overrepresented. Veterans of World War II and Korea are less likely to be homeless than their non-veteran counterparts. (The same cohort effect is not as evident for women veterans.) Four studies of homeless veterans, two of male veterans and two of female veterans,

---

DID YOU KNOW?

[Congress Hears about Homeless Veterans] Testimony of the National Coalition for Homeless Veterans before the U. S. Senate Committee on Banking, Housing, and Urban Affairs. Subcommittee on Housing Transportation and Community Development

Nov. 10, 2009

NCHV acknowledges the leadership role of this subcommittee, and that of the full committee, in this noble effort. There are three key bills that lay the foundation on which we, as a nation, can build a successful, comprehensive campaign to end and prevent homelessness among veterans. . . .

S. 1547—Zero Tolerance for Veteran Homelessness Act of 2009

For several years the homeless veteran assistance movement NCHV represents has realized there can be no end to veteran homelessness until we develop a strategy to address the needs of our former guardians before they become homeless—victims of health and economic misfortunes they cannot overcome without assistance.

The causes of all homelessness can be grouped into three primary categories: health issues, economic issues, and lack of access to safe, affordable housing for low- and extreme-low income families. . . .

The additional stressors veterans experience are prolonged separation from family and social support networks while engaging in extremely stressful training and occupational assignments; war-related illnesses and disabilities—both mental and physical; and the difficulty of many to transfer military occupational skills into the civilian workforce.

Victory in this campaign requires success on two fronts—effective, economical intervention strategies that help men and women rise above adversity . . . and prevention strategies that empower communities to support our wounded warriors and their families. . . .

We believe the *Zero Tolerance for Veteran Homelessness Act* addresses needs on both fronts.

- The Act provides for . . . a total of 60,000 housing vouchers for veterans with serious mental and emotional illnesses, other disabilities, and extreme low-income families that will need additional services to remain housed. . . . ***This Act would, therefore, effectively end chronic veteran homelessness within the next five years.***
- This Act provides authorization for up to $50 million annually to provide supportive services to low-income

veterans to reduce their risks of becoming homeless, and to help those who are find[ing] housing. . . . For many among the nation's 630,000 veterans living in extreme poverty (at or below 50% of the federal government poverty level), this aid could mean the difference between achieving stability and continuing on the downward spiral into homelessness.

- The Act would modernize the extremely important and successful VA Grant and Per Diem Program (GPD) to allow for the utilization of innovative project funding strategies. . . .
- The Act calls for the Secretary of Veterans Affais to study the method of reimbursing GPD community providers for their program expenses and report . . . his recommendations for revising the payment system.
- The Act calls for an increase in the annual GPD authorization to $200 million . . . which could provide additional funds for outreach through community-based veteran service centers and mobile service vans. . . .
- The Act would establish within HUD a Special Assistant for Veterans Affairs to ensure veterans have access to housing and homeless assistance programs . . . [in] the Department.

S. 1160—The Homes for Heroes Act of 2009

. . . [L]ong-term housing ranks in the top 10 reported unmet needs of veterans. Finding and obtaining safe and secure housing is often the biggest obstacle veterans in recovery face. This bill will allow low- and extremely low-income veterans to access housing. . . .

. . . [T]he Homes for Heroes Act would:

- Provide $200 million annually for the development of supportive housing for veterans who need case management and wrap-around services to remain housed.
- Fund 20,000 rental assistance vouchers for extremely low-income veteran families (those living at or below 50% of the federal poverty level). . . . These individuals represent those . . . at highest risk of becoming homeless. . . .
- Create the position of veteran liaison with the Department of Housing and Urban Development to ensure veteran inclusion in all HUD housing programs, and require inclusion of veteran data in local housing plans.

S. 1237—Homeless Women Veterans with Children Act of 2009

. . . According to VA data . . . the highest unmet needs of homeless single veterans with dependent children are:

provide evidence of this overrepresentation and increased likelihood of experiencing homelessness.

Overrepresentation of Male Veterans

Two national studies . . . found that male veterans were overrepresented in the homeless population. In addition, researchers in both studies determined that the likelihood of homelessness depended on the age of the veterans. . . . The odds of a veteran being homeless were highest for veterans who had enlisted after the military transitioned to an all-volunteer force (AVF) in 1973. These veterans were 20–34 at the time of the first study, and age 35–44 at the time of the second study.

In the first study, researchers found that 41% of adult homeless men were veterans, compared to just fewer than 34% of adult males in the general population. Overall, male veterans were 1.4 times as likely to be homeless as non-veterans. Notably, though, those veterans who had served after the Vietnam War were four times more likely to be homeless as non-veterans in the same age group. Vietnam era veterans, who are often thought to be the most overrepresented group of homeless veterans, were barely more likely to be homeless than non-veterans (1.01 times). . . .

In the second study, researchers found that nearly 33% of adult homeless men were veterans, compared to 28% of males in the general population. Once again, the likelihood of homelessness differed among age groups. Overall, male veterans were 1.25 times more likely to be homeless than non-veterans. However, the post-Vietnam birth cohort, like that in the 1994 study, were most at risk of homelessness; they were over three times as likely to be homeless as non-veterans in their cohort. Younger veterans, those [of] age 20–34 in 1996, were two times as likely to be homeless as non-veterans. And Vietnam era veterans were approximately 1.4 times as likely to be homeless as their non-veteran counterparts.

Overrepresentation of Female Veterans

Like male veterans, women veterans are more likely to be homeless than women who are not veterans. A study published in 2003 examined two surveys, one of mentally ill homeless women, and one of homeless persons generally, and found that 4.4% and 3.1% of those homeless surveyed were female veterans respectively (compared to approximately 1.3% of the general population), Although the likelihood of homelessness was different for each of the two surveyed populations, the study estimated the female veterans were between two and four times as likely to be homeless as their non-veteran counterparts. Unlike male veterans, all birth cohorts were more likely to be homeless than non-veterans....

Why Are Veterans Overrepresented in the Homeless Population?

As the number of homeless veterans has grown, researchers have attempted to explain why veterans are homeless in higher proportions than their numbers in the general population. Factors present both prior to military experience, and those that developed during or after service, have been found to be associated with the veterans' homelessness....

Factors Present During and After Military Service

- Child care assistance
- Legal aid for credit repair and child support issues
- Access to affordable housing

S. 1237 would authorize up to $10 million in grants to community- and faith-based organizations to provide critical, specialized supports for these deserving men and women as they work their way out of homelessness.

In Summation

... These three bills are vital for the ... Plan to move forward. From the increase in the number of ... [housing] vouchers, and the ability to provide supportive services for low-income and women veterans, to the improvement and expansion of the GPD program, these bills provide real opportunities to ... fulfill the historic mission to end homelessness among America's ... [veterans] in five years.

Source: Testimony of the National Coalition for Homeless Veterans before the U.S. Senate Committee on Banking, Housing, and Urban Affairs, Subcommittee on Housing, Transportation and Community Development, November 10, 2009, "National Coalition for Homeless Veterans; Policy & Legislation." Available online at http://banking.senate.gov/public/index.cfm?FuseAction=Hearings.Hearing&Hearing_ID=5440a0bd-ab35-49c4-85cc-d8b80e368b55.

Although researchers have not found that military service alone is associated with homelessness, it may be associated with other factors that contribute to homelessness. [The study] found an indirect connection between the stress that occurs as a result of deployment and exposure to combat, or "war-zone stress," and homelessness. Vietnam theatre and era veterans who experienced war-zone stress were found to have difficulty readjusting to civilian life, resulting in higher levels of problems that included social isolation, violent behavior, and, for white male veterans, homelessness.

[A] 1994 study of Vietnam era veterans ... evaluated 18 variables that could be associated with homelessness. The study categorized each variable ... according to when they occurred in the veteran's life: pre-military, military, the one-year readjustment period, and the post-military period subsequent to readjustment. Variables from each time period were found to be associated with homelessness, although their effects varied. The two military factors—combat exposure and participation in atrocities—did not have a direct relationship to homelessness. However, those two factors did contribute to (1) low levels of social support upon returning home, (2) psychiatric disorders (not including Post Traumatic Stress Disorder (PTSD)), (3) substance abuse disorders, and (4) being unmarried (including separation and divorce). Each of these four post-military variables, in turn, contributed directly to homelessness. In fact, social isolation, measured by low levels of

The presence of many homeless veterans in the United States is a matter of public record and is well-known in the United States. What people tend to overlook when thinking or talking about homeless veterans is that not all homeless veterans are men. Some are women. Margaret Ortiz spent her entire life savings on alcohol and drugs after she returned from Iraq and has been called "one of the new faces of America's homeless veterans population." (AP/Wide World Photos)

support in the first year after discharge from military service, together with the status of being unmarried, had the strongest association with homelessness of the 18 factors examined in the study.

Post-Traumatic Stress Disorder (PTSD). Researchers have not found a direct relationship between PTSD and homelessness. [One] ... study "found no unique association between combat-related PTSD and homelessness." ... Homeless combat veterans were no more likely to be diagnosed with PTSD than combat veterans who were not homeless. However, [the study] found PTSD was significantly related to other psychiatric disorders, substance abuse, problems in interpersonal relationships, and unemployment. These conditions can lead to readjustment difficulties and are considered risk factors for homelessness.

Factors that Pre-Date Military Service. [One] study found that three variables present in the lives of veterans before they joined the military had a significant direct relationship to homelessness. These were exposure to physical or sexual abuse prior to age 18; exposure to other traumatic experiences, such as experiencing a serious accident or natural disaster, or seeing someone killed; or placement in foster care prior to age 16. The researchers also found that a history of conduct disorder had a substantial indirect effect on homelessness. Conduct disorder includes behaviors such as being suspended or expelled from school, involvement with law enforcement, or having poor academic performance. Another pre-military variable that might contribute to homelessness among veterans is a lack of family support prior to enlistment.

The conditions present in the lives of veterans prior to military service, and the growth of homelessness among veterans, have been tied to the institution of the all-volunteer force (AVF) in 1973.... The overrepresentation of veterans in the homeless population is most prevalent in the birth cohort that joined the military after the Vietnam War. It is possible that higher rates of homelessness among these veterans are due to "lower recruitment standards during periods where military service was not held in high regard." Individuals who joined the military during the time after the implementation of the AVF might have been more likely to have characteristics that are risk factors for homelessness....

Veterans of the Wars in Iraq and Afghanistan

As veterans return from Operation Iraqi Freedom (OIF) and Operation Enduring Freedom (OEF), just as veterans before them, they face risks that could lead to homelessness. To date, 300 OEF/OIF veterans have used VA [Veterans Administration] services for homeless veterans, and the VA has classified 1,049 as being at risk of homelessness. The National Coalition for Homeless Veterans, in an informal survey of service providers, estimated that 1,260 veterans of the Iraq War sought assistance from Grant and Per Diem Programs in 2006. Approximately 686,302 OEF/OIF troops have been separated from service since 2002. If the experiences of the Vietnam War are any indication, the risk of becoming homeless continues for many years after service. After the Vietnam War, 76% of Vietnam combat troops and 50% of non-combat troops who eventually became homeless reported that at least ten years passed between the time they left military service and when they became homeless.

Among troops returning from Iraq, between 15% and 17% have screened positive for depression, generalized anxiety, and PTSD. Veterans returning from Iraq also appear to be seeking out mental health services at higher rates than veterans returning from other conflicts. There is some concern that the VA may not be able to meet demand. Access to VA health services could be a critical component of reintegration into the community for some veterans.... For some veterans, health issues, particularly mental health issues, may arise later, and there is concern that they might not be aware of available VA health programs and services. S[enate Bill] 1384, introduced on May 14, 2007, would institute a demonstration program in which the VA and DOD [Department of Defense] would work together to identify returning members of the armed services who are at risk of homelessness.

Another concern is that returning National Guard and Reserve troops may not be able to access services as readily as members of the Army or Marines. Members of the Guard and Reserve do not necessarily live near military bases, where services for returning personnel are provided. They could be largely separated from support networks. . . . In addition, members of the Guard and Reserve are half as likely to file claims for disability and pension benefits as those in the regular forces.

Female Veterans

The number and percentage of women enlisted in the military has increased since previous wars. . . . The number of women deployed to war is also on the rise. . . . The number of women veterans can be expected to grow commensurately. . . . At the same time, the number of male veterans is expected to decline.

Women veterans face challenges that could contribute to their risk of homelessness. Experts have found that female veterans report incidents of sexual assault that exceed rates reported in the general population. The percentage of female veterans seeking medical care through the VA who have reported that they have experienced sexual assault ranges between 23% and 29%. Female active duty soldiers have been found to suffer from PTSD at higher rates than male soldiers. Experience with sexual assault has been linked to PTSD, depression, alcohol and drug abuse, disrupted social networks, and employment difficulties. These factors can increase the difficulty with which women veterans readjust to civilian life, and could be risk factors for homelessness.

Women veterans are estimated to make up a relatively small proportion of the homeless veteran population. Among veterans who use VA's services for homeless veterans, women are estimated to make up just under 4% of the total. As a result, programs serving homeless veterans may not have adequate facilities for female veterans at risk of homelessness, particularly transitional housing for women and women with children. Currently, eight . . . programs provide transitional housing for female veterans and their children. The VA Advisory Committee on Homeless Veterans noted in its 2006 report that the . . . programs for women have been "slow to materialize" and recommended that the Special Needs grant be renewed and expanded.

SOURCE: Libby Perl, *Veterans and Homelessness: CRS Report for Congress*, RL34024. Prepared for Members and Committees of Congress. May 31, 2007. Available online at http://www.fas.org/sgp/crs/misc/RL34024.pdf.

ANALYSIS

Unfortunate aftershocks seem to accompany soldiers returning from war—even if they have been victorious. While these situations are always unpleasant, they are especially disturbing to a successful army and a country that has triumphed in war. Everyone expects victory to produce positive results, and negative outcomes seem discordant.

Nevertheless, some unpleasant consequences seem to follow every war—and stagger a society. One of the most stunning of these is the appearance on the streets of homeless veterans. The expectation of society is that the troops have just been victorious; therefore, they should feel buoyant and elevated by their success. But, at least some returning soldiers are not.

One result of every major U.S. war during the past 150 years has been the appearance of a substantial number of homeless veterans. After the Civil War, so many veterans seemed unable to readjust to civilian society that the federal government and some state governments established soldiers' homes. By the late 1920s, the federal system had 17 homes, and 43 states had set up 55 homes.

In 1933, thousands of homeless veterans converged on Washington, DC, to ask Congress for the bonus promised them in 1924. As a way of rewarding Americans who had participated in World War I, Congress voted a bonus to everyone who had fought in the war—but it would not be paid for 20 years. Each individual would receive a certain amount for every day that he had served overseas and a slightly smaller amount for every day he had served in the United States. As the Depression worsened in the early 1930s, thousands of veterans—many of them thought to be homeless—marched on Washington and petitioned Congress to give them their bonuses immediately rather than making them wait another decade.

As the end of World War II was beginning to be visible, Congress enacted the "Servicemen's Readjustment Act" of 1944, partly as a way of forestalling the conflict that had surrounded the Bonus Bill, but also partly to reward the several million Americans who had served in the military during the war. Generally referred to as the "G.I. Bill of Rights," it offered several important benefits that ultimately had tremendous effects on the United States. It offered to pay the college expenses of any serviceman or servicewoman, thus making college education available to millions of people who could not, by themselves, afford to attend a college or university. By 1947, almost half of all college students in the United States were veterans taking advantage of the GI Bill. The legislation also promised to guarantee mortgages on houses bought by veterans. This provision made homeownership a reality for millions of Americans who would not have been able to finance the purchase of a house without this assistance. By 1952, the Veterans' Administration had guaranteed mortgages for about 2.4 million GIs because the government guarantee encouraged lending agencies to finance their home purchases. The bill also had the effect of creating jobs by reviving the construction industry, which had just about died during the Depression and World War II, as well as those industries that produced construction materials. Finally, the law provided a weekly allowance to any veteran who was unemployed, although less than 20 percent of the funds allocated for this purpose were ever used.

Congress renewed and revised the GI Bill of Rights in 1958 to ensure that veterans would continue to have the same benefits originally provided for them. And, in 2008, Congress reworked the law once again. The latest version provides greater benefits for any veteran who served on or after September 11, 2001 (9/11). It offered to cover a larger part of an individual's educational expenses, provided a living allowance, gave money for books, and made it possible to transfer leftover benefits to a veteran's wife and children.

The issue of homeless veterans became especially controversial in the years after the Vietnam War. During those years, the number of homeless veterans seemed to increase rapidly and dramatically. By the time that it ended, the Vietnam War had become so unpopular that negative opinions of soldiers had also become common, and a negative point-of-view was attached to anything having to do with them. At first, the widely held interpretation was that these veterans were suffering from injuries received in battle—mental rather than physical injuries, but real nonetheless. Evidence also came out that many Vietnam veterans were addicted to alcohol, drugs, and other substances, and the general belief was that the horrors of war had affected them mentally and pushed them into socially negative and personally self-destructive behaviors.

In addition, veterans were increasingly being diagnosed with a newly discovered mental illness—post-traumatic stress disorder (PTSD)—an anxiety disorder that can develop after a person is exposed to a terrifying event in which people were brutally killed and the individual himself or herself was implicitly placed in a situation of grave danger. The widespread public belief was that Vietnam veterans suffered from PTSD because of the horrific events that they had witnessed in battle, and this belief contributed to public hostility to the war. When anger in the United States about the war had dissipated, and researchers were able to examine PTSD scientifically, they discovered that most veterans suffering from PTSD had never actually been engaged in combat situations and that those experiencing PTSD were generally soldiers who had entered the all-volunteer military after most of the fighting had ended.

The most recent wars fought by the United States are those against terror and the wars in Iraq and Afghanistan. Although the wars are still being fought, hundreds of thousands of men and women have already returned to the United States. Some of them have begun to show signs that they are at risk of homelessness, and researchers are attempting to determine what distinguishes the veterans who become homeless from the veterans who do not experience homelessness. This document is an excerpt from a report prepared for Congress by its research agency, the Congressional Research Service, and it attempts to tell Congress why some people become homeless, why others do not, and what might be expected to happen to veterans of the Iraqi and Afghanistan Wars during the next 10 years.

FURTHER READING

Cunningham, Mary, Meghan Henry, and Webb Lyons. *Vital Mission: Ending Homelessness among Veterans.* Washington, DC: The Homelessness Research Institute at the National Alliance to End Homelessness, 2007.

Robertson, Marjorie J. "Homeless Veterans: An Emerging Problem." In Richard D. Bingham, Roy E. Green, and Sammis B. White, *The Homeless in Contemporary Society.* Newbury Park, CA, and London: Sage Publications, 1989, 64–81.

Robertson, Marjorie J., and Emily Abel. "Homeless Veterans in Los Angeles County." Paper presented at the Annual Meeting of the American Public Health Association, Washington, DC, 1985.

Rosenheck, R. A., et al. "Homeless Veterans." In Jim Baumohl (ed.), *Homelessness in America.* Phoenix, AZ: Oryx Press, 1996.

Rosenheck, R. A., L. K. Frisman, and A. Chung. "The Proportion of Veterans among the Homeless." *American Journal of Public Health*, 84, 3 (1994), 466–68.

Seibyl, R. A., et al. *The Thirteenth Progress Report on the Domiciliary Care for Veterans Program.* West Haven, CT: Northeast Program Evaluation Center, 2002.

"Veterans." In Steven VanderStaay, *Street Lives: An Oral History of Homeless Americans.* Philadelphia, PA, and Gabriola Island, BC: New Society Publishers, 1992, 99–116.

37

HOMELESS PEOPLE
IN RURAL AREAS

Rural Homelessness Puts Victims Out of Sight, Out of Mind

- *Document:* This document describes homelessness in a rural area of Pennsylvania.
- *Date:* The document was first published on January 29, 2006.
- *Where:* The document was initially published in a newspaper in Pittsburgh, Pennsylvania.
- *Significance:* This document reveals the existence of another group of [homeless] people who are frequently not recognized by the general public—homeless people in rural areas. The document examines the reasons for the existence of rural homelessness and describes the nature of such people's lives and some of the causes of their homelessness. It reveals some of the differences between urban and rural poverty, but it also points out some of their similarities.

DOCUMENT

Michelle hauled the heavy trash bag up the stairs of the homeless shelter. Inside it was nearly everything she owned, and she struggled under the weight, her grip tearing holes in the plastic.

Michelle's daughter, Brianna, 8, waited at the top of the stairs, anxious to see her toys again, and ready to change out of the clothes she had been wearing for three days.

The two had arrived at the Emergency Shelter Project Family House in Altoona [Pennsylvania] last Sunday night, having left Michelle's boyfriend and their home behind.

"He's a heroin addict, and that ain't a life for me or for her," said Michelle, 31, who requested that her last name not be used.

If not for the 16-bed shelter, the only facility in Blair County that houses homeless families, they would be "out on the streets, literally," Michelle said. But here, in this nondescript house where no one but staff answers the door, the two will be safe and warm for the next 27 days.

This is what rural homelessness looks like.

The stereotype of homeless people—transient single men roaming the streets or sleeping under bridges, mentally ill or drug-addicted, begging for change, their lives contained in a shopping cart—does not conform to rural reality. Rural homelessness is the invisible kind, experts say.

Out here, shelters are few and far between. Public services are spare. Homeless people in rural areas are more likely to be sleeping in cars or campers, crowded or dilapidated structures, or on the couches of friends or relatives. According to the Rural Poverty Research Center, they are more likely to be women, married with children, currently working, and homeless for the first time. The Rural Poverty Research Center is an institute spearheaded by the U.S. Department of Health and Human Services, which examines the causes of rural poverty and helps to shape public policies concerning the issue.

Often thought to be an urban phenomenon, homelessness is an issue even in such places as rural Bedford County, where cows outnumber people. There is one shelter in Bedford County, and it is designated for abused women. Somerset County has one small shelter for families; cases of domestic abuse are referred to Cambria County. Blair County's emergency men's shelter in Altoona burned down in 2004; its replacement has yet to open its doors.

"It's rough around here," said Angelo Donia, a transitional housing case manager for Somerset County's Tableland Services. "Around here, they're not considered homeless because they're not sleeping on a storm grate. You won't believe the places I pull these guys out of."

The rural homeless might be invisible, but their ranks are growing. Social service agencies in predominantly rural counties report drastic increases in requests for aid from the Homeless Assistance Program and other services.

In Somerset County, the number of people receiving HAP aid has spun steadily upward from 165 in

DID YOU KNOW?

Rural Homelessness

Homelessness is often assumed to be an urban phenomenot because homeless people are more numerous, more geographically concentrated, and more visible in urban areas. However, people experience the same difficulties associated with homelessness and housing distress in America's small towns and rural areas as they do in urban areas. Problems defining, locating, and sampling have made enumerating the homeless population with certainty virtually impossible, with estimates commonly relying on counts of persons using services that are inaccessible. Some of what has been learned in recent years about the causes, consequences, and strategies for combating homelessness in rural areas is summarized below....

Definitions and Demographics

Understanding rural homelessness requires a more flexible definition of homelessness. There are far fewer shelters in rural areas than in urban areas; therefore, people experiencing homelessness are less likely to live on the street or in a shelter and more likely to live in a car or camper, or with relatives in overcrowded or substandard housing. Restricting definitions of homelessness to include only those who are literally homeless—that is, on the streets or in shelters—does not fit well with the rural reality, and also may exclude many rural communities from accessing federal dollars to address homelessness.

Rurality is typically defined in contrast to urbanicity. The most commonly used definitions are based on population density and proximity to metropolitan areas.... Rural communities constitute all "territory, population, and housing units not classified as urban."...

[The definition of a homeless person used in] The McKinney-Vento Homeless Assistance Act ... has created an atmosphere in which most rural communities do not count persons living in rural substandard structures as homeless, leaving a portion of those who are homeless in rural areas unidentified while their counterparts are being counted in urban communities.

Studies comparing urban and rural homeless populations have shown that homeless people in rural areas are more likely to be white, female, married, currently working, homeless for the first time, and homeless for a shorter period of time.... Other research indicates that families, single mothers, and children make up the largest group of people who are homeless in rural areas.... Homelessness among Native Americans and migrant workers is also largely a rural phenomenon. Findings also indicate higher rates of domestic violence and lower rates of alcohol and substance abuse. . . .

Policy Issues

Efforts to end rural homelessness are complicated by isolation, lack of awareness, and lack of resources. Helpful initiatives would include broadening the definition of homelessness to include those in temporary and/or dilapidated facilities, increasing outreach to isolated areas, and increasing networking and awareness on a national level. Ultimately, however, ending homelessness in rural areas requires jobs that pay a living wage, adequate income supports for those who cannot work, affordable housing, access to health care, and transportation.

Source: National Coalition for the Homeless. "Rural Homelessness," NCH Fact Sheet #11 published by the Nation Coalition for the Homeless. Available at http://www.nationalhomeless.org/factsheets/rural.html. Used by permission of the National Coalition for the Homeless.

1996–97 to 685 in 2003–04, according to state Department of Public Welfare statistics.

"The definition of homelessness in an urban area is people sleeping in boxes and in alleys. We really don't have that," said Jennifer Vought, community services program director for Somerset County's Tableland Services. "[Here,] they try to hide that they're homeless. They go to abandoned houses. They pull their vehicles into junk yards to disguise their situation. It's definitely a big difference."

Sister Celeste Ciesielka, a caseworker for Catholic Charities, which serves the Altoona-Johnstown diocese and often refers homeless people to the Emergency Shelter Project, said the shelter was full most of the time.

Bev Patton, of Love, Inc., a faith-based agency in Bedford County, must sometimes refer homeless people to a rescue mission in Cumberland, Md. Love Inc. has gotten several calls from elderly people who can't afford to pay their taxes, and whose homes were going to be auctioned in a sheriff's sale.

The causes of rural and urban homelessness are the same: poverty, a lack of affordable housing, mental illness, and drug and alcohol abuse. But the rural poor are hamstrung by transportation issues, such as high gas prices, infrequent bus service, geographic isolation from job centers, and a lack of health and social services.

Blair County's poverty rate has hovered from 11 percent to 13 percent in recent years, higher than the state average of about 10 percent. In 1999, Blair, Armstrong, and Fayette counties had more than 20 clients per 1,000 residents receiving homeless assistance, double the statewide ratio. That same year, according to an analysis by the Center for Rural Pennsylvania, rural areas had one emergency shelter unit for every 130 residents, while urban areas enjoyed the benefits of one unit for every 17 residents.

According to a 2002 study by the National Health Care for the Homeless Council, there are fewer actual homeless people in rural areas than in urban centers. But the proportionate incidence of homelessness in some rural counties is equal to or greater than what is found in major metropolitan areas. The study concluded that rural homeless people are less well-educated than their urban counterparts, but more likely to be employed, albeit in part-time or seasonal work with no benefits. They are more likely to take cash assistance from friends, and less likely to receive it from the government.

And because small, rural communities tend to be less socially diverse and more traditional, residents place a premium on ideals of self-sufficiency. As a result, rural homelessness is often less anonymous and carries a bigger social stigma.

Michelle feels she cannot depend on relatives to help her get back on her feet.

"My family is the type who says, 'You did it to yourself, now find a way out,'" she said.

For now, her way out starts with the Emergency Shelter Project. The rooms are clean and spartan, with small sinks, roll-away cots and cribs, old sofas slip-covered in bed sheets, and baskets of toys.

"The kids don't have anything else, but they do have toys," Director Carol Bravin said. "It's not fancy, but it's adequate."

Lists of house rules are posted on nearly every wall, mirror, and major appliance. Some residents, accustomed to independence, chafe at the curfews and chores.

Heroin use is a growing problem in Altoona, said Ms. Bravin, who has been robbed at gunpoint for drug money. Drugs play a major role in Blair County's homeless problem. The shelter does random drug testing; all clients must be clean in order to stay there.

A few years ago, a woman was staying at the shelter with her young son and concealing a drug habit.

"She was really addicted—12 bags a day." Ms. Bravin said. "Every morning, as soon as she would wake up, she would tie a belt around her arm and shoot up."

One day, the woman walked into the shelter's kitchen and saw her son at the table, tying something around his arm, a child's innocent mimicry of his mother.

"That's when it hit her," she said.

During the 30 days that families are sheltered here, the Emergency Shelter Project works with other social service agencies, both governmental and faith-based, to help families with whatever they need: rental assistance or transitional housing, employment services, drug and alcohol counseling, and "life skills" training, such as cooking and budgeting.

Families come to Altoona from places such as Claysburg, population 1,503; Roaring Spring, population 2,341; and other small farming towns in Blair County to receive these services, said Natalie Hockenberry, case manager for the shelter.

"For the most part, they've already exhausted this couch and that couch, this floor and that floor," she said.

DID YOU KNOW?

All Homelessness Is Not the Same

Homelessness in Rural America

Although normally associated with urban areas, homelessness is pervasive throughout rural America. Urban homelessness often receives more national attention, as homeless people are more geographically concentrated and more noticeable. Rural homelessness, however, is a serious condition affecting thousands of individuals and families. Studies have assessed that rural homeless individuals make up nine percent of the approximately 600,000 homeless throughout the United States.

Rural and urban homelessness share common root causes: poverty and a lack of affordable housing. In 1995, studies revealed that people in rural areas were 1.2 and 2.3 times more likely to be poor than those in metropolitan areas. . . . Recent economic trouble, including mounting housing costs, disappearing farms and closing factories, have increased the number of rural residents living in precarious housing situations. Rural homelessness occurs most frequently in predominantly agricultural regions or regions where economics revolve around declining industries such as timber or mining. Secondly, a deficit of adequate affordable housing triggers both rural and urban homelessness. . . .

Rural homelessness tends to have a distinctive profile vis-à-vis its urban counterpart. Most rural homeless individuals are experiencing homelessness for the first time and tend to remain homeless for shorter periods. Most rural homeless are married, white, working females—often with families. Also, rural America experiences homelessness among large Native American and farm labor populations. Rural areas tend to have fewer shelters or resources for people to turn to during emergencies, but individuals possess more extended family and friend networks. Therefore, the homeless rarely live on streets or in shelters. Most rural people without homes live in cars, with relatives in overcrowded settings, or in substandard housing.

Source: CARH (Council for Affordable Rural Housing), "Homelessness in Rural America." CARH News, January/February 2007, p. 16. Used by permission of CARH.

DID YOU KNOW?

Rural Homelessness

America's small towns and communities are not immune to the problem of homelessness. The number of people who experience rural homelessness is unknown, but the last national count of homeless people found that 7 percent live in rural areas.

Advocates and researchers often refer to people who experience rural homelessness as the "hidden homeless." Many rural homeless people live in places we do not see; they often are sleeping in the woods, campgrounds, cars, abandoned farm buildings, or other places not intended for habitation. Many more individuals and families in rural areas live in substandard housing or are doubled up. These households are at risk of homelessness.

The same structural factors that contribute to urban homelessness—lack of affordable housing and inadequate income—also lead to rural homelessness. Historically, the greatest housing concern for rural Americans has been poor housing quality.

Insufficient income, high rates of poverty, and unemployment also lead to rural homelessness. Rural homelessness is most dramatic in areas that experience high economic growth, thus driving up housing costs, and in areas of high rates of unemployment because of declining industries such as farming, timber, mining, or fishing. The lack of available jobs and steady incomes means that household income is significantly lower in rural areas; according to the latest report by the U.S. Census Bureau, the median income for households living in non-metropolitan areas was $40,785, compared to $51,853 for metropolitan areas.

Poverty is a persistent problem in rural America. The national poverty rate is 12.9%, whereas the poverty rate in rural areas is 15.1% and 189 of the poorest counties [in the United States] are rural. Perhaps most staggering is the problem of child poverty. More than 19% of rural children live in poverty (an increase of over 3% from 2000).

One of the key differences between rural and urban homelessness is a lower capacity in the homeless service provider infrastructure in rural areas as opposed to urban areas. Additionally, homeless people in rural areas tend to be homeless for shorter periods of time and are less likely to have health insurance and access to medical care.... Other predictors of homelessness such as substance abuse and mental illness, contribute to rural homelessness. Those who experience rural homelessness report higher rates of alcohol abuse and domestic violence, but

But these services are in demand. Tyrone and Hollidaysburg have a limited amount of public housing. The Section 8 program, administered through the Altoona Housing Authority, is not accepting applications, Mrs. Hockenberry said. Their wait list is "well over 1,000 people."

There are also no openings for transitional housing, a two-year program in which recipients pay 30 percent of their income toward a subsidized rent. There is heavy competition for these slots, and many people have a poor history of paying their utilities, due to a combination of low income and shoddy rental housing.

"One woman had a house with a hole in the roof," Mrs. Hockenberry said. "Her utilities were $600 a month; the heat went out the hole, and the gas company shut her gas off."

Rental assistance programs, which give clients their first month's rent plus security deposits, is sometimes not enough to get a low-income homeless person back on track. Many of the available jobs in Altoona are in retail or restaurants making $6 or $7 an hour.

"It's a struggle to get them emplacement that would pay the $400 a month rent," she said. "After the first month, you really have to watch your pennies, which is difficult when you have little education."

With such a thin margin of error, a lot of people are one paycheck, one illness, one gas bill or one bad decision away from being homeless, Ms. Bravin said, and she doesn't see it getting any better.

She opened the door to one of the shelter's empty bedrooms. The woman who stays in this room works full time, she said. On the bedside table was a waitress' check tablet, stamped with the logo of a nearby chain restaurant.

"The people we have here want to work," Ms. Bravin said. "For the most part, they're all employable."

SOURCE: Caitlin Cleary, "Rural Homelessness Puts Victims out of Sight, Out of Mind," *Pittsburgh Post-Gazette*, January 29, 2006. Used by permission of the *Pittsburgh Post-Gazette*.

ANALYSIS

To an extent, all homelessness is invisible. Sometimes people do not see it, either on purpose or accidentally. Sometimes, homeless people prefer not to be seen for any number of reasons—for privacy, to avoid being hassled by the police, because they are ashamed, or for many other reasons. But rural homelessness is invisible for a reason all its own. Rural areas have open space and a low density of population. Therefore, the potential audience to view homeless people is diminished, and most people never enter the rural world where they come into contact with homeless people. In this environment, homeless people are invisible because there is often no one to see them.

Although most people would probably not understand this, simply because they do not recognize the existence of rural homelessness, there are great differences between rural and urban homelessness. For one thing, services for homeless people are much less common. This scarcity exists because the people who need them, the homeless, escape detection by other people in society. Just as important, the absolute number of homeless people in a rural area pales when compared to the number of homeless people in a large metropolis. As a result, the need for homeless services also gets overlooked, or it is not recognized that there is a demand for those services, or providing them is not seen as being profitable. Consequently, little appropriate housing is provided for homeless people; there are no shelters or missions at which they can generally count on finding a place to sleep. Also, there are no cheap diners, markets, or other sources of food similar to the places available to urban homeless people—cheap diners and cafes, not to mention free meals at a mission or Salvation Army home.

Because of the lack of available, affordable housing, the rural homeless sleep in different places from the urban homeless. They sleep in cars—either their own or a deserted vacant car—and they squat in old abandoned buildings. They build huts out of whatever material is available at no cost. The rural homeless are much more likely to lack even a doorway or alleyway in which to sleep simply because there are so few doors and almost no alleys, and there are no large urban sites (department stores, libraries, police stations) where they can find a place to sleep and use a restroom. As a result, the rural homeless generally have a much greater likelihood of sleeping in a place that provides no real shelter at all.

Also, the rural homeless have much less access to services that are made available to homeless people in cities. Because they lack transportation, they are unable to

lower rates of mental illness and drug abuse than the urban homeless population. However, more recent research suggests that, when looking at substance use trends for the entire population, there is no difference in reported substance abuse between rural and urban residents.

There are numerous barriers to serving rural homeless people, including a negligible amount of available affordable housing, limited transportation methods, and that federal priorities and programs tend to be awarded in criteria that favor urban areas. Additionally, because rural areas face persistent poverty, a high number of people are continually at risk of homelessness.

Due to the aforementioned barriers, one of the most important strategies in ending rural homelessness is prevention. Preventing the occurrence of homelessness is the most economic way of ending homelessness. For communities that have limited funding providing people at risk of homelessness with prevention services, such as paying back rent or utilities and case management, can significantly decrease the number of people moving into homelessness.

Source: National Alliance to End Homelessness, "Fact Sheet: Rural Homelessness." Updated January 2010. Available at http://www.endhomelessness.org/content/article/detail/1613. Used by permission of the National Alliance to End Homelessness.

DID YOU KNOW?

Preventing and Recovering from Homelessness

In 2009, Maine Housing commissioned a comprehensive report on the nature of rural homelessness in that state. The final report contained a number of suggestions—some concrete and some very abstract—about how to end rural homelessness. The list included the following suggestions.

Preventing Homelessness

§ Recommendation: create a statewide "Don't Wait too Late" ad campaign to reach out to families living on the edge. The campaign would encourage families to seek help before their circumstances became dire, and direct them where to go for assistance.

§ Recommendation: establish a flexible fund in each rural county that can be used to fund critical gaps that can prevent homelessness or help families obtain housing.

§ Recommendation: create and fund a single point of contact within rural counties, especially those without general shelters, to prevent homelessness, and to support families who become homeless transition to housing stability. This position could oversee use of the flexible funds mentioned in the first bullet.

§ Recommendation: work with the G[eneral] A[ssistance] system to improve access to these funds for preventing and resolving family homelessness.

§ Recommendation: support data collection efforts in rural counties . . . to improve knowledge about the numbers of families needing assistance.

§ Recommendation: support rural housing and service providers in articulating the continuum of care that exists within their counties or regions to assist families facing homelessness.

Moving from Homelessness to Stable Housing

§ Recommendation: improve the availability of affordable housing construction and rehabilitation in rural towns, particularly where jobs and services are concentrated.

§ Recommendation: recruit and educate landlords about . . . housing quality standards, and provide support when families' behavior threatens their tenancy.

§ Recommendation: create a more seamless system for helping people who are homeless access available vouchers and use them to live near jobs and services.

§ Recommendation: work with telephone companies to provide voice mailboxes or provide phone access for

access health care or participate in the informal labor market in which homeless people can occasionally find part-time work, regardless of how unpleasant and unrewarding it may be.

In terms of their demographics, the rural homeless differ greatly from the urban homeless. They are much more likely to be white, female, married, currently working, experiencing homelessness for the first time, and to have been homeless for a shorter time. Contemporary research clearly shows that families, single mothers, and young children make up a much larger proportion of the rural homeless than of the urban homeless.

The rural homeless also have fewer social contacts than do the urban homeless. They encounter fewer people in the course of a day than do homeless people in cities, and, because there are so many fewer homeless people in a rural location than in a city, they are unable to develop peer groups with whom they can interact successfully. In fact, given the relative homogeneity of rural areas, and the stigma so often placed on homeless people, many of them prefer to keep their homelessness covert, and that fact alone makes it more difficult for them to create social relationships much less social networks.

And yet, despite those tremendous differences, important similarities between the rural and urban homeless populations do exist. Homeless people, wherever they are located, share two common traits: They are poor and they lack decent living accommodations. During the last 10 years or so, analysts, commentators, and observers have begun to develop a common interpretation of both the nature and the causes of homelessness, emphasizing these two basic characteristics. One advocate for the homeless wrote that "the primary causes of homelessness are the lack of affordable housing, the lack of living wage jobs or sufficient income, and the lack of adequate health and supportive services." Another has said that "rural and urban homelessness share common root causes: poverty and a lack of affordable housing." Still a third analysis, this one produced by the National Coalition for the Homeless, states that "rural homelessness, like urban homelessness, is the result of poverty and a lack of affordable housing."

FURTHER READING

Aron, Laudan Y., and Janet M. Fitchen. "Rural Homelessness: A Synopsis." In Jim Baumohl (ed.), *Homelessness in America*. Phoenix, AZ: Oryx, 1996.

Burt, Martha L. *Rural Homelessness: A Report on the Findings of RECD's Rural Homelessness Conferences:* Washington, DC: US Department of Agriculture, 2001.

Johnson, Kenneth. *Demographic Trends in Rural and Small Town America*. Durham, NH: University of New Hampshire, Carsey Institute, 2006.

National Coalition for the Homeless. "Rural Homelessness" (NCH Fact Sheet #11). Washington, DC: National Coalition for the Homeless, 2006.

Robertson, Marjorie, et al. "Rural Homelessness." In Deborah Dennis, Gretchen Locke, and Jill Khadduri (eds.), *Toward Understanding Homelessness: The 2007 National Symposium on Homelessness Research* Washington, DC: U.S. Department of Health and Human Services and U.S. Department of Housing and Urban Development, 2007. Available at http://aspe.hhs.gov/hsp/homelessness/symposium07/.

Wasserman, Keith. "Developing Plans to End Homelessness in Rural Communities." Presented at the National Alliance to End Homelessness Annual Conference, Washington, DC, 2006.

families for time limited periods in order to expedite communication with landlords and employers.

§ Recommendation: develop an online common application, not unlike the colleges that use a common application form, to facilitate the application process for housing.

§ Recommendation: research the feasibility and cost-effectiveness of issuing "smart cards" to families that can save this information electronically.

§ Recommendation: invest in training, and in updated hardware and software, to help rural providers use their scarce time more efficiently.

§ Recommendation: use technology to increase opportunities for rural providers to participate in mainstream resources trainings or other planning and information sharing sessions.

§ Recommendation: create additional transitional housing opportunities, or create staffing that can provide supports to young families to help them learn skills that will prevent future homelessness.

§ Recommendation: work to create new resources such as the flexible fund ... and to better integrate available programs and resources to improve their accessibility to families who do not meet HUD's homeless definition.

Source: Anne Gass, *Home to Stay: Helping Families Avoid or Recover from Homelessness in Maine's Rural Areas.* Study Commissioned by Maine Housing, Februrary 2009, 1–3.

38

HOMELESS PEOPLE OF COLOR

Racial Equity and Homelessness

- *Document:* The document is part of a report on the racial and ethnic composition of homeless people in Seattle, King County, Washington.
- *Date:* The document was written in October 2008.
- *Where:* The document was written in Seattle, Washington.
- *Significance:* The document compares homelessness data about different racial and ethnic groups in Seattle and shows the disparities among them. It raises the interesting and important question of why different ethnic groups, all made up largely of poor people, experience different rates of homelessness. The article also provides information about differentials in income and homeownership among different racial or ethnic groups. The complete document, in a later section not given here, offers suggestions about effective ways to alleviate homelessness.

DOCUMENT

. . . If we are truly committed to ending homelessness in King County [Washington], we need to examine the factors contributing to specific groups in our community experiencing this phenomenon [homelessness] at disproportionate rates.

Homelessness and income insecurity are social problems disproportionately experienced by persons of color.

The embedded racial inequities in the housing and economic systems have produced an accumulation of advantages for whites while simultaneously disadvantaging people of color. Historically, we can look at policies and practices that have created and exacerbated the economic disparity gap, including the GI Bill, various legislation affecting Native people, various forms of housing discrimination and inequities in employment hiring and compensation practices.

Barriers to Equal Opportunity

Housing Discrimination

Up until 1968, it was legal to discriminate against people on the basis of their race when renting or selling property in King County. Historically, these laws, policies, and practices have negatively affected access to affordable housing for people of color.

Land developers, realtors, and neighborhood associations wrote racial restrictions into the property deeds in order to maintain racial segregation in King County neighborhoods.

Other forms of discrimination were more covert. Steering, for example, and the practice of realtors unofficially agreeing to not show houses in white neighborhoods to people of color, and steering white homeowners into predominantly white neighborhoods. This resulted in confining black residents to certain neighborhoods.

In 1950, the Central District was home to 78% of the City's black population. Even though in 2000 this neighborhood housed just over 30% of the King County black population, the historical legacy of segregation has prevented land and homes in the Central District from appreciating at the same rate as more white neighborhoods.

In addition to housing segregation, historical discrimination in lending has negatively impacted communities of color.

- The term "redlining" comes from maps which indicated minority geographic regions by coloring them red or drawing a red line around them. Banks and other businesses used these maps to deny loans, insurance or other business services to people in less desirable neighborhoods. Discrimination in housing toward individuals was outlawed in 1968 and discrimination in lending based on neighborhood was outlawed in 1977. The practice of redlining includes

  - outright refusal of banks to lend in minority neighborhoods

  - procedures that discourage loan applications from minority areas, and

  - marketing policies that exclude such areas.

These practices reduce the home loan options for people in minority neighborhoods and weaken competition in the mortgage market. This results in higher mortgage costs and less favorable mortgage loan terms.

In effect, racial redlining discourages people of color from pursuing home ownership.

Currently, the number of loan applications to people of color is proportionate to the racial make-up of King County; however, people of color are receiving subprime lending at disproportionate rates compared to whites.

- In 2004, Hispanic households were 2 times as likely, and African-American households were 3 times as likely, as white households to have a sub-prime loan.
- 69% of census tracts with the highest levels of sub-prime home purchase and refinance loans are in predominantly minority or diverse areas.

These types of practices prevent people of color from benefiting in the housing market to the same extent as whites and those in predominantly middle-upper class neighborhoods.

In effect, people of color do not experience the same amount of economic accumulation that acts as a safety net to prevent homelessness or curtail intergenerational poverty.

The GI Bill

After World War II, the US government created a bill providing veterans with educational opportunities as well as home loan guarantees. This legislation enables millions of veterans to obtain a college education and become first-time home buyers. On the surface, these provisions extended to all veterans, but due to unequal practices in the lending and real estate markets, the majority of those who benefited were white veterans and their families.

The GI Bill, in the context of legal discrimination in that era created segregated, middle class, suburban neighborhoods made up of white families. This benefit catalyzed the process of wealth-building through homeownership for these families. In turn, they could then borrow from their home equity to send a first generation of family members to college, and this generation sequentially gave birth to today's professional class.

African Americans and Latin veterans and their families did not have access to these benefits. They remained renters and were confined to segregated neighborhoods with poor infrastructure and lack of access to adequate schooling, health care, and social services.

Their next generation had far less academic preparation or financial resources for higher education. Those who did not have sufficient resources to move from these segregated neighborhoods find their families today in areas where ongoing disinvestment guarantees unequal opportunities—few jobs, poorly performing schools, vulnerability to criminal victimization, lack of health care, etc.

Due to implicit inequality in the implementation of the GI Bill, people of color had a great disadvantage compared to whites in their ability to establish credit, equity, and asset accumulation—all of which constitute the cornerstones for intergenerational stability.

Relocation Programs of Native Peoples

In the early 1950s the U.S. government paid Native peoples to leave their reservations and resettle in five main urban areas, including Seattle. The Relocation Act ... guarantee[d] education, housing, and jobs for Native peoples if they moved into urban areas.

One year later, these promises were abandoned and Native peoples, having lost their reservation benefits, could not return to the reservations. With no housing, no education, and no employment, Native peoples found themselves homeless in Seattle and other major Western cities.

Simultaneous to these relocation programs, the US Congress passed a series of Termination acts which stripped tribes of recognition by the federal government, including their right to reservation land and federal support. With increasing poverty on reservations, Native people moved to urban areas seeking the promise of a more lucrative life in the city. They moved to cities with no financial resources, social support, or understanding of a culture and way of life vastly different from what they knew on the reservation.

As of 2004, over 164,000 Native American/Alaskan Native peoples lived in Washington State.

Of those, 33,000 dwell in King County and have a homeless rate three times their representation in the general population.

In effect, these policies, and many others, have created a disproportionate number of Urban Indians experiencing poverty and homelessness.

Discrimination and Disadvantages in Employment

Seattle did not pass legislation regarding employment discrimination based on age, sex, race, creed, color, or national origin until 1972. Before then, it was legal to refuse hiring a person, discharge or bar a person from a job, and discriminate in compensation or other terms of employment based on race. African Americans and Asian Americans were also excluded from most of the better paid and desirable jobs. Until World War II, even factory jobs were reserved for whites while most people of color were stuck in menial positions.

In the 1980s a shifting labor market away from manufacturing jobs occupied by people of color and other working class individuals towards a service-oriented and technologically-focused market demanding higher education and specialized training created a high incidence of unemployment for these groups. Furthermore, out-migration from urban areas due to deindustrialization particularly impacted people of color as their neighborhood infrastructure crumbled.

Unemployment affects all people, but due to the structure of the labor market, recessions affect people of color at higher rates. In part, this vulnerability derives from workers of color being overrepresented in part-time, temporary, and low-wage work, and therefore ineligible for unemployment insurance and health care benefits.

When a recession occurs, whites are more likely to receive unemployment benefits, and hence less likely to fall into poverty or homelessness. Of course, income level and asset wealth also serve as a buffer for these risks.

When the racial income gap persists, people of color are forced to live pay-check to pay-check and are therefore unable to save any money for these setbacks. According to the table below, people of color, especially African Americans and American Indians, are overrepresented in the lower income categories and underrepresented in the higher income categories.

Percent of Total Population by Race in Income Categories

	Less than $15,000	$15,000 to $24,999	$25,000 to $34,999	$35,000 to $49,999	$50,000 to $99,999	Greater than $100,000
Hispanic/Latino	14.2	14.3	15.1	18.3	27.1	10.47
African American	19.4	13.2	13.6	17.0	26.1	10.8
American Indian	20.0	11.4	14.2	17.4	26.5	10.5
Asian	13.9	8.2	9.3	14.1	33.6	20.9
Pacific Islander	10.7	11.5	13.8	18.4	35.6	10.0
White	7.9	7.7	9.2	14.5	35.4	25.2
Other	13.1	13.9	15.0	20.8	27.2	9.9
Two or More	15.4	11.5	12.5	16.7	29.5	14.4

Income and employment disparities tell only part of the story. Wealth, that is assets and liabilities that determine one's net worth, is the other piece.

The importance of wealth cannot be underestimated as it is a vital component of a family's standard of living. Wealth can allow a family to have consistent access to health care, education, safe and economically viable neighborhoods, and provide a safety net in times of economic hardships.

Homeownership is the most important asset for most families in the United States

In the 2000 King County census, homeownership rates varied across race, with the white population experiencing the greatest percent of homeownership. (68%) and blacks the least (37%).

The median value of homes in different neighborhoods sheds light on the racial disparities that have plagued the housing market in King County. In 2006, the average price per square foot of a home in South King County, the most ethnically diverse region in the county was $166; while in East King County [predominantly white] it was $264/square foot. As white families continue to increase their wealth through the increasing price of housing in affluent areas and other venues, people of color who own homes see less appreciation of land value or are unable to benefit from the housing market and continue to lose rent money to land owners. Over time, whites continue to accumulate wealth at far greater rates than people of color.

Consequences of Unequal Opportunity

High Rate of Homelessness for People of Color

Homelessness does not affect all groups of people equally. People of color are much more likely to experience homelessness than whites.

In the 2004 Status Report on Hunger and Homelessness, the U.S. Conference of Mayors found that people of color make up 65% of all homeless persons staying in shelters and transitional housing programs nationwide, and yet comprise only 31% of the U.S. population.

Homelessness in King County paints a similar picture. According to the 2007 One Night Count of Homeless Persons in King County, people of color represent well over half (58%) of the homeless population receiving services although they make up less than a third (27%) of county residents.

Three Census racial classification groups are overrepresented in the homeless population in King County (African Americans, Native Americans and Latinos).

- African Americans have the highest representation in the homeless population in King County of all communities of color, comprising 35% of homeless persons even though they represent only 5.4% of residents in the County.
- The percentage of Native Americans (3%) who are homeless is three times greater than their share of the total population living in King County (0.9%).
- The percentage of Latinos who are homeless (10%) [is] almost twice their share of the total population (5.5%).
- As a whole, Asians are underrepresented in the homeless population (4% homeless vs. 11.3% of total population), but this data could be confounded by the aggregation of all Asian groups into one category. It is likely that some Asian-Americans and Asian immigrant groups are overrepresented in the homeless population in King County considering the effects of embedded racial inequities. Unfortunately, few studies have been done that examine homelessness rates among the various Asian groups.

Further compounding the risk of homelessness for people of color, the unemployment rates are also higher for these communities.

Looking at the 2000 King County Census, the unemployment rates from highest to lowest were

- American Indian/   11.1%
  Alaskan Native
- Blacks   9.5%
- Multi-racial   6.8%
- Hispanics/Latinos   6.4%
- Asians & Pacific   5.0%
  Islanders
- Whites   3.9%

If people of color are experiencing both homelessness and unemployment at disproportionate rates to whites, then access to health care, nutritious food, social support and resources age also limited.

Disproportionate Rates of Poverty for People of Color

Segregation in the job market, under-compensation for labor and lack of accumulated wealth contribute to poverty rates higher for people of color than whites.

In 2000, King County whites had a poverty rate of 6.2%, a rate lower than every other racial group.

Poverty affects one's mobility and prevents families from leaving high poverty concentrated neighborhoods. Poverty often continues to become concentrated in certain neighborhoods, as people who can afford to move out. Then business, housing, and infrastructure investments decrease and more people move out if they can. The families with the least resources are left behind.

The intergenerational effects of poverty become an inheritance of unequal opportunities, including:

- under funded schools that do not provide the same skills for inner-city youth to be competitive in the job market
- lack of social capital and access to good jobs and job networks
- lack of education/college financing for children

Overall, the disproportionate experience of homeless and income insecurity by people of color in our community reinforces racial inequalities in other areas of life: health, education, safety, arrests, incarceration, and intergenerational disadvantages.

Without equal access to shelter, housing, and economic security, people of color are at greater risk for disparities in these various areas affecting one's ability to succeed and for future generations to prosper.

SOURCE: United Way of King County. King County Review of Health and Human Services. Community Assessment. "Racial Equity and Homelessness." (Seattle, WA: United Way of King County, October 2008). Used by permission.

ANALYSIS

Although there have been many studies of the effects of race on homelessness (i.e., Do individuals of some races have higher or lower percentages of homelessness than people of other races?) there have been relatively few studies that have compared more than two races. The most common pattern is to compare the white population against one other racial group: Asians or Asian Americans, Africans or African Americans, and so on.

The study from which this document was taken is almost unique in comparing a number of different racial groups—white, African American, and Asian American— the three groups most commonly considered as races, but it also compares Native Americans, Pacific Islanders, and most importantly, Hispanic/Latinos. Many social scientists might not consider Hispanic/Latinos as a separate race, but in a study like this, which tries to consider the largest number of people possible, and in which everyone in the population must be assigned a race for completeness' sake, considering them as a separate race is a useful fiction. Our society does not consider Latinos to be white. It treats them as a separate group, and they have certainly been victimized by racial prejudice and hostility, but they do not really fit into either the categories Asian American or African American, so it makes sense to consider them separately.

The document has several significant features. Obviously, the first is the one just mentioned—it considers a wider range of racial groups than most similar documents and tries to provide economic and social information about seven different racial groups, not two or three. By doing that, this study gives a broader overview of the subject and allows greater generalizations to be made. Most especially, it allows comparisons to be made between whites and persons of color, a much broader category than blacks or African Americans, even though information about that group is still provided.

Secondly, the article does not simply give figures about racial differences in housing. It gives a brief overview of how governmental and social policies have caused some groups to suffer homelessness at disproportionate rates. It explains how land developers, real-estate agents, and neighborhood organizations kept people of color from living in certain areas, and it talks about how the real estate practice of "steering" has been used to direct persons of color toward finding housing in certain other areas of the city.

But it also points out other important circumstances that are not as widely recognized. For example, the article makes the strong point that while discriminatory practices of the past have been outlawed, they are still having a serious effect. They created situations that have survived a long time and are extremely difficult to eradicate despite all good intentions. Also, since one effect of discriminatory practices in the construction and real estate businesses was to relegate minorities to less desirable residential land in central cities and propel large numbers of whites into much more desirable suburban or outlying areas, the housing that minorities did acquire has not appreciated at nearly the same rate as the residences of the white population, thus increasing the disparity of wealth between the white majority and people of color.

The article also points out that the GI Bill of Rights, one of the most popular and highly praised federal programs ever created, has had a negative impact on minority housing and contributed to the amount of homelessness. White veterans often had enough savings that they could qualify for government-backed mortgages and then take advantage of government-subsidized college educations. Both of these added to their wealth in two ways—one by enabling them to buy real estate that increased in value, and two, by allowing them to acquire a college degree that, in most cases, increased their regular incomes. Minorities were unable to do either of these things. Having much fewer resources to begin with, they were unable to purchase housing and gain from the increase in real estate values. Also, having greater resources at the beginning of the cycle, white veterans were able to take the time to attend college—sometimes at night and sometimes as part-time students—but minorities were unable to do either of these things. Their economic situations were so fragile that they could not afford to work less to be able to attend college, nor were they able to afford the costs of attending college, even if they were subsidized by the government.

The article then analyzes the condition of Native Americans and their housing in Seattle (Kings County). In puts that story into the context of the relations between Native Americans and the government of the United States and explains the laws and policies that within the past several decades sentenced Native Americans to a much lower standard of both housing and income.

FURTHER READING

Gilliam, A. "Homeless Women with Children." In R. L. Braithwaite and S. E. Taylor (eds.), *Health Issues in the Black Community*. San Francisco, CA: Jossey-Bass, 1992.
Molina, Edna. "Informal Non-Kin Networks among Latino and African-American Men." *American Behavioral Scientist*, 43, 4 (2000), 63–85.

39

HOMELESS LATINOS AND A DIFFERENT PERSPECTIVE

Homelessness Defined Differently

- **Document:** The document is part of an analysis of Mexican migrant workers to the United States. It argues that they do not define home—and therefore homelessness—in the same way that most Americans do.
- **Date:** The article was published in 2003, and the research for it was done between 2000 and 2002.
- **Where:** The article was published in the United States, and it concerns some migrants who went from Mexico to Texas to Ohio.
- **Significance:** Once again, this document raises the question of how to define home. It shows how different definitions of home can create conflict within an individual migrant or between Mexican migrant workers and the larger society. Implicitly, it raises the question of how, or even whether, a diverse society can reach consensus about an abstract concept like homelessness.

DOCUMENT

. . . Hector describes his experiences as a migrant agricultural worker. The life of the migrant worker has many aspects of homelessness. . . . [Many people] ascribe their problems of health, educational attainment, and crime to their homelessness for, in many ways, these *are* the homeless life they appear to lead.

The word home, to many people in the United States is a symbol of freedom, choice, and power. It is a physical space that one shapes the way one wants, reflecting the "inner" person, and where individuals may act as they choose without pretense or role playing. Often, home signifies a commodity, an object of monetary value that reflects the owner's value. To others, however, home is a conceptual or an emotional space used to represent relationships. We believe migrant workers such as Hector also think of homes in terms synonymous with the word family where it shares a conceptual space that defines roles and relationships. Home in this sense is *not* a creation that reflects individuality but an institution that shapes the identities of those within it. In much of the rhetoric surrounding homelessness the first conceptualization of home as a place seems to be dominant. In our work with Latino/a agricultural workers, the second sense of the word is apparent. Home means family for many migrant workers and is, in part, detached from space and place and these families often choose to be "homeless," in the sense that we usually think of the term, in order to maintain their "home," of family structure. In particular, choosing to be in the United States . . . involves choosing family over "home." . . .

The migrant farmer worker experience

Both my parents were born in Mier, Mexico but later moved to Ciudad Miguel Aleman. They met and married at a very young age, my dad was 20 and my mom 15. Neither finished school so they moved to Houston to find work and my dad ended up working different jobs in construction and carpentry. This is where my brother and I were born but soon after that we moved to Roma, a small border town in the Texas valley, so we could be closer to family. My dad continued traveling to Houston so he could find construction work while me, my mom, my brother, and eventually my third and youngest brother would remain at home.

The problems I saw were in the drugs, crime, unemployment, and poverty that plagued Roma. Despite being surrounded by it, I was always able to keep myself out of trouble. But this trouble finally landed in our house when I was 12 and my dad was arrested for selling drugs. Among the group caught, my father was the only one that returned to court for his trial after being released on bail. Because of this the judge cut his initial sentence of 5 to 8 years to half that time. While in jail, my mom and dad divorced, and when he was released deported

DID YOU KNOW?

The Special Circumstances of Homeless Latinos Research Report on Homeless Latino Immigrants

. . . Nearly 80% or recent Latino immigrants live in crowded conditions, and nearly 70% have less than a high school diploma.

Living in impoverished conditions, facing low paid and unstable work opportunities combined with a series of recent measures that have restricted their rights and access to public services and benefits, Latino immigrants may often find themselves sleeping on the streets or crowded into low-end hotel rooms with their families. . . . The situation of homeless Latino immigrants is rarely addressed in public policy discussions about homelessness. This is true even in San Francisco, a city with a substantial Latino immigrant population.

To further exacerbate the policy discussions' neglect of issues faced by homeless Latino immigrants, homeless policy forums rarely involve input from immigrants facing homelessness. Homeless Latino immigrants are triply marginalized from policy arenas: first, because they are homeless; second, because many did not arrive in the United States through official documented channels, and thus lack the legal rights of residency or citizenship; and third, because their primary language is Spanish.

Basic Demographic Findings

Most Homeless Latino Immigrants have lived in the United States for a substantial period of time.

The average time that the homeless Latino immigrants interviewed have lived in the United States is 9 years, and half have lived in the United States for 5 years or more. . . .

Homeless Latino immigrants contribute to the economy, often working in the lowest paid and most unstable jobs.

The occupations which immigrants reported are (in order of frequency): general labor/day labor, construction assistance/carpentry, restaurant work, cleaning, painting, gardening, moving, and janitorial jobs.

The instability and poor quality of these jobs, however, often leads to homelessness or makes it near impossible to exit homelessness.

69% of the homeless Latino immigrants said that they are either currently unable to find work or are unable to find stable work. The inability to find work is reflected in respondents' answers to the question of why they are homeless. The most [common] reasons given for their homelessness were: the lack of work, inability to afford rent, low-paying jobs, the lack of job stability, and the high cost of housing.

Many homeless Latino immigrants are chronically homeless.

The average time homeless Latino immigrants have been homeless is 1.5 years. (This figure does not include people living in SROs, who reported living in SROs for twice as long). Nearly half have been homeless for one year or longer, and 27% have been homeless for two years or more.

Homeless Latino immigrants face severe barriers to exiting homelessness, including legal status, racism, and language.

Legal Status:

80% of homeless Latino immigrants are without legal immigration documents. This lack of documentation was repeatedly stated as one of the largest problems that homeless immigrants feel they face.

Racism:

80% of homeless Latino immigrants interviewed felt that racism is a cause of homelessness. Racism and discrimination are among the major problems that homeless immigrants fell they face.

Language:

Spanish was the first language of all the immigrants interviewed, except for one who spoke Portuguese. Language barriers are another problem that homeless immigrants feel they face.

Source: Coalition on Homelessness San Francisco. "Hidden Voices: The Realities of Homeless Families and Homeless Immigrants." September 2004. Available online at http://www.cohsf.org/reports/2004/hiddenVoices.pdf.

back to Mexico. My dad was never a U.S. citizen. He was a resident alien and at the time, federal law said that any alien convicted of a federal offense had to be deported.

After my dad's arrest, things really changed. We went from having the money that drugs provided to having nothing. My mom proved strong though and went back to school, finished high school, got a nursing degree, and supported us on her own. But I could see it was a struggle for her. When I was 14, I began to migrate so I could help my mom out with money. She didn't want me to go. She thought that it might be too tough for me since I had never been exposed to such a thing. But I decided to go anyway. So when school let out I headed over to west Texas and the town of Loveland with some of my extended family and we would find jobs cleaning cotton and picking onions. But I would always leave after school had let out and return before school began. My mom insisted on that. She thought education was real important.

It was during this time that my mom met my step-dad and my half-brother was born. Well he owned a car wash in Roma that wasn't doing too well and since my mom had gotten pregnant with my baby stepbrother, he decided that the whole family was going to migrate to work in the fields and earn some money. So that summer it wasn't just me but my whole family that headed west to work in the cotton and onions. But the following summer my stepdad decided to take us all the way up to Illinois. See, that last summer he had heard about Illinois and the detasseling you could get for good pay. . . . We were such good workers that the company offered my stepfather a job for the whole year. So he took it and that's where my family's been this past year.

Even though I value the experiences I've had as a migrant and it made me appreciate what it takes to earn a living and support a family, it was pretty tough. Besides the weather being incredibly hot or the rain making it difficult to even move through the fields, I had other stuff I had to do also. Living in apartments or trailers means pretty cramped quarters so we all had to chip in and keep things clean. And since I was the oldest and my mom was pregnant I was also in charge of doing laundry, helping out with all the meals, keeping up the equipment that we were using in the fields and making sure that we had plenty of water for the next day's work. Yea, I guess going into the fields means a lot more than just working in them. (Juan Escalante)

Juan's story is in many ways typical of the migrant workers we interviewed. . . . [We discovered] differences between migrant and non-migrant farm worker children and, in doing so, the need for special social services and educational programs for the former. Perhaps the most important difference, in the sense of governmental services, is in household income: 82% of migrant farmworker children live in households that have below poverty incomes, compared with 33% of non-migrant farmworker children.

. . . Many of the hardships associated with the migrant cycle arise from maintaining the family, keeping everyone together as a unit. Troubles with transportation—multiple vehicles are needed for the numbers of people often working different jobs, driving through horrible weather to get north—for they have to be at particular places at particular time, long hours in the field, poor living conditions, and struggles with money arise because the family is maintained with everyone traveling together. All of these hardships threaten family survival as the obvious answer to many of their problems is to break up the family. Finally all of the things that a migrant mother, father, son, or daughter must do to help get

> ## DID YOU KNOW?
>
> ### Need to Be Interpreted Carefully—and so Do Behaviors
>
> Government statistics both nationwide and in the city of New York indicate that a very low percentage of homeless people living in shelters are Hispanic or Latin American immigrants.
>
> But recent studies by academic institutions and non-profits say the population of homeless Hispanics is underestimated because of their tendency to remain outside common governmental entities dealing with the problem.
>
> "Mexican-born homeless may be systematically undercounted in homeless samples because they are more likely to exist outside traditional homeless spaces," concludes a study called "Hidden Hispanic Homelessness in Los Angeles: the 'Latino Paradox' Revisited". . . .
>
> According to the Caritas foundation . . . "the lack of bilingual staff is one reason some Hispanics and agency providers believe that the Hispanic homeless population is underestimated and underserved."
>
> But the language barrier is not the only reason that it is difficult to gauge the extent of homelessness among Hispanics.
>
> A lot of families would qualify for homeless programs but don't apply for them because they aren't comfortable living in shelters. Hispanics place a high value on keeping families together, and many shelters separate men, women, and children.
>
> *Source:* New America Media, "Homeless Hispanics in New York Face Somber Future," *LaPrensa-San Diego*, November 10, 2008. Available online at http://news.newamericamedia.org/news/view_article.html?article_id=f8a2b5e7e37f20ea50ac64e844b5d3e9.

through these difficulties (quitting school to work, fixing a broken-down truck, visiting social and migrant services, etc.) reflects choosing to maintain the family as a whole. . . . In this way, the family is not only a focal point but also the construct in which these constructs lie. . . . In Juan's narrative it is because social relations are prioritized that hardships occur. Juan begins migrating at 14 to help his mother. He continues to go into the fields to help the family. Juan's family migrates as a group. Juan makes sacrifices to help the family with everyday needs when in Illinois. The family makes sacrifices so that Juan can go to school, for when he goes to school, he is no longer contributing his paycheck to the family budget. To construct programs and services to address these hardships as well as create access for migrants to aspects of mainstream American life (such as public schooling), it is important to acknowledge the logic of the actions that lead to the experiences.

Homeless and Homeless Again

Well, I knew that if I wanted to make something of myself and not work in the fields, I had to have an education. Actually, it's kind of weird 'cause mostly everybody you talk to, wants to earn money. They want to be where the money is but not me. And it's actually, it's kind of, I don't know, I think it's kind of ironic—I come from a low income family so it would be [normal] for me to have, like, this dream of becoming someone important and earning money, something that my parents didn't have much of. But no, to me what's most important is doing something I like and helping people, you know. . . . Or if, if you come from, um, a minority group migrating, you know, you don't really have that many alternatives if you don't have an education. So when you have an education you have so many doors open to you and you can do whatever you want. . . .

My mom told my sisters that I was gonna leave. [My parents are] like, "She's gonna go, this is her second year, you know she's a junior now and she just needs two more years and then she'll . . . be off to college and she's gonna graduate, hopefully meet some guy at college. You know, someone successful," and this and that. (Clara Garcia)

Struggling to return to Texas in order to start school in just a few weeks, rather than months, late involved facing the loneliness of being there alone—in effect, returning "home" to Texas meant becoming "homeless" in the sense that Clara now was without her family. To make herself feel better and avoid the emptiness of the house between phone calls from her parents in Ohio, Clara would spend all her time in her parents' room sleeping or reading. "I would stay in their room I guess to feel closer to them."

* * *

We introduced this paper describing different ideas about home: home as a place or home as a relationship between people. We argue that for migrant workers home is synonymous with family. The migrant workers are homeless in the sense of place in order to maintain their lived home—their family. Realizing this causes us to understand how many societal institutions in the United States assume the first definition of home and by doing so disrupt the migrant worker family—they break the worker's "home" by insisting on a connection to place. In many ways migrant workers are forced into "homelessness." Many of them left home when they left Mexico. They leave "home" again in a cultural sense when they leave the Spanish-speaking communities in which they have lived within the United States, and when we ask them to break the family structure to go to school or for some other purpose we cause individuals to become homeless in a most fundamental way—an emotional rootlessness. We think that once we acknowledge other images of "home" and the values and priorities that follow, policies and services for migrant workers and their children might take a different form. These might then serve our purposes (education) and their purposes (such as preserving the family) better. When policies and institutions ask a migrant family to choose between what they value (family) and what we value any good intended is undermined.

SOURCE: Kozoll, Richard H., Margery D. Osborne, and Georgia Earnest García, "Migrant Worker Children: Conceptions of Homelessness and Implications for Education." *Qualitative Studies in Education*, 16, 4 (July–August 2003). Used by permission of Taylor & Francis Group, http://www.informaworld.com.

ANALYSIS

The number of Latinos who experience homelessness in the United States has puzzled analysts for several decades. The puzzle develops because the rate of homelessness discovered by researchers is usually fairly low, around 12 percent. This figure differs so starkly from the rates of homelessness experienced by African Americans that the question inevitably rises about why such a disparity exists. If homelessness is at least partly a function of poverty, then Latinos should have a higher rate of homelessness. Some students of homelessness find the rates so surprisingly low that they have taken to talking about the *Latino Paradox* or *Hispanic Paradox*, terms that are also used to categorize an analogous situation when considering rates of mortality and health rates among Latinos.

Analysts of Latino culture have posited several explanations. Some have argued that the measures used to determine the homeless Chicano population are not accurate. In particular, they say that the nature of Latino homelessness—where Latinos stay—varies tremendously from the expectations of researchers. Therefore, when they go counting, they simply do not find the locations where the Latinos are located. Another widely accepted explanation is that Latinos have stronger support systems than white Americans and African Americans. The strength of the Latino family allows them to "double-up" and crowd their homes with more people than other groups are willing to do.

This article makes a similar argument about the strength of the Latino family, but it develops the idea differently. It argues that the difference is actually a difference in the way words are used, that in the Latino community family is, in effect, a synonym for home. When a Latino/a describes himself or herself as homeless, he or she is actually saying that he or she is separated from family. The authors of the article based this conclusion on intensive interviews with Latino immigrants and exploring their understanding of the two words. The selections taken from the article are transcriptions of small parts of two of those interviews.

But the authors of the article go further than that. They say that what would readily be called homelessness in the larger U.S. society is really a deliberate strategy that results from a conscious choice—to leave home to continue as a unified, rather than a separated—family. That is, to leave home to avoid being homeless.

In the two interviews contained in the document, families leave their homes and go to other places to be able to provide for the family and keep it intact. Had they remained "at home," they would not have had resources adequate for the family to stay together. Therefore, leaving home to keep the family together was a way of avoiding homelessness.

This argument has important implications that should not be overlooked. The people who do depart from "home" are not being buffeted by powerful social and economic forces over which they have no control. They are leaving to maintain the institution that defines "home" for them—the family. They are active agents in their own lives.

This contention has tremendous implications for the appropriate government policy toward homelessness. First, it raises the question of whether other groups also define *home* in some way that means something other than a physical abode. Are there other definitions of *home* that need to be found and explored before appropriate policies can be adopted? Second, additional definitions of *home* mean that when government is attempting to end "homelessness" for a group of people who have a different definition, policies other than providing decent housing might be more appropriate—strategies that would enable families to remain intact rather than have to separate to subsist economically.

FURTHER READING

Baker, S. G. "Homelessness and the Latino Paradox." In Jim Baumohl (ed.), *Homelessness in America*. Phoenix, AZ: Oryx Press, 1996.

Molina, Edna. "Informal Non-Kin Networks among Latino and African-American Men." *American Behavioral Scientist*, 43, 4 (2000), 63–85.

40

STAYING ALIVE—HOMELESS PEOPLE COPE

How Old Homeless Men Survive

- *Document:* The document describes how homeless men in New York City take care of their daily needs for food, shelter, and other necessities without having an adequate income.
- *Date:* This analysis was written in 1989.
- *Where:* The events took place in New York City and were described by writers from the New York area.
- *Significance:* The selection partly answers the question of how homeless people are able to survive with none of the infrastructure that most Americans take for granted. Even though the document was written two decades ago, its general conclusions and discussion of "survival strategies" is still valid and generally accepted by students of homelessness.

DOCUMENT

Money

Although a majority of men are obtaining some form of settlement, most are receiving inadequate amounts. Among those men living on the street, half live on approximately $100 per month. Consequently, the Bowery man spends a considerable portion of his time looking for alternative sources of income. While extra money may be used for basic survival, often the money goes toward alcohol as well, although alcohol is usually perceived by the men as part of their basic survival. . . .

The most ancient of extant methods of obtaining money is begging. Uncle Ed describes the art of panhandling:

I'd usually go down to Houston Street . . . and I'd bum a card [panhandle]. I go up to the cars and I tell 'em. "Excuse me, sir. Could you pardon me? I'm thirty-five cents short on a drink. Could you help me out?" I found out that they think more of you if you were man enough to ask them towards a drink instead of coming up with the old bullshit you need a quarter for a cup of coffee.

. . . Another way to "hustle" for money is to become a runner. One of the Bowery's premier runners is Roland. Runners are the lifeline for many of the older men who are sick, who go on drinking binges, or who are simply too depressed to leave their room. The runner goes out for food, cigarettes, or booze for either a set fee (usually from a quarter to a dollar), or they will be allowed to keep the change.

. . . Many of the men used to be able to get odd jobs through employment agencies or in taverns. Ed recalls the old days and contrasts it with today's Bowery.

There ain't no more employment agencies here no more either. Louie's shipped upstate and I don't want to go upstate. Sophie's used to be on the corner. She used to send me out everyday, you know, spot jobs, dishwashin' or shit like that. Now, if you go to an employment office, you've got to put down money before they send you out. . . . I've got no money to put down for a job.

When men are eager to work and there is little available in the city, some of the men can still obtain jobs in the kitchens or doing maintenance in the Catskills resort hotels. . . .

Another traditional option for men is to go to a pawn or "buy and sell" shop. There's only one left on the Bowery now, but several are near its perimeter. . . .

Other men, who have no possessions to pawn or fear that they won't be able to pay for its return, sell their food stamps to other men. . . . Commonly, men will make the round of missions to obtain second-hand clothes, only to sell it as soon as possible. Although many men . . . feel degraded by scavenging through litter baskets for returnable cans and bottles, cash redemption of these cans and bottles is one of the popular ways to make a few dollars. . . .

. . . For many years, one of the most popular ways to earn money was by selling blood. However, the blood banks that used to dot skid row are gone. . . .

Other men steal items uptown and bring them to the second-hand stores on the Bowery. . . . Finally, the most common way men obtain a few dollars is through loans from other men, or pooling money together, usually for booze but sometimes for food as well. . . .

Food

Nearly two fifths of the men reported that they weren't eating well. . . . Nearly half the men said that they sometimes go without meals. Among street men, two thirds reported that they sometimes go without meals.

The nonstreet men were considerably more likely to obtain a daily hot meal than the street men (61% to 41%). This reflected the fact that 26% of nonstreet men had access to hot plates or stoves, and 17% had access to a refrigerator. The nonstreet men also had higher income, and therefore 38% were able to go daily to restaurants

To survive at a decent level, homeless people need to find ways of acquiring a long list of goods and services that most middle-class Americans take for granted. Food, shelter, and money are only the most obvious of these. Like everyone else in society, homeless people need clothing, ways of keeping themselves and their clothes clean, acceptable toilet facilities, forms of recreation, and social activities—just to name a few of their needs. When you think about it carefully for a moment, you realize that homeless people have to find uncommon ways of getting just about every object that most Americans rarely have to think about, regardless of whether an item is tangible or intangible, common or rare, cheap or expensive. In this picture, two homeless men are receiving towels at a shelter where they have come to take showers. (AP/Wide World Photos)

or cafeterias, and another 34% ate in these restaurants at least once a week. . . . One means to cope with the problem of obtaining food was to rely on one's social support network. . . .

. . . Another primary source for obtaining hot meals was the local social service agency meal program. . . . Roughly half of the men went to such programs daily, and an additional one fourth went there at least weekly. Clearly, such programs were the bulwark of nutritional survival for these men. . . .

. . . Another alternative for meals is the mission. However, "the price of a meal is a 90-minute Bible Meeting." Other men, however, have been able to rationalize the mission routine. "They do not make you go to mass. They do not put no gun, knife, pistol, or stick on you." . . .

There are still some men who use another time-honored method for procuring food: the hand-out. For example, John . . . leaves his hotel at 4 a.m., and he begins his half-hour trek to the Fulton Fish Market. "They'd be unloadin' fish, and they drop a whole lot on the ground. Very seldom do they pick it up since they ain't gonna put it out for merchants, so they give it to me." . . .

Last, there are still a few "bums" on the Bowery who, because of their suspiciousness and fears, lack of initiative, or physical disabilities will not regularly use formal agencies. . . .

I found [him] going through garbage cans just off the Bowery in Chinatown. He says he lives in various places, sometimes in a box in the Chinese park, or near the Brooklyn or Manhattan Bridge. He gets food from garbage or from people at a Chinese restaurant who gives him scraps. . . .

Shelter

. . . For street and flophouse men, an apartment even in the Bowery area is often considered a significant step toward returning to respectability. Unfortunately, the men's ability to obtain an apartment is markedly curtailed by the limitation of having to provide both rent and security. . . .

In rating the quality of life in the flops, it was not unexpected, given the close quarters of cubicles and dormitories, to find that half the men complained of high noise level and two fifths of them complained of disturbed sleep . . . due to noise. Surprisingly, only one sixth of the men complained of inadequate heat during the winter. . . . On the other hand, many of the men are passive and predisposed to resignation. For instance, nearly two thirds of the men reported mice or roaches in their dwelling; however, only one in five men considered it a problem.

Their response to problems in the hotel reflects their sense of powerlessness and fear. Particularly vulnerable to being abused by hotel clerks, the old men have learned through bitter experience that complaints about even irrational violence yield little satisfaction. . . .

. . . Virtually all men recognize the extreme dangers of flopping in the street. . . . Most men in this situation will have in their minds a series of street flops which are perceived in relative degrees of safety from the weather and from harassment. In the winter, places with solid enclosures such as abandoned buildings, empty trucks, all-night movies, railway stations or the subway are preferred places. Lucky individuals will be befriended by a doorman who will let them sleep in a storage room or behind stairs. Most of these free indoor flops have different types of risks. In public buildings, one risks persecution by workers or the police. To sleep all night in the subway invites being mugged. . . . Places such as abandoned buildings and trucks offer little chance of escape if muggers appear, and the high rate of arson in New York City makes the former locale a possible site for a fiery demise. . . .

Other alternatives for street living include finding places such as park benches or the high grass under the Brooklyn Bridge. . . . Most habitual street men will have several such possible flops in mind for a given night and make a choice based on their perception of its safety for that night. Typically, in checking out one of their nonpark sleeping sites, they will not get to the designated spot until late at night when nobody would normally be around. If any young men are spotted nearby, they will go to their next spot. In the dead of winter, the cold can be more lethal than thugs. . . . Survival depends on finding several layers of warm clothing at a mission and a thick packing crate.

Parks are easier to define as a sleeping place. How well lit is it? What type of people hang out there? How often do police patrol the park, and are they particularly brutal? These factors can change precipitously. Much of the conversation people . . . have with other street people concerns ferreting out whether there have been any changes in the safety of a particular park.

. . . Despite the public image of the street man as being a lone psychotic individual, most of the older street men that we encountered were neither isolated nor psychotic. . . . Many of the men in order to attain some degree of security would sleep in pairs or groups. "It's dangerous by yourself. So it's better to sleep with a couple of other people." . . .

A final consideration must be protection from the elements. On nights that it rains, [some men] stand under some scaffolding. Other men will find a warm doorway, one that has a radiator. Or they might try to get into a cellar. Some men bundle themselves inside of a big cardboard box. . . .

Other places to go in inclement weather include subways, railroad stations, movie theaters, missions, and places "upstate." . . .

Grand Central and Penn stations are also popular shelters for these men, although the opportunities for sleeping are practically nil. One street man told an interviewer, "At Penn Station every second hour or so the cops come around and tell you if you ain't got a ticket to take a walk. And when they'd leave the waiting room then you'd come back in."

. . . Mission living as an alternative to street living has never been looked on favorably by the skid row culture. As Samuel Wallace commented more than two decades ago (1965),

It is all right to attend mission services now and then when one is really desperate or perhaps simply in need of some diversion. To make such attendance a regular habit, however, to take part in the services, or even worse to take up regular lodging in a mission—to become a mission stiff—makes one an outcast on skid row, possibly the lowest stage imaginable.

Hygiene

For hotel and restaurant men, keeping clean is relatively easy because of the availability of toilet and shower facilities in their residences. More of a problem in the hotels is lice or bedbug infestation. . . .

For street men, keeping clean, as with most things in their lives, demands considerably more effort than it does for the average person. . . . Virtually all of the public baths and toilets in the city have been closed, and some of the street men . . . have abandoned any attempt at personal hygiene. The typical result is matted hair, filthy clothes, skin crawling with lice, and an odor so offensive that some of the men brag that it is strong enough to ward off would-be muggers.

Many men make use of several of the local agencies for showers, especially the Holy Name Mission. . . . Uncle Ed used the Holy Name during the time he was living on the subway. He would get off the train about quarter to six and go to the Holy Name to take a bath, shower, and shave. . . .

As for laundering, most men use either coin-operated or Chinese laundries just off the Bowery. . . .

Whether a man has one suit or two suits of clothing is often crucial in determining his level of hygiene. Those men with two suits . . . can wear the second suit when the first becomes soiled and requires laundering. The one-suit man either must wash his clothes in parts, find a place where he can simultaneously disrobe and wash his clothes, or wear his clothes until their stench or their shabbiness necessitate the procurement of new clothes. . . .

Crime

Crime is far and away the major fear of older Bowery men. . . . Two thirds of men felt afraid of crime. . . . A startling 59% of the street men and 51% of the nonstreet men were crime victims during the previous year (e.g., mugging, assault, robbery). Moreover, 37% of street men and 33% of the nonstreet men reported having been involved in a crime in which they sustained personal injury during the previous year. . . .

Although "jackrollers" (men who rob other men . . .) have been associated with skid rows since their origins, the general opinion is that the quantity and viciousness are substantially higher than in the past. . . .

. . . Unprovoked, irrational violence finds everyday expression on the Bowery. Scars from knifings are a common sight on the bodies of older men. In the worst of the flophouses, assault on older men is a common occurrence. . . . Workers at such places sit behind wire barriers and have baseball bats or police billy clubs nearby for protection. . . .

To men sleeping on the streets at night, being jackrolled is a way of life. Hopefully, they will not be physically harmed.

Worse than losing some money can be the loss of the ID cards that help these men secure medical assistance, food stamps, and the like. . . .

The fear of streets after dark is reflected in the fact that 56% of the nonstreet men did not go out in the evening. [One man said that] "At night, no one is safe from them [jackrollers] unless he wears a police uniform or travels in a group."

. . . Although violent street crime is the most pronounced problem for these men, they are also victimized through various "white collar" crimes. . . . Many [loansharks] work in the hotels or taverns. . . . The usual rate was $14 back for every $10 borrowed (48% annual interest). Even more insidious is that most of these loansharks often have the men's checks turned over to them. So they extract the amount owed, and then he is already short for that month and often has to borrow again. . . .

Recreational Activities

When homeless men are not just trying to survive, what are their favorite pastimes? Casual conversation was virtually a universal form of activity....

Other common activities in which ... men engaged on at least a monthly basis included reading newspapers or books (78%), watching TV/listening to the radio (82%), or playing cards (47%)....

Although many men frequent "OTB" (Off-Track Betting parlors), occasionally visit a bookie, or gamble small sums of money in card games, there is a small, but not insubstantial number of men who are addicted to gambling. Whereas most of the addicted old men on the Bowery are hooked on alcohol, gambling is the second potential monkey on the back that leads men to skid row.

SOURCE: Carl I. Cohen and Jay Sokolovsky. *Old Men of the Bowery: Strategies for Survival among the Homeless.* New York and London: The Guilford Press, 1989. Used by permission of Guilford Press.

ANALYSIS

Questions frequently asked about homeless people include, How do they survive? How do they take care of all the actions and dealings that middle-class Americans do every day without consciously thinking about them? Where do they sleep if they don't have a place to live? Where do they keep their possessions? Where do they get food or prepare food or eat food? Where do they wash themselves? How do they get access to toilet facilities? How do they get money to pay for medical services or transportation, or entertainment or anything else that they desire?

People who are not well-informed about homeless persons frequently answer these questions by resorting to commonly accepted stereotypes—the homeless sleep on park benches, they keep their possessions in shopping carts, they find food in garbage cans, they do not keep themselves clean, they get money by panhandling, and they pee in alleys or shrubbery. But, in fact, while some homeless people *do* do some of these things occasionally, most homeless people rarely take care of their needs in such rudimentary ways.

Analysts, observers, and students of homelessness have identified myriad strategies used by homeless people to fulfill all of their basic needs. Some of their strategies can be seen easily if one only looks for them, and others have a more secret existence because homeless people, like everyone else, want to maintain at least some degree of personal privacy and dignity. They do *not* want to be considered, or to consider themselves, uncivilized or less-than-fully human.

Nevertheless, homeless people do perform some day-to-day behaviors in ways that many Americans define as improper, demeaning, or low-class. In places where large numbers of homeless people have gathered, it is not uncommon for them to use public restrooms, to wash in fountains or other public water facilities, and to ask restaurants for leftover or uneaten food. While many Americans have negative attitudes about these behaviors, they seem different if one remembers that some homeless people have no other way of satisfying their need for food and thinks about these activities as ways of providing essential requirements of life.

In fact, some social conflict about some of these issues does exist. For example, what a police officer might define as shoplifting or petty thievery, a social worker might consider a survival strategy for someone with no money. What a nutritionist might regard as unhealthful, outdated garbage that should be destroyed, a hungry and homeless person might consider a feast. Yesterday's newspaper that one person tosses into the garbage can, a person who has no access to any source of current information might consider a treasure. It can be difficult to examine and evaluate the alternative interpretations, and people who accept the more positive views are frequently said to be romanticizing homelessness and advocating "liberal" views of illegal or improper behavior—but that view, too, needs to be evaluated.

It does seem to be beyond question that homeless people have to find unusual ways of satisfying their needs that differ from ways generally used by people without their problems. This is especially true of daily activities—finding shelter, obtaining food, locating places for hygiene. But some analysts have taken a broader view of survival strategies and applied the same kind of interpretations to activities such as creating social networks or asserting some degree of control over a physical space.

In one important article, two sociologists have asked the question of how homeless people are able to negotiate their access to a space that they can occupy. Given the heavy demand in cities to remove homeless people from particular places and render them invisible, and given such pervasive attitudes of NIMBY ("Not in My Back Yard"), many observers ask how homeless people are able to negotiate this divide. They answer that question by showing how the city contains different kinds and levels of space—what they term prime, transitional, and marginal space. In short, homeless people respond to their need for space, but since they are excluded almost completely from some space (prime) and largely excluded from other space (transitional), homeless people react by determining what space is accessible and limiting their lives to locations where they are less likely to encounter resistance. What happens when a homeless person violates this rule is humorously presented in a movie made some years ago, *Down and Out in Beverly Hills*. In it, a homeless man takes up sleeping in a service alley behind the houses of some wealthy people. After they discover him, the movie depicts the interactions of these two different kinds of people as a clash of cultures.

In another article, a sociologist describes and analyzes how three different groups of homeless men in Los Angeles—English-speaking Latinos, Spanish-speaking Latinos, and African Americans—create different kinds of social networks. The author describes how these men of three differing racial/ethnic groups create "informal non-kin networks" whose differences can be seen by looking at such characteristics as the nature of the relationships in a network, the length of time that a network can last, the extent of intimacy of the people within a network, and the degree of reciprocity among the people in the network.

Perhaps the most significant aspect of these two articles, and the document in this chapter, is that all of their authors treat homeless people as competent, rational agents who are capable of analyzing problems, determining the potential costs and benefits of alternative solutions, and making logical choices about what to do based on that analysis. The authors do not portray homeless people as being totally at the mercy of society and other people.

The document presented in this chapter comes from one of the early studies of homeless people's survival strategies. Published in 1989, the book describes and analyzes the lives of homeless men in a district of New York City called the Bowery. For about 150 years, this district has been perceived as a center of poverty and dereliction inhabited by down-in-the-mouth alcoholics who will not work. In trying to understand these men more objectively, and by making fewer moral judgments about them, the two authors depict them differently from the usual portrayal. One important chapter of the book (presented here) describes and analyzes "How Old Homeless Men Survive." In answering that question, they focus on aspects of daily life and show an alternative explanation for behaviors that are frequently criticized—obtaining money, food, shelter, hygiene, crime, and recreation.

FURTHER READING

Cohen, C., and J. Sokolowsky. *Old Men of the Bowery: Strategies for Survival among the Homeless.* New York: Guildford Press, 1989.

Dordick, G. A. *Something Left to Lose: Personal Relations and Survival among New York's Homeless.* Philadelphia, PA: Temple University Press, 1997.

Duneier, M. *Sidewalk.* New York: Farrar, Straus and Giroux, 1999.

Gaetz, S., and B. O'Grady, "Making Money: Exploring the Economy of Young, Homeless Workers." *Work, Employment, and Society,* 16, 3 (2002).

Molina, Edna. "Informal Non-Kin Networks among Homeless Latino and African-American Men: Form and Functions." *The American Behavioral Scientist,* 43, 4 (January 2000), 663–85.

Snow, David A., et al. "Material Survival Strategies on the Street: Homeless People as *bricoleurs.*" In Jim Baumohl (ed.), *Homelessness in America.* Phoenix, AZ: Oryx Press, 1996. 86–96.

Snow, David A., and Michael Mulcahy. "Space, Politics, and the Survival Strategies of the Homeless." *The American Behavioral Scientist,* 45, 1 (September 2001), 149–62.

Underwood, J. *The Bridge People: Daily Life in a Camp of the Homeless.* Lanham, MD: University Press of America, 1993.

41

HOUSING FOR THE HOMELESS

NYU Study Says Affordable Housing Is Best Cure for Family Homelessness

- *Document:* This press release from New York University reports that a new study is about to be published that will challenge prevailing ideas about how to treat homeless people and suggest a different way of helping them escape from homelessness.
- *Date:* The press release was issued on November 1, 1998, and the study was published in the *American Journal of Public Health* a few days later.
- *Where:* The release and the study were both published in New York City, and the study was based on research that took place in New York City.
- *Significance:* The study shows how thinking about homelessness has been changing and developing in new ways. In particular, it offers a radically different solution for homelessness and suggests that all homeless people have not experienced homelessness in exactly the same way. The study reaches the extraordinary conclusion that the best way of ending a family's homelessness is by making it possible for them to afford a place to live.

DOCUMENT

New York University researchers, following poor and homeless New Yorkers for five years, found that the main cause of family homelessness is the scarcity of affordable housing. Furthermore, their study found that drug addiction, mental illness and other social problems were not main causes of homelessness among families living in NYC.

A key finding was that regardless of social disorders, 80% of formerly homeless families with subsidized housing stayed stably housed.

The study's findings will be published in the November issue of *The American Journal of Public Health*. The main authors are NYU psychology professor Marybeth Shinn and professor Beth C. Weitzman of NYU's Wagner Graduate School of Public Service.

Professor Shinn said, "For the past six years, government and private foundations have worked under the assumption that behavioral disorders are the root cause of homelessness and that an individual cannot be stably housed until these disorders have been addressed.

"Our research refutes that assumption. We found that subsidized housing succeeds in curing homelessness among families, regardless of behavioral disorders or other conditions. Whatever their problems—substance abuse, mental illness, physical illness or a history of incarceration—nearly all of the families in our study became stably housed when they received subsidized housing."

Professor Weitzman said, "Our research indicates that homelessness is not a permanent condition. People do get themselves out of the problem. But it only happens when some intervention occurs that provides them with access to the housing market.

"That said, the scariest finding to emerge from our study is the extraordinary number of poor people in New York City who are badly housed and therefore at risk of becoming homeless. For example, we know that 13% of families on the city's welfare caseload don't have their own apartment and are living doubled up with families. And we know that doubling up—always a fragile social arrangement—often precedes entry into the shelter system. Under these conditions, our results suggest, family homelessness will endure."

The researchers conducted interviews with 266 homeless families as they requested shelter and with a comparison sample of 298 families selected at random from the welfare caseload. These interviews were conducted in the first half of 1988. Respondents were then interviewed again five years later.

The object was to examine 4 factors—persistent poverty, behavioral disorders, impoverished social networks and housing conditions—as predictors of entry into shelter and subsequent housing stability.

DID YOU KNOW?

Decreases in Publicly Assisted Housing Results in a High Housing Cost Burden and High Rates of Homelessness, Disproportionately Affecting Racial Minorities

30. . . . [S]ince 2001, a number of government policies have led to reductions in the stock of publicly assisted housing and the number of eligible persons served over the last several years. While the federal government appropriates $38 billion to housing and community development, only 25 percent of the eligible renter households receive assistance. The effects . . . [have left] a high number of households with high housing cost burden and high rates of homelessness, disproportionately affecting racial minorities.

31. Three principle government programs affect the access to affordable housing:

- **Public Housing** is government-funded, multi-unit housing. Eligibility is limited to low income families. . . . Many housing authorities target units to households and families at very low income (VLI) levels . . . and/or extremely low income (ELI). . . .
- **Housing Choice Voucher Program (Section 8)** provides vouchers which allow renters to pay 30% of their income for rent, with the voucher reimbursing private landlords the remainder of the far market rent. . . . By law, 75 percent of vouchers must be targeted to ELI households. . . . Approximately 1.3 million families are served by this program.
- **Privately-owned, government-subsidized multifamily stock**, today comprising some 1.7 million low income families, serve those earning less than 80 percent AMI [Area Median Income]. . . .

Policy Recommendations

36. . . . The United States is not meeting its obligations to guarantee the enjoyment of equal rights to housing for racial minorities, because reductions in housing aid have had a disparate impact on minority populations. . . . The state is obligated to . . . amend laws and policies which perpetuate racial discrimination . . . and to take affirmative steps to . . . protect the enjoyment of equal rights. . . . Such steps should include:

- Create a National Affordable Housing Trust Fund that does not depend on appropriations but receives a dedicated source of funding . . . for the creation, rehabilitation, and preservation of rental housing that is affordable for low income families.

- Adequately fund the Housing Choice Voucher Program (Section 8) and public housing such that the waiting lists for these programs are progressively lessened through the adequate housing of all needy families.

Source: US Human Rights Network Housing Caucus. "Homelessness and Affordable Housing; Response to the Periodic Report of the United States to the United Nations Committee on the Elimination of Racial Discrimination." February 2008.

The main findings of the NYU study are as follows:

Homelessness was a stage that families passed through, not a permanent state: four-fifths of families who entered shelter had their own apartments 5 years later, and three-fifths were in stable housing.

Some 80 percent of the sheltered families that received subsidized housing became stable (that is, they had been living in their own residences for at least the previous 12 months). In contrast, only 18 percent of the families that did not receive subsidized housing were stable by study's end.

Receipt of subsidized housing depended primarily on waiting in shelter long enough to come to the top of the queue for subsidized housing, and on being assigned to a non-profit shelter that provided relatively extensive housing services. Women who experienced domestic violence were less likely than others to receive subsidized housing.

The housing characteristics that predicted homelessness were widespread in the overall welfare caseload. Thirteen percent of families on the overall welfare caseload in New York City in 1988 were doubled up in somebody else's apartment. Almost half lived in crowded conditions, with more than 2 people per bedroom. National data also suggest a large pool of ill-housed poor people. Under these conditions, the researchers suggest, family homelessness will endure.

The ability to identify families at risk of homelessness is not enhanced by examining social factors beyond housing. A main objective of the study was to determine what factors put families at risk of homelessness. To this end, the researchers developed a profile based on housing factors (frequent moves, overcrowding, poor building conditions) and baseline demographic factors (age, ethnicity, etc.) that identified 65% of families requesting shelter by targeting 10% of families on public assistance. When the profile was expanded to include all other factors—persistent poverty, behavioral disorders, and impoverished social networks—the percentage of homeless families identified increased to only 66%.

SOURCE: New York University, "Study Challenges Notion That Substance Abuse, Mental Illness and Other Social Issues are Root Causes of Problem." November 1, 1998. Accessed online at http://www.nyu.edu/publicaffairs/newsreleases/b_NYU_S5.shtml.

ANALYSIS

The rediscovery in the 1980s and 1990s of large numbers of homeless people shocked the United States. Since the end of World War II, nearly 40 years previously, middle-class Americans had generally anticipated long-term economic growth for the nation and upward social and economic mobility for most Americans (especially themselves). Economic downturns did happen—one had just occurred in the early 1970s—but Americans considered hard times to be just a blip on the radar, nothing of too great a concern. The economy was self-regulating, and, if left alone, or given a little fine-tuning by the government, would repair itself. After all, Americans thought, if the United States could pull out of the Great Depression and create the kind of economic growth that occurred during the 1950s and first half of the 1960s, the country could weather any kind of storm. Americans still associated the Depression and the 1930s with Franklin Roosevelt and the New Deal, and often thought that Roosevelt and the New Deal had solved the Depression, not yet understanding that the Depression lasted until the outbreak of World War II caused the economic growth that brought renewed prosperity.

Of course, Americans understood the existence of poverty and that it existed in the United States. But, in most of their minds, poverty was something that happened to other people, especially to other people about whom they cared very little, and about whom they knew little—people categorized as minorities, especially African Americans, Latinos or Hispanics, and Asians. Furthermore, because of the *de facto* housing segregation that existed in U.S. cities, combined with the transportation system that eliminated the need for most Americans to venture into some parts of the city, middle-class or affluent Americans rarely came into contact with racial minorities, never saw the poverty that so many of them experienced, and thought little about them. In a way, poor Americans were an abstraction that people knew existed but were somehow not real.

If middle-class Americans gave any thought to "homelessness," they frequently identified it with Skid Row. Some version of Skid Row existed in every large U.S. city. This was another area entered by few Americans unless they absolutely had to. They did not like the setting—old, dirty, and crumbling—and they did not like the people whom they perceived there—older white men whom they saw as drunk, disheveled, and dirty.

Perhaps the first indication that substantial poverty existed elsewhere than Skid Row occurred in 1962. That year, Michael Harrington published a short book called *The Other America*. In it, he

DID YOU KNOW?

Low-Cost Housing Issue Confronts Santa Paula; Residents Divided over Effects of Proposed Ban on New Units

Hundreds of Santa Paula residents are seeking a moratorium on low-income housing in the county's poorest city at a time when state law requires more help for the needy.

Backers say it's time for other cities in Ventura County [California] to do their fair share of providing housing the poor can afford. Otherwise, growing numbers of low-income people could bankrupt the town, said businessmen Larry Sagely and Steve Smead, who circulated a petition that's drawn 375 signatures.

"We just want to be in the middle," said Snead, a lifelong resident and insurance agent. "We want a housing balance so we can pay our bills."

... "Basically, instead of having one or two families living in one house, we ... have three or four families," said Al Guilin, a retired executive in the area's agriculture industry, who has lived in Santa Paula for 42 years. "If the work is there, the workers will be here, and they'll just live more closely together, or we won't be growing the crop."

... By law, [cities in California] must identify where year-round emergency shelters for the homeless can be built, count the number of extremely poor residents and show how they are trying to house them.

But the petition claims Santa Paula has done too much. The signers, who pledged they were registered voters in the city, want to stop construction of both subsidized and market-rate low-cost housing. The ban would last until such housing makes up no more than 15 percent of the total housing stock in the city of 30,000 where perhaps half the population is low-income.

Sagely and Smead, among others in town, point to Moorpark—a town some Santa Paulans used to call "Poorpark"—as a model of what Santa Paula should do. The east county community turned its fortunes around by bringing in higher-income housing bought by people with money to spend, Smead said.

... For some poor residents, [this] debate is hardly academic. Homemaker Lorena Ramirez, 38, moved into one of the city's affordable complexes, Courtyard by Harvard. So did her two young sons and her husband, Gerardo Mendez....

They left a one-bedroom apartment in Santa Paula, where the entire family had slept in one room on two mattresses, she said.

Another tenant, Lisbeth Diaz, 28, said multiple paychecks didn't solve her family's housing problem in a town where a two-bedroom apartment rents from $975 to $1100 a month.

Diaz shared a one-bedroom apartment with her father, husband, and two sons before moving to the complex near downtown. All three adults worked, but they still could not afford comfortable, market-rate housing, she said.

Source: Kathleen Wilson, "Low-cost housing issue confronts Santa Paula; Residents divided over effects of proposed ban on new units," *Ventura County Star,* July 6, 2008. Available online at http://www.vcstar.com/news/2008/jul/06/na1fcfairshare06/?print=1. Used by permission of the Ventura County Star.

documented the existence of widespread poverty throughout the United States, frequently in out-of-the-way places not often visited by most Americans, either physically or mentally. The book became highly influential and was reprinted seven times before 1971.

However, even reading a book like *The Other America* kept most Americans personally removed from the poorest part of the population. While the book provided them with factual knowledge about real social conditions, most Americans still never witnessed them personally, and they remained abstractions to which most people had no emotional attachments. That situation began to change as the 1960s wore on. President Kennedy read Harrington's book and was so stunned by its revelation that there were 40 to 50 million poor Americans that he created a task force to investigate its allegations and suggest policies to end poverty. Kennedy was assassinated before he could follow any of the panel's recommendations, but his successor, President Lyndon B. Johnson, declared a War on Poverty and established a whole host of programs meant to combat it. In the meantime, the civil rights movement publicized the poverty being experienced by African Americans and included economic equality in its demands, along with social and political equality.

Americans began to acknowledge the existence of poverty during the latter part of the 1960s, but it still had an abstract quality—until television brought the urban riots of the 1960s into their homes and they got a firsthand look at living conditions in central cities and began to see for themselves the squalor being experienced by tens of thousands of Americans. But, even then, those Americans who cared about social issues thought about the problem as one of poverty, not one of housing. Only when homeless people began appearing in *their* parts of cities and intruding into their lives did many Americans conceptualize homelessness as a serious social problem.

Also playing into their consciousness was the realization that homelessness did not just affect the men on Skid Row whom they considered to be derelict, lazy drunken bums. They slowly became aware that there were other homeless people—people whom they could not stigmatize as being unworthy or undeserving, but, rather, women, children, veterans, and mentally ill persons, as well as minorities who were by now being viewed more favorably, and with less hostility, even if only slightly. Once Americans began to feel poverty and to recognize who was actually experiencing it, attitudes began to change—slowly.

One other agent played a crucial role in changing attitudes toward poverty and homelessness, and that was media discussion in general and television in particular. As the number of homeless people multiplied, and as they began to be seen more frequently in public places, they received attention in newspapers and on television. These presentations—even if frequently hostile toward the homeless—at least raised the question of how they should be treated. Media attention gave Americans a chance to think about homeless people and their appropriate position in society—to consider whether homeless people should be institutionalized, incarcerated, driven from the streets, or if they should be treated with compassion, concern, and some degree of sympathy. Americans could begin wondering if homelessness resulted from some failing or deficiency in an individual's personal character or if homelessness and poverty resulted from society's failure to provide for them.

The document in this chapter is a press release telling about an about-to-be-published study concerning homeless families. According to this study, homeless families who were provided with subsidized housing developed stable living patterns and remained in that housing for lengthy periods of time. This idea flew in the face of most contemporary theory that said that people could not move out of homelessness unless their other problems were solved first. The new study said, quite clearly, that the best way of making a family un-homeless was to make it possible for them to afford a place to live.

DID YOU KNOW?

Results of the election in Ventura County, California on November 7, 2006

MEASURE K6. AFFORDABLE HOUSING—CITY OF SANTA PAULA

Shall an ordinance authorizing the Santa Paula Housing Authority to develop, construct or acquire in the City of Santa Paula, with federal or state financial assistance, low rent housing not to exceed in the aggregate 150 dwelling units for living accommodations for persons of low/very low income at sites yet to be determined and subject to all required discretionary city approval be adopted?

[The Measure Failed to be Adopted]

Yes	2,740	48.37%
No	2,925	51.63%

Source: League of Women Voters [of Ventura County, California], "Ventura County Ballot; November 7, 2006 Election" (Ventura County, CA: League of Women Voters of California Election Fund, 2006).

42

CRIMINALIZING THE HOMELESS

Homes Not Handcuffs

- *Document:* The document is a report prepared by two of the most important organizations that advocate for the homeless. It concerns the prevalence of one of the most frequent actions taken by U.S. cities when they deal with the problem of homelessness—criminalization. The report discusses the problems caused by criminalizing homelessness and also suggests some more successful ways of handling the problem.
- *Date:* The report was published in 2009.
- *Place:* The national headquarters of both of the authoring organizations are located in Washington, DC, and the report was presumably written there.
- *Significance:* The report highlights the serious problems that occur when cities attempt to respond to homelessness by criminalizing homeless people for their behaviors. It also suggests ways of combating criminalization and offers some more helpful means to deal with the issue.

DOCUMENT

Executive Summary

Even though most cities do not provide enough affordable housing, shelter space, and food to meet the need, many cities use the criminal justice system to punish people living on the street for doing things that they need to do to survive. Such measures often prohibit activities such as sleeping/camping, eating, sitting, and/or begging in public spaces and include criminal penalties for violations of these laws. Some cities have even enacted food sharing restrictions that punish groups and individuals for serving homeless people. Many of these measures appear to have the purpose of moving homeless people out of sight, or even out of a given city.

...*Homes Not Handcuffs* is the National Law Center on Homelessness & Poverty's (NLCHP) ninth report on the criminalization of homelessness and the National Coalition for the Homeless' (NCH) fifth report on the topic. The report documents cities with the worst record related to criminalizing homelessness, as well as initiatives in some cities that constitute more constructive approaches to street homelessness. The report includes reports of research regarding laws and practices in 273 cities around the country; as well as descriptions of lawsuits from various jurisdictions in which those measures have been challenged.

Types of Criminalization Measures

The criminalization of homelessness takes many forms including:

- Enactment and enforcement of legislation that makes it illegal to sleep, sit, or store personal belongings in public spaces in cities where people are forced to live in public spaces.
- Selective enforcement of more neutral laws, such as loitering, jaywalking, or open container laws, against homeless persons.
- Sweeps of city areas in which homeless persons are living to drive them out of those areas, frequently resulting in the destruction of individuals' personal property such as important personal documents and medication.
- Enactment and enforcement of laws that punish people for begging or panhandling in order to move poor or homeless persons out of a city or downtown area.
- Enactment and enforcement of laws that restrict groups sharing food with homeless persons in public spaces.
- Enforcement of a wide range of so-called "quality of life" ordinances related to public activities and hygiene (i.e., public urination) where no public facilities are available to people without housing.

Prevalence of Laws that Criminalize Homelessness and Poverty

City Ordinances frequently serve as a prominent tool for criminalizing homelessness. Of the 235 cities surveyed for our prohibited conduct chart

- 33% prohibit "camping" in particular public areas in the city and 17% have citywide prohibitions on "camping."
- 30% prohibit sitting/lying in certain public areas.
- 47% prohibit loitering in particular public areas and 19% prohibit loitering citywide.
- 47% prohibit begging in particular public places: 49% prohibit aggressive panhandling and 23% have citywide prohibitions on begging.

The trend of criminalizing homelessness continues to grow. Based on information gathered about the 224 cities that we included in our prohibited conduct charts in both our 2006 report and this report:

- There has been a 7% increase in laws prohibiting "camping" in particular public places.
- There has been an 11% increase in laws prohibiting loitering in particular public places.
- There has been a 6% increase in laws prohibiting begging in particular public places and a 5% increase in laws prohibiting aggressive panhandling.

Examples of Mean Cities

Since the beginning of 2007, among others . . . measures taken in the following cities stand out as some of the worst examples of cities' inhumane treatment of homeless and poor people.

- **Los Angeles, CA**. According to a study by UCLA released in September 2007, Los Angeles was spending $6 million a year to pay for fifty extra police officers as part of its Safe City Initiative to crack down on crime in the Skid Row at a time when the city budgeted only $5.7 million for homeless services. Advocates found that during an 11-month period 24 people were arrested 201 times, with an estimated cost of $3.6 million for police, the jail system, prosecutors, public defenders and the courts. Advocates [for the homeless] asserted that the money could have instead provided supportive housing for 225 people. Many of the citations issued to homeless people were for jaywalking and loitering—"crimes" that rarely produce written citations in other parts of Los Angeles.
- **St. Petersburg, FL**. Since early 2007, St. Petersburg has passed 6 new ordinances that target homeless people. These include ordinances that outlaw panhandling throughout most of downtown, prohibit the storage of personal belongings on public property, and make it unlawful to sleep outside at various locations. In January 2007, the Panellas-Pasco Public Defender announced that he would no longer represent indigent people arrested for violating municipal ordinances to protest what he called excessive arrests of homeless individuals by the City of St. Petersburg. According to numbers compiled by the Public Defender's Office, the vast majority of people booked into the Pinellas County Jail on municipal ordinances were homeless individuals from St. Petersburg.
- **Orlando, FL**. In 2006 the Orlando City Council passed a law that prohibited groups sharing food with 25 or more people in downtown parks covered under the ordinance from doing so more than twice a year. A member of one of the groups that shares food regularly with homeless and poor people in Orlando parks was actually arrested under the ordinance for sharing food. A federal district court found the law unconstitutional; however, the City of Orlando has appealed the decision.

Policy and Legal Concerns

These common practices that criminalize homelessness do nothing to address the underlying causes of homelessness. Instead they actually exacerbate the problem.

Cities across the country have tried a number of different ways to end homelessness. One common practice has been to enact harsh laws outlawing various behaviors common among homeless people. In late 2006, Los Angeles followed a practice adopted by many other cities and enacted a municipal ordinance making it illegal to sleep on city sidewalks during daytime hours. The result was situations in which police officers arrested people who violated the law, and they also confiscated and destroyed those people's personal possessions, calling them "trash." (AP/Wide World Photos)

They frequently move people away from services. When homeless persons are arrested and charged under these ordinances, they may develop a criminal record, making it more difficult to obtain the employment and/or housing that could help them become self-sufficient.

Criminalization measures also raise constitutional questions, and many of them violate the civil rights of homeless persons. Courts have found certain criminalization measures to be unconstitutional. For example:

- When a city passes a law that places too many restrictions on begging, such restrictions may raise free speech concerns as courts have found begging to be protected speech under the First Amendment.
- When a city destroys homeless persons' belongings, such actions may violate the Fourth Amendment rights to be free from unreasonable searches and seizures.
- When a city enforces a law that imposes criminal penalties on a homeless person for engaging in necessary life activities such as sleeping in public,

such a law could violate that person's Eighth Amendment right to be free from cruel and unusual punishment if the person has nowhere else to perform the activity.

- When a city passes a law that does not give people sufficient notice of what types of conduct it prohibits, or allows for arbitrary enforcement by law enforcement officials, such a law can be found to be overly vague in violation of the Constitution. Courts have found certain loitering and vagrancy laws to be unconstitutionally vague.

In addition to violating domestic law, criminalization measures can also violate international human rights law.

Constructive Alternatives to Criminalization

While many cities engage in practices that exacerbate the problem of homelessness by criminalizing it, some cities around the country have pursued more constructive approaches to homelessness:

- **Daytona Beach, FL**. In order to reduce the need for panhandling, a coalition of service providers, business groups, and the city of Daytona Beach began a program that provides homeless participants with jobs and housing. While in the Downtown Street Team program, participants are hired to clean up downtown Daytona Beach and are provided initially with shelter and subsequently with transitional housing. A number of participants have moved on from the program to other full-time jobs and housing.
- **Cleveland, OH**. Instead of passing a law to prevent groups that share food with homeless persons, the City of Cleveland has contracted with the Northeast Coalition for the Homeless to coordinate outreach agencies and food-sharing groups to prevent duplication of food provision, to create a more orderly food sharing system, and to provide an indoor food sharing site to groups who wish to use it.
- **Portland, OR**. As part of its 10-year plan, Portland began "A Key Not a Card," where outreach workers from five different service providers are able to immediately offer people living on the street permanent housing rather than just a business card. From the program's inception in 2005 through spring 2009, 936 individuals in 451 households have been housed through the program, including 216 households placed directly from the street.

Recommendations

Instead of criminalizing homelessness, local governments, business groups, and law enforcement officials should work with homeless people, providers, and advocates for solutions to prevent and end homelessness.

Cities should dedicate more resources to creating more affordable housing, permanent supportive housing, emergency shelters, and homeless services in general. To address street homelessness, cities should adopt or dedicate more resources to outreach programs, emergency shelter, and permanent supportive shelter.

Business groups can play a positive role in helping to address the issue of homelessness. Instead of advocating for criminalization measures, business groups can put resources into solutions to homelessness.

When cities work with homeless persons and advocate for solutions to homelessness, instead of punishing those who are homeless or poor, everyone benefits.

SOURCE: The National Law Center on Homelessness and Poverty, and The National Coalition for the Homeless, "Homes Not Handcuffs: the Criminalization of Homelessness in U.S. Cities," Washington, DC: The National Law Center on Homelessness and Poverty, and The National Coalition for the Homeless, 2009. Available online at <http://www.nationalhomeless.org/publications/crimreport/crimreport_2009.pdf>. Used by permission.

ANALYSIS

When the National Law Center on Homelessness and the National Coalition for the Homeless issued this joint report in 2009, cities had been trying to figure out what to do about homelessness and what to do with homeless people for decades and had not found workable, affordable, constitutional mechanisms to help homeless people.

In 1984, a magazine article described how San Francisco got "Tough with the Homeless." Near its beginning, the article pointed out to its readers that "San Francisco's fairy-tale setting belies an often nightmarish street scene. The city's generous welfare policies and limitless tolerance have drawn an army of vagrants, addicts, and hippie wannabes eager to recreate the summer of love [1968]." The article then explained in vivid detail how a series of mayors attempted to use the police to drive the homeless from the city. One instance occurred in August 1994, when Mayor Jordan announced the institution of Matrix,

a month-long program for enforcing in the downtown area 18 city and state ordinances that had fallen into disuse. Designed to ensure order in public places, they [the 18 laws] covered offenses such as public drunkenness, public urination and defecation, trespassing, street sales of narcotics, dumping of refuse, graffiti vandalism, camping and lodging in public parks, and obstructing sidewalks.

Teams of 12 to 18 officers made regular tours through the Civic Center Plaza, a four-block stretch of Market Street and Union Square

On September 1, Jordan announced that the program would be extended for another month. Just a week later, in response to public demand, the police declared that Matrix would become part of regular law enforcement city-wide.

The Matrix enforcement effort unfolded like a military campaign, retaking the city block by block. Every ten days or so, Matrix teams would announce a sweep of an additional area, chosen on the basis of citizen complaints. Cleaning up Civic Center Plaza took ten intensive days. . . .

... The elimination of a large encampment in Golden Gate Park [was one of the more dramatic events]. ... For years the encampment had rendered one end of the park off limits to normal use. The city concluded that the settlement had to be bulldozed to clear away heaps of hazardous debris. "I walked in myself and almost threw up," said [the Head Gardener]. ...

... With characteristic feistiness [Mayor] Jordan refused to apologize for either the means or the timing of the clean-up. "If the encampments are depositories of human feces, rain-soaked garbage and trash, discarded needles, and other disgusting waste, we will not hesitate to use extraordinary measures to clean up the mess."

Traditionally, throughout U.S. history, local governments have been responsible for caring for needy citizens so Jordan's actions should not surprise; his action repeated what had taken place on many previous occasions. This situation prevailed until the Great Depression of the 1930s. At that time, economic problems so exceeded the ability of local government to take responsibility for social welfare—and the economic problems were so obviously national and not just local—that Roosevelt and the federal government intervened. This involvement of the national government in providing social and economic benefits to U.S. citizens was not without its critics then, and there are still citizens who strongly oppose the federal government giving aid to anyone, although Social Security, Medicare, and a few other similar programs have become so institutionalized and so widely taken for granted that it seems highly unlikely that these programs could ever be eliminated.

But, until Congress passed the McKinney-Vento Homeless Assistance Act in 1987 and President Reagan signed it into law, the federal government never played an important role in caring for the social and economic well-being of U.S. citizens as individuals. Up until then, the care of individuals was considered first to be their own responsibility, then that of their family and friends, and then of their local communities—which could do as much or as little as it thought appropriate.

For better or worse, cities and other local communities have not generally accepted this responsibility willingly or happily. Their basic response to homelessness has been to get rid of it—not by ending the condition of homelessness by providing places to live, but by criminalizing it and by punishing homeless people to one degree or another. Most localities seem to have thought that the best way to rid themselves of homeless people was to remove homeless people to another place. This might have solved the problem of local homelessness, but in no way did it solve the problem of homelessness, reduce the number of homeless people, or do anything to assist any individual person who had no home.

In one of its milder forms, getting rid of homelessness—actually getting rid of homeless people—has meant forcing them to move to parts of the city where they would be less visible and not such an eyesore. This strategy has been especially important in cities having large and profitable tourist industries and where the goal of keeping public areas pleasant and comforting has been paramount. However, there have been many other means used to criminalize homelessness that have been tried by hundreds of towns and cities in the country. These have been carefully and fully documented in the reports published over the last 20 years by the National Law

Center on Homelessness and Poverty and the National Coalition for the Homeless. The document in this chapter is drawn from the most recent of the reports that was sponsored by and published jointly by the two organizations.

In seeking to understand not just homelessness but why homelessness is a crucial issue confronting our society, it is essential to recognize that the treatment of homeless individuals by any level or branch of government raises fundamental questions about the relationship between the government and members of the society. How much power does government have over the individual and how much power can the government use to enforce its demands? Asking those questions raises even more. How does (or how should) government respond positively to the interests of some groups and individuals and to the disadvantage of others? For example, in the illustration given above, the author notes that homeless people are especially a problem in cities where tourism is an important economic activity. Tourists do not want to see dirty unkempt individuals in a place, such as San Francisco, where they have gone to have a good time. They do not want to be faced with unpleasant sights. Whose interests should the municipal government consider in an issue such as that one—the interests and desires of the tourists? Or, the interests and desires of local citizens who hope to profit from the ongoing presence of tourists? Or, the interests of homeless people who have no place other than the street to sleep, no place other than the garbage can to find food, and nowhere else but the public restroom in the public library to wash and clean themselves?

Everyone has desires and needs to be satisfied, but sometimes the satisfaction of one person's needs and the satisfaction of another person's are incompatible and contradictory; they are mutually exclusive, and, almost by definition, satisfying one person automatically means dis-satisfying some one else. On what basis is it determined to settle the conflict? How will the society decide whom to advantage and whom to disadvantage? What are a society's fundamental priorities? Are they race, ethnicity, religion, gender, age, wealth, place of residence, or any other demographic characteristic?

That is the fundamental problem that homelessness presents to U.S. society. Who receives assistance and how is that determined? The document about Los Angeles cleaning up its Skid Row points out that restrictions on individual behavior there would never be imposed or enforced in other parts of the city. Is that acceptable? Most people would almost certainly answer, "Of course not." And yet, such circumstances arise over and over again when cities and the country consider the homeless. The easiest road to take is the one most often taken—end the problems caused by homelessness—get rid of the homeless people—not by providing them with homes but by removing them to a place unseen. Unfortunately, that solution removes homeless people to a less highly valued place, but it does not end homelessness, and it is almost certainly an unconstitutional act of the government to forcibly expel or exile a person.

FURTHER READING

Butterfield, F. "Prisons Replace Hospitals for the Nation's Mentally Ill." *New York Times* (March 5, 1998), p. A1.

National Law Center on Homelessness and Poverty. *Out of Sight—Out of Mind. A Report on anti-Homeless Laws, Litigation, and Alternatives in 50 United States Cities.* Washington, DC: National Law Center on Homelessness and Poverty, 1999.

Takahashi, L. *Homelessness, AIDS, and Stigmatization: The NIMBY Syndrome in the United States at the End of the Twentieth Century.* Oxford, UK: Clarendon Press, 1998.

43

WASHINGTON TAKES THE LEAD

Executive Summary

- **Document:** This document is part of a plan developed by the United States Interagency Council on Homelessness (USICH) to end homelessness in the United States in the next 10 years.
- **Date:** In 2009, Congress legislated that USICH would write this report, and it was finished and released by the end of May 2010.
- **Where:** Like most documents produced by federal agencies, it was written and published in Washington, DC.
- **Significance:** This document represents the first attempt by any agency of the federal government to take any responsibility for the existence of homelessness in the United States. In receiving this report, President Obama called the existence of homelessness "unacceptable," and he made ending homelessness a "priority." If he succeeds, it will be an extraordinary accomplishment and will almost certainly be seen in the future as one of the great achievements of his administration. If he fails, historians will be trying to decide if the plan failed because of internal problems, because homelessness cannot be eradicated, or if it failed because the country's leaders didn't have the political skills needed to work together to solve a major social problem.

DOCUMENT

Our nation has made significant progress over the last decade reducing homelessness in specific communities and with specific populations. Communities across the United States—from rural Mankato, Minnesota to urban San Francisco—have organized partnerships between local and state agencies and with the private and nonprofit sectors to implement plans to prevent, reduce, and end homelessness.

These communities, in partnership with the federal government, have used a targeted pipeline of resources to combine housing and supportive services to deliver permanent supportive housing for people who have been homeless the longest and are the frailest. The results have been significant.

In many respects, this current period of economic hardship mirrors the early 1980s when widespread homelessness reappeared for the first time since the Great Depression. Communities will need all of the tools in our grasp to meet the needs of those experiencing homelessness, including families and far too many of our nation's Veterans. In particular, we are concerned that recent national data shows a significant rise in family homelessness for 2008 to 2009.

HUD [Housing and Urban Development] Secretary Shaun Donovan, HHS [Health and Human Services] Secretary Kathleen Sibelius, VA [Veterans Affairs] Secretary Eric K. Shinseki, and Labor Secretary Hilda Solis declared the vision of the Plan to be centered on the belief that "no one should experience homelessness—no one should be without a safe, stable place to call home." The Plan is focused on four key goals: **(1) Finish the job of ending chronic homelessness in five years; (2) Prevent and end homelessness among Veterans in five years; (3) Prevent and end homelessness for families, youth, and children in ten years; and (4) Set a path to ending all types of homelessness.**

The goals and timeframes we aspire to in this Plan are an important target for the nation. They demonstrate the Council's belief that ending homelessness in America must be a priority for our country. As President Barack Obama has said, in a nation as wealthy as ours, "it is simply unacceptable for individuals, children, families, and our nation's Veterans to be faced with homelessness." We believe it is important to set goals, even if aspirational, for true progress to be made.

This Plan is a roadmap for joint action by the 19-member United States Interagency Council on Homelessness [USICH], along with local and state partners in the public and private sectors. It will provide a reference framework for the allocation of resources and the alignment of programs to achieve our goal to prevent and end homelessness in America. The Plan also proposes the realignment of existing programs based on what we have learned and the best practices that are occurring at the local level so that resources focus on what works. We will take action in partnership with Congress, states, localities, philanthropy, and communities around the country.

From years of practice and research, we have identified successful approaches to end homelessness. Evidence points to the role housing plays as an essential platform for human and community development. Stable housing is the foundation upon which people build their lives—absent a safe, decent, affordable place to live, it is next to impossible to achieve good health, positive educational outcomes, or reach one's economic potential. Indeed, for many persons living in poverty, the lack of stable housing leads to costly cycling through crisis-driven systems like foster care, emergency rooms, psychiatric hospitals, emergency domestic violence shelters, detox centers, and jails. By the same token, stable housing provides an ideal launching pad for the delivery of health care and other social services focused on improving life outcomes for individuals and families. More recently, researchers have focused on housing stability as an important ingredient for the success of children and youth in school. When children have a stable home, they are more likely to succeed socially, emotionally, and academically.

Capitalizing on these insights, this Plan builds on the significant reforms of the last decade and the intent by the Obama administration to directly address homelessness through intergovernmental collaboration. Successful implementation of the Plan will result in stability and permanency for the more than 649,000 men, women, and children who are homeless on a single day in America. At the same time, its execution will produce approaches to homelessness that are cost-effective for local, state, and federal government. The Plan's content presents initial goals, themes, objectives, and strategies and was generated through the collaboration and consensus of the 19 USICH member agencies. Since the Homeless Emergency Assistance and Rapid Transition to Housing (HEARTH) Act requires USICH to update the Plan annually, the substance of this Plan represents the beginning of a process toward our goal of preventing and ending homelessness.

The Affordable Care Act (Health Reform), a landmark initiative of the Obama administration, will further the Plan's goals by helping numerous families and individuals experiencing homelessness to get the health care they need. Medicaid will be expanded to nearly all individuals under the age of 65 with incomes up to 133% of the federal poverty level (currently about $15,000 for a single individual). This significant expansion will allow more families and adults without dependent children to enroll in Medicaid in 2014. In addition, Health Reform will support demonstrations to improve the ability of psychiatric facilities to provide emergency services; it will also expand the availability of medical homes for individuals with chronic conditions, including severe and persistent mental illness. Expansion of Community Health Centers is another major change that will serve many vulnerable populations, including those who are homeless or at risk of being homeless.

The Plan proposes a set of strategies that call upon the federal government to work in partnership with state and local governments, as well as the private sector to employ cost effective comprehensive solutions to end homelessness. The Plan recognizes that the federal government needs to be smarter and more targeted in its response and role, which also includes supporting the work that is being done on the ground. The federal government's partners at the local level have already made tremendous strides, with communities across the nation—including over 1,000 mayors and county executives across the country—having developed plans to end homelessness. The Plan highlights that by collaborating at all levels of government. The nation can harness public resources and build on the innovations that have been demonstrated at the local level and in cities nationwide to provide everyone—from the most capable to the most vulnerable—the opportunity to reach their full potential.

The Plan includes 10 objectives and 52 strategies. The objectives and strategies contribute to accomplishing all four goals of the Plan.

The first section details the development of this first-ever comprehensive federal plan to prevent and end homelessness. This section sets out the core values reflected in the Plan and the key principles that guided the process. It also describes the opportunities for public comment offered during the development of the Plan.

The second section of the Plan provides an overview of homelessness in America. Since homelessness takes many different forms by population or geographic area, we provide a synopsis of the issues facing these varying groups experiencing homelessness. The section also addressed the sources of data used throughout the Plan.

The third section represents the core of the Plan including the objectives and strategies to prevent and end homelessness. It provides the logic behind each objective, the departments and agencies involved, the key partners, and strategies to achieve the respective objectives.

The Plan concludes with a section that defines the steps USICH partners will take next, providing a framework for action. This includes the impact we aspire to have that will require active work from many partners at all levels of government and across the private sector. This section provides a brief summary about the context in which we move forward in terms of the economic, policy, and political challenges and opportunities. There is a discussion of the measures that will be used to track progress over time toward the Plan goals. Initiatives currently under way that help advance the Plan goals are summarized. Finally, the section lays out the documents USICH will produce to provide information and transparency to the public, Congress, and our partners going forward.

Vision

No one should experience homelessness—
no one should be without a safe, stable place to call home.

Goals

- **Finish the job ending homeless in 5 years**
- **Prevent and end homelessness among Veterans in 5 years**
- **Prevent and end homelessness for families, youth, and children in 10 years**
- **Set a path to ending all types of homelessness**

Themes

Increase Leadership, Collaboration, and Civic Engagement

Objective 1: Provide and promote collaborative leadership at all levels of government and across all sectors to inspire and energize Americans to commit to preventing and ending homelessness.

Objective 2: Strengthen the capacity of public and private organizations by increasing knowledge about collaboration, homelessness, and successful interventions to prevent and end homelessness.

Increase Access to Stable and Affordable Housing

Objective 3: Provide affordable housing to people experiencing or most at risk of homelessness.

Objective 4: Provide permanent supportive housing to prevent and end chronic homelessness.

Increase Economic Security

Objective 5: Increase meaningful and sustainable employment for people experiencing or most at risk of homelessness.

Objective 6: Improve access to mainstream programs and services to reduce people's financial vulnerability to homelessness

Improve Health and Stability

Objective 7: Integrate primary and behavioral health care services with homeless assistance programs and housing to reduce people's vulnerability to end the impacts of homelessness

Objective 8: Advance health and housing stability for youth aging out of systems such as foster care and juvenile justice

Objective 9: Advance health and housing stability for people experiencing homelessness who have frequent contact with hospitals and criminal justice

Retool the Homeless Crisis Response System

Objective 10: Transform homeless services to crisis response systems that prevent homelessness and rapidly return people who experience homelessness to stable housing.

Development of the Plan

The President and Congress charged USICH to develop "a national strategic plan" to end homelessness with the enactment of the Homeless Emergency Assistance and Rapid Transition to Housing (HEARTH) Act in May 2009. This Federal Strategic Plan to Prevent and End Homelessness reflects agreement in the agencies on the Council on a set of priorities and strategies including activities initiated by the President in the budget for fiscal years 2010 and 2011.

The Council affirmed six core values to be reflected in the Plan:

- Homelessness is unacceptable.
- There are no "homeless people," but rather people who have lost their homes who deserve to be treated with dignity and respect.
- Homelessness is expensive; it is better to invest in solutions.
- Homelessness is solvable; we have learned a lot about that work.
- Homelessness can be prevented.
- There is strength in collaboration and USICH can make a difference.

The Council decided the **development of the Plan should be guided by key principles**. It should be:

- Collaborative
- Solutions-driven and evidence-based
- Cost effective
- Implementable and user-friendly

- Lasting and scalable; and
- Measurable, with clear outcomes and accountability

We stressed the importance of transparency. We encouraged multiple opportunities for input, feedback, and collaboration in the development of the Plan from researchers, practitioners, state and local government leaders, advocates, people who have experienced homelessness, and federal agency staff.

Four workgroups were convened to **analyze specific populations:**

- Families with children
- Youth
- Veterans
- Individuals experiencing chronic homelessness

A fifth workgroup (Community) analyzed how the federal government can better support communities (including public and private sectors) in their efforts to prevent and end homelessness. Workgroup members from Council agencies reviewed the literature and talked with experts for additional insights into the scope of the problem, its causes and consequences, and best practices. They synthesized the information into recommendations for the Plan.

SOURCE: [United States Interagency Council on Homelessness]. *Opening Doors: Federal Strategic Plan to End Homelessness*. Washington, DC (451 7th St., SW, Suite 2200, Washington 20410), U.S. Interagency Council on Homeless, 2010. pp. 4–8.

ANALYSIS

On June 22, 2010, the U.S. Interagency Council on Homelessness (USICH) released "Opening Doors: Federal Strategic Plan to Prevent and End Homelessness." The Council had been charged to produce this report 13 months earlier when President Obama signed into law the Homeless Emergency and Rapid Transition to Housing (HEARTH) Act. That act contained the provision that "not later than 12 months after the date of the enactment of the Homeless Emergency Assistance and Rapid Transition to Housing Act of 2009, develop, make available for public comment, and submit to the President and to Congress a National Strategic Plan to End Homelessness, and shall update such plan annually."

The USICH issued its report 13 months later with great fanfare. It did not simply release "Opening Doors" with a press release or notice in the Federal Register. Rather, it "unveiled" the report at a ceremony presided over by Barbara Poppe, the Executive Director of the USICH. Ms. Poppe was accompanied by several other members of the Commission including the Secretaries of Housing and Urban Development (HUD), Labor, Health and Human Services (HHS), and Veterans Affairs (VA) who were all members of USICH (along with the Secretaries of Agriculture, Commerce, Defense, Education, Energy, Homeland Security, Interior, Justice, and Transportation, not to mention the Commissioner of the Social Security

Administration, the Chief Executive Officer of the Corporation for National and Community Service, the Administrator of the General Services Administration, the Director of the Office of Management and Budget [OMB], among others). Poppe presented the report to the Domestic Policy Council Director Melody Barnes, who accepted it on behalf of President Obama.

In delivering the report to the President, Shaun Donovan, Chair of the USICH and Secretary of HUD, heaped praise on it. It was, he said, "the most far-reaching and ambitious plan to end homelessness in our history," and it would "strengthen existing programs and forge new partnerships." He enthusiastically declared that "Congress, state, and local officials, faith-based and community organizations, and business and philanthropic leaders across our country" would "harness public and private resources" to end homelessness. "No one," he said, "should be without a safe, stable place to call home and today we unveil a plan that will put our nation on the path toward ending all types of homelessness."

Executive Director Poppe, too, applauded the report, saying that "for the first time the nation will have goals, strategies, and measurable outcomes that will guide us toward a fiscally prudent government response." And Secretary of Labor Hilda Solis, who was also the vice-chair of USICH, emphasized the cooperative nature envisioned in the report. "Achieving the goals in 'Opening Doors' will require strong partnerships with Congress, states, localities, philanthropy, faith-based and community organizations across the country," she said.

Response to the report nationally was quick. The National Alliance to End Homelessness issued a brief press statement that same afternoon "welcom[ing the] first-ever comprehensive federal commitment to end homelessness." "The plan has a time-frame and clear national goals; these will help to drive an organized and committed federal response." Nan Roman, President of the National Alliance to End Homelessness, elaborated more that afternoon. She thought that the plan "set ambitious national goals that will be the key to driving progress. They include ending **veterans' homelessness in five years**, ending **chronic homelessness in five years**, and ending **family and youth homelessness** in ten years." She went on to comment that "unambiguous goals, coupled with an ambitious, but do-able, time-frame are critical to success."

Neil J. Donovan, another advocate for the homeless and Executive Director of the National Coalition for the Homeless (NCH), also "congratulate[d]" USICH for introducing the Strategic Plan, and he "embrace[d]" its "vision that no one should experience homelessness and no one should be without a safe place to call home." He went on to praise President Obama for declaring in his message accepting the Plan that "ending homelessness in America must be a national priority." He called the plan "groundbreaking," but he clearly did have reservations. In specific he criticized the vagueness of the plan. As he put it, "many of the methods outlined are vague and without firm commitment to allocate funds and implement strategies. There will certainly be continued need for further discussion and action to address this national priority." The plan, he said, "must not create a double standard and [must] hold itself to the same strict standard that it holds for local communities, clear number goals, timetables, and identify funding and implementing bodies to ensure they move from planning to action."

Jeremy Rosen, Policy Director of the National Law Center on Homelessness and Poverty, took almost the same line as that put forth by Neil Donovan. He averred that the plan did "a great job of outlining the issues" and declared that "it's comprehensive, covers all populations, and acknowledges different federal definitions of homelessness and their importance." The goals were also "good," and the NLCHP praised "Opening Doors" as "the first federal government document to explicitly call for preventing and ending family homelessness in ten years."

But he then went on to raise substantial criticisms. The strategies in the plan, he said, "are vague." The plan contained "lots of talk about dissemination of best practices to states and localities, about more research, about reviewing federal programs to remove barriers that prevent homeless people from accessing housing or services." And these, Rosen agreed, were "all very important things." But, he pointed out, the plan contained "no specifics as to how the plan will be funded." The plan also cited "a need for new housing subsidies, but fails to describe how many are needed and how we will get them." In summation, Rosen thanked USICH for its work but said that "if we really want to end homelessness it's going to take more than just a plan—we'll need specific strategies and the promise of enough money to accomplish them."

Analysts such as Nan Roman, Neil J. Donovan, and Jeremy Rosen—all strong advocates for homeless people—praised USICH for its position, but they also criticized the report for being too ambiguous about how the federal government was going to achieve its objectives and how it was going to pay for them. Nevertheless, the structure of their responses tended to emphasize the positive aspects of the report by first expressing strong approval of its goals and only secondarily explaining their qualms in a straightforward, non-accusatory tone.

Perhaps Tony Pugh, a reporter for the McClatchy Newspapers, most clearly adopted this style of writing. He set the tenor of his column by titling it "Obama Administration Vows to End Homelessness," thus giving credit to the President and his administration, and he continued in this manner by almost immediately quoting Nan Roman to the effect that the plan was "a significant breakthrough because there's never been a comprehensive effort to end homelessness with a timeline and measurable goals." Only then did he bring up any criticisms, but he also subordinated them to positive statements. For example, he began his first paragraph discussing qualms by initially noting that "other advocates also lauded the plan's goals," and only then did he report that "they questioned the lack of details about how some of the proposals would be paid for." Moreover, the first critic whom he mentioned was Maria Foscarinis, the Executive Director of the National Law Center on Homelessness & Poverty, who certainly favored federal action to end homelessness. In quoting her, Pugh pointed out that her criticisms were more aimed at the question of whether government officials would have the will to implement the plan, not whether she agreed with the plan. "The big question is whether preventing children and families in the U.S. from becoming homeless is important enough for Congress' to increase homeless-program funding. Foscarinis expressed doubt that 'they'll do that without enough pressure and leadership from the White House.... In order to achieve these goals,' she said, 'the funding has to be there, and that means the administration has to really be firm and advocate.'"

About a week after USICH released its report, some journalists began to express criticisms more forcefully and with much more hostility. Michael Medved, writing for aolnews online, called the report "Obama's Flimflam Plan to End Homelessness." The first paragraph of his column immediately launched into a sarcastic attack by commenting that "Opening Doors" might have "produced a deafening national chorus of hoots and guffaws, except for the embarrassing fact that the press paid scant attention to this sweeping initiative to end homelessness." He immediately thereafter asked the question "who could report with a straight face on a costly fresh effort that solemnly promises to 'wipe out' all 'chronic homelessness' by 2015" given the current national circumstances: "soaring deficits, a teetering world economy, a failing war in Afghanistan, a catastrophic oil spill, a surging Republican opposition, and a chief executive with precipitously plummeting approval ratings?"

Medved's sarcastic questioning continued in the next paragraph when he asked if "any sane observer above the age of 14 [could] honestly believe that a new federal program would succeed in achieving this noble goal," and he wondered "even more outlandishly, [if] the latest bureaucratic prescription would finally succeed in its broader purpose: to 'end' homelessness of every sort within the next ten years." Medved continued in this tone for about two pages, ultimately directly attacking the President and his entire domestic agenda. "The reliance on federal power illustrates the twisted thinking that undergirds every aspect of the president's domestic agenda. Would even the glib and accomplished commander in chief be able to explain why acute local troubles—like homelessness, or the provision of medical care, or struggling schools—require ministrations and money from far away Washington, instead of the more flexible and accountable efforts of public servants who are closer (in every way) to the pressing problems?"

Others quickly fell in line behind Medved. Writing in the *Washington Times*, Deborah Simmons called "the quest to end homelessness . . . unrealistic." And, Sonja Fitz, writing for the *Berkeley [California] Daily Planet*, adopted the same tone as Medved even though she expressed her disdain of the Plan from the left rather than the right. To her, the Plan "taste[d] suspiciously like stone soup . . . warmed over nuggets of existing wisdom from service providers around the country floating in a pale federal broth." Fitz was skeptical, she said, "as [she] shove[d] aside the stack of 5, 10, and 15 year plans [that she'd] encountered since entering this field in 1986," and she wanted to know, "Where's the beef?" And, continuing her sarcasm, she said that since she was a vegetarian she'd "take the liberty of inventing a different catchphrase, where's the hot sauce?" And, she "mean[t] that quasi-literally: where's the *heat* that underscores the core emergency behind the neatly packaged bundle of factors that create and sustain homelessness: *lack of housing?*"

She answered her question in the next paragraph.

Oh yes, here it is on page 36, under the second goal, two lines in the second strategy, " . . . low cost capital for new construction" and "fund the National Housing Trust Fund," And, again on page 39, under the third strategy (after "improving targeting and prioritizing" and "creating protocols and incentives" for people to move out of supported housing and into independent housing when ready): "expand the supply of permanent affordable housing." Thank you, Captain Obvious! Good objectives, but nothing new, and nothing concrete about how to make it happen. Do you think people haven't been *trying* hard enough to build new housing?

The conflicts over the USICH Plan strongly suggest how difficult it will be for the federal government to develop a plan that might actually end homelessness. Government officials, news analysts, journalists, and political commentators are unable to agree on a definition of homelessness, unable to agree whether on whether homelessness can be eradicated, and unable even to agree if the federal government should take any responsibility for ending homelessness. They disagree about the causes of homelessness, and they disagree about the moral worth of homeless people and their rights. Most of all, though, they seem to subordinate policy issues, such as homelessness, to political interests such as maintaining their own personal power and that of their political party. To succeed, the recent 10-year plan to end homelessness will have to overcome all of these disagreements and somehow find a place where everyone is willing to listen to everyone else, put their own interests aside, and decide to work for the well-being of homeless people.

BIBLIOGRAPHY

Allen, John. *Homelessness in American Literature: Romanticism, Realism and Testimony*. New York, NY and London: Routledge, 2004.

Aydelotte, Frank. *Elizabethan Rogues and Vagabonds*. New York, NY: Barnes & Noble, Inc., 1967.

Bahr, Howard (ed.). *Disaffiliated Man: Essays and Bibliography on Skid Row, Vagrancy, and Outsiders*. Toronto, ON.: University of Toronto Press, 1970.

Baldwin, Stanley. *Poverty and Politics: The Rise and Decline of the Farm Security Administration*. Chapel Hill, NC: University of North Carolina Press, 1968.

Barak, Gregg. *Gimme Shelter: A Social History of Homelessness in America*. New York, NY: Praeger, 1991.

Baum, Alice S., *A Nation in Denial: The Truth about Homelessness*. Boulder, CO; San Francisco, CA; and Oxford, UK: Westview Press, 1993.

Baumohl, Jim (ed.). *Homelessness in America*. Phoenix, AZ: Oryx Press, 1996.

Bingham, Richard D., Roy E. Green, and Sammis B. White. *The Homeless in Contemporary Society*. Newbury Park, CA and London: Sage Publications, 1987.

Blau, Joel. *The Visible Poor: Homelessness in the United States*. New York, NY and Oxford, UK: Oxford University Press, 1992.

Burt, Martha. *America's Homeless: Numbers, Characteristics, and Programs that Serve Them*. Washington, DC: Urban Institute, 1989.

Burt, Martha. *Over the Edge: The Growth of Homelessness in the 1980s*. New York, NY: Russell Sage Foundation, 1992.

Cloke, Paul J., Paul Milbourne, and Rebekah Widdowfield. *Rural Homelessness: Issues, Experiences, and Policy Responses*. Bristol, UK: Policy Press, 2002.

Cotton, Eddy Jo. *Hobo: A Young Man's Thoughts on Trains and Tramping in America*. New York, NY: Harmony Books, 2002.

Cresswell, Tim. *The Tramp in America*. London: Reaktion Books, 2001.

Crouse, Joan M. *The Homeless Transient in the Great Depression: New York State, 1929–1941*. Albany, NY: State University of New York Press, 1986.

Dear, Michael, and Jennifer Wolch. *Landscapes of Despair: From Deinstitutionalization to Homelessness*. Princeton, NJ: Princeton University Press, 1987.

DePastino, Todd. *Citizen Hobo: How a Century of Homelessness Shaped America*. Chicago, IL and London: University of Chicago Press, 2003.

Dickson, Paul, and Thomas B. Allen. *The Bonus Army: An American Epic*. New York, NY: Walker and Company, 2004.

Gregory, James N. *American Exodus: The Dust Bowl Migration and Okie Culture in California*. New York, NY: Oxford University Press, 1989.

Hamburger, Robert. *All the Lonely People: Life in a Single Room Occupancy Hotel*. New Haven, CT and New York, NY: Ticknor & Fields, 1983.

Higbie, Frank Tobias. *Indispensable Outcasts: Hobo Workers and Community in the American Midwest, 1880–1930*. Urbana, IL: University of Illinois Press, 2003.

Hoch, Charles, and R. Slayton. *New Homeless and Old Community and the Skid Row Hotel*. Philadelphia, PA: University of Pennsylvania Press, 1989.

Hombs, Mary Ellen. *American Homelessness: A Reference Handbook* (3rd ed.). Santa Barbara, CA; Denver, CO; and London: ABC-CLIO, 2001.

Hombs, Mary Ellen. *Homelessness in America: A Forced March to Nowhere*. Washington, DC: Community for Creative Non-Violence, 1982.

Hope, Marjorie, and James Young. *The Faces of Homelessness*. Lexington, MA: Lexington Books, 1986.

Hopper, Kim. "Homelessness Old and New: The Matter of Definition." *Housing Policy Debate*, 2, 3 (1981), 757–814.

Hopper, Kim. "Housing the Homeless." *Social Policy*, 28, 3 (Spring 1998), 28, 64–67.

Hopper, Kim. "Public Shelter as 'a Hybrid Institution': Homeless Men in Historical Perspective." *Journal of Social Issues*, 46, 4 (Winter 1990), 3–29.

Hopper, Kim. *Reckoning with Homelessness*. Ithaca, NY: Cornell University Press, 2003.

Hopper, Kim, and Jim Baumohl. "Held in Abeyance." *American Behavioral Scientist*, 37, 4 (February 1994), 522–54.

Hopper, Kim, and J. Hamberg. "The Making of America's Homeless: From Skid Row to New Poor, 1945–1984." In *Critical Perspectives on Housing* (ed. Rachel Bratt, Chester Hartman, and Ann Meyerson). Philadelphia, PA: Temple University Press, 1989, 12–40.

Jencks, Christopher. *The Homeless*. Cambridge, MA: Harvard University Press, 1994.

Kusmer, Kenneth L. *Down and Out, on the Road: The Homeless in American History*. New York, NY: Oxford University Press, 2003.

Lee, Barrett A., Kimberly A. Tyler, and James D. Wright. "The New Homelessness Revisited." *Annual Review of Sociology*, 36 (2010), 501–21.

Liebow, Elliot. *Tell Them Who I Am: The Lives of Homeless Women*. New York, NY: Penguin Books, 1995.

Miller, Ronald J. *The Demolition of Skid Row*. Lexington, MA, and Toronto, ON: Lexington Books, D.C. Heath and Company, 1982.

Monkkonen, Eric H. (ed.). *Walking to Work: Tramps in America, 1790–1935*. Lincoln, NE and London: University of Nebraska Press, 1984.

O'Connor, John, and Lorraine Brown. *Free, Adult, Uncensored: The Living History of the Federal Theatre Project*. Washington, DC: New Republic Books, 1978.

Redburn, F., and T. Buss. *Responding to America's Homeless: Public Policy Alternatives*. New York, NY: Praeger, 1986.

Rosenthal, Rob. *Homeless in Paradise: A Map of the Terrain*. Philadelphia, PA: Temple University Press, 1994.

Rossi, Peter. *Down and Out in America: The Origins of Homelessness*. Chicago, IL: University of Chicago Press, 1989.

Schneider, John C. "Skid Row as an Urban Neighborhood." *Urbanism Past and Present*, 9, 1 (1984), 10–20.

Shinn, Marybeth, and Colleen Gillespie. "The Roles of Housing and Poverty in the Origins of Homelessness." *American Behavioral Scientist*, 37, 4 (February 1994), 505–21.

Shinn, Marybeth, Jim Baumohl, and Kim Hopper. "The Prevention of Homelessness Revisited." *Analyses of Social Issues and Public Policy*, 1, 1 (December 2001), 95–128.

Snow, David A., and Leon Anderson. *Down on Their Luck: A Study of Homeless Street People.* Berkeley, CA and Oxford, UK: University of California Press, 1993.

Sommer, Heidi. *Homelessness in Urban America: A Review of the Literature.* Berkeley, CA: Institute of Governmental Studies Press, 2000.

VanderStaay, Steven. *Street Lives: An Oral History of Homeless Americans.* Philadelphia, PA: New Society Publishers, 1992.

Wasserman, Jason Adam, and Jeffrey Michael Claire. *At Home on the Street: People, Poverty, and a Hidden Culture of Homelessness.* Boulder, CO: Lynne Rienner Publishers, 2010.

Watson, Sophie, with Helen Austerberry. *Housing and Homelessness: A Feminist Perspective.* London and Boston, MA: Routledge, and Kegan Paul, 1986.

Williams, Clifford. *One More Train to Ride: The Underground World of Modern American Hoboes.* Bloomington, IN: Indiana University Press, 2003.

Wolch, Jennifer, and Michael Dear. *Malign Neglect: Homelessness in American Cities.* San Francisco, CA: Jossey-Bass, 1993.

Wormser, Richard. *Hoboes: Wandering in America, 1870–1940.* New York, NY: Walker and Co., 1994.

Wright, James. *Address Unknown: The Homeless in America.* Hawthorne, NY: Aldine de Gruyter, 1989.

Wright, James, Beth Rubin, and Joel Devine. *Beside the Golden Door: Policy, Politics, and the Homeless.* New York, NY: Aldine de Gruyter, 1998.

INDEX

Activities, Bowery men, 342
Adler, Herman, 99
Adolescents, 289
Affordable Care Health Reform
  Act, 366
Afghanistan War. *See* Operation
  Enduring Freedom (OEF)
African Americans: employment
  discrimination, 321; and the GI
  Bill of Rights, 320; in the homeless
  population, 266, 267; King County
  homeless, 323; King County
  unemployment rate,
  323; special populations research,
  278–79
Age: as grouping cohorts, xiv; and
  homeless population, 266, 267;
  homeless veterans, 299–300;
  subgroup dimension, 272–75
Agricultural workers: country lodging
  diary, 53–54, 56; Grape strike,
  190–92; Mexican migrants, 328;
  wages of, 204
Agriculture: agribusiness, 55; Great
  Depression, 118–21
Agriculture Resettlement
  Program, 150
Alcohol abuse: homeless veterans,
  300; rural homeless, 310, 312–13;
  special populations research, 280
Alcohol use: country lodging, 55, 56;
  daily survival needs, 336, 342
All-volunteer force (AVF), 300, 303
Allen, John, 102

Almshouse: eighteenth century, 17;
  emergence of, xviii
Ambulatory automatism, 21
American Civil Liberties Union
  (ACLU), 159, 160
American Federation of Labor
  (AFL), 95
American Indians. *See* Native
  Americans
American Individualism (Hoover), 140
American Journal of Public Health,
  346, 347
American Songbook (Sandburg), 87
Anacostia flats, 132, 136
Anacostia River, 134, 138
Anderson, Nels: on hobo gender roles,
  77; hobo jungle document, 66–69;
  on intellectual hoboes, 102; and
  participant observation practices,
  241; on train ride, 28
Anderson, Sherwood, 103
Annual Homeless Assessment Report
  (AHAR): analysis of
  characteristics, 267–68; analysis of
  homeless estimate, 257–61;
  homeless characteristics, 264, 265–
  67; homeless estimate, 254–57
Arent, Arthur, 209
"Arkies," 121, 160–61
Arvin Migratory Labor Camp:
  description of, 167, 171–73, 175;
  songs, 211; success of, 194
Asian/Pacific Islanders, 323
Aspinwall, William, 36

Assembly Bill 980, 156
Assembly Bill 1356, 157
Assembly Bill 2459, 156
Atlantic Monthly, 90–93
Automobiles: continental travel, 108;
  and Great Depression homeless,
  xxi–xxii; Lange photos, 200

Babb, Julia, 168
Babb, Sanora, 116, 173, 209
Baker, Susan Gonzalez, 279
Baking, 53, 55
Baldy, 73
Bales, Andy, 259
Ball, 73
Banking system, 129–30
Bassuk, Ellen L.: analysis of testimony,
  292–93; as homeless activist, 294;
  testimony of, 288–92, 294–95
Batter, 73
Beck, Frank O., 99
Berrigan, Daniel, 243
Berrigan, Philip, 243
"Big Rock Candy Mountain,
  The," 87
"Bindle stiffs," 28
Bishop, Isabel, 211
"Black Monday," 127
"Black Tuesday," 127
"Blackie and Joe Take a Ride," 34–35
Blacks. *See* African Americans
Blanket stiff: labor force, 91; tramp's
  jargon, 73
"Blind baggage," 33, 73, 158

Bloke, 73

Blood banks, 337

Bok, Derek, 283

"Bonanza farms," 55

Bonus Army, article about, 132–40; description of, 132, 133–34, 146–47; and homeless veterans, 305

Bonus Bill, 147–48, 149

Bonus Marchers, 132

Boston, 49

Bowery: daily survival needs, 336–42, 344; main stem, 61

Boxcar Bertha, 24, 292–93

Boy and Girl Tramps of America (Minehan), 293

Bradley, Preston, 99

Brady, Frank, 54

Bravin, Carol, 311, 312

Bridewell, David, 128

Broward Outreach Center, 292

Brown, Jesse, 281–82

Bruns, Roger, 94

Bughouse, 73

Bull, 73

"Bum blockade," 159, 160

Bum Brigade: migrant unpopularity, 194; term, 158, 160

"Bum lumps," 66

Bums: as intermittent labor force, xix, 18; OED definition, 4–5, 9; Reitman's definition, 20, 21, 23

"Bumpers," 33

Bundle, 73

"Bundle stiffs," 182

Bureau of Economic Analysis, 128

Bureau of Labor Statistics (BSL), 190

Burgess, E. W., 99

Burns, Robert L., 155

Burt, Martha R.: homeless activist, 294; homeless scholar, 257; soup kitchen/shelter survey, 251

"Buy and sell" shop, 337

"Buzzing," 68

"Cage," 61

California: attitude toward migrants, 195; blocking transients, 154–60; during the Great Depression, 112; homeless population, 265; migration to, 116, 121, 159–60

California Citizen Association, 158

Call of the Wild, The (London), 29

Cannery and Agricultural Workers Industrial Union (C&A.W.I.U.), 191

Cannery Row (Steinbeck), 209

Carleton, H. A., 154–55

Census, Hooverville (Seattle), 187

Census Bureau: homeless estimates, 16, 258; SBE, 255

Cerf, Bennet, 173

Chaplin, Ralph, 86, 103

Chavez, César Estrada, 203

Cheke, Sir John, xxviii

Chesebro, Ray L., 156–57

Chew the rag, 73

Chicago: affordable housing, 265; number sheltered, 47

Chicago Bureau of Charities, homeless men, 5

Chicago Tribune, xxix

Child homelessness: Bassuk's testimony/analysis, 288–93; in homeless population, 266; in Lange photos, 201, 203–7; numerical estimate, 13, 14; as special populations research, 273; and USICH plan, 366–67

Christensen, P. P., 155, 156

Chronic homeless, 369

Ciesielka, Sister Celeste, 310

Cities: constructive approaches, 358; criminalization of homeless, 356

Citizen Hobo (DePastino), xv

Civilian Conservation Corps (CCC): camps, 150–51; creation of, 149, 219

Civil rights movement, 221

Civil rights violations, 357–58

Civil War: family-centered ideology, xix; and homeless veterans, 305; the identifiable homeless, 23; and the Southern migration, xv

Cleveland (OH), 358

Clothing, 338

Coal miners, 48

Coalition to End Homelessness, 292

"Code of fair practice," 146

Coffeyville (KS) model jungle, 70

Cohen, Barbara E., 251

Collins, Tom: Arvin Camp, 171, 172, 194; song lyrics, 211; and Steinbeck, 113, 168

Colonial era homelessness, xvii–xviii, 17, 22–23

Commercial lodging houses, 61–62

Commission on Industrial Relations, 42, 69

Committee for Food and Shelter (ICF), 250–51

Communication system, 77, 78–79

Community Health Centers, 366

Community of Creative Non-violence (CCNV): HUD report, 246, 247–48; and Mitch Snyder, 238, 243

"Company Housing for Cotton Workers," Lange photos, 204

"Compensation certificates," 137

Conduct disorder, 302–3

Conference of Mayors, 258–59

Congress of Industrial Organizations (CIO), 95

Congressional Research Service: homeless veterans report, 298–304; report analysis, 304–6

Constitution, 16

Continuous jungle camps, 67

Continuum of Care applications, 256

Continuum of Care Programs, 235

Cooking equipment, 70

Cooler, 73

Coplen, G. W., 179–80

Cotton mill workers, 48

Coughlin, Father Charles, 112, 219

Country lodging: analysis of diary entries, 55–57; Dodge's diary entries, 52–55

Covenant House, 291, 292

"Cow-catcher," 34

Coxey, Jacob, 93–94

Coxey's Army, 93–94

Crack cocaine, 280

Crane, Stephen, 102

Crash of 1873, 46

Crib, 73

Crime: assaults on homeless mothers, 289; assaults on homeless youth, 274; Bowery men's fear of, 341; and homeless, 343

Criminals, 270, 282–83

Criminal tramp, 21

Croak, 73

Crocus, 73

Crooner, The (film), 210

Cross, Homer, 155

Crouse, Joan, xv

Cubicles, 61–62

Curtis, Charles, 133–34, 138
Cutting, Bronson, 216, 218

Daily needs: Bowery men, 336–42; homeless persons, 342–44
Dakota Territory, 52
Damnedest Radical, The (Bruns), 94
Darrow, Clarence, 103
"Date picker's home," Lange photos, 202
Davis, James E., 155, 156, 158–59, 160
Daytona Beach (FL), 358
De Caux, Len, 95
"Death of the Hired Man" (Frost), 7–8
DePastino, Todd, xv
Depression life photographs, Lange, 198–208
"Derelict," 107
Developmental delays, 290
Diaz, Lisbeth, 349–50
Dicer, 73
Dickens, Charles, 226, 228–29
"Dictionaries," 79
Dill Pickle Club/Society, 22, 103
Dip, 73
Disabled homeless population, 266
Discrimination, 319
Displaced persons, xiv–xv
Disruption, 290
"Doing the Math to Reduce Homelessness," 257
Dombey and Son (Dickens): selection, 226–28; selection analyzed, 228–29
Domestic violence: and housing subsidies, 348; and rural homeless, 310, 312–13; special populations research, 276, 277
"Don't Wait too Late," 314
Donia, Angelo, 309
Donovan, Neil J., 370, 371
Donovan, Shaun, 365, 370
Douglas, D., 158
Dow Jones Industrial Average (DJIA), 127
Down and Out in Beverly Hills (film), 343
Down and Out, On the Road (Kusmer), xv
Dreiser, Theodore, 102
"Drought refugees" photo, 199
Drug trafficking, 274
Dump, 73
"Dust Bowl," 119, 120–21

"Dust Bowl Ballads," 210
Dust storms, xxi, 116–18, 120

Eads, William. *See* How, William Eads
Edge, William, 76
Education, 299–300
Eisenhower, Dwight D., 139, 146
Elderly, 274–75
Electric refrigerators, xix
"Eleven Cent Cotton and Forty Cent Meat," 211
Emergency and Transitional Shelter Population 2000, 257
Emergency Shelter Grant Program, 235
Emergency Shelter Project Family House, 308–9, 310, 311
Emergency shelters, 265
Employment: daily survival needs, 337; education requirements, 265; and female veterans, 299; and racial/ethnic discrimination, 321, 322
Employment agency, 61
EPIC, End Poverty in California, 219
Epstein, Jesse, 181–82
Escalante, Juan, 329–31
Ethnicity, and homeless populations, 318–26; subgroup dimension, 272–73, 278–79, wage gap, 265
Evans, Walker, 211–12
Executive Order 6101, 149
Executive Summary (AHAR): homeless characteristics, 264–67; homeless characteristics analysis, 267–68; homeless estimate, 254–57; homeless estimate analysis, 257–61
"Extra gang," 41

Factories in the Field (McWilliams): analysis of selection, 173–75; selection, 170–73
Factory workers, xxi
"Fairbanks family," Lange photos, 208
"Fakirs," 28
Families: AHAR homeless estimates, 256; in the homeless population, 266, 268; and homeless trends, 266–67; homeless veterans, 300; Latino immigrants, 331, 332; and nineteenth-century ideology, xviii–xix; "rediscovery" of homeless, 292; special populations

research, 271, 277–78; USICH plan, 369
Farm Security Administration (FSA): Lange photos, 198–202; model camps, 113
Farm workers, Grape strike, 190–92; as transient population, xx–xxi
Fawny man, 73
Federal Emergency Relief Act (1933): passage of, 216; termination of, 219
Federal Emergency Relief Administration (FERA): FTS liquidation, 216, 220; limited tenure, 160; and transient numbers, 218
Federal Emergency Relief Agency (FERA): Care of Transient and Homeless, 145; New Deal program, 112, 113, 149, 150–51
Federal Home Loan Bank: housing crisis document, 124–26; housing crisis document analysis, 128–30
Federal Theater Project, 209
Federal Transient Program (FTP): Care of Transient and Homeless, 144; end of, 219, 220; limited tenure, 160; as New Deal program, 112, 113, 150–51
Federal Transient Service, 216–18
Filipino grape pickers, 191–92
Fitz, Sonja, 372–73
Flagged (jargon), 74
Floater custom, 68
"Floaters," 91
Flophouse, 339
"Flops," 61
Florida, 265
Flynt, James, 241
Flynt, Josiah, 79
Food, 337, 338
Ford, Henry, xxi, 91
Foreclosure, 124–26, 128
Foreign immigrants: California's treatment of, 195; in Hooverville (Seattle), 185, 187
Foscarinis, Maria, 371
Free speech, 24
Fresno (CA) grape strike, 190, 191
Frost, Robert, 7–8, 229

Gag (jargon), 74
Galway (jargon), 74
Gambling, 342

Garcia, Anastasia, 291
Garcia, Angela, 291, 292
Garcia, Clara, 332
Garden, Mary, 99, 100
Garrett, Priscilla, 292
Garrison, Walter E., 192
Gateway district, 60
Gay, Earl C., 155
Gelder, Ken, 78
Gender: hobo gender roles, 77;
    homeless population division,
    265–66; subgroup dimension,
    272–73, 275–77
Ghost-story (jargon), 74
GI Bill of Rights: provisions of, 305;
    and segregated middle class, 320,
    325
Gifford, Walter, 179
Gilded Age depressions, 61
Girl, The (LeSueur), 209
Glassford, Pelham D., 133, 134–35,
    137
Glossary, 73–76
Godden, Richard, 207
Goldman, Emma, 24, 103
Gordon, Linda, 208
Grafter (jargon), 74
Grand Central Station, 340
Grapes of Wrath, The (Steinbeck),
    113, 116, 121, 164, 168, 173, 209
Grape Strike, document, 191–93;
    document analysis, 193–95
Grasshopper plague, 120
"Gray cats," 28
Great Depression: causes of, 118–19,
    127; end of, 349; GDP decline,
    127–28; and homelessness, xiv,
    111–12; and search for work, xx;
    and Stock Market Crash, 127
Great Plains drought, xiv, xxi, 119
Gress, Jim, 291
Gropper, William, 211
Gross Domestic Product (GDP), 127
"Guerilla picketing," 192
Guilin, Al, 349
Gunnels, 26
Guthrie, Woody, 210

Haines, Patrick, 54
Hand-out: Bowery jargon, 338–39;
    tramp's jargon, 74
Hang-out (jargon), 74
Harborview Hospital, 186

Harman, S. L., 156
Harrington, Michael, 350
Harvest Gypsies, The (Steinbeck), 121
"Harvest Gypsies, The": document,
    164–67; document analysis,
    167–68
Health care reform, 366
Health problems, 299
Health status, 272–73, 280–81
Hebdige, Dick, 77–78
Hecht, Ben, 103
"Hellelujah," hobo song, 82–83, 86
Henry, Dutch, 54
Henson, David, 291, 292
Heroin addiction, 311
Hession, Jess, 155
Hewitt, Christopher, 252, 257
"Hidden" homeless, 13
Higashi, Daryl, 256
Higbie, Frank, xv
"Hi-jacking," 68
Hill, Joe: biography, 94–95; as
    songwriter, 86
Hispanic Paradox, 333
Hispanics. See Latinos
History of Vagrants and Vagrancy and
    Beggars and Begging, A (Ribton-
    Turner), xxvi–xxix
HIV infections, 281
Hobo: intermittent labor force,
    xix–xx, xxi; OED definition, 5;
    Reitman's definition, 20, 21, 22, 23
Hobo College: and Ben Reitman, 24,
    document, 97–101; document
    analysis, 102–3; and William Eads
    How, 24, 98–100, 102–3
Hobo College Campus, 100
Hobohemia: breaking ties, 100; as
    distinct subculture, 77, 78;
    document, 106–8; document
    analysis, 108–10; main stem
    document, 60–62; main stem
    document analysis, 62–63; political
    component, 93; subculture of, 108;
    term, xx
Hobo jargon, 72–76
Hobo jungle: document, 66–69;
    document analysis, 69–70
"Hobo jungles," rural lodgings, 62;
    term, 18
Hobo labor force, 92–93
"Hobo lumber jack," 91
"Hobo miner," 91

Hobo News, The, 103
Hobo politics: IWW article, 90–93;
    IWW article analyzed, 93–95
Hobo songs: analysis, 85–87; lyrics,
    81, 82–85
Hobo's Prayer, 100–101
"Hobo's Recollections, A": analysis of,
    42–43; article, 40–42
Hobo subculture, 72–76
Hobo, The (Anderson), 77
Hollenbeck Voluntary Board, 159
Hollywood Open Forum, 159
Holy Name Mission, 341
Hombs, Mary Ellen, 240–41, 243, 244
Home: as American symbol, 328; and
    Mexican migrant workers, 328–34;
    nineteenth-century ideology,
    xviii–xix; OED definition, 7–8;
    word element, xiii, 7
Homeless: during the Great
    Depression, 112, 121; and
    Homeless Assistance Act, 232,
    234, 235; number during 1890–
    1925, 46–49; OED definition, 4;
    reappearance of, xxii; Snyder's
    estimates, 238–41
Homeless Assistance Act, 239;
    document, 232, 233–34; document
    analysis, 234–35; HUD estimate,
    246–47; misconceptions about,
    272; and reconciliation estimate
    document, 250–51; reconciliation
    estimate document analysis, 252;
    six dimensions, 272–73;
    subpopulations, 265–67
Homeless Assistance Program (HAP),
    309–10
Homeless Count Report, 258
Homeless Emergency Assistance and
    Rapid Transition to Housing
    (HEARTH), 366, 368, 369
Homeless in America (Hombs/Snyder),
    240–41, 243
Homeless individuals: AHAR
    executive summary, 254; AHAR
    estimates, 256–61
Homeless Management Information
    System (HMIS), 256
Homelessness: as absence of
    permanent abode, 22; advent of,
    xiv–xv; appropriate word?, 290;
    and causation, xv–xvi;
    criminalization of, 354–59;

as cultural expression, 209; demographic characteristics, xiii–xiv; 1890–1925 study/analysis, 46–50; factors implicated in, xvi–xxii; and geographic location, xv, 265, 266; during the Great Depression, 128; in large urban areas, 222; interrogatory examination, xi–xxii; and Latino immigrants, 329–30; measuring methodology, 12–13, 242–43; and Mexican migrants, 333; national estimates of, 13–14; OED definitions, 4–9, 226, 228; preventing rural, 314–15; recent debates, xxiii; risk of, 295; rural definition, 309–10; and seasonal workers, 233; and Seattle Native Americans, 321; social construction of, 235; and veterans, 132; word elements, xi–xiii, 7

Homeless Person's Survival Act, 235

Homeless Transient in the Great Depression, The (Crouse), xv

Homeless veterans: characteristics of, 298–99, 300; military factors, 301–2; over representation of, 299–301; pre-service factors, 302; women, 300

Homeless Women Veterans with Children Act, 300–1

Home ownership, 322

Homes for Heroes Act, 300

Homes Not Handcuffs, 354–59

Hoosier, 74

Hoover, Herbert: banking regulation, 130; Bonus Army, 132–33, 135, 137–40, 146; and Hoovervilles, 179, 184, 187; presidential campaign, 147

"Hoover versus radicalism," 133, 137

"Hooverville," 138; document, 178–87; document analysis, 187–88; illustration, 184; New York City, 183

Hopkins, Harry, 148

Hopper, Kim, 294

Hotels, 340

"House," 7

Housekeeping, 67

"Houselessness," xiii

Housing: affordable, 265; and child homelessness, 290–91; 1890–1929 production, 48–49; and farm workers, 193–94; and homelessness, 222; *Homes Not Handcuffs*, 358; Hoovervilles, 179–82; Lange photos, 198, 202–5, 207; and musical genres, 210; New York University study, 346, 347–48; and rural homeless, 311, 312, 313, 314, 315; special populations research, 270, 271

Housing and Urban Development (HUD) report: homeless characteristics, 264, 265–67; characteristics analysis, 267–68; homeless estimate/analysis, 246–48; homeless estimate summary, 254–57; homeless estimate summary analysis, 257–61; and reconciliation estimate, 250

Housing Choice Voucher Program, 347, 348

Housing crisis, 124–25, 128–30

Housing discrimination, 319–20

Housing segregation, 349. *See also* Segregation

How the Other Half Lives (Riis), 49

How, William Eads, 24, 98–100, 102–3

Humanists, xvi

Hunger, 265

Hunger and Homelessness Survey, 258–59

Hunter, Robert, 48

Hurley, Patrick, 133, 135, 136, 139, 147

Hurricane Katrina (2005), xiv

Hygiene, daily survival needs, 340

"I Ain't Got No Home," 210

Illegal immigrants, 270, 282–83

Illness, 166–67

Income: racial/ethnic distribution, 322; special populations research, 271–72

Indispensable Outcasts (Higbie), xv

Infant homelessness, 291–92

Intelligence tests, 100

International Brotherhood of Welfare Assistance, 86, 98–99, 103

International Workers of the World (IWW): hobo politics, 90–95; hobo songs, 86, 93

Interrogatory words, xi

Iraq War. *See* Operation Iraqi Freedom (OIF)

Itinerant vagrants, 21

"It's only a Shanty in Old Shanty Town," 210

Ives, Burl, 87

"Jackrollers," 341

Jackson, Jessie, 178–87

Jencks, Christopher, 8, 251, 257

Jiggered (jargon), 74

Job seeking, 61, 63

Johnson, Lyndon B., xxii, 380

Joint (jargon), 74

Joslin, Theodore, 147

Journal of Public Policy, 46

"Jungle buzzard," 92

Jungle camps, 67

Jungle crimes, 68

Jungle etiquette, 67, 68

Jungle friendliness, 69

"Jungles," 6

Jungle sociability, 67

Kansas Transient Service, 145–46

"Key Not a Card, A," 358

Keyssar, Alexander, 48

King County (WA): racial/ethnic disparity report, 318–24; racial/ethnic disparity report analysis, 324–26

"King of the hoboes," 20, 24, 99

Kip-house (jargon), 74

Kip town (jargon), 74

Kirman, Richard, 158

Kulhane, Dennis, 294

Kusmer, Kenneth, xv

Labor Commission on Industrial Relations, 42

Labor force: post-1920, 111; post–World War II, 106–7, 109

Labor market, 60–61

Labor Unionism in American Agriculture, 190

Landeson, John, 99

Lange, Dorothea: Depression life photographs, 198–208, 212; Depression photographer, 161, 211–12; and photos as evidence, 241

Language: hobo subculture, 78, 79; and Latino immigrants, 330, 331

"Latino Paradox," 279, 331, 333

Latinos: basic demographic findings, 329–30; and employment

discrimination, 321; and GI Bill of Rights, 320; King County homeless, 323; King County unemployment rate, 323; special populations research, 278, 279–80

Laundry, Bowery hygiene needs, 341; country lodging, 55

Leather (jargon), 74

Lee, Thomas' recollections, 40–42, 43

Leslie, Dorla, 291

LeSueur, Meridel, 209

"Letters from a Tramp," 32–34

Lewis, Evan, 155

Lewis, Ted, 210

Lighthouse (jargon), 74

Lindsay, Vachel, 103

"Lingo," 72

Loan sharks, 341

Loans, 337

Location, xv, 265, 266

Lodge houses, 92

Lodging houses, 61–62

Lodi (CA): Filipino grape pickers, 191–92; Grape strike, 190, 191–92

London, Jack: biographical data, 29; on Hobohemia 102; and Hobo jargon, 78–79; participant observation practices, 241; and "Rods and Gunnels," 26–28; text analysis, 28–29

Long, Huey, 112, 219

Long term homeless, 257

Los Angeles, as mean city, 356, 357, 361

Los Angeles *Herald-Express*: blocking transients article, 154–59; blocking transients analysis, 159–61

Los Angeles Homeless Assistance Authority (LAHSA) report, 259–60

Love, Inc., 310

Lubin, Simon J., 168, 207

MacArthur, Gen. Douglas, 135, 136, 139, 146, 147

MacDonald, Commissioner, 191

Main guy (jargon), 74

Main stem: Chicago term, 102; defined, 61; disappearance of, 108; as geographic location, 59, 60–62; term, 18

Make-shift housing, 13

Mantis, Patricia, 292

Marine Hospital, 186

Mark (jargon), 74

Markham, Jim, 54

Marsh, Reginald, 211

Martin, Charles H., 158

Matrix enforcement program, 359–60

"Mayor of Hooverville," 183

McClintock, Harry K., 86

McCook, J. J.: "Train-jumping," 32–35; text analysis, 36

McKinney, Stewart B., 235

McKinney Homeless Assistance Act, 232–33, 235

McKinney-Vento Homeless Assistance Act: passage of, 232–33, 235; and Reagan administration, 360; and rural homeless, 309

McLean, Evalyn Walsh, 133

McWilliams, Carey, agricultural housing, 193, 194–95; *Factories in the Field*, 170, 173, 175

Meal-ticket (jargon), 74

Mean cities, *Homes Not Handcuffs*, 356

Medved, Michael, 372

Mellon, Andrew, 140

Men, daily survival needs, 336–42, 344; homeless veterans, 299, 300

Mental illness homeless, help for, 257; in the homeless population, 265; special populations research, 271, 276, 280

Merriam, Frank F., 155, 157

"Mexican field laborers' houses," Lange photos, 203

Mexican migrants, 328–34

"Migrant agricultural worker's family," Lange photo, 201

Migrant Farm Worker, A," text, 40–42: text analysis, 42–43

"Migrant Mexican children," Lange photos, 205–06

"Migrant potato pickers living conditions," Lange photo, 200

Migrant workers, during the Great Depression, xx, xxi; foreign, 174; the Mexican experience, 328, 329–32; recommendations for, 146; reduction of, 106; and the rural homeless, 309–10

"Migratory Camps, The," 175

Miller, Bill, 53

"Millionaire Hobo," 103

Minehan, Thomas, 293

Minorities, 347

Mission living, 338, 340

Mitchell, William, 135

Mobility: OED characteristic, 9; and Thomas Lee, 43; train-riding, 28–29

Moeur, B. B., 157–58

Monkey (jargon), 74

Monroe, Harriet, 103

Mooch (jargon), 74

Moocher (jargon), 75

Mooney, Tom, 91

"Mother," xviii–xix

Motherhood, 276, 289

Motor car, and the intermittent labor force, xx

Muckrakers, 169

Mug (jargon), 75

"Mulligan fund," 92

"Mulligan stew," 70

Multifamily stock, 347

"Musher," 28

Mush-fakir (jargon), 75

Music, hobo subculture, 85

"My Wandering Boy," 83–84, 86

Nation, The, Bonus Army article, 132–37

National Affordable Housing Trust Fund, 347–48

National Alliance to End Homelessness: on HUD estimates, 260–61; on "Opening Doors," 370

National Bureau of Economic Research, 251

National Center on Family Homelessness: findings 289–91; goals, 294; recommendations, 291–92

National Coalition for Homeless Veterans (NCHV): congressional testimony, 299–301; estimate of homelessness, 303

National Coalition for the Homeless (NCH): document, 12–14; document analysis, 14–16; and *Homes Not Handcuffs*, 354; report analysis, 359–61; and rural homeless, 314

National Committee on the Care of Transient and Homeless: report analysis, 146–51; report selection, 144–46

National Council on Family Homelessness, 46

National Guard/Reserves, 303–4

National Health Care for the Homeless Council, 310

National Housing Association, 49

National Institutes of Mental Health, 280

National Law Center on Homelessness and Poverty (NLCHP): homeless estimates, 13; *Homes Not Handcuffs*, 354–61

National Survey of Homeless Assistance Providers and Programs, 13, 14, 284–85

National Symposium on Homeless Research: analysis of research, 284–85; special populations, 270–84

National Union of Social Justice, 219

National Youth Administration (NYA), 219

Native Americans: employment discrimination, 321; King County homeless, 323, 225–26; King County unemployment rate, 323; resettlement programs, 320–21; rural homeless, 309–10

"Nativity," xiv

Natural disasters, xiv

Neuropathic tramp, 21

New Deal: and CCC, 149; homeless legislation, 112

"New wave" immigrants, 48–49

New York City: homeless population, 265; population density, 49; shelter residents, 47, 48; transients in, 217

New York City Municipal Lodging House, 47, 48

New York Stock Exchange (NYSE), 127

New York Times homelessness references, 243

New York University study: press release, 346–48; press release analysis, 348–51

New York Welfare Council, 218–19

Norris, Frank, 102

Obama, Barack, 365

Occupations, 329

Odell, Sheriff, 192

Office (jargon), 75

Of Mice and Men (Steinbeck), 209

"Okies," 121, 160–61, 168

Oklahoma migrations, 116

"Oklahoma potato picker's family," Lange photos, 206

"One Big Union," 91

One Night Count of Homeless Persons, 323

"One-third of a Nation," 209

On the Farm: document, 116–18; document analysis, 118–21

On the hog (jargon), 75

"Opening Doors," 369–72

Operation Enduring Freedom (OEF), 303

Operation Iraqi Freedom (OIF), 303

Orlando (FL), mean cities, 356

Ortiz, Margaret, 302

Other America, The (Harrington), 350

Oxford English Dictionary (OED): analysis of definitions, 6–9; homeless definitions, 4–6, 226, 228; homeless entry, xxix

Panhandlers, xxii

Panhandling, 336–37

Paper (jargon), 75

Parker, Carleton H., 93, 95

Parker, Cornelia Stratton, 95

Parks, 340

Parsons, Lucy, 103

Patman, Wright, 137, 138, 147

Patton, Bev, 310

Patton, Gen. George, 139, 146

Pawn shops, 337

"Peace faction," 192

Pen (jargon), 75

Pennsylvania salve (jargon), 75

Penn Station, 340

Pennyweighters (jargon), 75

Period prevalence counts, 12–13

Permanent jungle camps, 67, 68

Photographers, Great Depression, 211–12

Photographs: Depression life, 198–208; as evidence, 241

Pictorial language, 77

Pierce, Samuel, 247–48

"Place of birth," xiv

Point-in-time (PIT): AHAR counts, 255; defined, 12–13; estimate, 264

Police stations, 47

Poor, attitude toward, 283

Poorhouses, 47

Poppe, Barbara, 369, 370

Portland (OR), 358

Post-traumatic stress disorder (PTSD), 281, 302, 304, 306

Potter, Dr. Ellen, 220

Poverty: attitudes toward, 349–51; criminalization of, 355; and homelessness, 48, 222; and Latino immigrants, 331; in New York City, 347; post–World War II, xxii; racial/ethnic disparity, 323; and rural homeless, 311; special populations research, 270, 277

Poverty line, 48

Poverty rate: Chicago, 265; King County, 324

"Preacher and the Slave, The," 84–85, 86, 87

Proposition 187, 282

Prostitution: and homeless youth, 274; Reitman's view of, 24

Prushun (jargon), 75

Psychiatric disorders, 280

Public housing: Human Rights Network Housing Caucus, 347; subsidized, 223

Pugh, Tony, 371

Pun and plaster (jargon), 75

"Punching the wind," 27

Push (jargon), 75

Queer, the (jargon), 75

Race: King County homeless populations, 318–26; subgroup dimension, 272–73, 278

Racism, 330

Railroads: disappearance of Hobohemia, 109, 111; and hobo jungles, 66, 69; and Hoboes riders, 47, 92; and intermittent labor force, xix, xx, 111; and the main stem, 62; workers earnings, 48

Ramirez, Lorena, 349

Reader's Guide to Periodical Literature homelessness references, 243

Reagan, Ronald: and homelessness, 234, 235; and Mitch Snyder, 240

Recent Trends in American Housing, 49

Reconstruction Finance Corporation, 150

Redlining, 319

Reitman, Dr. Ben, biographical information, 23–24: Boxcar Bertha,

24, 292–93; and Coxey's Army, 94; definitional quotations, 20–22; and Hobo College, 99, 103; office of, 22; poem about, 21, text analysis, 24

Relationship: among hoboes, 36, 62

Repeater (jargon), 75

Republican Party, 194

Restaurants, 340

"Rialto, the," 62

Ribton-Turner, C. J., xxvi

"Riding the rods," 26, 27, 34–35

Riis, Jacob, 47, 49

"Road," 7

Rod(s), 27, 34–35

"Rods and Gunnels," 26–28

Roman, Nan, 370, 371

Roosevelt, Eleanor, 148

Roosevelt, Franklin D.: and Bonus Army, 146–49; federal relief programs, 219; international problems, 194; and job creation, xxii

Rosen, Jeremy, 371

Ross, Peter H., 251, 257

Rothstein, Arnold, 211–12

Rotman, David, 99

Rouges, xvii, xxix

Route 66, Lange photos, 198

"Roving Bill," 35

Rube (jargon), 75

Rules, 70, 77

Runner, 337

Rural homeless: characteristics of, 311–13, 314; document, 308–12; document analysis, 313–15

Rural Poverty Research Center, 309

Rural Rehabilitation Administration, 219

Rykwert, Joseph, 7

Sagely, Larry, 349

Salvation Army, 85, 86, 186

Sandburg, Carl, 87, 103

San Francisco, 359, 361

San Francisco earthquake, xiv

Santa Paula (CA) low-cost housing, 349–50, 351

Saps (jargon), 75

Scavenging, 337, 339

Schaub, E. L., 99

Schneider, John, 63

Scoff (jargon), 75

Scollan, Thomas, 155

Screw (jargon), 75

Seattle Housing Authority, 179–80, 181–82

Seattle Port Commission, 178, 179, 187

Sea-Wolf, The (London), 29

Second Bonus Army, 148, 149

Section 8, 347

Segregation: and King County homeless, 319; housing, 279

Service Based Enumeration (SBE), 255

"Servicemen's Readjustment Act," 305

Set-down (jargon), 75

Sex, xiii–xiv

Sexual assault, female veterans, 304, homeless mothers, 289

Shahn, Ben, 211–12

Shake (jargon), 75

Share Our Wealth Program, 219

Shaw, Frank L., 156–57

Shelter, survival need, 339

Sheltered homelessness: AHAR estimates, 257–58; and Latino immigrants, 331

Shelter Plus Care Program, 235

Shinn, Marybeth, 294, 347

Shinseki, Eric K., 365

Shove (jargon), 75

"Shovel bums," 28

Shover (jargon), 75

Sibelius, Kathleen, 365

Signs, 77, 79

Simmons, Deborah, 372

Sinclair, Upton, 102, 219

Single Room Occupancy Program, 235

Sinker (jargon), 75

Sister of the Road (Reitman), 24

Skid Row: NYU study analysis, 349, 350; stem displacement, 107–8, 111

Slaves, xix

Slopping-up (jargon), 76

"Smart cards," 315

Smead, Steve, 349

Snipe (jargon), 76

Snyder, Mitch: biography, 243–44; congressional testimony, 238–39; *Homeless in America* selection, 240–41; on HUD report, 248

Social Realism, 211

Social Security Act, 150, 219

Social Service Review, The, 220

Social status dimension, 272–73, 281–82

Social unit dimension, 272–73, 277–80

Soldiers' Bonus, 137

Solis, Hilda, 365, 370

Solkmore, Justice, 192–93

Song and dance (jargon), 76

Songs: hobo subculture, 82–83; about homelessness, 210–11

South of Market, 60

Spark (jargon), 76

Speek, Peter, 42–43

Spiel (jargon), 76

Spiked (jargon), 76

Squatters conditions, 164–67

St. Petersburg (FL), mean cities, 356

Stake men, 28, 76

"Stale-beer dives," 61

Stall (jargon), 76

Staple, Demali, 291, 292, 293

Staple, Jabari, 291

State Immigration and Housing Commission (CA), 90, 95

Status Report on Hunger and Homelessness, 322–23

Steichen, Edward, 201

Steinbeck, John: FSA camp, 113; homelessness representations, 209; Pulitzer Prize, 121, 173; squatters' camp, 164–68; and Tom Collins, 113, 168

Steinbeck, John, works: *Cannery Row,* 209; *Grapes of Wrath, The,* 113, 116, 121, 164, 168, 173, 209; *Harvest Gypsies, The,* 121; *Of Mice and Men,* 209; *Their Blood Is Strong,* 168; *White Fang,* 29

Stem: Chicago term, 102; description of, 59, 62–63; disappearance of, 106, 108, 111

"Stew bums," 28

Stiff (jargon), 76

Stock Market Crash (1929), 127

"Street counts," AHAR, 255

"Street definition," xi

Stryker, Roy, 212

"Subculture geographies," 78

Subcultures, 77–78

Sub-prime loans, 320

Subsidized housing, 223, 347, 348

Substance abuse: homeless population, 265; and rural homeless, 310, 312–13; special populations research, 276, 280
Sucker (jargon), 76
Suhr, Herman, 91
Supplemental social security income (SSI), 271
Supportive Housing Program, 235
"Survival strategies," 294

Tableland Services, 309
"Tactical orders," 156
Taft, Clinton J., 159
Tawney, R. H., xxviii
Taylor, Paul S.: agricultural economist, 161; refugee photos, 199, 200
Technology: and hobo labor force, xix–xx, xxi; as labor replacement, 107, 108, 109; and rural homeless, 315
Temporary jungle camps, 67
"Tenderfoot," 72
Termination acts, 321
"Texas tenant farmer," Lange photos, 207
Thaw, Harry, 91
Theft, 337
Their Blood Is Strong (Steinbeck), 168
"This World Is Not My Home," 210
Thompson, Florence, Lange photo, 201
Threshing crews, 53
Timber (jargon), 76
Tomato-can vag (jargon), 76
"Train jumping," 32–35
Train-riding, 26–28
Tramp(s), in country lodging, 52, 55; as intermittent labor force, xix–xx; OED definition, 5, 9; Reitman's definition, 20, 21–22, 23; term, 5
"Tramp menace," xix, 17
Tramp's jargon: analysis, 76–79; glossary, 72–76
"Tramp speak," 71
Transient(s), California's blocking of, 154–59; community view of, 217; during the Great Depression, xx, xxi; OED definition, 5; recommendations, 145–46
Transportation, 310, 313–14
Tucker, Irving St. John, 99

Tugwell, Rexford, 212
Tully, Jim, 99
"Tunnel-dwellers," xii, xiii
"Turf, the," 7, 76
Turner, Frederick Jackson, 48

Unemployed, *OED* definition, 5
Unemployment: and the Great Depression, 128; and Latino immigrants, 330; during the Progressive era, 48; and the rural homeless, 312
Union Rescue Mission, 259
United Farm Workers, 203
United States Employment Service, 170
United States Interagency Council on Homelessness (USICH), 233; document, 364–69; document analysis, 369–73
"Unsheltered, the," 13
Urban Institute, 13
Urban migration, 49
Urban renewal, 109–10
Urgent Relief for the Homeless Act, 235
USA Today, 13

Vagabond(s), in medieval England, xvii, xxix; OED definition, 5–6, 9
Vagrant(s): OED definition, 6, 9; in medieval England, xvii, xxix; Reitman's definition, 21
Venereal disease, 24
Veterans: and the Bonus March, 132–34, 136, 137, 140; Civil War, xix; and homeless population, 266; homeless report, 298–302; and Hooverville, 186; special populations research, 270, 281–83; and USICH plan, 369; Vietnam, 300, 301, 303, 305–6
Victimization, 289–90
Vietnam veterans, 300, 301, 303, 305–6
Violence: and Bowery men, 341; and the homelessness, 289–90
Visual artists, 211
Vocabulary, 79
Vought, Jennifer, 310

Wages: housing market, 265; rural homeless, 312

Wagner Graduate School of Public Service, 347
Wallace, Samuel, 340
"Warn people out," xviii
"Warn them out," colonial era, 17
War of 1812, xv
War on Poverty, xxii, 350
War refugees, xiv–xv
"War-zone stress," 301
Waters, Walter, 137, 138
Wayfarer's Lodge, 47
Weitzman, Beth C., 347
Western migration, 112
Wheatland Riot, 90
White, Stanford, 91
White Fang (London), 29
White unemployment rate, 323
Whitman, Walt, 120–21
Whose Names Are Unknown (Babb), 173, 209
Willard, Josiah Flynt, 79
Wolcott, Margaret Marion Post, 211–12
Women: current homeless population, 275–77; homeless veterans, 300–301, 302, 304
"Women on the Breadlines," 209
Woods, Edith, 49
Woodward, Mary Dodge, analysis of diary entries, 55; Dairy entries, 52–55
Work, OED characteristic, 9
Workforce: average 1904 yearly earnings, 48; during the nineteenth century, xix, 17
Workforce Investment Act, 234
Workhouse: in the eighteenth century, 17; emergence of, xviii
Works Progress Administration (WPA): blocking transients, 154; employable workers relief, 219; and FTS termination; 217; for needy unemployed, 150
World War I veterans, 305
World War II: demand for workers, 221; employment opportunities, 106, 221; and homeless veterans, 305; and job creation, xxii

Youth: special populations research, 274; USICH plan, 369

Zero Tolerance for Veteran Homelessness Act, 299–300

ABOUT THE AUTHOR

NEIL LARRY SHUMSKY, PhD, teaches history at Virginia Tech, Blacksburg, Virginia. He has been a member of the history department at Virginia Tech since 1972. He earned his doctoral degree at the University of California, Berkeley, where he emphasized American social history in general and the history of American cities and the history of immigration to the United States in particular. Shumsky has published numerous books and articles regarding both urban history and immigration history.

CPSIA information can be obtained at www.ICGtesting.com
Printed in the USA
BVOW09*1001170116

433093BV00006B/11/P